Management Dynamics in Strategic Alliances

A volume in
Research in Strategic Alliances
T. K. Das, *Series Editor*

Research in Strategic Alliances

T. K. Das
Series Editor

Published

Forthcoming volumes

Management Dynamics in Strategic Alliances

Edited by

T. K. Das
City University of New York

INFORMATION AGE PUBLISHING, INC.
Charlotte, NC • www.infoagepub.com

Library of Congress Cataloging-in-Publication Data

Management dynamics in strategic alliances / edited by T. K. Das.
     p. cm. – (Research in strategic alliances)
  Includes index.
  ISBN 978-1-61735-754-1 (pbk.) – ISBN 978-1-61735-755-8 (hardcover) –
ISBN 978-1-61735-756-5 (ebook)
  1. Strategic alliances (Business) 2. Organizational behavior. 3.
Management. I. Das, T. K.
  HD69.S8M325 2012
  658'.046–dc23
                                                          2011052475

CONTENTS

FOREWORD TO THE SERIES

Relationships have been important to commercial activity and economic transactions for thousands of years. Yet the development of a global competitive landscape has substantially enhanced the importance of partnerships between economic entities. These partnerships, referred to as strategic alliances, provide access to resources and capabilities that allow firms to gain economies of scope and to increase their productivity and innovation. The economies, productivity, and innovations are necessary to at least maintain competitive parity and especially to achieve a competitive advantage in the often highly competitive global markets. Strategic alliances have also become a prominent means of entering new markets, especially foreign markets. Therefore, alliances and the networks of firms of which they are a part have become essential for the conduct of business for all types of firms—large, small, established, and new.

Because of their growing importance, research on strategic alliances has increased markedly in the last 2 decades. Yet there is need for an authoritative compendium of strategic alliance research and knowledge. This book series on *Research in Strategic Alliances* fills this critically important gap in our field. It provides a thorough examination of significant topics that provide complete and up-to-date knowledge on strategic alliances. This book series will serve as a catalyst for more effective management of strategic alliances and will guide future research on them. I commend it to you.

—**Michael A. Hitt**
Distinguished Professor and Joe B. Foster Chair in Business Leadership at Texas A&M University, and Past President of the Academy of Management and the Strategic Management Society.

Management Dynamics in Strategic Alliances, page vii
Copyright © 2012 by Information Age Publishing

ABOUT THE SERIES

The globalization of markets has led to increased interdependence among business firms, leading to an explosion in the number of strategic alliances. Strategic alliances, briefly, are cooperative arrangements aimed at achieving the strategic objectives of two or more partner firms. These interfirm arrangements can range from joint R&D to equity-based joint ventures. However, the scholarship relating to strategic alliances remains largely dispersed in the literatures of traditional academic disciplines such as strategic management, marketing, economics, and sociology. This book series on strategic alliances will cover the essential progress made thus far in the literature and elaborate upon fruitful streams of scholarship. More importantly, the book series will focus on providing a robust and comprehensive forum for new scholarship in the field of strategic alliances. In particular, the books in the series will cover new views of interdisciplinary theoretical frameworks and models (dealing with resources, risk, trust, control, cooperation, learning, opportunism, governance, developmental stages, performance, etc.), significant practical problems of alliance organization and management (such as alliance capability, interpartner conflict, internal tensions, use of information technology), and emerging areas of inquiry. The series will also include comprehensive empirical studies of selected segments of business, economic, industrial, government, and nonprofit activities with wide prevalence of strategic alliances. Through the ongoing release of focused topical titles, this book series will seek to disseminate theoretical insights and practical management information that will enable interested professionals to gain a rigorous and comprehensive understanding of the field of strategic alliances.

CHAPTER 1

ALLIANCE FORMATION AND STRUCTURE CHOICE

The Roles of Entrepreneurial Orientation and Institutional Environments

Pat H. Dickson
K. Mark Weaver

ABSTRACT

The choice of whether to form an alliance as well as the choice of governance structures for alliances formed has often been characterized as a strategic choice made by firm managers. This characterization has yielded much to our understandings of alliance formation and structure, and it has propelled us toward deeper questions regarding the underlying dynamics of these choices associated with this strategic behavior. Two such questions are the focus of this chapter and the research that motivates it. First, to what extent does the nature of the institutional environment of a small- to medium-sized enterprise (SME) play in shaping the alliance choice decisions made by SME decision leaders? Second, to what extent does the nature of individual key decision leaders in the SME impact alliance choice decisions and, more specifically to this investigation, does the entrepreneurial orientation of firm

Management Dynamics in Strategic Alliances, pages 1–21

1

leaders have an impact on alliance choice above and beyond that associated with the institutional environment. The answers to these questions are explored through an analysis of survey responses from over 2,000 firms located in eight countries.

INTRODUCTION

There has been important research into the motivation of firms to form alliances (Ghemawat, Porter, & Rawlinson, 1996; Park, Chen, & Gallagher, 2002; Sakakibara, 2002). Alliance formation is often seen as a critical strategic behavior necessary in the obtaining of support and resources for both survival and growth. One theme that seems to be emerging from the varied research aimed at understanding alliance motives is an understanding that the choice to form an alliance is an adaptation choice (Koza & Lewin, 1998). In an attempt to adapt to uncertainty (Dickson & Weaver, 1997), firm leaders choose to enter alliances as a means to enhance the firm's competitive position (Kogut, 1988) or to reduce transaction costs (Williamson, 1985).

Once the choice is made by a firm to form an alliance relationship, the governance form chosen for an alliance relationship is particularly important in influencing the success of the alliance (Osborn & Baughn, 1990). Tallman and Shenkar (1994), in explaining why certain alliance structures are chosen over others, argue that the choice is a result of an attempt to reduce uncertainty and improve organizational performance. Two important theories utilized in understanding strategic decisions—transaction cost economics (TCE) (Williamson, 1985) and resource dependence theory (RDT) (Pfeffer & Salancik, 1978)—argue a direct link between the environment and strategic decisions. While both theories provide powerful potential explanations for the strategic choice of alliance structures, to date, the research exploring these explanations has been limited. The specific focus of this chapter and the supporting research is not only the exploration of the role of the institutional environment of the firm but also the behavioral orientations of the firm leaders in determining both the strategic choice to form an alliance as well as the choice of structures to govern the alliance.

Institutional factors have long been hypothesized as impacting strategic choice (DiMaggio & Powell, 1991). Institutional factors are those attributes of the firm's environment that exert normative pressures on the firm (Barringer & Harrison, 2000). Of lesser consideration in prior research is the role of individual behavioral orientations in the alliance choice process. Palich and Bagby (1995) suggest that individual characteristics of organizational leaders must also be considered if we are to have a complete picture. In specific, these researchers argue that the risk propensity or entrepreneurial orientation (EO) of firm leaders will impact how they frame the environment and in turn the strategic choices that they make.

Due to significant methodological challenges, research jointly exploring the role of institutional factors and individual behavioral characteristics on the choice to form alliances and the choice of alliance structures has been limited. This chapter provides a discussion of research that has sought to overcome those challenges and to provide a richer understanding of the role of institutions and behavioral orientations on alliance choice. SMEs have been chosen as the focus for this discussion and for the associated research for an important methodological reason. One of the difficulties in exploring the impact of the behavioral attributes of individuals on firm-level strategic choices is the need to isolate those individuals that clearly have an impact on firm-level behavior. The challenges of this type of research are clearly argued by Nielsen (2010). The difficulty of linking individual behavior to firm decisions is to some extent lessened by the focus on SMEs. Classical economic theory has traditionally assumed that, in firms of this size (fewer than 500 employees), the owner and the firm are synonymous (Lumpkin & Dess, 1996). Based on this argument, we can assume that behavioral attributes of the owner are determining or at least impacting the firm-level strategic choices of the firm. While the discussion and associated research are focused on SMEs, implications for larger firms can be drawn.

The chapter will proceed in the following fashion. First, the nature of alliance formation and structure and research that supports our understandings of these strategic choices by firms will be reviewed. Second, drawing on institutional theory, a set of institutional factors that appear to influence alliance behavior, both formation and choice of structures, will be suggested. Third, drawing on research focusing on the role of the behavioral attributes of decision leaders in impacting strategic choice, one such behavioral orientation—an orientation toward risk, innovation, and creativity—will be explored as a possible predictor of alliance choice. Fourth, a research study designed to test these relationships will be described, and finally, the results and implications of that study will be discussed.

INSTITUTIONAL AND INDIVIDUAL PREDICTORS OF ALLIANCE CHOICE

Alliance Formation

Alliance formation is arguably one of the most utilized strategies for resource acquisition and leveraging by both large and small firms (Baum, Calabrese, & Silverman, 2000; Miles, Preece, & Baetz, 1999). Firms have used alliance relationships for resource acquisition, information exchange, technology transfer, and risk management (Deeds & Hill, 1999), among other motives. Alliances, although potentially providing the resources needed by the firm, are a two-edged sword (Deeds & Hill, 1999). In order to access the resources an alliance relationship may provide, the firm must often open itself up to the potential for opportunistic behavior by alliance partners (Das & Teng, 2000, 2001a, 2001b). Such behavior may involve the loss of information about proprietary technologies and capabilities (Osborn & Baughn, 1990).

In this chapter, alliances are conceptualized as voluntary interfirm agreements that establish exchange relationships between firms but which involve no joint ownership (Barringer & Harrison, 2000; Dickson & Weaver, 1997). Although such agreements, unlike joint ventures, do not establish a jointly owned entity, there are often significant resources required in attracting alliance partners, structuring relationships, managing relationships, and extracting value from the exchanges over time (Todeva & Knoke, 2005).

Alliance Structure

Because alliances are built around knowledge-based resources, there is an ever-present danger that may result from the opportunistic behavior of an alliance partner in the unintended transfer of knowledge-based resources that were not part of the original alliance bargain (Das & Teng, 2000). Conventional wisdom, drawing principally upon the tenets of transaction cost theory, suggests that the greater the level of control in the form of contributed assets specific to the alliance relationship, as in equity-based alliances, the less likely will be the potential for opportunistic behavior (Williamson, 1983). A low level of behavioral uncertainty, following the logic of TCE, is primarily an attribute of alliance relationships marked by sufficient levels of firm assets that are specific to the relationship (Williamson, 1985). This lack of uncertainty regarding how alliance partners will behave evolves from the presence of credible commitments and/or contractual safeguards specifying remedies for opportunistic behavior (Williamson, 1985; Zaheer & Venkatraman, 1995). Equity commitments require an investment at the beginning of the alliance relationship. Typically, these commitments, because they are specific to the alliance relationship, are not recoverable and lose value should the alliance relationship be damaged by the opportunistic behavior of the alliance participants (Williamson, 1985). Equity commitments, while providing the highest level of potential loss should an alliance partner behave in a manner that is not in the best interest of the alliance, also imply some level of ownership. Ownership often requires a much higher level of disclosure by a firm regarding the technologies and processes of the firm than the firm leadership is willing to make. This requirement may in fact result in a greater potential for opportunistic behavior since relationships involving equity commitments generally require greater levels of disclosure in the relationship. In an effort to manage the level of disclosure, firms involved in alliances often choose more arm's-length and informal controls to govern their alliance relationships (Deeds & Hill, 1999). Although this strategy may reduce the required levels of disclosure, it may open firm leaders to higher levels of uncertainty regarding the potential behavior of partners to the alliance unless there are strong relational controls in place.

Institutional Environment and Alliance Choice

In the study serving as the foundation for this chapter, the first question addressed is, "Does the nature of the institutional environment impact the decision by SME owners to form an alliance and, if they choose to do so, to utilize equity-based or agreement-only forms of alliances?" According to Hitt, Ahlstrom, Dacin, Levitas, and Svobodina (2004), institutional forces have great power in shaping economic activity and the strategic choices of firms. Institutional theory suggests that certain aspects of the institutional environment of firms exert pressures toward complying with accepted norms in order to appear legitimate (Barringer & Harrison, 2000; DiMaggio & Powell, 1991). Proponents of the role of institutional factors in influencing firm behavior argue that the strategic choices available to firms are not unlimited, and that firm leaders, in order to manage risk and achieve goals, choose actions from a defined set of legitimate options. A review of existing research in this area suggests three important institutional factors that might play a role in the strategic choice of SME owners to form an alliance and, if the choice to form is made, the choice of agreement or equity-based alliance structures (Dickson & Weaver, 2011). These factors include the nature of the economic system in which the firm operates, the nature of the risk associated with the economic environment of the firm, and the nature of the legal system governing interfirm transactions for the firm.

Firms from smaller economies are at a distinct disadvantage in acquiring the resources they need to achieve strategic goals, while firms from larger, more munificent economies have increased access to pools of resources and more extensive technological infrastructures (Hagedoorn & Narula, 1996; Walsh, 1988). Keats and Hitt (1988) argue that a munificent environment—an environment characterized by a broad range of resources supporting growth (Dess & Beard, 1984)—will tend to support growth and the achievement of strategic goals. Taken collectively, these arguments suggest that when resources can be acquired from the external markets, there will be less need for the firm to seek out resources through quasi-market transactions such as the formation of interfirm alliances, particularly given the hazards that often accompany alliance relationships. If this logic holds true, it indicates that the greater the munificence of the environment, the less likely firms might be to form alliances.

The role that environmental munificence plays in the choice of an agreement-based alliance over an equity-based alliance is somewhat more problematic. According to Gulati (1995), if the costs associated with the transactions in an exchange are too high to place them within an agreement-only-based alliance, then equity-based alliances will be utilized. Williamson (1985) suggests that the more uncertain the nature of a firm's environment, the more likely the firm will be to form more highly structured and equity-based alliances. For SMEs, resource dependency rather than resource sufficiency is often the norm (Calof, 1993). The ability for such firms to contribute resources or to make equity investments in alliance relationships is potentially limited. For SMEs in economies providing limited resources, as previously noted, the motivation for forming alliances is often driven by the need to acquire resources, limiting their ability to invest significant resources themselves. These understandings of SMEs and the nature of environmental munificence would suggest the following hypotheses for exploration:

> **Hypothesis 1:** *The more munificent the environment of the SME, the less likely the firm will be to choose to form strategic alliances.*

> **Hypothesis 2:** *The more munificent the environment of the SME, the more likely, if alliances are formed, that they will be equity based.*

Environmental risks, particularly those associated with the economic environment of the firm, have long been suggested to influence the interactions of firms (Ghoshal, 1987). Rasheed (2005) conceptualizes such risks as encompassing ownership, control, operational transfer, and investment risks. Firms that choose to form alliance relationships want to know that their investments in those alliances will be protected. There is evidence that economic instability deters foreign investment (Oxley, 1999), particularly in those national settings in which there is a history of government expropriation of foreign-held assets. SMEs located in high economic risk areas will be less attractive to potential alliance partners. Likewise, if alliances are formed in environments characterized by high risk, as noted above, then firms would seem likely to prefer more highly structured and equity-based alliances. These arguments would suggest the following hypotheses:

Hypothesis 3: *The higher the level of economic risk of the home country of the SME, the less likely the firm will be to form strategic alliances.*

Hypothesis 4: *The higher the level of economic risk of the home country of the SME, the more likely, if alliances are formed, that they will be equity based.*

The legal systems governing the firm's transactions have been viewed as providing powerful normative pressures in shaping strategic choice (Oxley, 1997, 1999). The elements of legal systems govern both organizational and industry actions through establishing the basis for production, exchange, and distribution with the intent of establishing order (Davis & North, 1971; Yiu & Makino, 2002). The elements of legal systems most often regarded as impacting the transactions of firms include such laws as those pertaining to intellectual property protection and of the financial investments of both individuals and firms (La Porta, Lopez-de-Silanes, Shleifer, & Vishny, 1997). The strengths or weaknesses of laws governing interfirm transactions may encourage or discourage the making of investments and co-specialized assets often necessitated in the alliance process. In a like manner, the nature of the legal system may also impact the choice of alliance structures.

Since legal systems are complex, it has proven difficult to measure which aspects of the system most influence transactions. La Porta, Lopez-de-Silanes, and Shleifer (1999) argue that the primary issue determining the strength of enforcement of contracts and property rights is the origins of the legal system. The stream of research motivated by La Porta et al. groups legal systems into four primary groups based on origin. These include English Common Law and French, German, and Scandinavian Civil Law. Their work suggests that in general, French Civil Law countries have the lowest quality of legal enforcement in terms of contracts and property rights (La Porta et al., 1999, 2002). Their work, using this broad measure of the origin of laws, would suggest that firms in French Civil Law countries would be less likely to form alliances, but should they form alliances, they would more likely be equity based. Based on these arguments, the following hypotheses are suggested:

Hypothesis 5: *In comparison to SMEs in French Civil Law countries, SMEs in countries with laws founded upon other legal systems will be more likely to form alliances.*

Hypothesis 6: *In comparison to SMEs in French Civil Law countries, SMEs in countries with laws founded upon other legal systems will be less likely to use equity-based alliances.*

Entrepreneurial Orientation and Alliance Choice

In this study, the second question addressed is, "Does the orientation of the SME owner or key decision leader toward innovation, creativity, and risk impact the decision to form an alliance and, if they choose to do so, to utilize equity-based or agreement-only forms of alliances?" The beliefs, values, and predispositions of key decision leaders of firms can have an important effect on firm-level strategic decisions, according to Tyler and Steensma (1995). The entrepreneurial orientation of the key decision leader has been proposed as one variable differentiating firms that choose cooperative behavior from firms that choose to go it alone (Covin & Slevin, 1989; Shan, 1990). Dickson and Weaver (1997) suggest that the key decision leader's entrepreneurial orientation may also influence the choice of cooperative strategies. Lumpkin and Dess describe an entrepreneurial orientation as an orientation that is characterized by "autonomy, innovativeness, risk taking, proactiveness, and competitive aggressiveness" (1996, p. 162). Both Palich and Bagby (1995) and Covin and Slevin (1989) conclude that a decision leader's entrepreneurial orientation has an important impact on how the leader views the firm's environment. Palich and Bagby argue that entrepreneurially oriented leaders are not necessarily more willing to take risks but are more likely to frame seemingly risky and uncertain environments in a more positive light than are more conservatively oriented leaders. Their research indicates that the manner in which a more entrepreneurially oriented decision leader frames his or her environment is quite different from the manner in which a less entrepreneurially oriented leader might frame the same environment. As previously noted, alliance relationships are not without risk to both parties to the relationship. It would seem reasonable to conclude from the characterization of an entrepreneurial orientation that firm leaders with a greater tolerance for risk and a willingness to seek out innovative and creative solutions would be more likely to be willing to form strategic alliance relationships. This logic would also seem to suggest that in general, the more entrepreneurially oriented and risk taking the decision leader, the less likely he or she will be to feel the need to form more structured equity-based alliances. The following hypotheses are suggested by these assumptions:

> **Hypothesis 7:** *The greater the entrepreneurial orientation of the key decision leader in the firm, the more likely the firm will be to form strategic alliances.*

> **Hypothesis 8:** *The greater the entrepreneurial orientation of the key decision leader in the firm, the less likely the firm will be to form equity-based alliances.*

The preceeding hypotheses collectively build a framework suggesting that both the nature of the institutional environment as well as the nature of the key decisions leader will have important implications on both the choice to form an alliance and the choice of whether to utilize more highly structured equity-based relationships. The following sections of this chapter describe the research that was designed to test these hypotheses, the results that were obtained from this research, and the implications of the findings.

RESEARCH DESIGN

Sample

Our research was begun with the collection of survey data from SME manufacturing and service firms in eight countries that included Australia, Finland, Greece, Indonesia, Mexico, the Netherlands, Norway, and Sweden. A key informant design was used in which surveys were sent to the owners or general managers of firms with no more than 500 employees but no fewer than 6 employees. Although a single informant design was utilized, there is strong theoretical support to conclude that firms of this size are, in general, extensions of the individuals in charge (Lumpkin & Dess, 1996), and it is this assumption that allows us to utilize EO as a measure at the individual level of analysis and a key motivation behind utilizing SMEs for the study. A subsequent analysis of the differences in response across those respondents indicated that full ownership of the firm with those with only partial ownership showed no significant differences. The firms were randomly selected from 12 different industry classifications and 1 inclusive classification for service firms. Lists of firms were developed through the use of commercially available database listings and organizational affiliation roles. For example, KOMPASS On-Line systems was utilized for SME listings in the European Markets. KOMPASS is considered to be a reliable source of names and addresses of registered businesses. In other countries, membership roles from Chambers of Commerce, Chambers of Importers and Exporters, industry trade groups, and such were utilized and cross-referenced to develop master lists from which the sample was drawn. The total number of SMEs selected for inclusion in each country was based on available resources and the judgment of research associates in each country.

The surveys were originally developed in English and then translated through a back-translation process. Every effort was made to make the data-collection process equivalent. In most countries, the surveys were delivered via mail. In Mexico, Indonesia, and Greece, the surveys were delivered by hand. In all countries, the surveys were delivered in two separate waves to allow for an early-late response assessment as well as an assessment of nonrespondents. In the first wave, surveys were delivered to all SMEs randomly selected for the study. In the second wave, bad-address and out-of-business returns were excluded. In the countries in which surveys were hand delivered, all SMES were contacted by phone and asked to cooperate in the study prior to delivery. The representative nature of the sample was assessed through both an analysis of variance procedure, testing based on survey wave, as well as a random telephone survey of a select group of nonrespondents in each country. The results suggested no significant differences between early and late respondents or between respondents and nonrespondents.

Study Measures

The study-dependent variables were "alliance use versus nonuse" and "nonequity only versus at least one equity-based alliance." No assessment was made in advance to determine if firms held alliance relationships, but rather surveys were sent to all firms randomly selected for the study. Respondents were asked to indicate if their firm currently maintained an alliance relationship, and if so, how many and what types of alliances did the SME maintain. The survey provided the respondents with a list of various types of alliances, with the respondent being ask to indicate if his or her firm currently held such an alliance and if so, how many. The alliance types provided included marketing, distribution and production agreements, licensing, outside contracting, export management or trading alliances, R&D process or product alliances, and purchaser-supplier alliances. Each type of alliance was clearly presented with separate questions. In order to arrive at the study-dependent variables, responses across all alliance-use questions were totaled and dichotomized into a yes/no variable for the "alliance use" measure. Alliance relationships were coded as either equity-based relationships with equity investments or as nonequity agreements. Strong support for this coding scheme is found in Gulati's (1995) work. Because the level of analysis for this study was the firm, it was assumed that those SMEs maintaining both types of alliances would be significantly different from those SMEs maintaining agreement-based alliances exclusively. Gulati supports this assumption and consistent with his methodology, the mixed group (both equity based and agreement based) and those that held equity-only agreements were combined to form an equity-based group. The firm-level of analysis, while somewhat problematic, provides a richer view of the full range of characteristics of SMEs holding multiple alliances than does a level of analysis that attempts to characterize the firm based on a single alliance relationship. Additionally, it should be noted, that there is a broad body of research focusing on the role of contracts in providing control within strategic alliances (Mellewigt, Madhok, & Weibel, 2007) and the role of trust in substituting for contracts (Klein Woolthuis, Hillebrand, & Nooteboom,

2005; Luo, 2002). For purposes of this study, the choice was made to focus exclusively on equity investments as a control mechanism, given the rich history of this variable as a strong predictor of alliance outcomes.

Variables for the institutional environment of the SME were collected from various sources and included based on prior use. Market munificence was measured using market size as an indicator of munificence. Market size is the natural log of the 5-year average, ending with the year of data collection in each country, of the real GDP in 1990 U.S. dollars. Data for this measure was drawn from the United Nations Department of Economic and Social Affairs (UNESCO) Statistical Yearbook (2002). The accuracy of these numbers was verified through various other sources. The economic risk measure was based on an economic risk index developed and published by *Euromoney* (1998). The measure is based on a rating of a nation's debt in the international financial markets. The index rates countries on a scale of 0–100, with higher levels indicating greater stability and lower risk. This particular risk measure has been validated by studies replicating the measure using objective economic and political data (Cosset & Roy, 1991; Oxley, 1999). Oxley (1999) argues that this measure combines elements of both political and economic risk, and that it has been shown to be highly consistent with objective economic and political data. For purposes of this analysis, this measure was reverse coded. The measure of legal risk and/or uncertainty used in this study was based on the origin of the legal system of each country and was drawn from La Porta et al. (1998, 1999, 2002). A dummy coding scheme was utilized in which SMEs were coded as being from a "French Civil Law," "Scandinavian Civil Law," or "English Common Law" country.

The entrepreneurial orientation of the key decision leader was measured using a scale developed and tested by Covin and Slevin (1989). The items measure the firm's tendencies toward innovation, proactiveness toward competitors, and tendencies toward risk taking (a = .79 to .81). Although a firm-level measure, based on our assumption of the key decision leader being equivalent with the firm for firms of the size utilized in this study, the scale is used to measure individual orientations toward innovation, creativity, and risk—the components of entrepreneurial orientation.

Control Measures

To provide a rigorous test of the hypothesized relationships in this study, a wide range of control variables were used. To control for differences at the industry level, 12 separate industry groups were sampled in the study. In order to aid in the stability of the regression analysis, these 12 industry groups were collapsed into 4 industry groupings based on the level of technological sophistication, since a number of studies have shown high correlations between the level of technology in an industry and alliance formation. The categorization scheme was based on one provided by the Organization for Economic Co-Operation and Development (OECD): Science, Technology and Industry Scoreboard (2003). A dummy coding scheme was used for the four industry groups that were designated as "high tech," "medium high tech," "medium low tech," and "low tech."

A number of firm-level differences were also controlled. These included the size of the firm, the financial capacity of the firm, and the export intensity of the firm. Firm size was measured using the natural log of the total number of employees. Firm financial capacity was assessed using a financial performance measure drawn from Covin, Slevin, and Schultz (1994). The measure is composed of seven "satisfaction" with financial performance metrics and seven corresponding "importance" of financial performance metrics. In order to obtain the overall financial performance score, the seven satisfaction scores were multiplied by the importance scores to obtain a weighted average financial capacity index ($\alpha = .78$ for importance measures; $\alpha = .91$ for satisfaction measures). This type of financial measure has been extensively used, shown to correlate highly with objective type financial measures, and proven to result in higher response rates from smaller firms (Covin & Slevin, 1989). Export intensity was a ratio of the export sales of the firm to total firm sales as reported by the respondent. Lee and Park (2008) present research that strongly suggests that international exposure and involvement by top managers is positively associated with alliance formation.

To control for potential individual differences across respondents, both the age and gender of the respondent was entered into the analysis. It was also deemed reasonable to control for individual differences across SME owners and managers in how they view the necessity for alliance activity. A 4-item scale developed by Steensma, Marino, Weaver, and Dickson (2000) was utilized ($\alpha = .80$). The four items tap the respondent's belief in the importance of entering into strategic alliances, the inability of SMEs to be self-reliant, and the necessity to align with both large and small firms in the future. Finally, controls for the perceptions of the respondent regarding environmental conditions that might impact their strategic choice to enter alliances were included. The general uncertainty regarding market conditions and how those conditions might change over time (Poppo & Zenger, 1998) and the uncertainty regarding technological complexity and volatility (Hagedoorn, 1993) have all been shown to be associated with the strategic choice to form alliances in past research. Measures for each of these perceptions were drawn from the work of Covin and Slevin (1989) and Schultz, Slevin, and Covin (1995).

Analyses

The relationship of the institutional variables as well as the entrepreneurial orientation of the firm owner/manager to the dichotomous outcome variables—alliance use/nonuse and agreement-based-only versus equity-based alliances—was measured through the use of a logistic regression procedure. The beta coefficients provided by a logistic regression procedure give the change in log odds of obtaining the outcome variable when there is a change of one unit in the predictor variable. If the logistic coefficient for a variable is significant and positive, it suggests that the variable increases the odds of obtaining the outcome variable, while a negative coefficient indicates a decrease in the odds. Based on the advice of Hosmer and Lemeshow (1989), the study variables were entered into the logistic regression in stages in order to assess the relative impacts. In order to provide the more rigorous test possible for both the institutional variables and EO, all control variables were estimated first, followed by the institutional variables, and lastly the EO measure.

STUDY RESULTS

Sample Demographics

Table 1.1 provides the sample demographics for this study, including the number of firms surveyed by country, the response rate by country, and a breakdown of the number of surveyed firms with alliances and of those with alliances the number that hold equity-based alliances. Additional information regarding the nature of a number of the measures used in the study is also provided.

Tests of Hypotheses

Table 1.2 provides a summary of the results of the logistic regression for both alliance use and alliance structure as well as a brief analysis of the possible meanings of the results obtained. In addition to the outcome variables for the study, Table 1.2 also provides a list of those control variables that were found to be significant and that proved to be of particular interest to this study.

The results of the logistic regression analysis, while broadly supporting the hypothesized relationships, did reveal a few surprises. The results suggest that for firms of the sizes surveyed in this research, the greater the environmental munificence, as reflected by the size of the economy, the less

TABLE 1.1 Study Demographics

Country[a]	Total Sampled	Completed Surveys	Percent Responding	No Alliances	One or More Alliances	At least one Equity Alliance	Average Firm Size
Australia	1,373	313	22.8	137	176	22	84.38
Finland	400	121	30.8	14	107	16	55.02
Greece	400	228	57.0	56	172	25	35.28
Indonesia	890	285	32.0	149	136	42	69.28
Mexico	650	363	56.0	173	190	62	120.84
Netherlands	300	131	43.7	44	87	21	36.42
Norway	2,465	433	17.6	88	345	61	63.81
Sweden	600	180	30.0	28	152	38	65.32
Totals	**7,078**	**2,054**[b]	**23.9**	**689**	**1,365**[c]	**287**[c]	**62.51**

[a] The home markets for the companies included in this analysis have an average GDP ranging from a low of $97,075 (in millions of U.S. dollars) for Greece to a high of $383,303 for Australia. Economic risk indices range from 96.92 for Sweden, based on a 100-point scale, with the highest scores equaling the lowest risk, to 43.56 for Indonesia as ranked by the Euromoney Country Risk Index. Australia has as its legal foundation English Common Law. Greece, Indonesia, Mexico, and the Netherlands are based on French Civil Law. Finland, Norway, and Sweden are based on Scandinavian Civil Law.

[b] 53 surveys were excluded in the regression analysis due to missing data.

[c] 22 surveys from firms with at least one equity-based alliance were excluded in the regressions analysis due to missing data.

TABLE 1.2 Summary of Regression Analysis Results

Predictor Variables	Formation	Structure	Result Analysis
Market munificence	− − −	+ +	The larger, more munificent the economy, the less likely the firm is to form a strategic alliance. For firms that do form alliances, the more munificent the economy, the more likely the firm is to have at least one equity-based alliance.
Economic risk	− − −	+	The greater the economic risk, the less likely the firm is to form a strategic alliance. For firms that do form alliances, the greater the economic risk, the more likely the firm is to have at least one alliance that is equity based.
English Common Law	N.S.	N.S.	In comparison to firms in French Civil Law countries, firms in English Common Law countries are no more or no less likely to form strategic alliances. There is also no significant difference in the use of equity-based alliances.
Scandinavian Civil Law	− −	−	In comparison to firms in French Civil Law countries, firms in Scandinavian Civil Law countries are less likely to form strategic alliances. Of the firms that do form alliances, the firms in Scandinavian Civil Law countries are less likely to have at least one equity-based alliance.
Entrepreneurial Orientation	+ + +	N.S.	The greater the entrepreneurial orientation of the owner/general manager, the more likely the firm is to form a strategic alliance. The entrepreneurial orientation of the owner/general manager has no impact on the choice of equity or nonequity alliances.

Control Variables of Significance

Predictor Variables	Formation	Structure	Result Analysis
Firm size	+ + +	+ +	The larger the firm, the more likely it is to both form alliances and to form at least one equity-based alliance.
Export intensity	+ + +	+	The greater the level of export intensity, the more likely the firm is to form alliances and to form at least one equity-based alliance
Technological uncertainty	+ + +	+ +	The greater the perception of the owner/general manager of the uncertainty of the technological environment, the more likely the firm is to form alliances and to form at least one equity-based alliance.

(continued)

TABLE 1.2 (continued)   Summary of Regression Analysis Results

Predictor Variables	Formation	Structure	Result Analysis
Alliance necessity	+++	++	The greater the belief of the owner/ general manager that alliances are necessary strategic activities, the more likely the firm is to form alliances and to form at least one equity-based alliance.

Note: N = 2,001 for alliance formation model. Nagelkerke R^2 = .241 for alliance formation model

N = 1,343 for alliance structure model. Nagelkerke R^2 = .116 for alliance structure model

+++ indicates that the relationship is positive and significant at the $p < .001$ level

++ indicates positive and significant at the $p < .01$ level

+ indicates positive and significant at the $p < .05$ level

--- indicates negative and significant at the $p < .001$ level

-- indicates negative and significant at the $p < .01$ level

- indicates negative and significant at the $p < .05$ level

N.S. indicates that the relationship is not significant

likely the owners of SMEs are to form strategic alliances. Similarly, the greater the level of economic risk in the environment, the less likely is the formation of alliances by SMEs. While the results did not support a significant difference in alliance formation by companies located in English Common Law countries in comparison to those in French Civil Law countries, it did indicate a significant difference between firms in Scandinavian Civil Law and French Civil Law countries. Contrary to expectations, firms in Scandinavian countries were less likely to form alliances. Importantly, the results suggest that the higher the proclivity toward risky behavior, innovation, and creativity (EO), the more likely the SME owner is to form strategic alliances.

In regard to alliance structure, the results of the analysis suggest that the greater the market munificence and the greater the level of economic risk, the more likely that all or at least some of the SME alliances would be structured based on equity investments. Similar to alliance choice, there was no significant difference between firms in English Common Law and French Civil Law countries, while there were differences between Scandinavian and French Civil Law. As predicted, SMEs in Scandinavian Civil Law countries were less likely to have at least some alliance relationships involving equity investments. Surprisingly, unlike the choice to form alliances, the level of EO of the SME owner was found to have no significant impact on the choice of alliance structures.

Finally, the control variables utilized in this study did provide some additional interesting results. The size of the firm, the level of export intensity of the firm, the perceptions of the SME owner regarding the uncertainty of the technological environment, and the necessity for alliances as a strategic choice were all positively and significantly related to both the decision to form alliances and the choice of equity-based alliance structures. In general, the larger the firm, the more heavily involved the firm is in exporting; and the greater the owner's perception of technological uncertainty and alliance necessity, the more likely the alliance owner is to form alliances and to form at least some equity-based alliances.

DISCUSSION AND CONCLUSIONS

Theoretical frameworks have long suggested that both the strategic choice to form alliance relationships and the choice of alliance structures may be strongly influenced by the nature of the environment of the firm (Gulati, 1995). The individual differences of strategic decision leaders of firms has more recently been argued to also have important implications for strategic behavior and in specific alliance choice (Covin & Slevin, 1989; Palich & Bagby, 1991). The research findings discussed in this chapter suggest that both perspectives—that institutions matter and that individual orientations matter—may be true. While both perspectives are supported by the results, the findings regarding the impact of individual orientations on alliance choice have not, to the authors' knowledge, been previously shown. The findings provide support to the notion that the greater the proclivity of the individual owner toward risky behavior, innovation, and creativity (EO), the more likely she or he is to seek out alliance relationships. Surprisingly, this same relationship does not hold true, once an alliance is formed, in the decision to utilize more structured equity-based alliances.

Implications

The results of the research reported in this chapter have important implications for both theory and practice. The findings of this research suggest the importance of considering not only the impact of the firm's environment on alliance choice, as suggested by theoretical frameworks focusing on the firms and markets, but also the impact of the behavioral orientations of individual owners and managers in determining strategic decisions regarding alliance formation.

The findings of the research also have important implications for policy. In motivating alliance formation, institutions appear to matter. This is of importance to policymakers seeking to support alliance formation as an industry or national strategy for growth and development. The results of the research also emphasize the importance of understanding the role of individual differences in alliance choice. Individual differences across firm owners and managers may lead to important variance in response to changes in the institutional environment.

Limitations

The study that provides the foundation for this chapter provides one of the broadest surveys of SMEs, including SMEs from eight countries and twelve industries. In spite of the breadth of companies surveyed, generalizations made to countries, industries, and firms with more than 500 employees must be made with caution. The study utilizes survey methodology that while providing unique knowledge of independently owned SMEs, has important limitations. Every effort was made in the study to mitigate these potential limitations. Finally, another limitation, potentially present in all cross-national research, is the possibility of misinterpretation of questions by the respondents and misinterpretations of the responses by researchers. The care taken in survey development and translation by the researchers as well as the use of local teams of experts in the interpretation of the results hopefully has minimized these additional limitations.

REFERENCES

Barringer, B. R., & Harrison, J. S. (2000). Walking a tightrope: Creating value through interorganizational relationships. *Journal of Management, 26,* 367–403.

Baum, J. A., Calabrese, T., & Silverman, B. S. (2000). Don't go it alone: Alliance network composition and startups' performance in Canadian biotechnology. *Strategic Management Journal, 21,* 267–294.

Calof, J. L. (1993). The impact of size on internationalization. *Journal of Small Business Management, 31,* 60–69.

Cosset, J., & Roy, J. (1991). The determinants of country risk ratings. *Journal of International Business Studies, 22,* 135–142.

Covin, J. G., & Slevin, D. (1989). Strategic management of small firms in hostile and benign environments. *Strategic Management Journal, 10,* 75–87.

Covin, J. G., Slevin, D. P., & Schultz, R. L. (1994). Implementing strategic missions: Effective strategic, structural and tactical choices. *Journal of Management Studies, 31,* 481–505.

Das, T. K., & Teng, B. (2000). A resource-based theory of strategic alliances. *Journal of Management, 26,* 31–61.

Das T. K., & Teng, B. (2001a). Relational risk and its personal correlates in strategic alliances. *Journal of Business and Psychology, 15,* 445–461.

Das, T. K., & Teng, B. (2001b). A risk perception model of alliance structuring. *Journal of International Management, 7,* 1–29.

Davis, L. E., & North, D. C. (1971). *Institutional change and American economic growth.* Cambridge, England: Cambridge University Press.

Deeds, D., & Hill, C. (1999). An examination of opportunistic action within research alliances: Evidence from the biotechnology industry. *Journal of Business Venturing, 14,* 141–163.

Dess, G. G., & Beard, D. W. (1984). Dimensions of organizational task environments. *Administrative Science Quarterly, 29,* 52–73.

Dickson, P. H., & Weaver, K. M. (1997). Environmental determinants and individual-level moderators of alliance use. *Academy of Management Journal, 40,* 404–425.

Dickson, P. H., & Weaver, K. M. (2011). Institutional readiness and small to medium-sized enterprise alliance formation. *Journal of Small Business Management, 49,* 126–148.

DiMaggio, P. J., & Powell, W. W. (1991). Introduction. In W. W. Powell & P. J. DiMaggio (Eds.), *The new institutionalism in organizational analysis* (pp. 1–38). Chicago, IL: University of Chicago Press.

Euromoney (1998). *Country risk revisited.* London, England: Euromoney.

Ghemawat, P., Porter, M., & Rawlinson, R. (1996). Patterns of international coalition activity. In M. E. Porter (Ed.), *Competition in global industries* (pp. 345–365). Boston, MA: Harvard University Press.

Ghoshal, S. (1987). Global strategy: An organizing framework. *Strategic Management Journal, 8,* 425–440.

Gulati, R. (1995). Does familiarity breed trust? The implications of repeated ties for contractual choice in alliances. *Academy of Management Journal, 38,* 85–112.

Hagedoorn, J. (1993). Understanding the rationale of strategic technology partnering: Interorganizational modes of cooperation and sectoral differences. *Strategic Management Journal, 14,* 371–385.

Hagedoorn, J., & Narula, R. (1996). Choosing organizational modes of strategic technology partnering: International and sectoral differences. *Journal of International Business Studies, 27,* 265–284.

Hitt, M. A., Ahlstrom, D., Dacin, M. T., Levitas, E., & Svobodina, L. (2004). The institutional effects on strategic alliance partner selection in transition economies: China vs. Russia. *Organization Science, 15,* 173–185.

Hosmer, D. W., & Lemeshow, S. (1989). *Applied logistic regression.* New York, NY: Wiley.

Keats, B., & Hitt, M. (1988). A causal model of linkages among environmental dimensions, macro organizational characteristics, and performance. *Academy of Management Journal, 31,* 570–598.

Klein Woolthuis, R., Hillebrand, B., & Nooteboom, B. (2005). Trust, contract and relationship development. *Organization Studies, 26,* 813–840.

Kogut, B. (1988). A study of the life cycle of joint ventures. In F. Contractor & P. Lorange (Eds.), *Cooperative strategies in international business* (pp. 169–185). Lexington, MA: Lexington Books.

Koza, M., & Lewin, A. (1998). The co-evolution of strategic alliances. *Organization Science, 9,* 255–264.

La Porta, R., Lopez-de-Silanes, F., & Shleifer, A. (1998). Law and finance. *Journal of Political Economy, 106,* 1113–1155.

La Porta, R., Lopez-de-Silanes, F., & Shleifer, A. (1999). Corporate ownership around the world. *Journal of Finance, 54,* 471–517.

La Porta, R., Lopez-de-Silanes, F., & Shleifer, A. (2002). Investor protection and corporate valuation. *Journal of Finance, 57,* 1147–1170.

La Porta, R., Lopez-de-Silanes, F., Shleifer, A., & Vishny, R. W. (1997). Legal determinants of external finance. *Journal of Finance, 52,* 1131–1150.

Lee, H., & Park, J. (2008). The influence of top management team international exposure on international alliance formation. *Journal of Management Studies, 45,* 961–981.

Lumpkin, G. T., & Dess, G. G. (1996). Clarifying the entrepreneurial orientation construct and linking it to performance. *Academy of Management Review, 21,* 135–172.

Luo, Y. (2002). Building trust in cross-cultural collaborations: Toward a contingency perspective. *Journal of Management, 28,* 669–694.

Mellewigt, T., Madhok, A., & Weibel, A. (2007). Trust and formal contracts in interorganizational relationships—Substitutes *and* complements. *Managerial and Decision Economics, 28,* 833–847.

Miles, G., Preece, S. B., & Baetz, M. C. (1999, April, 20–29). Dangers of dependence: The impact of strategic alliance use by small technology-based firms. *Journal of Small Business Management.*

Nielsen, B. B. (2010). Multilevel issues in strategic alliance research. In T. K. Das (Ed.), *Researching strategic alliances: Emerging perspectives* (pp. 1–26). Charlotte, NC: Information Age.

OECD. (2003). *OECD science, technology and industry scoreboard.* Paris, France: Organization for Economic Co-operation and Development.

Osborn, R., & Baughn, C. (1990). Forms of interorganizational governance for multinational alliances. *Academy of Management Journal, 33,* 503–519.

Oxley, J. E. (1997). Appropriability hazards and governance in strategic alliances: A transaction cost approach. *Journal of Law, Economics and Organization, 13,* 387–409.

Oxley, J. E. (1999). Institutional environment and the mechanisms of governance: The impact of intellectual property protection on the structure of inter-firm alliances. *Journal of Economic Behavior & Organization, 38,* 283–309.

Palich, L. E., & Bagby, D. R. (1995). Using cognitive theory to explain entrepreneurial risk-taking: Challenging conventional wisdom. *Journal of Business Venturing, 10,* 425–438.

Park, S. H., Chen, R., & Gallagher, S. (2002). Firm resources as moderators of the relationship between market growth and strategic alliances in semiconductor startups. *Academy of Management Journal, 45,* 527–545.

Pfeffer, J., & Salancik, G. R. (1978). *The external control of organizations.* New York, NY: Harper and Row.

Poppo, L., & Zenger, T. (1998). Testing alternative theories of the firm: Transaction cost, knowledge-based, and measurement explanations for make-or-buy decision in information services. *Strategic Management Journal, 19,* 853–877.

Rasheed, H. S. (2005). Foreign entry mode and performance: The moderating effects of environment. *Journal of Small Business Management, 43,* 41–54.

Sakakibara, M. (2002). Formation of R&D consortia: Industry and company effects. *Strategic Management Journal, 23,* 1033–1050.

Schultz, R. L., Slevin, D. P., & Covin, J. G. (1995). *The strategic management profile: An executive questionnaire.* [Unpublished questionnaire]. Joseph M. Katz Graduate School of Business, University of Pittsburgh, Pennsylvania.

Shan, W. (1990). An empirical analysis of organizational strategies in entrepreneurial high-technology firms. *Strategic Management Journal, 11,* 129–139.

Steensma, H. K., Marino, L., Weaver, K. M., & Dickson, P. H. (2000). The influence of national culture on the formation of technology alliances by entrepreneurial firms. *Academy of Management Journal, 43,* 951–973.

Tallman, S. B., & Shenkar, O. (1994). A managerial decision model of international cooperative venture formation. *Journal of International Business Studies, 25,* 91–113.

Todeva, E., & Knoke, D. (2005). Strategic alliances and models of cooperation. *Management Decision, 43,* 123–148.

Tyler, B. B., & Steensma, H. K. (1995). Evaluating technology collaborative opportunities: A cognitive modeling perspective. *Strategic Management Journal, 16,* 43–70.

UNESCO. (2002). *UNESCO statistical yearbook.* New York, NY: United Nations Department of Economic and Social Affairs.

Walsh, V. (1988). Technology and competitiveness of small countries. In C. Freeman & B. Lundvall (Eds.), *Small countries facing the technological revolution* (pp. 37–66). London, England: Pinter.

Williamson, O. E. (1983). Credible commitments: Using hostages to support exchange. *American Economic Review, 73,* 519–540.

Williamson, O. E. (1985). *The economic institutions of capitalism.* New York, NY: Free Press.

Yiu, D., & Makino, S. (2002). The choice between joint venture and wholly owned subsidiary: An institutional perspective. *Organization Science, 13,* 667–683.

Zaheer, A., & Venkatraman, N. (1995). Relational governance as an interorganizational strategy: An empirical test of the role of trust in economic exchange. *Strategic Management Journal, 16,* 373–392.

CHAPTER 2

VALUE CREATION IN ALLIANCE PORTFOLIOS

Integrating Configurational and Managerial Aspects

Andreas Al-Laham
Florian Zock

ABSTRACT

Whereas a vast amount of research has indicated that single strategic alliances create value for the focal firms, sparse work has been conducted on the mechanisms of value creation within a firm's alliance portfolio. This chapter will address this gap in the literature by merging both configurational and managerial aspects of value creation in alliance portfolios, which have so far always been regarded separately. We develop a conceptual framework based on theoretical considerations embedded in the knowledge-based view and the dynamic capabilities view. In particular, we analyze the impact of multi-level alliance portfolio configuration on firms' innovation performance. Also, we investigate the role of alliance portfolio capabilities by examining its moderating effect on that relationship as well as its direct influence on a firm's innovation performance. We assume three inverted U-shaped relationships

Management Dynamics in Strategic Alliances, pages 23–51

between alliance portfolio configuration and firm innovation performance indicating that a balanced portfolio has the highest innovative outcome. Furthermore, we presume that portfolio capabilities per se strengthen firm innovation performance. Finally, we hypothesize that alliance portfolio capabilities positively moderate those three inverted U-shaped relationships between alliance portfolio configuration and a firm's innovation performance.

INTRODUCTION

Apple's business model is acclaimed by scholars and practitioners in the strategic management field for its value creation potential (Ozcan & Eisenhardt, 2009). In fact, many best practices can be derived from the company's turnaround from almost bankruptcy to record performance in 2010. In this turnaround, network embeddedness has been playing a central role. Apple's interorganizational alliances with EMI, Google, Infineon, Salesforce.com, Microsoft, and other firms (Burrows, 2007) were strategic key factors for its success. Taken together, these ties helped Apple to focus on its core competencies (i.e., R&D, design, marketing) while exploiting their alliance partners' resources, capabilities, and market positions. However, Apple is far from being the only firm that dedicates much strategic attention toward partnering within their business model in order to create value. In the past decade, the majority of firms operating in key industries, such as hardware and software, automotive, and pharmaceuticals have strengthened their alliance activity to enhance performance outcomes (Wassmer, 2010).

In particular, biotechnology has been identified as the industry with the greatest partnering affinity (Hagedoorn, 2002). Firms operating in this field rely on knowledge-extensive capabilities that transform scientific know-how in products. Thereby, their attempts are not only directed toward generating new products but also toward new methods and processes to discover them (Powell, Koput, & Smith-Doerr, 1996). Thus, commercialization heavily depends on core competences dealing with scientific discoveries (Amburgey, Al-Laham, Tzabbar, & Aharonson, 2008). For such a business model to create value, partnering is indispensible in order to source specialized knowledge from external institutions such as universities. As a result, by today, biotechnology firms are engaged in multiple simultaneous alliances in R&D, marketing, or sales (Al-Laham & Amburgey, 2010; Amburgey et al., 2008).

The Apple and biotech examples do not represent unique phenomena but rather reflect the general trends in business. In fact, today's competitive environments have forced firms to develop core competencies and rely on external sources for supplementary and complementary capabilities and knowledge (Santoro & Chakrabarti, 2002). As a result, through outsourcing, firms have reduced the depth of value adding resulting in alliances, which have become a central element of business models and strategy aiming at value creation (Contractor & Lorange, 2002; Das & Teng, 2000a; Gulati, 1998; Gulati, Nohria, & Zaheer, 2000). In knowledge-intensive industries, there is ample evidence that firms do not only enter in one strategic alliance but into multiple simultaneous alliances (Hagedoorn, 2002; Hoang & Rothaermel, 2005; Kale, Dyer, & Singh, 2002; Rothaermel & Deeds, 2004; Stuart, 2000). Consequently, those firms are engaged in the challenge to build up, configure, manage, and control a complex alliance portfolio (Gulati, 1998; Hoffmann, 2007; Lavie, 2007; Marino, Strandholm, Steensma, & Weaver, 2002).

Although partnering has obviously become a significant strategic weapon for numerous firms across industries aiming at value creation, its actual practice is a challenging task. In fact, studies have shown that firms engaged in large alliance portfolios do not necessarily perform better than those with smaller portfolios (Heimeriks, Duysters, & Vanhaverbeke, 2007). This is due to the fact that alliance failure rates are generally high, ranging from 40% to 70% (Heimeriks, Klein, & Reuer, 2009). The literature has identified two main factors for that failure of executing alliances: ineffective partner selection (Lavie, 2009) and inefficient management of the alliance portfolio (Ireland, Hitt, & Vaidyanath, 2002). Thus, engaging in extensive alliance portfolio activity does not ultimately create value for the focal firms. Value generation and performance enhancement, rather, depend on effective and efficient strategic decisions on the alliance portfolio configuration and management. Thus, from a strategic management perspective, the central question is how firms can configure and manage their alliance portfolios to overcome those failures and in turn, create value. Our chapter aims to answer this question. Specifically, we want to explore how alliance portfolio configuration and management influence firms' innovation performance.

Therefore, the chapter is organized as follows. First, we provide a review of the literature and prior research on alliance portfolios, including an outline of their antecedents and an identification of the specific research gap we aim to fill. Next, we introduce the concepts that are central to this chapter. Based on the theoretical rationale of the knowledge-based view and the dynamic capabilities view, we then develop an integrative conceptual framework of value creation in alliance portfolios. By merging configurational and managerial aspects within this framework, we deduce assumptions that might guide future empirical research. We end up with a conclusion that includes theoretical contributions, managerial implications, and avenues for further research.

LITERATURE REVIEW AND RESEARCH GAP

Antecedents of Alliance Portfolio Research: Alliance and Network Research

Research on cooperative strategies has proliferated in correspondence with their increasing emergence in business (Lavie, 2007; Powell, 1990). Relevant studies can be categorized into two streams of literature: on the one hand research dealing with single alliances, on the other hand studies preoccupied with (social) networks. By definition, alliances are voluntary arrangements among independent firms to exchange or share resources and engage in the co-development or provision of products, services, or technologies (Gulati, 1998). Brass, Galaskiewicz, Greve, and Tsai (2004) generally define a (social) network as "a set of nodes and the set of ties representing some relationship...between the nodes." Thereby, nodes can be perceived as individuals, formally defined groups (like firm departments), organizations (like a firm), or other collective social units (like stakeholders). Ties may include buying and selling, sharing of information, transfer of resources and of knowledge.

Within the literature focusing on the single dyadic alliance as the principal unit of analysis, the research focus has been on determinants of alliance formation, governance, management, and performance (Gulati, 1998). Therefore, the main focus has been on explaining value creation in alliances (Das & Teng, 2000a) and identifying anticipated beneficial outcomes from being engaged in alliances (Ireland et al., 2002). Thus, alliances generate value through several ways, including scale economies, effective risk management, efficient market entries as well as learning from alliance partners (Alvarez & Barney, 2001; Kogut, 1988). Furthermore, alliances assist firms to cope with uncertainty, reduce their resource dependency, and strategically reposition themselves in dynamic environments and markets (Das & Teng, 1996, 2000b; Spekman, Forbes, Isabella, & MacAvoy, 1998; Young-Ybarra, & Wiersema, 1999).

The second stream of research adopts a network perspective, exploring structural or relational aspects of networks (Granovetter, 1985). Structural embeddedness studies highlight actors' positions in the overall network structure and identify benefits that social network membership can provide for those actors referred to as social capital (Portes, 1998). These benefits derive from closed network structures that link actors (Coleman, 1988), from central network positioning (Bonacich, 1987; Podolny, 1993), or from brokerage positions that bridge disconnected actors (Burt, 1992). Social capital may contribute to firm performance by enhancing innovation (Ahuja, 2000; Tsai & Ghoshal, 1998), knowledge transfer (Burt, 1992; Inkpen & Tsang, 2005), intellectual capital (Nahapiet & Ghoshal, 1998), and efficiency (Baker, 1990; Burt, 2000). Relational embeddedness studies, in turn, examine the nature of relationships, considering for instance, the strength of ties and the evolving trust between actors (Granovetter, 1973; Podolny, 1994; Powell, 1990; Uzzi, 1996).

Review of Alliance Portfolio Research

The research discussed so far is valuable, as it can enhance our understanding of the cooperative paradigm in general (Powell, 1990). However, both perspectives suffer from conceptual shortcomings that restrict their explanatory power for the strategic management field. On the one hand, alliance research has focused exclusively on the dyadic level and on atomistic, isolated events, neglecting synergies resulting from social embeddedness (Lavie, 2007; Wassmer, 2010). On the other hand, network research has been preoccupied with structural and relational properties, assuming away differences in the inherent attributes of actors (Rowley, Behrens, & Krackhardt, 2000) and neglecting the firm-level perspective. The recently emerging alliance portfolio perspective can address these shortcomings. This stream of literature takes a firm-level perspective. At the same time, it also considers social network embeddedness due to simultaneous strategic alliances taken by the focal firm. By definition, an alliance portfolio describes a focal firm's ego-network of alliances, those still active as well as those terminated earlier on, spanning a variety of dimensions (i.e., partners, contents, scope) (Lavie, 2007). The scarce existing body of research can be organized in a conceptual map comprising three major areas, each representing an important phase and challenge in the life cycle of an alliance portfolio. These three areas are the emergence, configuration, and management of alliance portfolios (Wassmer, 2010). However, most of the issues in these three research areas have not yet been investigated or have only been addressed peripherally. We want to advance alliance portfolio research by exploring how alliance portfolio configuration and management create value.

Identification of Research Gap

With regard to alliance portfolio configuration and its effect on performance outcomes, structural portfolio properties (Gulati, 1999), relational (Rowley et al., 2000) and partner characteristics (Lavie, 2007) have been examined. As a major limitation, the few existing studies have solely taken a one-dimensional approach (partner dimension, or alliance/dyadic dimension or portfolio structure/network dimension). A multilevel conceptualization integrating the three dimensions of portfolio configuration has not been provided yet. We fill that gap by examining the relationship between multilevel alliance portfolio configuration and firm innovation performance. In addition, we aim to merge alliance portfolio configuration with broader management challenges, which have so far always been regarded in separation (Wassmer, 2010). To that end, we also illuminate the influence of a distinct set of dynamic capabilities (Eisenhardt & Martin, 2000; Teece, Pisano, & Shuen, 1997) the focal firm needs to develop for the purpose of enhancing innovation performance: alliance portfolio capabilities (Kale et al., 2002; Sarkar, Aulakh, & Madhok, 2009).

Hence, we first discuss how multilevel alliance portfolio configuration impacts firm innovation performance. Second, we examine how portfolio capabilities per se influence innovation performance. Third, we investigate how the multilevel portfolio configuration-innovation performance link is moderated by alliance portfolio capabilities. Before we are able to address these so far unsolved questions, we have to provide an understanding for the most central constructs: alliance portfolio, value creation, multilevel alliance portfolio configuration, and alliance portfolio capabilities.

CONCEPTUAL BACKGROUND

Alliance Portfolio

By definition, an alliance portfolio describes a focal firm's ego-network of alliances, those still active as well as those terminated earlier on, spanning a variety of dimensions (i.e., partners, contents, scope) (Bae & Gargiulo, 2004; Hoffmann, 2005; Lavie & Miller, 2008). However, a focal firm's alliance portfolio does not represent an atomistic, isolated entity (Granovetter, 1985). The respective ego-network is rather embedded in a global network of firms spanning many industries and countries (see Figure 2.1). Neglecting those networks in which alliance portfolios are embedded can lead to an incomplete understanding of alliance portfolios (Gulati, 1999). We emphasize this thought below.

Value Creation

For decades, the core interest of strategic management has been in value creation. Researchers from diverse theoretical backgrounds, such as industrial organization (Porter, 1980), resource-based view (RBV) (Barney, 1991), and relational view (Dyer & Singh, 1998), have discussed the antecedents of competitive advantage and superior firm performance in order to grasp the concept of value creation. This also applies to alliance portfolio literature where various performance constructs have been explored: firm survival (Baum & Oliver, 1991), growth rates (Powell et al., 1996), and financial performance (Lavie, 2007; Lavie & Miller, 2008).

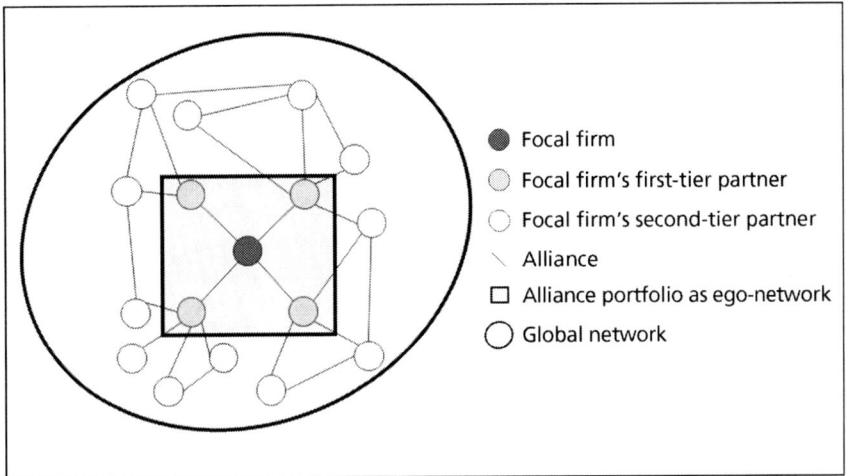

Figure 2.1   Focal firm's alliance portfolio as ego-network embedded in a global network.

In today's hypercompetitive environment (D'Aveni, 1994), the sustainable generation of value mainly depends on continuous innovative output. For that reason, we conceptualize value creation as innovation performance. Therefore we link innovation performance to the knowledge-based view in strategic management. The view that innovation arises from the recombination of existing knowledge is now well-established (Grant, 1996; Spender, 1996; Spender & Grant, 1996). The study of innovation has conceptualized the innovation process as the accumulation and recombination of knowledge embodied in science and technology (Van de Ven, 1986). More specifically, innovation is seen as an outcome of a process involving the development, diffusion, and application of knowledge embedded within particular social and institutional contexts (McLoughlin, 1999). Drawing upon Schumpeter's (1934) classical contribution, several recent studies have confirmed the central role knowledge transfer, recombination, and integration play in the firm's ability to generate innovations (Henderson & Cockburn, 1994; Phene, Fladmoe-Lindquist, & Marsh, 2006; Rosenkopf & Nerkar, 2001). Several other studies have emphasized the critical function of accessing and recombining both internal and external knowledge for innovation (DeCarolis & Deeds, 1999; Kogut & Zander, 1992).

Multilevel Alliance Portfolio Configuration

From a strategic management perspective, focal firms can actively build up and structure their alliance portfolios. Such strategic action refers to alliance portfolio configuration. Prior research has argued that firms can configure three dimensions of their portfolios: a partner dimension (Lavie, 2007), a relational dimension (Rowley et al., 2000), and a structural dimension (Gulati, 1999). These three dimensions of alliance portfolio configuration span multiple levels of analysis. In fact, the partner dimension is at the partner firm level of analysis, whereas the relational dimension is at the dyadic level of analysis, and the structural dimension of alliance portfolios is at the global-network level of analysis. Hence, alliance portfolio configuration is a multidimensional and multilevel construct (see Figure 2.2)[1.]

At the partner firm level of analysis, the focal firm can decide which alliance partners it wants to add to its portfolio. In order to conceptualize this partner dimension, we point to the degree of variance in partners' resources, capabilities, and knowledge, referred to as partner diversity (Lavie, 2007). Specifically, we suggest analyzing partner diversity with regard to their international diversity. This refers to the degree of internationalization of a firm's portfolio partners coming from various countries of origins, which differ in national culture, as well as providing additional knowledge about customer preferences, market structures, and governmental regulations (Lavie & Miller, 2008). Prior research has indicated that international partners provide a fruitful learning arena for a focal firm due to the heterogeneity in the partners' knowledge base (Al-Laham & Amburgey, 2010).

At the dyad level of analysis, the focal firm can arrange its portfolio with regard to tie strength[2] (Granovetter, 1973), which is generally perceived as frequency of interaction (McEvily & Zaheer, 1999). In our framework, we conceptualize tie strength as multiplexity (Wasserman & Faust, 1994). Multiplexity refers to the number of relations within a given link (Galaskiewicz & Wasserman, 1993). Intuitively, the concept describes the tendency for

Dimension	Level of analysis	Variable	Conceptualization
Partner	Firm level	Partner international diversity	Degree of internationalization of a firm's alliance portfolio partners
Relational	Dyadic level	Tie strength	Degree of multiplexity of an alliance referring to the tendency that two or more different alliance types (i.e., R&D and marketing) occur together
Structural	Network level	Partner network status	Degree of influence of a firm's alliance portfolio partners on the larger global network in which the portfolio is embedded

Figure 2.2 Overview of multilevel alliance portfolio configuration.

two or more different alliance types to occur together between two specific partners.[3]

At the network level of analysis, the focal firm can arrange its alliance portfolio with regard to the positional embeddedness of their first-tier portfolio partners (see Figure 2.1) (Gulati & Gargiulo, 1999), referring to their structural position within the larger network. Among features characterizing network positions, research suggests that network status is the most valuable (Bonacich, 1987; Podolny, 1993). Thus, status involves prestige or simply influence. Thus, the focal firm can add partners to their portfolio that differ in the degree of influence on the larger network; high-status partners are those that are linked to many partners that are, in turn, linked to several other partners.

Alliance Portfolio Capabilities

According to the RBV, firms in the same industry perform differently because they differ in resources they control (Barney, 1991; Wernerfelt, 1984). Despite its significance, the RBV is criticized to be static in nature, thereby neglecting the impact of dynamic environments (Barreto, 2010). In order to address this shortcoming, Teece et al. (1997) have proposed the dynamic capabilities approach. This explicitly acknowledges the importance of dynamic processes, including the development and maintenance of differential bundles of capabilities over time (Galunic & Eisenhardt, 2001; Henderson & Cockburn, 1994; Kogut & Zander, 1992; Zander & Kogut, 1995). We concentrate on one specific set of such capabilities literature has characterized as important: alliance portfolio capabilities.

Consistent with our process-based approach to conceptualizing dynamic capabilities, we perceive alliance portfolio capabilities as the collection of managerial routines that are available to the focal firms to deal with the inherent challenges of alliance portfolio management (Eisenhardt & Martin, 2000). Through experiential learning (Cyert & March, 1963; Levitt & March, 1988; Martin & Salomon, 2003; Nelson & Winter, 1982; Pennings, Barkema, & Douma, 1994), these routines result from and develop with accumulated experience in building and managing alliance portfolios. Recently, Sarkar et al. (2009) have identified three specific process dimensions of alliance portfolio capabilities, which they call partnering proactiveness, relational governance, and portfolio coordination. Partnering proactiveness refers to a firm's efforts to identify and exploit alliance opportunities. Relational governance points to a firm's engagement in activities for developing informal safeguards in their alliances. Finally, portfolio coordination refers to a firm's measures to integrate and synchronize knowledge and activities across the portfolio.

VALUE CREATION IN ALLIANCE PORTFOLIOS: THE ROLE OF MULTILEVEL PORTFOLIO CONFIGURATION

Multilevel Alliance Portfolio Configuration and Firm Innovation Performance

After having provided a common understanding for the most central constructs, we now turn to developing our integrative framework of value creation in alliance portfolios, which we introduce in Figure 2.3. We aim to build that framework stepwise, by deriving specific assumptions on how multilevel alliance portfolio configuration, portfolio capabilities, and firm innovation performance relate to each other. To that end, we first analyze how portfolio configuration influences focal firm innovation performance. Following the knowledge-based view in strategic management, a firm's alliance portfolio is an important external source of knowledge in order to foster innovation (Arora & Gambardella, 1990; Hitt, Hoskisson, Johnson, & Moesel, 1996) as well as to develop innovative capabilities (Chaudhuri & Tabrizi, 1999). We presume that the partner, the relational, and the structural characteristics of the portfolio determine the degree of knowledge flows. In the following, we hypothesize upon to what extent the three dimensions provide sources of knowledge in order to strengthen innovation.

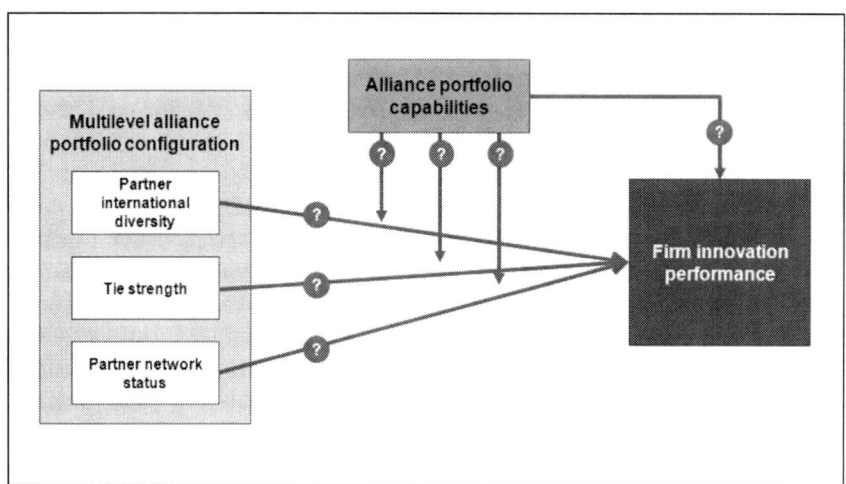

Figure 2.3 Integrative framework of value creation in alliance portfolios.

Alliance Portfolio Configuration at the Firm Level: Partner International Diversity and Firm Innovation Performance

The first dimension of alliance portfolio configuration refers to the diverse set of a firm's portfolio partners. From a knowledge-based view, there are several reasons for the positive innovation performance effects of international diversity. Generally, firms tend to search for new knowledge in the neighborhood of their current technological knowledge domain (Nelson & Winter, 1982). However, purely technologically local search restricts the possibilities for innovation through the recombination of knowledge (Leonard-Barton, 1995; Levitt & March, 1988). To overcome this restriction and to compete successfully over time, firms must move beyond technologically local search (McGrath, 2001; Rosenkopf, Metiu, & George, 2001), since the existence of heterogeneous knowledge enhances the likelihood for novel ideas to emerge (Henderson & Cockburn, 1996; Turner & Fauconnier, 1997). In particular, forming upstream alliances with foreign portfolio partners may offer untapped technologies and resources that could be limited in the firm's home country (Eisenhardt & Schoonhoven, 1996; Hagedoorn, 1993). In addition, a globally diversified alliance portfolio may provide local market knowledge that can help to bridge national boundaries and leverage firm's competitive advantage in foreign markets (Lavie & Miller, 2008). Thus, internationally diversified alliance portfolios may provide responsiveness to global market conditions and risk reduction (Eisenhardt & Schoonhoven, 1996; Hagedoorn, 1993; Kogut & Kulatilaka, 1993; Powell et al., 1996; Teece, 1992). Hence, partners' international diversity may offer opportunities for strengthening firm innovation performance resulting from additional access to knowledge.

However, by maintaining an alliance portfolio with diverse partners, firms also face conflicts (Madhok & Tallman, 1998; Park & Zhou, 2005; White & Lui, 2005) that result from differences in partner characteristics due to cultural divergence (Parkhe, 1991). Differences in national culture between the focal firm and its partners limit the scope of shared values and goals that are needed to absorb and transfer knowledge in alliances (Parkhe, 1991). Differences in value systems of culturally distant partners may result in divergent expectations and eventually in lack of commitment and unresolvable conflicts (Lane & Beamish, 1990). Overall, these liabilities reduce the effectiveness of collaboration with foreign partners (Barkema, Shenkar, Vermeulen, & Bell, 1997; Kumar & Nti, 1998; Lane & Lubatkin, 1998) and weaken the firm's ability to leverage knowledge from the alliance portfolio (Powell et al., 1996). Taken together, those factors tend to undermine the firm's innovation performance. Hence, firms face trade-offs as they increase the partner diversity of their alliance portfolio. Diversified partners provide access to enriched knowledge pools, which increases innovation performance. However, increased diversity can bring more complexity. The latter restricts the access to additional knowledge, which may decrease innovation performance. We thus assume an inverted U-shaped link between partner diversity and innovation performance.

> **Assumption 1A:** *The relationship between partner international diversity and firm innovation performance is curvilinear. The slope is positive at low and moderate levels of partner diversity and is negative at high levels of partner diversity.*

Alliance Portfolio Configuration at the Dyad Level: Tie Strength and Firm Innovation Performance

The second component of alliance portfolio configuration influencing firm innovation performance is the relational characteristics of alliance portfolios reflected by tie strength. Hence, focal firms can design the actual setting of their alliances by choosing between strong and weak ties. The impact of strong and weak ties on various firm performance measures has been widely discussed in the context of interfirm alliances (Kale, Singh, & Perlmutter, 2000; Larson, 1992; Uzzi, 1997). Recently, that relationship has also been regarded at the alliance portfolio level (Capaldo, 2007; Tiwana, 2008). Strong ties can stimulate close interaction and mitigate fear of opportunistic behavior (Kale et al., 2000; Zaheer, McEvily, & Perrone, 1998). As a result, focal firms adding strong ties to their portfolio can overcome the control systems usually set up in knowledge-intensive alliances to restrict information leakage (Capaldo, 2007). This is due to the fact that strong ties are implicitly trust based and characterized by the development of social content between alliance partners (Wassmer, 2010). In addition, by lowering various contracting and monitoring costs, those self-enforcing safeguards may lead to increased cross-fertilization of alliance portfolio members' knowledge bases, allowing for constant, steady flows of new ideas and innovation (Sarkar et al., 2009).

Increasing tie strength favors firm innovation performance. However, a portfolio composed of strong ties faces serious challenges as well, as the ego-network lacks the strength of weak ties (Granovetter, 1973). In fact, weak ties are able to foster and speed up innovation by connecting focal firms to otherwise difficult-to-reach knowledge areas (Rogers, 2003). By doing so, valuable nonredundant knowledge can be acquired (Burt, 1992). With increasing tie strength, focal firms cannot leverage those potentials for additional innovative impulses. Indeed, focal firms that are imprisoned in a small portfolio of strong ties risk being unable to face technological discontinuities and new market trends (Capaldo, 2007) resulting from non-redundancy of knowledge (Burt, 1992). As a result, we can argue that at intense levels of tie strength, usually more redundant information and knowledge results in decreasing innovation performance (Rowley et al., 2000).

To conclude, close interaction among the partners of the focal firm's alliance portfolio in the form of strong ties can offer steady flows of new knowledge augmenting firm innovation performance. However, focal firms relying on a portfolio composed of a great number of strong ties are restricted to tap into nonredundant, highly innovative knowledge. Hence, we assume a curvilinear relationship between tie strength and innovation performance, taking an inverted U-shape.

Assumption 1B: *The relationship between tie strength and firm innovation performance is curvilinear. The slope is positive at low and moderate levels of tie strength and is negative at high levels of tie strength.*

Alliance Portfolio Configuration at the Network Level: Partner Network Status and Firm Innovation Performance

The third dimension of alliance portfolio configuration refers to positional embeddedness or centrality of the focal firm's portfolio partners reflected by their network status. For building their portfolios, focal firms can choose between higher-status and lower-status portfolio partners. Compared to their lower-status counterparts, high-status portfolio partners provide two sets of knowledge stocks for focal firms. First, such high-status portfolio partners gain timely and easy access to resources that are embedded in the larger network (Powell et al., 1996), as lower-status firms in the global network are actively seeking an alliance involvement with them. In fact, in order to attract their attention, those lower-status firms offer them access to information or know-how (Madhavan, Koka, & Prescott, 1998). Second, those high-status portfolio partners can easily access human capital. This is due to the fact that highly qualified employees, such as specialized scientists, prefer to work for high-status firms (Frank, 1985). Thus, by adding high-status partners to their alliance portfolio, focal firms can tap into knowledge embedded in the larger network as well as into specialized know-how. Taken together, these additional sources of knowledge may enhance a firm's innovation performance.

However, the mentioned benefits of high-status portfolio partners are limited. Indeed, with the intensifying network status of their portfolio partners, focal firms are facing increasing threats to their innovative potential because of two main reasons: decreasing knowledge appropriation capacity and knowledge redundancy of their portfolio partners. First, a focal firm whose alliance portfolio comprises a considerable number of partners enjoying high network status may be unable to appropriate the knowledge benefits that its alliances in the portfolio produce (Bae & Gargiulo, 2004). The paradox here is that high-status partners who can make significant contribution to joint innovation creation may also be able to restrict the knowledge appropriation capacity for the focal firm (Lavie, 2007). This implies that firms may not be able to absorb valuable network knowledge, as their partners restrict access to it. Such limited knowledge-acquiring potential may undermine the firms' innovation performance. Second, an alliance portfolio composed of many high-status firms can be referred to as being structurally equivalent, insofar as a bulk of portfolio members occupies similar, namely, central positions (Burt, 1987). As a result, the information and knowledge flows within such a structurally equivalent alliance portfolio tend to be rather redundant than diverse (Burt, 1992). As a consequence, new and creative ideas are not exchanged between high-status portfolio partners. Thus, redundancy in knowledge resulting from intensive network status of focal firms' partners undermines focal firm innovation performance.

To sum up, we have argued that high-status partners provide access to knowledge in the form of network resources and human capital. As a result, increasing partner status has a positive influence on focal firm innovation performance. However, this relationship only holds true up to a certain point where further intensifying partner status has negative innovation performance implications. This is due to the decreasing knowledge-appropriation capacity and the hampered access to nonredundant knowledge. Thus, we assume an inverted U-shaped relationship between partner network status and firm innovation performance.

Assumption 1C: *The relationship between partner network status and focal firm innovation performance is curvilinear. The slope is positive at low and moderate levels of partner network status and is negative at high levels of partner network status.*

We illustrate the deduced assumptions characterizing the relationship between multilevel alliance portfolio configuration and focal firm innovation performance in Figure 2.4.

VALUE CREATION IN ALLIANCE PORTFOLIOS: THE ROLE OF PORTFOLIO CAPABILITIES

So far we have analyzed how portfolio configuration influences firm innovation performance. In the following, we investigate how the latter is

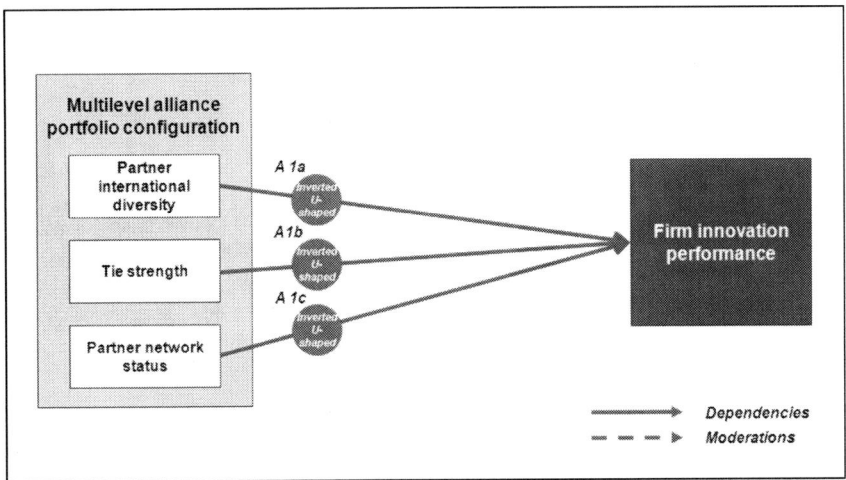

Figure 2.4   Multilevel alliance portfolio configuration and firm innovation performance.

impacted by alliance portfolio capabilities. In so doing, we can further develop and complete our integrative framework of value creation in alliance portfolios.

Alliance Portfolio Capabilities and Firm Innovation Performance

Prior research has indicated that alliance portfolio capabilities enhance firm performance (Heimeriks et al., 2009; Sarkar et al., 2009). From a learning perspective, an alliance portfolio represents a firm's accumulated alliance experience (Wassmer, 2010). Through experiential learning (Cyert & March, 1963; Levitt & March, 1988; Martin & Salomon, 2003; Nelson & Winter, 1982; Pennings et al., 1994), firms can leverage that experience to develop organizational routines. These routines, referred to as alliance portfolio capabilities, can assist the firm in strengthening its innovation performance. This is due to that fact that by learning from alliance portfolio experience, firms can strengthen their architectural competence (Henderson & Cockburn, 1994) or combinative capability (Kogut & Zander, 1992). Both concepts refer to the ability to recombine external and internal knowledge and in turn, foster innovation. As a result, firms that have superior portfolio capabilities to acquire and exploit new knowledge are expected to have superior innovation performance. These observations suggest the following basic assumption, which is illustrated in Figure 2.5:

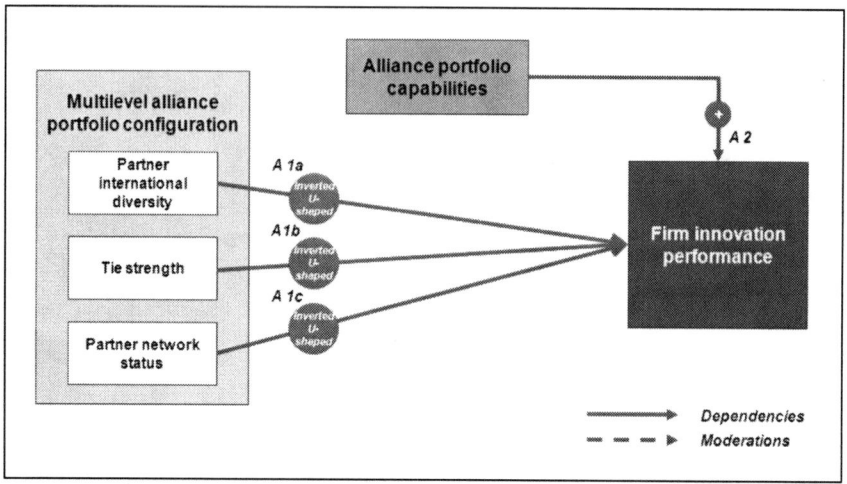

Figure 2.5 Alliance portfolio capabilities and firm innovation performance.

Assumption 2: *Alliance portfolio capabilities positively affect firm innovation performance.*

Moderating Effect of Alliance Portfolio Capabilities on the Relationship Between Multilevel Alliance Portfolio Configuration and Firm Innovation Performance

We have argued that a firm's innovation performance depends on its multilevel alliance portfolio configuration. In particular, we have proposed that a firm's innovation performance varies with the extent of partner international diversity, tie strength, and partner network status. This has been assigned to the respective interplay of specific opportunities and challenges for the access of knowledge provided by the individual alliance portfolio configuration dimension. However, the focal firm's capacity to extract those benefits and cope with those challenges may depend on or may be moderated by its alliance portfolio capabilities. Indeed, empirical research has shown that performance differences of alliance portfolios reflect variance in distinct alliance portfolio capability across firms (Anand & Khanna, 2000; Harbison & Pekar, 1998; Heimeriks & Duysters, 2007; Kale et al., 2002).

As mentioned, we conceptualize alliance portfolio capabilities as the collection of routines resulting from and developing with the focal firms' prior portfolio experience. In line with extant literature, we suggest that these managerial routines result in the formalization and internalization of alliance portfolio know-how (Heimeriks et al., 2007). In general, such know-how helps to solve repetitive problems through standardized processes. Such know-how helps to face new emerging challenges through established problem-solving routines that might be applicable to a range of portfolio management issues, such as portfolio configuration challenges. Collectively combined, that know-how resulting from routines can generate competitive advantage and thus, influence performance outcomes (Heimeriks et al., 2007; Ireland et al., 2002).

Each such routine can be broken down into its constituent skill-based competencies (Eisenhardt & Martin, 2000). These skills are referred to as the ability to select partners that are compatible for a given alliance with partners in other extant alliances; the ability to monitor various alliances; or the ability to coordinate activities and knowledge flows in the portfolio (Hoffmann, 2007). Building on and further refining the conceptualization of Sarkar et al. (2009) mentioned earlier, we argue that focal firms may develop and maintain three specific skills that aid their alliance portfolio management. We label them (a) partnering skills, (b) entrepreneurial skills, and (c) bargaining skills. We assume that they moderate the link between multilevel portfolio configuration and innovation performance.

Moderating Effect of Partnering Skills on the Relationship Between Partner Diversity and Firm Innovation Performance

At the partner firm level, we have suggested that innovation performance may decrease with increasing partner diversity. This has been explained by increasing complexity hampering knowledge integration and thus, undermining innovation performance. However, the focal firms may develop and maintain specific skills aimed at reducing conflicts between diverse partners. Such partnering skills may contribute to the firm's capacity to identify partnering opportunities; develop alliance relationships; and establish relational mechanisms that involve knowledge sharing, investments in relation-specific assets, complementary partner resources, and informal safeguards (Dyer & Singh, 1998; Kale et al., 2000; Lorenzoni & Lipparini, 1999). Thus, partnering skills can assist in attracting prospective partners and learning how to team up more effectively, which reduces the costs of coordinating activities with partners and facilitates resource sharing in the alliance portfolios (Das & Teng, 1998). Taken together, such partnering skills strengthen the focal firms' absorptive capacity (Zahra & George, 2002). The latter helps to understand partners' genuine national environments and consequently, to extract more knowledge from alliances with partners that are increasingly distinctive in their characteristics (Lavie & Rosenkopf, 2006).

Assumption 3A: *The relationship between partner diversity and focal firm innovation performance will be positively moderated by alliance portfolio capabilities (specifically through partnering skills).*

Moderating Effect of Entrepreneurial Skills on the Relationship Between Tie Strength and Firm Innovation Performance

At the dyad level, we have assumed that innovation performance may decrease with increasing tie strength. This has been explained by the lacking innovativeness of too many strong ties and the missing innovation potential of weak ties. However, focal firms may develop and maintain capabilities that aim to capitalize on the steady exchange of knowledge between partners forming strong ties. We assume that these skill-based routines, which we call entrepreneurial skills, are developed by the focal firms as a reaction to their inability to extract innovation from their strong ties. Such entrepreneurial skills, in the sense of strategic entrepreneurship (Ireland, Hitt, & Sirmon, 2003), aim at creating the architecture for opportunity seeking within long-time established strong ties, which usually hardly provide disruptive innovation potential. These entrepreneurial skills include the creation of interorganizational platforms for communication and cross-learning that may support the integration of knowledge dispersed across the alliance portfolio resulting in enhanced innovation outcomes (Argyris & Schön, 1978; Grant, 1996). In addition, such entrepreneurial skills refer to processes that enhance the entrepreneurial culture. An entrepreneurial culture develops in an organization wherein the employees have an entrepreneurial mindset. Such employees search for opportunities and determine the capabilities needed to successfully exploit them (Covin & Slevin, 2002; McGrath & MacMillan, 2000). As a result, diverse, nonredundant, and new knowledge may also be generated within strong ties through the development of entrepreneurial skills. The latter may enhance the degree of nonredundant knowledge within strong ties, thereby increasing the innovation performance trajectory.

Assumption 3B: *The relationship between tie strength and focal firm innovation performance will be positively moderated by alliance portfolio capabilities (specifically through entrepreneurial skills).*

Moderating Effect of Bargaining Skills on the Relationship Between Partner Network Status and Firm Innovation Performance

At the network level, we have argued that innovation performance may decrease with increasing partner network status. This has been explained by a decrease in the knowledge-appropriation capacity of the focal firms. However, their appropriation capacity mainly depends on relative bargaining power with reference to their alliance portfolio partners. This is due to the fact that the relative bargaining power affects the distribution of rents in alliances (Hamel, 1991) and can reduce the focal firms' share of common benefits relative to their share in joint investments (Khanna, Gulati, & Nohria, 1998). By definition, bargaining power is the ability to favorably change the terms of agreements, obtain accommodations from partners, and influence the outcomes of negotiations (Yan & Gray, 1994). We assume that such abilities resulting in bargaining power may be acquired through learning mechanisms. With increasing experience in dealing with high-status network partners aiming at appropriating knowledge from the alliance portfolio, the focal firms can develop specific skill-based routines for handling these situations. Such bargaining skills aid the focal firms' capacity to appropriate additional knowledge from the alliance portfolio themselves. Thus, focal firms that focus on developing and maintaining distinctive bargaining skills designed to increase their relative bargaining power may strengthen the extent of knowledge they can appropriate from their portfolio. Hence, bargaining skills may enhance the innovation performance trajectory.

Assumption 3C: *The relationship between partner network status and focal firm innovation performance will be positively moderated by alliance portfolio capabilities (specifically through bargaining skills).*

Figure 2.6 summarizes our conceptual thoughts and illustrates the complete integrative theoretical framework of value creation in alliance portfolios.

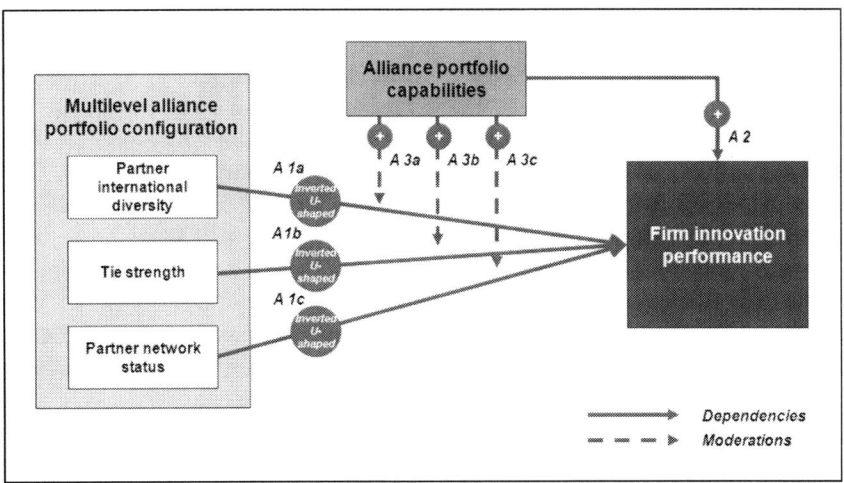

Figure 2.6 Moderating effect of alliance portfolio capabilities.

CONCLUSION

Theoretical Contributions

We conceptually investigate the role of multilevel alliance portfolio configuration and alliance portfolio capabilities on firm innovation. As such, our research provides several theoretical contributions to the strategic management literature. First, we advance alliance portfolio research in general by jointly examining configurational and managerial aspects of value creation in alliance portfolios that have so far always been regarded in separation. Specifically, we develop an integrated conceptual framework based on the knowledge-based view and the dynamic capabilities view. Emanating from these theoretical rationales, we can contribute that both configurational and managerial aspects are supposed to be indispensible for value creation in that they directly influence firm innovation performance; and that, theoretically, there are interaction effects between configurational and managerial value drivers that positively influence firm innovation performance. In so doing, we build on, reemphasize, and extend arguments dealing with the value creation potential of single strategic alliances proposed by, among others, Das and Teng (2000a, 2000b) in their prior work.

Second, we advance research dealing with alliance portfolio configuration. To begin with, this chapter is one of the first attempts to conceptualize alliance portfolio configuration as a comprehensive multidimensional construct. Whereas previous studies have mostly taken a one-dimensional approach, we develop a multilevel understanding of alliance portfolio configuration integrating three dimensions. In fact, it incorporates firm-, dyadic-, and network-level dimensions, in particular partner international diversity, dyadic tie strength, and partner network embeddedness. Therefore, we argue that the firm can strengthen its innovation performance by acquiring knowledge sourced along these three dimensions.

In addition, this chapter contributes to the notion of embeddedness (Granovetter, 1985). Recently, researchers have explicitly incorporated embeddedness logic in their understanding of questions related to the conduct and performance of firms (Gulati et al., 2000). For example, Williamson (2000) advanced transaction cost theory acknowledging that organizational governance was embedded in social norms and contexts. This influenced the way institutions should be managed. In addition, Johansson and Vahlne (2009) argued that the process of internationalization was motivated by existing ties, as these helped to gain especially knowledge and trust for additional global operations. We join this recent trend of integrating the advantages of embeddedness. Thus, we argue that the alliance portfolio is embedded in a larger global network. As a consequence, focal firms can source additional knowledge from that larger network via their partners' partners. In so doing, we can merge the ego-network perspective of existing alliance portfolio research with a social network perspective.

Fourth, our research suggests that an alliance portfolio configuration that is balanced concerning multiple dimensions at multiple levels results in superior innovation performance. Such multilevel balance refers to the combination of local and global partners, weak and strong alliances, as well as isolated partners and partners highly embedded in networks. As such, our research contributes to the concept of ambidexterity. Since Duncan (1976) introduced the term "organizational ambidexterity," the concept has become an ever-increasing field of research.[4] Alliance portfolio research has recently started to address the growing field as well. To give an example, research has shown that firms often use a mix of bridging ties (for structural holes) as well as strong ties to enhance their alliance ambidexterity and alliance performance (Tiwana, 2008). Our chapter adds to this research. We theoretically presume that an ambidextrous portfolio balancing partners' international diversity, tie strength, and partner network embeddedness results in the highest innovation performance outcomes.

Fifth, we contribute to the so-far scarce literature dealing with alliance portfolio management capabilities. Our chapter is one of the first attempts to investigate alliance portfolio capabilities as a moderating effect contextualizing the link between portfolio configuration and innovation performance. In addition, we further develop the conceptual understanding of alliance portfolio management capabilities per se by elaborating on three specific skills that are supposed to enhance focal firm innovation performance: partnering skills, entrepreneurial skills, and bargaining skills.

Managerial Implications

In modern business, continuous innovation is of crucial importance for strategic renewal and firm survival (IBM, 2006, 2010). As a result, managers aspire to identify strategic levers for achieving superior innovation performance. Our research indicates that the gestalt of and the lessons learned from the portfolio of alliances are such levers. As a practical consequence, managers should implement a holistic alliance portfolio management involving strategic and organizational aspects. Strategically, such integrated portfolio management includes effective partner selection and portfolio monitoring. For partner selection, a complex due diligence process should be installed, allowing for the compliance of multilevel portfolio balance. Also, the portfolio configuration should be rotationally monitored in order to control for dynamics in portfolio configuration and maintain multilevel balance. We assume that these strategic initiatives will increase innovation performance. Organizationally, such integrated portfolio management includes the establishment of a dedicated alliance function. The latter facilitates the implementation of the initiatives advised above. In addition, such an alliance function also bundles experience and allows for learning mechanisms to take effect. We presume that such organizational initiatives will also eventually improve not only innovation but more general firm-level performance.

Avenues for Further Research

Although this chapter highlights important insights about the influence of multilevel alliance portfolio configuration and portfolio management capabilities on firm innovation, we are just at the beginning of our research. Based on the conceptual thoughts developed throughout this chapter, the logical avenue for further research is empirically testing the derived framework and assumptions. To that end, a longitudinal analysis, such as an event history or panel data analysis, would be best-suited to identify significant effects of multilevel alliance portfolio configuration and portfolio capabilities on focal firm performance. Apart from that, we see several other avenues for further research on alliance portfolio configuration and management. In fact, little is still known on how alliance portfolio configurations change over time and what drives this evolution (Hoffmann, 2007). Most studies that have contributed to this line of research have taken a qualitative and case-based approach. Thus, to shed more light on alliance portfolio evolution, future research must implement large-scale empirical studies to test the theories developed in these case-based studies (Wassmer, 2010). Further research is also needed to better understand the antecedents and constituents of alliance portfolio capabilities that go beyond recent research (Heimeriks et al., 2009; Sarkar et al., 2009). In that regard, an additional interesting subject for further research is how alliance capabilities on the single alliance level are different from alliance capabilities on the portfolio level (Wassmer, 2010).

NOTES

1. This is due to the fact that a focal firm's alliance portfolio is composed of alliances with partners that are, in turn, embedded in the larger global network (see section "Alliance Portfolio").
2. The main relational configuration factor that has been examined in the extant literature is the tie strength of individual alliances (Wassmer, 2010).
3. For example, R&D alliance and marketing agreement between the focal firm and any partner at one time.

4. According to Raisch, Birkinshaw, Probst, and Tushman (2009), "the number of studies in leading management journals that explicitly refer to the ambidexterity concept increased from less than 10 in 2004 to more than 80 today" (p. 685). This clearly shows that ambidexterity has become an attractive research domain.

REFERENCES

Ahuja, G. (2000). Collaboration networks, structural holes, and innovation: A longitudinal study. *Administrative Science Quarterly, 45,* 425–455.

Al-Laham, A., & Amburgey, T. (2010). Who makes you central? Analyzing the influence of international alliance experience on network centrality of start-up firms. *Management International Review, 50,* 297–323.

Alvarez, S. A., & Barney, J. B. (2001). How entrepreneurial firms can benefit from alliances with large partners. *Academy of Management Executive, 15*(1), 139–148.

Amburgey, T., Al-Laham, A., Tzabbar, D., & Aharonson, B. (2008). The structural evolution of multiplex organizational networks: Research and commerce in biotechnology. *Advances in Strategic Management, 25,* 171–209.

Anand, B. T., & Khanna, T. (2000). Do firms learn how to create value? The case of alliances. *Strategic Management Journal, 21,* 295–315.

Argyris, C., & Schön, D. A. (1978). *Organizational learning: A theory of action perspective.* Reading, MA: Addison-Wesley.

Arora, A., & Gambardella, A. (1990). Complementarity and external linkages. The strategies of the large firms in biotechnology. *Journal of Industrial Economics, 38,* 361–379.

Bae, J., & Gargiulo, M. (2004). Partner substitutability, alliance network structure, and firm profitability in the telecommunications industry. *Academy of Management Journal, 47,* 843–859.

Baker, W. E. (1990). Market networks and corporate behavior. *American Journal of Sociology, 96,* 589–625.

Barkema, H., Shenkar, O., Vermeulen, F., & Bell, J. (1997). Working abroad, working with others: How firms learn to operate international joint ventures. *Academy of Management Journal, 40,* 426–442.

Barney, J. B. (1991). Firm resources and sustained competitive advantage. *Journal of Management, 17,* 99–120.

Barreto, I. (2010). Dynamic capabilities: A review of past research and an agenda for the future. *Journal of Management, 36,* 256–280.

Baum, J. A. C., & Oliver, C. (1991). Institutional linkages and organizational mortality. *Administrative Science Quarterly, 36,* 187–218.

Bonacich, P. (1987). Power and centrality: A family of measures. *American Journal of Sociology, 92,* 1170–1182.

Brass, D. J., Galaskiewicz, J., Greve, H. R., & Tsai, W. (2004). Taking stock of networks and organizations: A multilevel perspective. *Academy of Management Journal, 47,* 795–817.

Burrows, P. (2007, July 9). Welcome to Apple world. *BusinessWeek,* pp. 88–92.

Burt, R. (1987). Social contagion and innovation: Cohesion versus structural equivalence. *American Journal of Sociology, 92*, 1287–1335.

Burt, R. (1992). *Structural holes: The social structure of competition.* Cambridge, MA: Harvard University Press.

Burt, R. (2000). The network structure of social capital. *Research in Organizational Behavior, 22*, 345–423.

Capaldo, A. (2007). Networking structure and innovation: The leveraging of a dual network as a distinctive relational capability. *Strategic Management Journal, 28*, 585–608.

Chaudhuri, S., & Tabrizi, B. (1999). Capturing the real value in high-tech acquisitions. *Harvard Business Review, 77*(5), 123–130.

Coleman, J. S. (1988). Social capital in the creation of human capital. *American Journal of Sociology, 94*, 95–120.

Contractor, F. J., & Lorange, P. (Eds.). (2002). *Cooperative strategies and alliances.* Oxford, England: Pergamon.

Covin, J. G., & Slevin, D. P. (2002). The entrepreneurial imperatives of strategic leadership. In M. A. Hitt, R. D. Ireland, S. M. Camp, & D. L. Sexton (Eds.), *Strategic entrepreneurship: Creating a new mindset* (pp. 309–327). Oxford, England: Blackwell Publishers.

Cyert, R. M., & March, J. G. (1963). *A behavioral theory of the firm.* Englewood Cliffs, NJ: Prentice-Hall.

Das, T. K., & Teng, B. (1996). Risk types and interfirm alliance structures. *Journal of Management Studies, 33*, 827–843.

Das, T. K., & Teng, B. (1998). Between trust and control: Developing confidence in partner cooperation in alliances. *Academy of Management Review, 23*, 491–512.

Das, T. K., & Teng, B. (2000a). A resource-based theory of strategic alliances. *Journal of Management, 26*, 31–61.

Das, T. K., & Teng, B. (2000b). Instabilities of strategic alliances: An internal tensions perspective. *Organization Science, 11*, 77–101.

D'Aveni, R. (1994). *Hypercompetition: Managing the dynamics of strategic maneuvering.* New York, NY: Free Press.

DeCarolis, D. M., & Deeds, D. L. (1999). The impact of stocks and flows on organizational knowledge on firm performance: An empirical investigation of the biotechnology industry. *Strategic Management Journal, 20*, 953–968.

Duncan, R. B. (1976). The ambidextrous organization: Designing dual structures for innovation. In R. H. Killman, L. R. Pondy, & D. Slevin (Eds.), *The management of organization design* (pp. 167–188). New York, NY: North-Holland.

Dyer, J. H., & Singh, H. (1998). The relational view: Cooperative strategies and sources of interorganizational competitive advantage. *Academy of Management Review, 23*, 660–679.

Eisenhardt, K. M., & Martin, J. A. (2000). Dynamic capabilities: What are they? *Strategic Management Journal, 22*, 1105–1121.

Eisenhardt, K. M., & Schoonhoven, C. B. (1996). Resource-based view of strategic alliance formation: Strategic and social effects in entrepreneurial firms. *Organization Science, 7*, 136–150.

Frank, R. H. (1985). *Choosing the right pond: Human behaviour and the quest for relative wage.* London, England: Oxford University Press.

Galaskiewicz, J., & Wasserman, S. (1993). Social network analysis: Concepts, methodology, and directions for the 1990s. *Sociological Methods & Research, 22*(1), 3–22.

Galunic, D. C., & Eisenhardt, K. M. (2001). Architectural innovation and modular corporate forms. *Academy of Management Journal, 44*, 1229–1249.

Granovetter, M. (1973). The strength of weak ties. *American Journal of Sociology, 78*, 1360–1380.

Granovetter, M. (1985). Economic action and social structure: The problem of embeddedness. *American Journal of Sociology, 91*, 481–510.

Grant, R. M. (1996). Toward a knowledge-based theory of the firm. *Strategic Management Journal, 17*, 109–122.

Gulati, R. (1998). Alliances and networks. *Strategic Management Journal, 19*, 293–317.

Gulati, R. (1999). Network location and learning: The influence of network resources and firm capabilities on alliance formation. *Strategic Management Journal, 20*(5), 397–420.

Gulati, R., & Gargiulo, M. (1999). Where do interorganizational networks come from? *American Journal of Sociology, 104*, 177–231.

Gulati R., Nohria N., & Zaheer, A. (2000). Strategic networks. *Strategic Management Journal, 21*, 203–215.

Hagedoorn, J. (1993). Understanding the rationale of strategic technology partnering: Interorganizational modes of cooperation and sectoral differences. *Strategic Management Journal, 14*, 371–385.

Hagedoorn, J. (2002). Inter-firm R&D partnerships: An overview of major trends and patterns since 1960. *Research Policy, 31*, 477–492.

Hamel, G. (1991). Competition for competence and inter-partner learning within international strategic alliances. *Strategic Management Journal, 12*, 83–103.

Harbison, J. R., & Pekar, P. (1998). *Smart alliances: A practical guide to repeatable success.* San Francisco, CA: Booz Allen Hamilton.

Heimeriks, K. H., & Duysters, G. (2007). Alliance capability as a mediator between experience and alliance performance: An empirical investigation into the alliance capability development process. *Journal of Management Studies, 44*, 25–49.

Heimeriks, K. H., Duysters, G., & Vanhaverbeke, W. (2007). Learning mechanisms and differential performance in alliance portfolios. *Strategic Organization, 5*, 373–408.

Heimeriks, K. H., Klein, E., & Reuer, J. J. (2009). Building capabilities for alliance portfolios. *Long Range Planning, 42*, 96–114.

Henderson, R., & Cockburn, I. (1994). Measuring competence? Exploring firm effects in pharmaceutical research. *Strategic Management Journal, 15*, 63–84.

Henderson, R., & Cockburn, I. (1996). Scale, scope, and spillovers: Determinants of research productivity in the pharmaceutical industry. *RAND Journal of Economics, 27*(1), 32–59.

Hitt, M. A., Hoskisson, R. E., Johnson, R. A., & Moesel, D. D. (1996). The market for corporate control and firm innovation. *Academy of Management Journal, 39*, 1084–1119.

Hoang, H., & Rothaermel, F. T. (2005). The effect of general and partner-specific alliance experience on joint R&D project performance. *Academy of Management Journal, 48*, 332–345.

Hoffmann, W. H. (2005). How to manage a portfolio of alliances. *Long Range Planning, 38,* 121–143.

Hoffmann, W. H. (2007). Strategies for managing a portfolio of alliances. *Strategic Management Journal, 28*(8), 827–856.

IBM. (2006). *Global CEO Study.*

IBM. (2010). *Global CEO Study.*

Inkpen, A. C., & Tsang, E. W. K. (2005). Social capital, networks, and knowledge transfer. *Academy of Management Review, 30*(1), 146–165.

Ireland, R. D., Hitt, M. A., & Sirmon, D. G. (2003). A model of strategic entrepreneurship: The construct and its dimensions. *Journal of Management, 29,* 963–989.

Ireland, R. D., Hitt, M. A., & Vaidyanath, D. (2002). Alliance management as a source of competitive advantage. *Journal of Management, 28,* 413–446.

Johanson, J., & Vahlne, J.-E. (2009). The Uppsala internationalization process model revisited: From liability of foreignness to liability of outsidership. *Journal of International Business Studies, 41,* 1–21.

Kale, P., Singh, H., & Perlmutter, H. (2000). Learning and protection of proprietary assets in strategic alliances: Building relational capital. *Strategic Management Journal, 21,* 217–237.

Kale, P., Dyer, J. H., & Singh, H. (2002). Alliance capability, stock market response, and long-term alliance success: The role of the alliance function. *Strategic Management Journal, 23,* 317–343.

Khanna, T., Gulati, R., & Nohria, N. (1998). The dynamics of learning alliances: Competition, cooperation, and relative scope. *Strategic Management Journal, 3,* 193–210.

Kogut, B. (1988). Joint ventures: Theoretical and empirical perspectives. *Strategic Management Journal, 9,* 319–332.

Kogut, B., & Kulatilaka, N. (1993). Operating flexibility, global manufacturing, and the option value of a multinational network. *Management Science, 39,* 123–139.

Kogut, B., & Zander, U. (1992). Knowledge of the firm, combinative capabilities, and the replication of technology. *Organization Science, 3,* 383–397.

Kumar, R., & Nti, K. O. (1998). Differential learning and interaction in alliance dynamics: A process and outcome discrepancy model. *Organization Science, 9,* 356–367.

Lane, H. W., & Beamish, P. W. (1990). Cross-cultural cooperative behavior in joint ventures in LDCs. *Management International Review, 30,* 87–102.

Lane, P. J., & Lubatkin, M. (1998). Relative absorptive capacity and interorganizational learning. *Strategic Management Journal, 19,* 461–477.

Larson, A. (1992). Network dyads in entrepreneurial settings: A study of the governance of exchange relationships. *Administration Science Quarterly, 37,* 76–104.

Lavie, D. (2007). Alliance portfolios and firm performance: A study of value creation and appropriation in the U.S. software industry. *Strategic Management Journal, 28,* 1187–1212.

Lavie, D. (2009). Capturing value from alliance portfolios. *Organizational Dynamics, 38,* 26–36.

Lavie, D., & Miller, S. R. (2008). Alliance portfolio internationalization and firm performance. *Organization Science, 19,* 623–646.

Lavie, D., & Rosenkopf, L. (2006). Balancing exploration and exploitation in alliance formation. *Academy of Management Journal, 49,* 797–818.

Leonard-Barton, D. (1995). *Wellsprings of knowledge: Building and sustaining the sources of innovation.* Boston, MA: Harvard Business School Press.

Levitt, B., & March, J. G. (1988). Organizational learning. *Annual Review of Sociology, 14,* 319–340.

Lorenzoni, G., & Lipparini, A. (1999). The leveraging of interfirm relationships as a distinctive organizational capability: A longitudinal study. *Strategic Management Journal, 20,* 317–338.

Madhavan, R., Koka, B., & Prescott, J. E. (1998). Networks in transition: How industry events (re)shape interfirm relationships. *Strategic Management Journal, 19,* 439–459.

Madhok, A., & Tallman, S. B. (1998). Resources, transactions, and rents: Managing value through interfirm collaborative relationships. *Organization Science, 9,* 1–14.

Marino, L., Strandholm, K., Steensma, H. K., & Weaver, K. M. (2002). The moderating effect of national culture on the relationship between entrepreneurial orientation and strategic alliance portfolio extensiveness. *Entrepreneurship Theory and Practice, 26,* 145–160.

Martin, X., & Salomon, R. (2003). Tacitness, learning, and international expansion: A study of foreign direct investment in a knowledge-intensive industry. *Organization Science, 14,* 297–311.

McEvily, B., & Zaheer, A. (1999). Bridging ties: A source of firm heterogeneity in competitive capabilities. *Strategic Management Journal, 20,* 1133–1156.

McGrath, R. (2001). Exploratory learning, innovative capacity and managerial oversight. *Academy of Management Journal, 44,* 118–133.

McGrath, R. M., & MacMillan, I. C. (2000). *The entrepreneurial mindset.* Boston, MA: Harvard Business School Press.

McLoughlin, C. (1999). Culturally responsive technology use: Developing an online community of learners. *British Journal of Educational Technology, 30,* 231–243.

Nahapiet J., & Ghoshal, S. (1998). Social capital, intellectual capital, and the organizational advantage. *Academy of Management Review, 23,* 242–266.

Nelson, R., & Winter, S. (1982). *An evolutionary theory of economic change.* Cambridge, England: Harvard University Press.

Ozcan, P., & Eisenhardt, K. M. (2009). Origin of alliance portfolios: Entrepreneurs, network strategies, and firm performance. *Academy of Management Journal, 52,* 246–279.

Park, S. H., & Zhou, D. (2005). Firm heterogeneity and competitive dynamics in alliance formation. *Academy of Management Review, 30,* 531–554.

Parkhe, A. (1991). Interfirm diversity, organizational learning, and longevity. *Journal of International Business Studies, 22,* 579–601.

Pennings, J. M., Barkema, H. G., & Douma, S. (1994). Organizational learning and diversification. *Academy of Management Journal, 37,* 608–627.

Phene, A., Fladmoe-Lindquist, K., & Marsh, L. (2006). Breakthrough innovations in the U.S. biotechnology industry: The effects of technological space and geographic origin. *Strategic Management Journal, 27,* 369–388.

Podolny, J. M. (1993). A status-based model of market competition. *American Journal of Sociology, 98,* 829–872.

Podolny, J. M. (1994). Market uncertainty and the social character of economic exchange. *Administrative Science Quarterly, 39,* 458–483.

Porter, M. E. (1980). *Competitive strategy.* New York, NY: Free Press.

Portes, A. (1998). Social capital: Its origins and applications in modern sociology. *Annual Review of Sociology, 24,* 1–24.

Powell, W. W. (1990). Neither market nor hierarchy: Network forms of organization. In B. M. Staw & L. L. Cummings (Eds.), *Research in Organizational Behavior, 12,* 295–336.

Powell, W. W., Koput, K. W., & Smith-Doerr, L. (1996). Interorganizational collaboration and the locus of innovation: Networks of learning in biotechnology. *Administrative Science Quarterly, 41,* 116–145.

Raisch, S., Birkinshaw, J. B., Probst, G., & Tushman, M. L. (2009). Organizational ambidexterity: Balancing exploitation and exploration for sustained performance. *Organization Science, 20,* 685–695.

Rogers, E. (2003). *Diffusion of innovations.* New York, NY: Free Press.

Rosenkopf, L., & Nerkar, A. (2001). Beyond local search: Boundary-spanning, exploration, and impact in the optical disc industry. *Strategic Management Journal, 22,* 287–306.

Rosenkopf, L., Metiu, A., & George, V. (2001). From the bottom up? Technical committee activity and alliance formation. *Administrative Science Quarterly, 46,* 748–772.

Rothaermel, F. T., & Deeds, D. (2004). Exploration and exploitation alliances in biotechnology: A system of new product development. *Strategic Management Journal, 25,* 201–221.

Rowley, T., Behrens, D., & Krackhardt, D. (2000). Redundant governance structures: An analysis of relational embeddedness in the steel and semiconductor industries. *Strategic Management Journal, 21,* 369–386.

Santoro, M., & Chakrabarti, A. (2002). Firm size and technology centrality in industry-university interactions. *Research Policy, 31,* 1163–1180.

Sarkar, M. B., Aulakh, P. S., & Madhok, A. (2009). Process capabilities and value generation in alliance portfolios. *Organization Science, 20,* 583–600.

Schumpeter, J. A. (1934). *The theory of economic development: An inquiry into profits, capital, credit, interest, and the business cycle.* Cambridge, MA: Harvard University Press.

Spekman, R. E., Forbes, T. M., Isabella, L. A., & MacAvoy, T. C. (1998). Alliance management: A view from the past and a look to the future. *Journal of Management Studies, 35,* 747–772.

Spender, J. C. (1996). Making knowledge the basis of a dynamic theory of the firm. *Strategic Management Journal, 17,* 45–63.

Spender, J. C., & Grant, R. M. (1996). Knowledge and the firm: Overview. *Strategic Management Journal, 17,* 5–9.

Stuart, T. (2000). Interorganizational alliances and the performance of firms: A study of growth and innovation rates in a high technology industry. *Strategic Management Journal, 21,* 791–811.

Teece, D. (1992). Foreign investment and technological development in Silicon Valley. *California Management Review, 34*(2), 88–106.

Teece, D. J., Pisano, G., & Shuen, A. (1997). Dynamic capabilities and strategic management. *Strategic Management Journal, 18,* 509–533.

Tiwana, A. (2008). Do bridging ties complement strong ties? An empirical examination of alliance ambidexterity. *Strategic Management Journal, 29,* 251–272.

Tsai, W., & Ghoshal, S. (1998). Social capital and value creation: The role of intrafirm networks. *Academy of Management Journal, 41,* 464–476.

Turner, M., & Fauconnier, G. (1997). A mechanism of creativity. *Poetics Today, 20,* 397–418.

Uzzi, B. (1996). The sources and consequences of embeddedness for the economic performance of organizations: The network effect. *American Sociological Review, 61,* 674–698.

Uzzi, B. (1997). Social structure and competition in interfirm networks: The paradox of embeddedness. *Administrative Science Quarterly, 42,* 35–67.

Van de Ven, A. (1986). Central problems in the management of innovation. *Management Science, 32,* 590–607.

Wasserman, S. & Faust, K. (1994). *Social network analysis: Methods and applications.* Cambridge, England: Cambridge University Press.

Wassmer, U. (2010). Alliance portfolios: A review and research agenda. *Journal of Management, 36,* 141–171.

Wernerfelt, B. (1984). A resource-based view of the firm. *Strategic Management Journal, 5,* 171–180.

White, S., & Lui, S. S. (2005). Distinguishing costs of cooperation and control in alliances. *Strategic Management Journal, 26,* 913–932.

Williamson, O. E. (2000). The new institutional economics: Taking stock, looking ahead. *Journal of Economic Literature, 38,* 595–613.

Yan, A., & Gray, B. (1994). Bargaining power, management control, and performance in United States-Chinese joint ventures: A comparative case study. *Academy of Management Journal, 37,* 1478–1517.

Young-Ybarra, C., & Wiersema, M. (1999). Strategic flexibility in information technology alliances: The influence of transaction cost economics and social exchange theory. *Organization Science, 10,* 439–459.

Zaheer, A., McEvily, A. B., & Perrone, V. (1998). Does trust matter? Exploring the effects of interorganizational and interpersonal trust on performance. *Organization Science, 9,* 1–20.

Zahra, S. A., & George, G. (2002). Absorptive capacity: A review, reconceptualization, and extension. *Academy of Management Review, 27,* 185–203.

Zander, U., & Kogut, B. (1995). Knowledge and the speed of transfer and imitation of organizational capabilities: An empirical test. *Organization Science, 6,* 76–92.

CHAPTER 3

ANTECEDENTS TO VALUE CREATION AND VALUE APPROPRIATION OUTCOMES OF STRATEGIC ALLIANCES

The Moderating Role of Governance Mode

Adamantia Pateli
Spyros Lioukas

ABSTRACT

Research interest in the value derived from alliances has been expressed through investigation of multiple perspectives of the outcomes of alliances using terminologies such as performance, success, termination, effectiveness, strategic goal fulfillment, and achievement of partners' objectives. The present chapter considers the antecedents to value creation and appropriation and the moderating role of governance configuration of the alliances in the antecedents-outcomes relationship. To do so, it adopts the property rights theory, which is considered to extend transaction cost economics and

Management Dynamics in Strategic Alliances, pages 53–72
Copyright © 2012 by Information Age Publishing
53

resource-based view. According to our proposed model, value creation of alliances depends on a number of contingency factors related to alliance's history and orientation as well as partners' relatedness. Value appropriation of alliances also depends upon partners' relatedness, but it is only affected by other factors, such as firm's bargaining power and absorptive capacity. Through the proposed model, we argue that the choice of appropriate governance configuration moderates (strengthens or weakens) the effect of the above contingency factors on value creation and appropriation. In addition, we support that value creation affects value appropriation, and vice versa.

INTRODUCTION

Alliances can create value in different ways depending on the growth strategy that they serve and factors such as past relationships and relatedness of the partners involved. Different alliance content and contextual factors naturally affect the firms' individual expectations for value creation and capture, which in turn affect the ways in which alliances should be designed and managed. Thus, a first step in designing a strategic alliance is to identify the underlying value creation logic (Doz & Hamel, 1998) and the partners' strategic motives in forming the alliance (Tsang, 1998). Prior alliance research has assessed value creation in several ways. The most common measures, sourced from the literature of alliance performance and success, include alliance duration, stability, and termination as well as assessment of partners' ongoing relationship and fit.

Partners do not always extract commensurately equal value from an alliance (Gulati & Wang, 2003). As prior research suggests, there are many cases in which one partner may race to learn the other's skills, while the other has no such intentions. As a result, one partner may acquire greater value from the alliance than its partner. Recently, there has been an ever-increasing research interest in understanding why two firms experience differential wealth gains when they form an alliance (Adegbesan & Higgins, 2010; Gulati & Wang, 2003; Kumar, 2010).

A variety of measures has been suggested for measuring the ability of firms to capture value from alliances. The typical value capture measures comprise financial indicators denoting firms' performance and include firm's profitability, net income, growth of sales, return on investment or return on assets, and stock market gains. In addition to financial data, a set of subjective measures has been used, such as the managers' satisfaction with the outcome of the alliance and the firms' ability to meet its strategic objectives (Anand & Khanna, 2000).

Several researchers have tried to make sense out of the breadth of existing performance measures by arguing that a measure's appropriateness varies with the context or depend on the conceptual frameworks that categorize different perspectives of performance (Olk, 2006). Nevertheless, only a few studies have clearly distinguished between the value creation (VC) and the value appropriation (VA) outcomes. Although several researchers have empirically assessed the comparability of select measures, research studies examining how VC and VA outcomes are differentiated on the basis of the alliance's governance mode are missing.

While there are many empirical studies having investigated the alliance governance and alliance performance issues, very few have explored their interconnection. Most of the existing empirical works have drawn on transaction cost principles, the principal theoretical perspective of the alliance governance literature, in order to explain the differential impact of governance mode on performance (Leiblein, 2003). Specifically, these studies examine whether governance modes that deviate from transaction cost economics principles lead to poorer performance, what is called the "misalignment hypothesis" (Yvrande-Billon & Saussier, 2005). In her study of R&D alliances in the telecommunication industry, Sampson (2004) discusses the performance consequences of making the wrong choice of governance mode. Her results indicate that innovative performance is affected more by governance modes that impose excessive bureaucracy (equity alliances) rather than governance modes that allow excessive opportunism hazards (nonequity alliances). Using data on alliances in the German telecommunications industry, Hoetker and Mellewigt (2009) test the relationship between alliance content, the choice of governance mechanisms, and the performance of the alliance. They conclude that the optimal configuration of formal and relational governance mechanisms depends on the assets involved in an alliance, with formal mechanisms best-suited to property-based assets and relational governance best-suited to knowledge-based assets. Taken together, these studies suggest that future research would benefit from the definition of a model appropriate to assess either alliance or firm performance on the basis of alternative alliance governance modes.

In this chapter, our aim is to address this gap by providing a governance-moderating model of value creation and value appropriation. The model includes three types of relationships, each of which correspond to a different research question. First, we investigate the direct effects of several contingency factors, sourced from alliance literature, on a set of VC and VA outcomes, based on literature of organizational performance. Then we examine the moderating role of governance in each of the above effects, thus identifying a significant parameter indirectly affecting both value creation and value appropriation potential. In doing so, we wish to shed light on how equity alliances (joint ventures, minority investments) differ from nonequity alliances (contractual agreements) in their impact on value creation and value appropriation outcomes. Finally, we argue in favor of a bidirectional relationship between value creation and appropriation, or between common and private benefits accrued by an alliance. While these two concepts are commonly investigated, their relationship remains blurred. The ultimate goal of this research stream is to propose a model able to predict the value outcomes of alternative governance configurations ex ante, thus enabling firms to improve their decision making on the design and structure of their alliances. The governance literature constitutes the prime research area to which our investigations contribute.

The next section provides a comprehensive review of the alliance governance literature and presents the main findings of empirical studies regarding the prime determinants of alliance's governance mode. The third section of this chapter reviews the literature on value creation and value appropriation and ends by categorizing the associated performance outcomes. The section that follows introduces the proposed governance-moderating model of value creation and value appropriation. The chapter concludes by discussing the implications of this model and suggestions for further research.

THE ALLIANCE GOVERNANCE CHOICE

The term "governance" has been broadly defined as a "mode of organizing transactions" (Williamson & Ouchi, 1981). Stated differently, alliance governance defines how an alliance is managed, how it is organized and regulated by agreements and processes, and how the partners control and influence its evolution and performance over time (Doz & Hamel, 1998). Several theories have been proposed to explain the formation and governance of strategic alliances including, among others, the transaction cost economics theory, the resource-based view of the firm, the real options theory, and the property rights theory. Each of these provides a different perspective on why alliances occur and how firms choose to structure their alliance.

Alliance Governance Modes

Most studies of governance have been based on the dichotomy of equity versus nonequity alliances (Pangarkar & Klein, 2001; Pateli & Lioukas, 2011). Whereas equity alliances include joint ventures and minority investments, nonequity alliances refer to all other contractual arrangements that do not involve equity exchange. Equity alliances are seen as quasi-hierarchies, since they rely more on hierarchical governance mechanisms, while nonequity alliances are seen as quasi-markets, since they rely more on arm's-length market transactions.

Alliance governance modes are mainly discerned by their level of integration. Nevertheless, they also differ with respect to the set of mechanisms that they employ for coordinating and safeguarding exchanges among the collaborating parties. The mechanisms rule how the alliance parties integrate their contributions while ensuring equity, resolving conflicts, and mitigating opportunism. The following paragraphs discuss the primary features of each of the three above-defined governance modes, while Table 3.1 provides a summarized discrimination of them with regard to a number of governance dimensions (i.e., integration, command structure and authority, conflict resolution mechanism).

By forming a joint venture, partners agree to create a new entity that is owned jointly. The partners of joint venture are highly integrated, while

TABLE 3.1 Discrimination of Governance Modes

	Governance Modes		
Dimensions	Joint ventures	Minority investment	Contract-based agreements
Organizational Structure	Joint entity	Networked entities	Distinct corporate entities
Hierarchical Continuum	Quasi-hierarchy	Quasi-hierarchy (but less than JV)	Quasi-market
Integration	High	Medium	Low
Command Structure and Authority	Independent command structure and legitimate authority system	Via a joint board of directors	Ongoing activities jointly coordinated and decisions made ad hoc
Shared Ownership	Shared ownership of all assets	Each partner has minority equity in the other	Property rights legally specified
Control Over Resources and Outcomes	Residual control of the alliance's resources and outcomes	Mutual but shared control over the resources and outcomes	Agreement on their control rights over resources and outcomes
Scope of Alliance Activities	Wide	Limited (depending on the equity level)	Limited and specified a priori
Monitoring of Alliance Activities	High through joint managerial control	High through shared board membership	Low (legal contracts)
Incentive Systems	Concern about the value of the joint venture's equity	Partners' concern for the value of their equity	Few if any official mechanisms
Mechanisms for Dispute Resolution	By fiat	Through board member intervention	Reliance on contracts

Source: Adapted from Pateli & Lioukas, 2011

each of them contributes its own relative resources and knowledge to produce mutual benefits. The partners keep shared ownership of all corporate assets, while the joint venture keeps the residual control over the alliance's resources and outcomes. Compared with the other governance modes, joint ventures are more effective in transferring tacit knowledge.

Minority investments are partnerships in which firms agree to share equity with each other without creating any new entity, thus the partners are considered to be networked. The partners keep mutual but shared control over the resources contributed to the alliance as well as the alliance's outcomes. They are mostly preferred by large firms in order to acquire access to promising new technology or exceptional knowledge of smaller partners.

Finally, contract-based agreements involve legal contracts signed by partners on the production and transfer of their resources. Compared to equity alliances, contractual agreements are featured by low integration between partners. Partners *a priori* agree upon their control rights over the alliance's outcomes. Ongoing activities are jointly coordinated and decisions are made ad hoc. This mode may be preferred over joint ventures and minority investments due to its increased level of flexibility.

Contingency Factors of the Alliance Governance Choice

Most empirical studies on alliance governance ground their arguments on transaction cost economics (TCE). TCE proposes that choosing an appropriate alliance governance structure is an important mechanism that firms employ to protect themselves from partners' opportunistic behavior. Equity alliances are preferred in cases where there is a need for more protection than efficiency in partners' transactions. Based on TCE arguments, equity governance modes are preferred when alliances involve more than two partners (Colombo, 2003; Oxley & Sampson, 2004) or partners of different countries (Gulati & Singh, 1998; Teng & Das, 2008), include exchange of relation specific assets (Chen & Chen, 2003), or are formed under conditions of high partner behavioral uncertainty (Chen & Chen, 2003). Instead, nonequity alliances are preferred in industries featured by high R&D intensity (Hagedoorn & Narula, 1996; Osborn & Baughn, 1990).

Additional considerations from the resource-based view (RBV) and knowledge-based view (KBV) support governance forms that maintain a balance between allowing sufficiently open resource/knowledge/technology exchange to achieve alliance objectives, while controlling exchange flows to avoid unintended leakage of valuable resources/knowledge/technology (Colombo, 2003; Oxley & Sampson, 2004). Thus, empirical studies show that firms choose a more hierarchical governance mode (i.e., joint venture) when partners' strategic interdependence is expected to be high

(Gulati & Singh, 1998), alliance scope (range of activities involved in the alliance) is broad and involves a technology component (Gulati & Singh, 1998) or joint R&D activities (Colombo, 2003; Osborn & Baughn, 1990; Pangarkar & Klein, 2001). Instead, nonequity alliances are favored in cases where partners have similar capabilities (Colombo, 2003), complementary resources (Chen & Chen, 2003) and substantial competitive overlap in either the product or geographical market level (Oxley & Sampson, 2004).

Empirical studies supported by other theoretical perspectives, including social exchange theory, real options, and property rights theory, have either contradicted the above results or complemented them with a new set of governance antecedents. Grounded in social exchange theory, empirical work on alliance governance has shown that prior ties provide partners with more trust, thus rendering the use of more hierarchical modes less compelling (Gulati & Singh, 1998). Nevertheless, this finding is contradicted by researchers following either a competence-based perspective (Colombo, 2003) or a property rights perspective (Pateli & Lioukas, 2011). Using the real options perspective in combination with the transaction economics theory, Santoro and McGill (2005) have argued in favor of nonequity alliances in industries characterized by an increased level of technological uncertainty. Last, but not least, following a property rights approach, a recent empirical study on information technology alliances reveals that equity structures are preferred when partners keep a competitive relationship and follow a growth strategy, whereas nonequity structures are chosen when partners exhibit high resource complementarity (Pateli & Lioukas, 2011).

RESEARCH ON VALUE CREATION AND APPROPRIATION

Conceptualization of Value Creation and Value Appropriation

Value creation (VC) mechanisms enhance the firms' ability to generate value from their partners as they collectively pursue shared objectives and produce relational rents that cannot be generated independently by individual participants in alliances. In turn, value appropriation (VA), also commonly termed value capture, mechanisms do not create new value but instead determine the relative share of relational rents that each partner can appropriate. In other words, partners competitively pursue self-interested objectives in an attempt to increase their share of appropriated relational rent (Lavie, 2007).

The disparity between value creation and value appropriation is akin to the distinction between common and private benefits or between "size of the pie" and "share of the pie." Thus, VC mechanisms are collective processes that generate common benefits and contribute to the development of the largest possible size of the pie, whereas value appropriation mechanisms determine the distribution of these common benefits to individual partners as well as the capacity of partners to extract the largest possible share of the pie that has been jointly created. Stated differently, value creation is a cooperative effort of partners to maximize the value of alliances by serving the strategic imperatives that incited its formation, while value capture is the individual effort of partners to capture the greatest possible share of the value created. The aforementioned distinction makes it obvious that value creation is related to the agreed-upon (by the involved parties) purpose of alliance formation, while value capture is related to the value outcomes of the alliance for each individual partner (Doz & Hamel, 1998). Nevertheless, the combination of VC and VA mechanisms accounts for the contribution of the alliance to each partner's performance.

While there is increasing evidence that alliances are an important source of value creation and competitive advantage, we know less about how collaborating firms split the value (rents) generated as a result of the collaboration. Previous research on value of alliances has focused largely on measuring the benefits generated from the alliance at a collaborative level. But less attention has been paid to measuring the gains that are realized by individual firms in the alliance (Dyer, Singh, & Kale, 2008).

Measuring Value Creation and Value Appropriation

Prior alliance research has assessed value creation and value appropriation of alliances in several ways. Despite numerous studies and reviews (Olk, 2006), there remains no single view of how to measure them. Following, we present a review of relevant empirical studies. In order to improve organizing, and thus increase understanding of the associated performance measures, we have developed a two-dimensional framework. The first dimension of the framework concerns the "type of value" that is measured and includes either value creation or value appropriation. As said earlier, value creation measures benefits at the collaborative level, while value appropriation measures benefits at the individual level. The second dimension of the framework concerns the "multiplicity of the measures" employed and distinguishes between single measures (single variables) and multiple measures (constructs). The resulting framework is provided in Table 3.2. While only two dimensions are defined, in essence, a third dimension is also discussed; the distinction between objective and subjective evaluation measures.

According to Doz and Hamel (1998), researchers should employ a different set of measures for assessing the performance of alliances based on the value creation logic that alliances serve. Doz and Hamel group the value creation logic of alliances into three categories: (a) co-option, which

TABLE 3.2 Value Creation, Value Appropriation, and Associated Performance Measures

	Value Creation (collaborative level)	Value Appropriation (individual level)
Single Measures	• Stability • Duration • Termination • Partners' Aggregated Market-to-Book Value • Partners' Aggregated ROI or ROA	• Individual Firm's Market-to-Book Value • Individual Firm's ROI or ROA • Firm Profitability/Productivity • Innovation Outcome (e.g., patents) • Managers' Satisfaction with Alliance Performance
Multiple Measures	• Partners' Compatibility/Fit (operational, cultural, strategic) • Ongoing Relationship (trust, conflict, opportunistic behavior) • Alliance Effectiveness • Innovation Performance (e.g., patents, new products/services)	• Strategic Objectives' Achievement • Expected Alliance Value • Balanced Scorecard (financial, customer, process, growth)

motivates firms to join forces and thus collaborate for improving their competitive position in existing or new markets; (b) co-specialization, the synergistic value creation that results from combination of partners' resources, skills, and knowledge; and (c) learning, which considers alliances as an avenue for internalizing new skills and thus creating conditions for developing core competence.

VC outcomes are commonly sourced from literature on alliance performance and effectiveness. Existing literature has typically assessed the value creation potential of alliances by using an event-study methodology to examine stock market reactions to alliance announcements. Apart from the stock market reactions, a variety of other financial indicators, such as return on investment (ROI), return on assets (ROA), net income, and growth of sales, has dominated the alliance performance literature (Anand & Khanna, 2000; Combs & Ketchen, 1999; Gulati & Wang, 2003). These are usually calculated for each of the partners involved and then are summed to provide an aggregated measure. Apart from the above financial measures, a number of operational measures have also been employed to assess alliance performance; the most common of which include alliance's duration, termination, and stability (Lunnan & Haugland, 2008).

Although not a common practice, multiple measures have also been used to assess the value creation of alliances, such as partners' fit in terms of strategic, operational, and cultural compatibility (Futrell, Slugay, & Stephens, 2001) as well as assessment of partners' ongoing relationship in terms of trust, conflict resolution, and presence of opportunistic behavior (Olk,

2006). Realizing the multifaceted nature of alliance value on the one hand, and wishing to connect it with the firm's strategic motives for forming alliances on the other, prior research has provided a number of multidimensional constructs measuring the alliance effectiveness. One such example includes the expected alliance value (EAV) construct, used to measure the degree of attaining milestone goals set by each firm at the outset of the strategic alliance (Pateli & Giaglis, 2007). The EAV items have been defined based on alliance formation motives, being specified by studies on strategic alliances formation (Hagedoorn, 1993; Tsang, 1998; Vilkamo & Keil, 2003). The construct includes seven dimensions, considered as strategic contributions of cooperative arrangements (Contractor & Lorange, 1988)—risk reduction, economies of scale and/or rationalization, complementary technologies and patents co-opting or blocking competition, overcoming government-mandated investment or trade barrier, initial international expansion, vertical quasi-integration—and are represented by 20 evaluation items. Another way to measure value creation, commonly used for R&D and technology alliances, involves the estimation of alliance's innovative performance in terms of patents counts and citations, new products/services counts, and R&D expenditures (Hagedoorn & Cloodt, 2003; Jiang & Li, 2009).

To measure value appropriation, researchers commonly turn to models of firm performance. The abovementioned financial measures (e.g., growth of sales, market-to-book value, return on asset) are assessed by each individual firm. Since accurate data on the above financial indicators are onerous, if not impossible to collect, scholars have often looked at firms' expectation of whether and how much the firm will capture value from the alliance (Gulati & Wang, 2003). Thus, subjective measures of financial indicators in terms of predicted values are used instead of the objective measures. However, given the difficulties of forecasting the cash flows associated with an alliance with precision, several researchers have opted for the subjective nonfinancial measurement of alliance performance. Accordingly, subjective measures (management evaluations) of performance are preferred when non-financial performance is involved or when objective financial measures are not available (Geringer & Hebert, 1991). Moreover, partners are usually reluctant to provide objective measures of performance, and thus subjective measures, such as managers' satisfaction with the outcome of the alliance and firms' ability to meet the strategic objectives set at the outset of the specific alliance, are often employed.

Last, the Balanced Scorecard method has been used as a value assessment tool able to link a firm's expected benefits to its strategic motives for entering an alliance. The value items of this tool are categorized into the four dimensions of the Balanced Scorecard (Kaplan & Norton, 1996), and thus may include financial value items, such as cost economization or maximization of return on assets; customer value items, such as delivery of products/services at lower prices and improved after sales support; operational value items, such as access to new resources and capabilities and decrease of time-to-market; as well as growth value items, such as differentiation of products and services. Although the Balanced Scorecard has achieved widespread acceptance in the business world, in practice it has been criticized by scholars for requiring a large bulk of organizational information that is difficult to collect as well as for uncertainty as to how to combine these data into an overall performance (Meyer, 2002).

A GOVERNANCE-MODERATING MODEL OF VALUE CREATION AND APPROPRIATION

Examining the VC and VA outcomes under the moderating effect of the governance choice constitutes an underresearched field of the alliance literature. So far, research studies examining the relationship between alliance governance and performance has been oriented toward examining the cost of misaligned governance in terms of performance (Hoetker & Mellewigt, 2009; Sampson, 2004) as well as comparing the differences in performance between equity and nonequity alliances (Glaister & Buckley, 1998). In the last case, evaluation of performance has been limited to assessment of managers' satisfaction with the alliance. Taken together, these studies suggest that future research would benefit from the construction of integrated models of firms' governance choices and their performance implications. Hereinafter, we provide some first insight by investigating the way in which the choice of alliance governance mode affects the relationship of certain groups of antecedents with VC and VA.

In order to extract contingency factors, we follow the property rights theory, which is considered an extension of the most widely used resource-based view and transaction cost economics theories in a number of ways (Foss & Foss, 2005). Based on this theory, a firm's ability to create and appropriate value from an exchange depends on the property rights that it holds as well as on the transaction costs associated with the definition, protection, and exchange of these rights.

To develop our model, we have reviewed research on governance (Chen & Chen, 2003; Colombo, 2003; Pateli & Lioukas, 2011; Sampson, 2004; Santoro & McGill, 2005) as well as research on value creation and appropriation (Adegbesan & Higgins, 2010; Kumar, 2010; Ritala & Hurmelinna-Laukkanen, 2009). This research has indicated several VC and VA predictors, the most important of which have been grouped under three categories: (a) alliance history and orientation, (b) partners' relatedness, and (c) firms' power. The governance mode has been handled as moderator, due to its ability to either reinforce or weaken the relationship between antecedents and outcomes

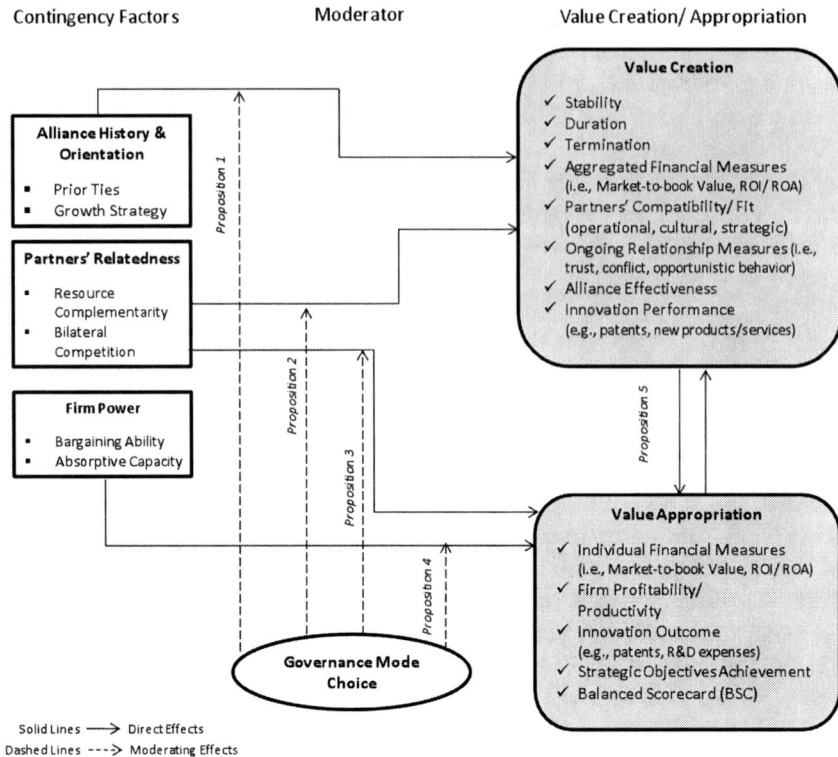

Figure 3.1   A governance-moderating model of value creation and appropriation.

of value creation and value appropriation. Thus, we argue that the relation between the groups of antecedents factors and the VC and VA outcomes is not equally strong for both equity and nonequity alliances. Instead, in some cases, this relation may become stronger for joint ventures and weaker for contractual agreements, or vice versa.

As Figure 3.1 depicts, the model comprises three sections of relationships. The first section includes the direct effects of key contingency factors on the value creation and appropriation potential. The second section comprises the moderating role of the governance mode choice in the relationship of three contingency factors with the VC and VA outcomes. The last section of the figure includes the bidirectional effect between the VC and VA outcomes.

Alliance History & Orientation and Value Creation

Alliance history is primarily referring to the number of prior ties between partners as well as the duration, the performance, and the governance of these ties. Studying these factors enables managers to estimate the contractual hazards involved as well as the opportunities that may emerge, and thus make their decisions on the best governance mode for a prospective alliance. On the other hand, alliance orientation concerns the ultimate goal for which the alliance has been formed, and usually this concerns a growth strategy, such as expanding into new market segments or new geographical areas, or even producing new products/services.

Joint ventures imply a wide scope of joint activities between partners, which enable them to increase experience of each other and even enhance trust between them. In cases where firms have cooperated more than once in the past, their integration through a joint venture structure may increase trust and decrease probabilities for conflicts and opportunistic behavior, thus affecting positively the VC-related performance measures. Moreover, in cases where alliances are formed to serve a common partner's goal for growth—in terms of either expansion into new markets or diversification of existing products/services to target new market groups—a hierarchical governance mode may enhance opportunities for sharing resources and dividing control rights, thus increasing common benefits accruing for all partners involved. Instead, the choice of a contractual agreement may decrease the effect of alliance history and orientation on VC outcomes, since it turns the primary interest of partners from achieving growth to protecting themselves from partners' opportunistic behavior, and thus hinders the generation of value. The above arguments lead to the formulation of the following proposition:

Proposition 1: *The alliance governance mode moderates the effect of alliance history and orientation (prior ties, growth strategy) on value creation.*

Partners' Relatedness and Value Creation

Partners' relatedness involves a comparison of partners in terms of several key features, such as competitive position, resource contribution, technological capabilities, and cultural compatibility. Hereinafter, we identify two features—resource complementarity and bilateral competition—that have been found in alliance literature (Chen & Chen, 2003; Hamel, Doz, & Prahalad, 1989; Hoffmann & Schlosser, 2001; Lavie, 2007; Ritala & Hurmelinna-Laukkanen, 2009) to affect critical alliance decisions, such as the selection of partners, the choice of governance mode, the size of partners' investment and their share over the total returns.

According to Lunnan and Haugland (2008), complementary resources positively affect short-term and long-term performance of alliances. However, if partners are competitors, then resource complementarity between them is rather low, thus decreasing possibilities for alliance stability and success. Equity alliances tend to be more robust than nonequity alliances when the initial contributors retain a competitive relationship (Pateli & Lioukas, 2011). The reason is that by applying the structural mechanisms (internal control, authority, and dispute resolution) of dealing with multiple transaction costs, joint ventures can reduce information asymmetry or partners' opportunism. Based on the aforementioned reasoning, choosing a hierarchical governance mode may increase the positive effects of both resource complementarity and competitive relationship on joint value creation. The above ideas are summarized in the following proposition:

> **Proposition 2:** *The alliance governance mode moderates the effect of partners' relatedness (resource complementarity, bilateral competition) on value creation.*

Partners' Relatedness and Value Appropriation

When there is some degree of resource complementarity between partners, then their partnership results in the generation of a surplus (Adegbesan & Higgins, 2010). The magnitude of the surplus created is proportional to the degree of complementarity between the partners, and the way it is split between them is indeterminate ex ante. On the other hand, collaborating with competitors has been found to negatively affect value appropriation potential (Ritala & Hurmelinna-Laukkanen, 2009).

In cases where partners are characterized by high resource complementarity, meaning that both partners contribute unique and highly valuable resources, contractual agreements enable firms to exploit their partner's unique resources without spending time and resources on assuring their property rights (Pateli & Lioukas, 2011). Legally reinforced agreements regarding their control rights over resources and outcomes provide a safe environment for them to produce new services and products without the fear of losing control over either their valuable resources or the final outcomes of their alliances. Instead, joint ventures, while assuring residual control of the alliance's resources and outcomes, do not involve explicit definition of the share of these control rights between partners. Moreover, given the wide scope of joint activities between partners of joint ventures, there is a great possibility for valuable knowledge and resources to leak. In that case, if partners hold competitive positions, the alliance may create disproportional opportunities for value capture. Hence, the foregoing proposition is developed.

> **Proposition 3:** *The alliance governance mode moderates the effect of partners' relatedness (resource complementarity, bilateral competition) on value appropriation.*

Firm Power and Value Appropriation

The firm power within an alliance is usually denoted by its contributed resources as well as its ability to learn from its partners, and thus enhance its competences. Current literature on value distribution of alliances combines bargaining ability with absorptive capacity in order to determine value appropriation (Adegbesan & Higgins, 2010; Dyer et al., 2008; Kumar, 2010).

Joint ventures are considered as a rather safe environment for firms to exchange valuable resources as well as to develop their learning and exploitation capabilities. Firms endogenously choose joint ventures over market contracts in situations where the knowledge bases to be combined are tacit and are not fully protected by patents and strong appropriability regimes (Kumar, 2010). Instead, given the incomplete nature of alliances' contracts, partners of contractual agreements become less interested in developing joint value and more keen on extracting private benefits for themselves. The above arguments suggest that joint ventures are likely to be inherently associated with greater potential for value appropriation than contractual agreements. This is due to the incompleteness of contracts and the opportunities that joint ventures provide for enhancing learning. We summarize the foregoing in the following proposition:

Proposition 4: *The alliance governance mode moderates the effect of firm power (bargaining ability, absorptive capacity) on value appropriation.*

Value Creation and Value Appropriation

As described above, value creation potential is influenced by a range of factors, some of which are in common with value appropriation potential. All factors affecting value creation are associated with features of the alliance unit (i.e., strategic goal, prior ties) or features deriving from comparison of partners (i.e., complementarity, competition). On the other hand, the value appropriation potential concerns individual firms and thus is primarily determined by firm's power in negotiation as well as in exploitation of resources.

While there are several studies investigating the factors of value creation, and fewer but quite a few recent studies investigating the factors of value distribution, their relationship has not been explicitly defined. A relevant attempt has been made by Dyer et al. (2008) in developing a contingency framework providing alternative scenarios for the stability of alliances with regard to both private and common benefits derived for partners. Nevertheless, the relationship between common and private benefits is not investigated. Moreover, in a recent work, Adegbesan and Higgins (2010) identify that value appropriation is not independent of value creation, and so they urge future research toward capturing the dynamic relationship between these two value outcomes. Hereinafter, we argue that as value creation potential increases, the size of the common pie to share also increases, thus opening up opportunities for firms to capture more private benefits. Also, as firms become able to extract more private benefits from a given partnership, they become willing to invest more of their resources and competences in keeping it alive. The above ideas lead to the formulation of the following proposition:

Proposition 5: *Value creation has a direct effect on value appropriation, and vice versa.*

DISCUSSION AND FUTURE RESEARCH

The intent of this chapter is to increase our understanding regarding the relationship of key antecedents of value creation and appropriation, the choice of governance mechanisms, and the performance of the alliance. Current research and practice has provided a great diversity of alliance performance measures in terms of collective and private benefits generated for the alliance's partners. Nevertheless, less attention has been paid on the way in which the initial choice of governance mode influences the effects of several prime contingency factors on value creation and appropriation. Therefore, this chapter proposes a model that draws from the property rights theory to describe the moderating role of the governance mode in the relationship of several contingency factors of value with performance measures used to assess value generation and distribution.

Our model comprises a first attempt toward developing an integrated governance-moderating model of value creation and value appropriation. The model can be improved by empirically testing its proposed relationships and exploring its implications for the design as well as the management of alliances. An assessment of the entire model will provide important findings in the alliance governance literature, since it will reveal the value potential of equity and nonequity alliances. Moreover, it will contribute to the alliance performance literature by differentiating the group of VC outcomes from the group of VA outcomes and identifying the contingency factors that affect each group.

Testing the model raises a number of challenging issues. On the one hand, the contingency factors of the model comprises three different groups of factors, each of which includes a set of antecedents, conceptualized as either single variable or constructs. On the other hand, the value parameters of our model are assessed with the use of several constructs, each of which includes multiple indicators. Each of these parameters provides insight into the diverse evaluation aspect of alliances. As such, all of them are considered as candidate-dependent variables. The moderating variable of the model includes the governance mode, which is usually conceptualized as either a binary variable (equity vs. nonequity alliance) or a categorical variable (joint venture, minority investment, contractual agreements). Thus, testing this model will likely require causal modeling. This method is well-suited for evaluating the effect of one or more independent variables on multiple dependent variables, conceptualized as constructs. Moreover, it enables the parallel testing of multiple moderating relationships. Nevertheless, the magnitude of the data-collection task means that either a large-sized sample will be used or the testing will be the result of more than one empirical study. It is possible that future research will end up splitting the model into sections and focusing on a subset of relationships each time.

To develop our model, we have primarily followed the considerations and arguments of the property rights perspective. Therefore, the model does not explore how contingency factors, resulting from other theoretical perspectives such as transaction cost economics (TCE) and resource-based view (RBV), may affect the VC and VA outcomes in a direct or indirect way. Future research that incorporates the influence of other antecedents (e.g., scope of activities, alliance management experience, and similarity of partners' technology capabilities) will enhance the power of the model and enable comparison of the power of each theoretical perspective in handling the difference between the performance outcomes of value creation and appropriation.

This model has implications for theories in the alliance governance field. The great majority of existing studies in the area have applied TCE in order to explain firms' decision making on the structure of their alliance by focusing on the cost of misaligning transaction with governance structures (e.g., Leiblein, Reuer, & Dalsace, 2002; Sampson, 2004; Yvrande-Billon & Saussier, 2005). Fewer but quite a few works integrate transaction cost perspective with resource-based perspective in order to balance the cost and resource considerations of various scholars in the alliance literature. As discussed above, this chapter applies a property rights perspective, which is considered to extend TCE and RBV, to explain the performance implication of diverse governance modes. When the model is tested and the relationships of the contingency factors, the governance mode, and the diverse value creation and appropriation outcomes become better known, the power of the property rights theory on the governance and performance field will be reinforced.

Finally, the propositions underlying our model could contribute to the alliance management research area. Alliances that last several years could change structure from time to time. Thus, a contractual agreement on developing new products/services may evolve into the establishment of a joint venture, which will commercially exploit the new products/services. The reverse transformation, evolving from an equity to a nonequity alliance, may be less frequent but not impossible. Thus, the model could capture changes in performance as the alliance evolves from one governance mode to another. To test such a model, longitudinal data for long-lasting alliances are required.

REFERENCES

Adegbesan, J. A., & Higgins, M. J. (2010). The intra-alliance division of value created through collaboration. *Strategic Management Journal, 32*, 187–211.

Anand, B. N., & Khanna, T. (2000). Do firms learn to create value? The case of alliances. *Strategic Management Journal, 21*, 295–315.

Chen, H., & Chen, T-J. (2003). Governance structures in strategic alliances: Transaction costs versus resource-based perspective. *Journal of World Business, 38*, 1–14.

Colombo, M. G. (2003). Alliance form: A test of the contractual and competence perspectives. *Strategic Management Journal, 24*, 1209–1229.

Combs, J., & Ketchen, D. (1999). Explaining interfirm cooperation and performance: Toward a reconciliation of predictions from the resource-based view and organizational economics. *Strategic Management Journal, 20*, 867–888.

Contractor, F. J., & Lorange, P. (1988). Why should firms cooperate? The strategy and economics basis for cooperative ventures. In F. J. Contractor & P. Lorange (Eds.), *Cooperative strategies in international business: Joint ventures and technology partnerships between firms* (pp. 3–30). Lexington, MA: Lexington Books.

Doz, Y. L., & Hamel, G. (1998). *Alliance advantage—The art of creating value through partnering.* Boston, MA: Harvard Business School Press.

Dyer, J. H., Singh, H., & Kale, P. (2008). Splitting the pie: Rent distribution in alliances and networks. *Managerial and Decision Economics, 29*(2–3), 137–148.

Foss, K., & Foss, N. J. (2005). Resources and transaction costs: How property rights economics furthers the resource-based view. *Strategic Management Journal, 26*(6), 541–553.

Futrell, D., Slugay, M., & Stephens, C. (2001) Becoming a premier partner: Measuring, managing, changing partnering capabilities at Eli Lilly and Company. *Journal of Commercial Biotechnology, 8*(1), 5–13.

Geringer, J. M., & Hebert, L. (1991). Measuring performance of international joint ventures. *Journal of International Business Studies, 22*, 249–263.

Glaister, K. W., & Buckley, P. J. (1998). Measures of performance in UK international alliances. *Organization Studies, 19*, 89–118.

Gulati, R., & Singh, H. (1998). The architecture of cooperation: Managing coordination costs and appropriation concerns in strategic alliances. *Administrative Science Quarterly, 43*, 781–814.

Gulati, R., & Wang, L. O. (2003). Size of the pie and share of the pie: Implications of network embeddedness and business relatedness for value creation and value appropriation in joint ventures. In V. Buskens, W. Raub, & C. Snijders

(Eds.), *Research in the sociology of organizations* (Vol. 20, pp. 209–242). Oxford, England: Elsevier Science.

Hagedoorn, J. (1993). Understanding the rationale of strategic technology partnering: Interorganizational modes of cooperation and sectoral differences. *Strategic Management Journal, 14,* 371–385.

Hagedoorn, J., & Cloodt, M. (2003). Measuring innovative performance: Is there an advantage in using multiple indicators? *Research Policy, 32,* 1365–1379.

Hagedoorn, J., & Narula, R. (1996). Choosing modes of governance for strategic technology partnering: International sectoral differences. *International Journal of Business Studies, 27,* 265–284.

Hamel, G., Doz, Y. L., & Prahalad, C. K. (1989). Collaborate with your competitors-and win. *Harvard Business Review, 67*(1), 133–139.

Hoetker, G., & Mellewigt, T. (2009). Choice and performance of governance mechanisms: Matching alliance governance to asset type. *Strategic Management Journal, 30,* 1025–1044.

Hoffmann, W. H., & Schlosser, R. (2001). Success factors of strategic alliances in small and medium-sized enterprises—An empirical survey. *Long Range Planning, 34,* 357–381.

Jiang, X., & Li, Y. (2009). An empirical investigation of knowledge management and innovative performance: The case of alliances. *Research Policy, 38,* 358–368.

Kaplan, R. S, & Norton D. P. (1996). *Balanced scorecard: Translating strategy into action.* Boston, MA: Harvard Business School Press.

Kumar, M. V. S. (2010). Differential gains between partners in joint ventures: Role of resource appropriation and private benefits. *Organization Science, 21,* 232–248.

Lavie, D. (2007). Alliance portfolios and performance: A study of value creation and appropriation in the U.S. software industry. *Strategic Management Journal, 28,* 1187–1212.

Leiblein, M. J. (2003). The choice of organizational governance form and firm performance: Predictions from transaction cost, resource-based, and real option theories. *Journal of Management, 29,* 937–962.

Leiblein, M. J., Reuer, J. J., & Dalsace, F. (2002). Do make or buy decisions matter? The influence of organizational governance on technological performance. *Strategic Management Journal, 23,* 817–833.

Lunnan, R., & Haugland, S. A. (2008). Predicting and measuring alliance performance: A multidimensional analysis. *Strategic Management Journal, 29,* 545–556.

Meyer, M. (2002). *Rethinking performance measurement: Beyond the balanced scorecard.* Cambridge, England: Cambridge University Press.

Olk, P. (2006). Modeling and measuring the performance of alliances. In O. Shenkar & J. J. Reuer (Eds.), *Handbook of strategic alliances* (pp. 397–412). Thousand Oaks, CA: Sage.

Osborn, R. N., & Baughn, C. C. (1990) Forms of interorganizational governance for multinational alliances. *Academy of Management Journal, 33*(3), 503–519.

Oxley, J. E., & Sampson, R. C. (2004). The scope and governance of international R&D alliances. *Strategic Management Journal, 25,* 723–749.

Pangarkar, N., & Klein, S. (2001). The impacts of alliance purpose and partner similarity on alliance governance. *British Journal of Management, 12,* 341–353.

Pateli, A., & Giaglis, G. (2007). Governance contingencies for strategic technology alliances—A case in wireless business. *International Journal of Technology Management, 40,* 310–329.

Pateli, A., & Lioukas, S. (2011). The choice of governance mode in ICT alliances: A property rights approach. *Information & Management, 48*(1), 69–77.

Ritala, P., & Hurmelinna-Laukkanen, P. (2009). What's in it for me? Creating and appropriating value in innovation-related coopetition. *Technovation, 29,* 819–828.

Sampson, R. C. (2004). The cost of misaligned governance in R&D alliances. *The Journal of Law, Economics, & Organization, 20,* 484–526.

Santoro, M. D., & McGill, J. P. (2005). The effect of uncertainty and asset co-specialization on governance in biotechnology alliances. *Strategic Management Journal, 26,* 1261–1269.

Teng, B., & Das, T. K. (2008). Governance structure choice in strategic alliances: The roles of alliance objectives, alliance management experience, and international partners. *Management Decision, 46,* 725–742.

Tsang, E. W. K. (1998). Motives for strategic alliance: A resource-based perspective. *Scandinavian Journal of Management, 14,* 207–221.

Vilkamo, T., & Keil, T. (2003). Strategic technology partnering in high-velocity environments: Lessons from a case study. *Technovation, 23,* 193–204.

Williamson, O. E., & Ouchi, W. G. (1981). The markets and hierarchies and visible hand perspectives. In A. H. Van de Ven & W. F. Joyce (Eds.), *Perspectives on organization design and behavior* (pp. 347–370). New York, NY: Wiley.

Yvrande-Billon, A., & Saussier, S. (2005). Do organizations matter? Assessing the importance of governance through performance. In J. Harvey (Ed.), *New ideas in contracting and organizational economics research* (pp. 69–86). New York, NY: Nova Science Publishers.

CHAPTER 4

THE DYNAMICS OF THE ALLIANCE DEVELOPMENT PROCESS

T. K. Das
Bing-Sheng Teng

ABSTRACT

One of the key issues in understanding the developmental processes of strategic alliances is how the alliance conditions change over the different stages of alliance development. A related question concerns the nature of the co-evolutionary dynamics of alliances in terms of their constituent partner firms. In this chapter, we propose an integrated process model of alliances that is based on alliance conditions, alliance developmental stages, and an alliance system comprising co-evolutionary elements. We suggest that alliance conditions, or the key characteristics of an alliance at any given moment, link the alliance environment (firm characteristics) and the alliance development process. We also explore how specific patterns of alliance conditions have differential impacts on the interactive elements of the alliance co-evolutionary system.

Management Dynamics in Strategic Alliances, pages 73–99
73

INTRODUCTION

Business organizations have inevitably to adapt to an increasingly diversifying world of accelerating business activities. Some notable trends in this endeavor include greater local responsiveness to international business developments, workforce diversity, and decentralization of management and corporate governance. Devising appropriate forms of management and organization is one way that firms adapt to this changing environment. One form of organization with the requisite internal variety is strategic alliances, or interfirm cooperative arrangements aimed at achieving the strategic objectives of the partners. Alliances have been proliferating in the last 20 years (Harbison & Pekar, 1998). Many researchers have viewed alliances as a hybrid form of organization because they blend the features of both market transactions and internalization (Powell, 1987; Thorelli, 1986). Alliances are regarded as an alternative mode of organization, that is, a network organizational form that is subject to the multipronged control of at least two partners (Jarillo, 1988). In addition, strategic alliances have considerable variety in their specific governance structures. Although alliances in the form of joint ventures are nothing novel in the arena of international business, the emergence of a whole range of alliance structures, such as joint marketing and cross-licensing, significantly adds to the variety of organizational forms. Also, these alliance forms may be arrayed along a continuum in terms of the degree of internalization.

Substantial research has been carried out on strategic alliances, especially their motivations, antecedents, formation, and outcome. However, with few exceptions (e.g., Ring & Van de Ven, 1994), researchers have paid far less attention to the developmental processes of strategic alliances, that is, the processes through which alliances are negotiated, formed, operated, evaluated, reformed, and terminated. Koza and Lewin (1998) list six important research streams in alliances, such as alliance phenomenon, choosing alliances over other governance structures, and alliance performance. None of these research streams, however, has a process orientation.

In recent years, increasing research attention has been focused on alliance development processes. Despite these efforts, however, our understanding of the alliance developmental processes remains quite limited. For example, although alliances are known to be highly evolutionary and unstable (Das & Teng, 2000a), it is still unclear how and why changes take place in alliances. Little is known about how alliances and their contexts, including the characteristics of the partner firms, co-evolve in a dynamic fashion. Co-evolution refers to the simultaneous development of organizations and their environment, independently as well as interactively. Koza and Lewin rightly note that "co-evolutionary research on alliances which incorporates . . . process variables remains an unexplored area of research" (1998, p. 258).

We believe that a more comprehensive conception of developmental processes is critical for an adequate understanding of strategic alliances. Alliances are significantly different from formal organizations or hierarchies in terms of their evolutionary processes. The developmental processes and stages in formal organizations (see, for example, Greiner, 1972) are thus not necessarily applicable to alliances. For instance, the initial negotiation stage among prospective partner firms is unique to strategic alliances. Also, the interactions between an alliance and its environment are much more complicated than in the case of single organizations as there are at least two firms involved in an alliance. Thus, understanding alliance developmental processes is more than merely envisioning several stages. It is also, importantly, about the dynamics of alliance conditions that influence the unfolding of these processes across stages in tandem with the co-evolution of the alliance and its constituent partner firms.

In this chapter, we suggest that alliances go through a development process consisting of the three stages of formation, operation, and outcome. We also discuss how the evolution of alliances along this process is dictated by the changing conditions of alliances as reflected by their collective strengths, interpartner conflicts, and interdependencies. Furthermore, alliances co-evolve with their environment, comprising the characteristics of the partner firms. The co-evolving dynamics can be examined through the alliance condition variables and selected firm characteristics.

We divide this chapter into four parts. We first review the alliance process models in the literature. Second, we propose the notion of alliance conditions—comprising collective strengths, interpartner conflicts, and interdependencies—and discuss how firm characteristics determine these conditions. In the third section, we examine the role of alliance conditions in the different stages of alliance development. Finally, we explore the co-evolution of alliances and their constituent partner firms.

ALLIANCE PROCESS MODELS

Several process models have recently been proposed in the alliance literature. We briefly review these and identify their major limitations. We adopt the definition of process proposed by Van de Ven (1992, p. 169): "a sequence of events that describes how things change over time." Our review centers on developmental stages, alliance conditions, and co-evolution (see Table 4.1).

TABLE 4.1   Approaches to Alliance Development

Authors	Process approaches		
	Developmental stages of alliances	Alliance conditions in the developmental process	Co-evolution of alliances and their environment
Ariño & de la Torre (1998)	Yes	Yes	Yes
Borch (1994)	Yes	No	No
Brouthers et al. (1997)	Yes	No	No
Das & Teng (1997)	Yes	No	No
Doz (1996)	Yes	Yes	No
Kanter (1994)	Yes	No	No
Koza & Lewin (1998)	No	No	Yes
Kumar & Nti (1998)	Yes	No	No
Larson (1992)	Yes	No	No
Niederkofler, 1991	Yes	Yes	No
Ring & Van de Ven (1994)	Yes	No	No

Developmental Stages of Alliances

Many researchers have focused on the developmental stages of alliances, that is, the process from initiation and negotiation to alliance evaluation and even termination (Borch, 1994; Kanter, 1994; Larson, 1992). We list several stage models of the alliance development process in Table 4.2. For example, Brouthers, Brouthers, and Harris (1997) propose a 5-stage process model that includes selecting the mode of operation, locating partners, negotiation, managing the alliance, and evaluating alliance performance. Similarly, Das and Teng (1997) suggest that the process may be divided into seven stages: choosing an alliance strategy, selecting partners, negotiation, setting up the alliance, operation, evaluation, and modification.

Ring and Van de Ven's (1994) framework probably best exemplifies this developmental stages approach. In a process model of interorganizational relationships, they discuss a repetitive process consisting of stages like negotiation, commitment, and execution. The overall process is moderated by continuous assessments based on efficiency and equity. Ring and Van de Ven identify key issues in each stage. The negotiation stage is highlighted by interactions between formal bargaining and informal sense making. The commitment stage is characterized by both formal legal contract and psychological contract between the partners. The execution stage contains both role interactions and personal interactions. Based on these stages and

TABLE 4.2 Selected Alliance Process Models

Models in the literature	Model summary		
	1. Formation	2. Operation	3. Outcome
Brouthers, Brouthers, & Harris (1997)	Selecting mode of operation Locating partners Negotiation	Managing the alliance	Evaluating performance
Das & Teng (1997)	Choosing an alliance strategy Selecting partners Negotiation Setting up the alliance	Operation	Evaluation Modification
D'Aunno & Zuckerman (1987)	Emergence of a coalition	Transition to a coalition	Maturity Crossroads
Kanter (1994)	Selection and courtship Getting engaged Setting up housekeeping	Learning to collaborate	Changing within
Ring & Van de Ven (1994)	Negotiation Commitment	Execution	Assessment
Spekman, Isabella, MacAvoy, & Forbes (1996)	Anticipation Engagement Valuation	Coordination Investment	Stabilization Decision

key issues, the authors explain the emergence, evolution, and dissolution of interorganizational relationships.

Although these frameworks reveal important stages and key issues within each stage, a significant limitation is that the underlying factors that may affect the entire developmental process are not examined. In other words, it is unclear whether an alliance will always move from one stage to the next and what factors may derail the sequence or the process.

Alliance Conditions in the Developmental Process

The second major approach incorporates alliance conditions in the entire developmental process. This is different from much of the extant alliance research that examines only the alliance formation condition, for example, Eisenhardt & Schoonhoven, 1996; Gulati, 1995; Oliver, 1990. The essence of this approach is that alliance conditions are the key to understanding the transition from one alliance stage to another. Alliance conditions inform the differences across alliances in terms of the particular stages of their developmental process. For example, we need to understand why some alliances are reformulated very soon after their formation while others remain relatively more stable. The answer is that each stage has its own necessary conditions, so that an alliance cannot move to the next stage unless certain conditions are present.

Based on several case studies, Niederkofler (1991) proposes an evolutionary framework of alliances that is based on two essential conditions, strategic fit and operational fit. Strategic fit refers to the necessary resource endowments of partner firms that are sufficient for pursuing mutual objectives. Operational fit is about the compatibility of the committed resources and the problems in operating the alliances. Changes in these two conditions prompt the alliance to go through either adjustment or renegotiation. A persistent misfit can lead to either dormancy or alliance exit. Inkpen and Beamish (1997) discuss how learning changes the bargaining power of partners (one specific condition), which affects the subsequent developmental process of alliances.

Doz (1996) proposes that there are several sets of alliance conditions: task definition; partners' routines; interface structure; and expectations of performance, behavior, and motives. These conditions determine how the learning process unfolds in an alliance; initial learning behavior changes these conditions, which in turn leads to certain changes in learning behavior. This way the developmental processes of alliances can be monitored through a close examination of alliance conditions. Doz's extensive field studies provide support for this view.

Although the alliance conditions approach recognizes the central role of alliance conditions in alliance development, a critical problem is that the key condition variables have not been developed. Also, existing research does not pay adequate attention to the determinants of alliance conditions, such as the characteristics of the partner firms. We will attempt to address both these problems.

Co-evolution of Alliances and Their Environment

The third major process approach emphasizes the co-evolution of alliances and their environment. This approach has only recently emerged in the alliance literature. The idea of co-evolution is rooted in the tradition of population ecology and evolutionary theory (Hannan & Freeman, 1977; McKelvey, 1982). Applied to strategic alliances, in this view, not only does the external environment affect the alliance developmental processes, but the alliance activities affect the internal alliance environment as well, for example, the resource profiles, strategic objectives, market positions, and reputation of the constituent partner firms.

Ariño and de la Torre (1998) test a model of alliance evolution that is based on the work of Ring and Van de Ven (1994) and Doz (1996). Following Doz, they included the factor "external change." However, the role of external change is very limited in their model, affecting only reevaluation in alliances. Thus far there is no research that describes a comprehensive co-evolution process of alliances and their environment.

As Table 4.1 shows, much of the alliance process research has adopted the approach relating to alliance developmental stages. A few have incorporated alliance conditions into the process. Only two articles have touched upon co-evolution, but have done so in a rudimentary manner. We suggest, therefore, that there are at least two major gaps in the alliance process literature. First, alliance conditions and their determinants have not received adequate research attention. Second, the co-evolution perspective needs to be developed much further. The essential elements in an alliance co-evolution framework are also unclear. Clearly, this co-evolution approach should integrate other process variables. Thus, we need an integration of the three major alliance process approaches. We attempt here to do so by discussing in some detail the nature of alliance conditions and their varying influences in the alliance developmental process (see Figure 4.1), and by proposing the idea of an alliance co-evolution system that comprises the separate and interwoven evolutions of the alliance and its constituent partner firms.

ALLIANCE CONDITIONS

Alliance conditions are the characteristics of an alliance at any given moment in the life of the alliance. They describe the state of an alliance. Researchers have talked about "initial conditions" and "revised conditions" of alliances (Doz, 1996; Gulati, 1998) as well as "preconditions" and "conditions to build" (Larson, 1992) and exchange conditions (Jones, Hesterly, & Borgatti, 1997) in networks. We designate all these terms collectively as "alliance conditions" irrespective of the particular stage of the alliance. We reason that, as Doz (1996) demonstrates, there are a common set of variables that capture the essence of alliance conditions across the developmental stages. Doz notes that alliance conditions, as measured by a set of variables, dynamically evolve over time as initial conditions are replaced by revised conditions. Ariño and de la Torre (1998) also find that alliance conditions are dynamic in nature throughout the life of an alliance because they "govern the interactions between the partners" (p. 308). The existence of such common condition variables is also clear in Kogut's (1988) observation that "the competitive conditions that motivate the creation of a joint venture may also be responsible for its termination" (p. 169). Based on a review of the literature, we propose that the following three variables systematically

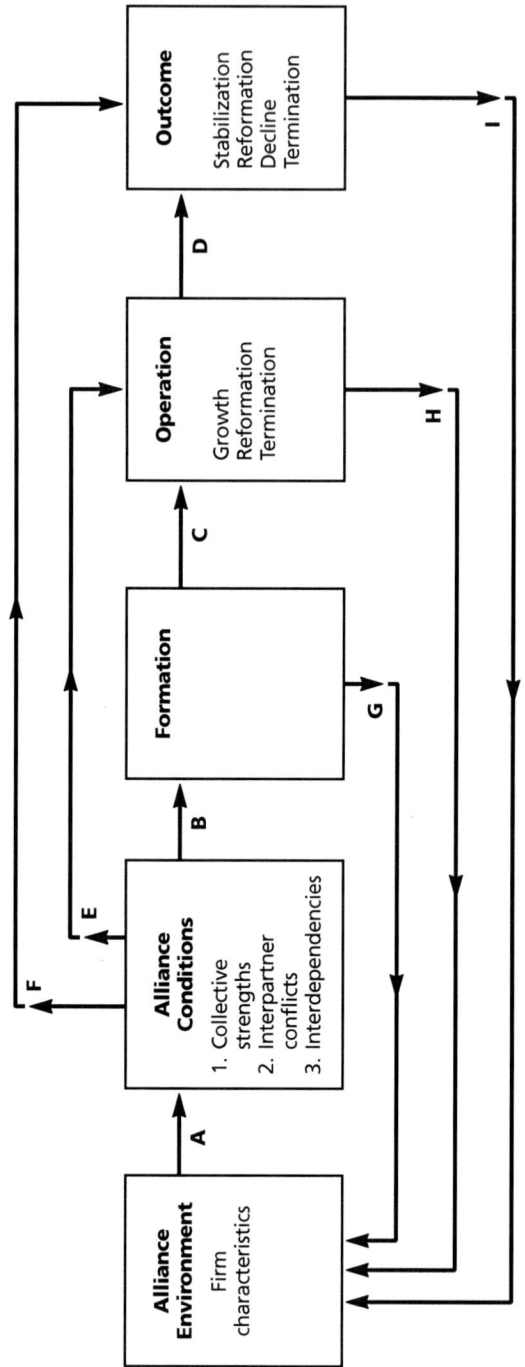

Figure 4.1 Alliance conditions and alliance development.

capture the key aspects of alliance conditions: collective strengths, interpartner conflicts, and interdependencies.

Together, these three condition variables seem to cover three critical aspects of alliances: positive effects of alliances (collective strengths), negative effects of alliances (interpartner conflicts), and the need for alliances (interdependencies). All three condition variables also deal with the interrelationships between the partners. By comparison, the alliance condition variables proposed by Doz (1996)—task definition, partners' routines, and interface structure—tend to focus more on the technical aspects of alliance operations and less on the relational aspects. As such, Doz's list seems to leave out a number of important issues, such as trust, commitment, and capabilities. Our list, in contrast, deals with these issues directly or indirectly. For example, trust and commitment are incorporated within the construct of interpartner conflicts, while capabilities are part of the collective strengths.

Collective Strengths

The collective strengths of an alliance are the aggregated resource endowments of partner firms in relation to the specific strategic objectives that they aim to pursue jointly. The resource-based view of the firm suggests that alliances are formed to obtain access to other firms' critical resources (Das & Teng, 2000b). The purpose is to have sufficient resources to pursue value-creating strategies. Bringing complementary resources into an alliance is considered a key determinant of economic rent generated from alliances. The chances of success increase when the collective strengths of the partner firms are enhanced by combining their market power, technology, and other key resources.

Interpartner Conflicts

The second alliance condition variable—interpartner conflicts—refers to the degree of divergence in partners' preferences, interests, and practices in an alliance (Hardy & Phillips, 1998; Kogut, 1989). Interpartner conflicts are an important aspect of alliances because effective cooperation demands a relatively low level of conflict. As such, conflict resolution has garnered considerable research attention.

While there are various reasons for interpartner conflicts, they seem to fall into three principal categories. First, partner firms may have very different organizational routines, technologies, decision-making styles, and preferences that do not fit very well (Olk, 1997). When firms are vastly different, it takes more money, time, and effort to coordinate their efforts. When firms scramble to have it their own individual way, conflicts inevitably arise. The second source of interpartner conflicts has to do with the private interests and opportunistic behavior of partner firms, which are emphasized in transaction cost economics. Firms may have incompatible goals in the alliance that prompt maximizing their private benefits without advancing the common benefits of partners. Firms may also behave opportunistically to appropriate partners' tacit knowledge and know-how and deliver substandard products. The third type of interpartner conflicts arises from outside the alliance. Partner firms may be fierce competitors in the same market, so their separate interests may clash.

Interdependencies

Interdependencies refer to a condition in which both parties benefit from dealing with each other (Levine & White, 1961). In technology-sourcing alliances, Steensma and Corley (2000) found that interdependencies critically moderate the performance of the alliances. According to the resource-dependence theory, firms attempt to manage their dependence on other firms by engaging in various interfirm relationships. In any relationship, the need for another firm's resources creates a sense of dependence. Although dependence on other firms is a prerequisite for a firm to consider alliances, unidirectional dependence or asymmetrical dependence is not always sufficient for alliance formation. The extreme of asymmetrical dependence is when A depends on B while B does not at all depend on A. No alliance will be formed under this condition. Only when the partners mutually depend on each other will cooperation take place. Empirically, Gulati (1995) confirms that interdependencies do contribute to alliance formation.

So far we have discussed the three alliance condition variables. We now examine a key determinant of alliance conditions in terms of the alliance environment, namely, the characteristics of the partner firms. The alliance environment as related to alliance co-evolution would generally include various aspects of the organizational, competitive, and institutional environment of the alliance. In this chapter, we focus on the organizational environment only (namely, the characteristics of the two or more potential partners) in order to keep our discussion reasonably brief in this initial effort. Accordingly, we select several key factors that exemplify the way that partner firm characteristics affect alliance conditions.

Firm Characteristics and Alliance Conditions

Market Commonality

In competitor analysis, market commonality is "the degree of presence that a competitor manifests in the markets it overlaps with the focal firm"

(Chen, 1996, p. 106). The notion is based on the comparative importance of an industry to the firms—that is, the percentage of their total revenue—and their market share in that industry. A high market commonality suggests that the partners have a high degree of overlap in their overall operations.

Market commonality is likely to be positively related to collective strengths. When partner firms compete mainly in the same market or industry, their combined market share and market power are likely to be high, as compared with two firms from different industries. A higher combined market share is an indicator of high collective strengths in the industry. That is the reason there are many alliances formed by direct competitors. However, this does not mean that the level of interdependencies necessarily goes up with market commonality. Firms with little operational overlap may well need each other as much as direct competitors.

Increasing market commonality will contribute to increased interpartner conflicts, as direct competitors are likely to have conflicting interests. When partner firms compete principally in the same industry, one partner's gain is often at the expense of the other. Even though the partners may find mutual interests in the alliance, potential conflicts may arise very easily, such as when there are geographic overlaps between the partners. Also, joint ventures formed by direct competitors are more likely to dissolve. In Table 4.3, we summarize the proposed relationships, that is, the direction of impact on alliance conditions when the partner firm characteristics change.

Competitive Positions

Eisenhardt and Schoonhoven (1996) find that a vulnerable strategic position leads to more alliance formation. We argued that, everything else being equal, weak companies need partners more than strong companies do. Thus, improving competitive positions will lead to a lower degree of interdependencies among partners. In contrast, individual partner firms with improving competitive positions will tend to achieve higher collective

TABLE 4.3 Partner Firm Characteristics and Alliance Conditions

Partner Firm Characteristics	Effects on Alliance Conditions		
	Collective Strengths	Interpartner Conflicts	Interdependencies
Market commonality (increasing)	Increases	Increases	No effect
Competitive positions (improving)	Increases	No effect	Decreases
Diverse resource profiles (accentuating)	No effect	Increases	Increases
Reputation (increasing)	Increases	Decreases	No effect

strengths. We do not expect any direct relationship between competitive positions and interpartner conflicts. Both strong and weak partner firms may have conflicting interests or incompatible resources and preferences.

Diverse Resource Profiles

Resource profiles of partner firms (and their potential fit) have received much attention in the literature (Medcof, 1997). Generally speaking, partner firms may have either similar or dissimilar resource profiles. This dimension of resource diversity determines the type of resource fit in the alliance, either complementary or supplementary. Most researchers seem to believe that a diverse resource profile is better because partners may contribute different resources to an alliance. This argument seems to be related only to interdependencies, that is, heterogeneous resource profiles enhance the need for each other. Similar resource profiles are more likely to create unidirectional dependence.

However, scholars have also argued that whether or not partners have diverse resource profiles is not important, the key point is the aggregate of the resources. In that sense, a supplementary resource alignment can be equally valuable in beefing up the collective strengths (Das & Teng, 2000b). Value can be created by bringing in similar resources to reach a critical competitive level. Thus, there will be no relationship between the type of resource profiles and the collective strengths of an alliance. Additionally, diverse resource profiles will have a direct impact on interpartner conflicts. As we noted earlier, one source of interpartner conflicts is having different resources contributed by partners that cannot work well together. Examples include incompatible technologies and different organizational routines. Thus, diverse resource profiles may invite more interpartner conflicts.

Reputation

A firm's reputation for trustworthiness is considered as a strategic asset. Because opportunism is a major concern in alliances, a firm's reputation helps in enhancing its partner firm's confidence in partner cooperation (Das & Teng, 1998). A reputation for trustworthiness may be the result of either direct interactions in the past, common partners in other relations, or the general image in the marketplace. Reputation may enhance the collective strengths because partners will be more willing to contribute sensitive resources. Zaheer, McEvily, and Perrone (1998) find that interfirm trust reduces negotiation costs, which add to collective strengths. By the same token, improving reputation may also reduce interpartner conflicts. Trusting partners are more likely to exercise mutual forbearance and cooperate in good faith. We expect no relationship between reputation and interdependencies, because trust itself does not create the need for each other. Dependence is based on resource needs.

ALLIANCE CONDITIONS AND ALLIANCE DEVELOPMENTAL STAGES

Referring to our earlier discussion of alliance process models and Table 4.1, one stream of alliance research focuses on the alliance developmental stages. Among the various stages suggested in the literature, three common stages can be discerned: formation, operation, and outcome stages. In Table 4.2, we have organized the seven alliance process models under these three stages. It is important to note that all models contain (a) a formation stage, in which an alliance strategy is formulated, partners identified, deals negotiated, and the alliance set up; (b) an operation stage, in which partners start to operate the alliance and implement the agreement; and (c) an outcome stage, in which results are obtained and evaluated, and the alliance either stabilizes or continues to change and reform. Although the three stages have distinct characteristics, they also have overlaps, as with any life-stages models. For example, an alliance may start to operate when formal agreements are in the process of being developed. Despite the overlaps, however, the basic idea is that alliances, like typical organizations, go through discernible stages during their operational lives.

We argue that the progress within the three alliance stages is significantly influenced by alliance conditions (see arrows B, E, and F in Figure 4.1). Researchers note that initial alliance conditions and revised conditions critically affect the way alliances proceed, and the same set of condition variables (while different from ours) can be used to describe the developmental process (Doz, 1996). Using the alliance condition variables we proposed earlier—collective strengths, interpartner conflicts, and interdependencies—we now examine the role of these variables in the three developmental stages.

Formation Stage

In the formation stage, partner firms approach each other and negotiate the alliance. Partner firms then carry out the agreement and set up the alliance by committing various types of resources. The alliance is initiated and put into operation. Alliances will be formed only under certain conditions (designated by arrow A in Figure 4.1). These conditions include a relatively high level of collective strengths, a low level of interpartner conflicts, and a high level of interdependencies.

First, a high level of interdependencies is needed for alliance formation because it provides the requisite rationale (Oliver, 1990). Given the managerial complexities of alliances, most firms would choose to stay away from alliances if they are not required to be truly interdependent for a given project. The level of interdependence will not change significantly in the formation stage, because the alliance is just beginning to take shape. Second, alliances tend to be formed with a relatively high level of collective strengths in relation to the intended strategic objectives. Clearly, the partners will need to be confident that the performance risk of the alliance is relatively low (Das & Teng, 1996, 2001a). The collective strengths are likely to go up slowly in the formation stage as the partners continue to bring in valuable resources. Third, alliance formation takes place when current and expected interpartner conflicts are perceived to be low. Partner firms need assurance that serious opportunistic behavior is unlikely, tantamount to a low level of perceived relational risk (Das & Teng, 1996, 2001a). However, during the formation process, it is quite possible that interpartner conflicts will go up gradually as interfirm diversity begins to affect smooth cooperation. Also, hidden agendas may be revealed during this stage, which will further heighten interpartner conflicts.

Operation Stage

Not only is the formation stage directly influenced by alliance conditions, the transition from the formation stage to the operation stage is also dictated by the same alliance condition variables (see arrow E in Figure 4.1). During the operation stage, partner firms collaborate and implement all agreements of the alliance. The alliance will likely grow rapidly in size during this stage, somewhat akin to the growth stage of organizational life cycles. Other than the growth route, an alliance may also be reformed and/or terminated at this stage.

We may call this transitional period early in the operation stage a "crossroads," borrowing the term from D'Aunno and Zuckerman (1987). During the crossroads period, the three alliance conditions may fluctuate significantly and thus lead the alliance to a quick termination. Or the alliance may undergo a reformation that may bring the alliance back on track. For example, interdependencies may suddenly go down during the operation stage. Researchers note that interdependencies can quickly change as a result of learning in alliances (Inkpen & Beamish, 1997). A direct result is a change in the bargaining power between the partners, which may lead to a renegotiation of the original deal. Other types of resource acquisition, for example, for the purpose of name recognition and market entry, if rapidly accomplished, may also lead to diminishing interdependencies. If so, chances are the alliance will not proceed along an extended operation stage, it will either need to be reformed or will head toward termination.

Similarly, the collective strengths of the alliance may take a downturn at the end of the operation stage. The reasons include, importantly, an exhaustion of resources and commitments. It is also possible that the initial match between the partner firms is no longer sustainable. The result, again, is a possible reformation or termination. Besides, an alliance may be destabilized during the initial crossroads period should significant interpartner conflicts arise. Opportunistic behavior of firms is likely to grow and its impact begin to be felt. For an alliance to proceed efficiently in the operation stage, initial disorder and conflicts of interest created by working with partner firms need to be severely curbed. If interpartner conflicts get out of control, the alliance will be on the way toward reformation or termination. It is in this sense that we suggest that alliance conditions have a direct impact on the operation stage of alliances.

If an alliance proceeds normally to growth in the operation stage, alliance conditions will evolve in a predictable fashion. First, interdependencies will tend to go down gradually. A continued appropriation of each other's resources will steadily erode the need for each other. However, an expeditious transfer of valuable resources is unlikely at this stage if it did not happen earlier during the initial crossroads period.

Second, collective strengths may continue to go up at this stage, although the pace is likely to slow down. Not only will the alliance be growing in size, its collective strengths will also increase as the partner firms find the best ways to join forces. Nakamura, Shaver, and Yeung (1996) note that partner firms may choose either convergent operation (based on learning each other's know-how) or divergent operation (which results in more specialization in the alliance). Either approach may produce significant absolute value.

Third, we expect the level of interpartner conflicts to go down during the operation stage. Initial problems and incompatibilities created by alliance diversity are likely to be eased through interfirm adaptation. Partner firms will try to work out ways to deal with opportunistic behavior (Das & Rahman, 2001). Conflict resolution techniques will also be developed in this stage. All types of management control in alliances, for example, output, behavior, and social control, should also help in coping with interpartner conflicts (Das & Teng, 2001b). The alliance will thus proceed toward the next crossroads period while entering the outcome stage.

Outcome Stage

During the outcome stage, alliance performance becomes tangible and can, thus, be evaluated with some certainty. There are four possible outcomes for an alliance at this stage: stabilization, reformation, decline, and termination. Of course, a combination of outcomes is also possible, such as a termination after reformation. It needs to be noted that alliance reformation and alliance termination do not necessarily signal alliance failure.

Reformation and termination may be the best option under certain circumstances, such as the achievement of preset alliance objectives. Alliance condition variables continue to play a decisive role in the outcome stage (see arrow F in Figure 4.1). The particular alliance outcome will depend on the conditions of the alliance.

The transitional period early in the outcome stage—in the nature of crossroads—will presage the likely outcome of an alliance. Just as with the first crossroads period at the beginning of the operation stage, an alliance will run into trouble if its collective strengths and interdependencies start to go down significantly and interpartner conflicts multiply. Reformation or termination will then be likely outcomes.

A more gradual deterioration in alliance conditions will lead to alliance decline. Researchers have paid considerable attention to organizational decline (Weitzel & Jonsson, 1989), which can be attributed to a shrinkage in the resource base or a diminishing ability to adapt to the environment. In a similar manner, strategic alliances may register a decline in their performance, resource base, and adaptive ability, and thus slide toward dissolution. We suggest that alliance decline is characterized by (a) a decrease in collective strengths, which diminishes the resource base; (b) an increase in interpartner conflicts, which diminishes each other's adaptive ability; and (c) a decrease in interdependencies, which diminishes commitment.

In the outcome stage, alliances may also stabilize and become mature. That means the alliance achieves a fit with its environment and successfully adapts to the environment on a continuous basis. In such a case, the three alliance condition variables will also show a stabilized pattern. The level of interdependencies will go down slowly, especially if a convergent operation is pursued. Collective strengths may continue to climb as the alliance grows and managers gain experience. Interpartner conflicts will move downward as conflict resolution techniques and control mechanisms are perfected.

In sum, while an alliance proceeds from the formation stage to the operation stage to the outcome stage, the alliance conditions substantively influence the unfolding of the overall developmental process (arrows B, E, and F in Figure 4.1).

So far we have discussed how alliance conditions affect the alliance developmental process. Because alliance conditions are the result of the firm characteristics that we discussed earlier, it is plain that these alliance conditions will shift whenever there are changes in the firm characteristics. In addition, we suggest that alliance evolution will, in turn, also affect firm characteristics (arrows G, H, and I in Figure 4.1). More importantly, we propose that an alliance and its constituent partner firms interactively co-evolve, and this co-evolutionary system can be explored in terms of the firm characteristics and alliance conditions. In the next section, we discuss these co-evolutionary processes.

CO-EVOLUTION OF ALLIANCES AND THEIR PARTNER FIRMS

Alliance co-evolution is of research interest because, after all, strategic alliances uniquely represent a system consisting of multiple elements, that is, the partners and the alliance *per se*. This multifaceted nature of alliances suggests that these elements will evolve separately as well as interactively. Although some scholars have studied the co-evolution of organizations and their environment (e.g., Levinthal & Myatt, 1994), the alliance literature has not paid much attention to alliance co-evolution. The few papers that discuss the notion of co-evolution in alliances do so only in relation to their environment (Ariño & de la Torre, 1998; Koza & Lewin, 1998). The literature has been unclear about the elements of an alliance co-evolutionary system. Here we propose the different elements of a co-evolutionary system as applicable to strategic alliances.

Co-evolution has its foundation in evolution. By definition, co-evolution takes place when different parts of a system evolve simultaneously and interact with each other so that one partner's evolution is affected by another partner's evolution. Because an alliance co-evolves with its constituent partner firms, the evolution of each entity influences the other's evolution, and vice versa.

Partner Firm Evolution Affecting Alliance Evolution

Market Commonality

Partner firm evolution, as described by the four firm characteristics, will greatly influence alliance evolution. If market commonality between partner firms goes up, collective strengths and interpartner conflicts will also go up (see Table 4.3). The likely result of having direct competitors with high operational overlap as partners is that the alliance will experience more instability. Although higher collective strengths mean more resources to proceed fast, higher interpartner conflicts based on partner self-interest suggest that collaboration will not be smooth. The alliance between Liz Claiborne and Avon, for example, encountered trouble when Avon acquired an upscale cosmetics company in an effort to enhance its image (Stafford, 1994). Because the acquisition increased the market commonality of the two partners, Liz Claiborne began to view Avon as more of a competitor than a partner. Because of this increased conflict, the alliance was soon dissolved through the acquisition of Avon by Liz Claiborne.

Competitive Positions

When partner firms achieve better competitive positions in the market, they will have higher collective strengths but lower interdependencies. High collective strengths suggest that the alliance will be able to proceed fairly successfully. According to Eisenhardt and Schoonhoven (1996), strong strategic positions diminish the need for alliances. Because of low interdependencies among the partners, the alliance is likely to be dissolved rather quickly.

Diverse Resource Profiles

Partner firms may develop more diverse resource profiles during the tenure of the alliance, which may or may not be the result of a convergent resource operation within the alliance. In that case, partner firms will have higher interpartner conflicts and higher interdependencies. On the one hand, diverse resource profiles will encourage the partners to acquire each other's valuable resources. Interpartner conflicts due to opportunistic learning will delay the progress of the alliance. On the other hand, because partner firms may become more interdependent, they will be more likely to be deeply embedded in the alliance.

Reputation

Finally, partner firms' reputation for trustworthiness also changes over time. Interactions in the alliance may increase perceived trustworthiness, however a firm's reputation may change when independent events happen outside the alliance. Higher trustworthiness results in higher collective strengths and lower interpartner conflicts (Zaheer et al., 1998). Accordingly, the alliance will progress faster. In addition, alliance stability will be enhanced.

Alliance Evolution Affecting Partner Firm Evolution

Formation Stage

The results of alliance progress and evolution directly affect partner firms' situation and characteristics. For example, Das, Sen, and Sengupta (1998) find that announcements of strategic alliances cause firm valuations to fluctuate in the stock market. During the formation stage, it is most likely that partner firms' market commonality and reputation will change as a result of alliance evolution. The other characteristics will tend to be more affected later in the process. For example, firms' competitive positions and resource profiles will not change quickly during alliance formation.

Alliance formation affects partner firms' market commonality almost immediately. Sometimes a partner firm does not originally operate in the industry of the alliance (such as when a bank forms an alliance in the insurance business). The formation of the alliance changes the situation because the firm then has a presence in that industry. If both partner firms operate in that industry, alliance formation also changes their relative market share in the industry and the importance of that industry to them. The result is inevitably a higher level of market commonality. High market commonality leads to greater collective strengths and interpartner conflicts (as we discussed earlier), which then impact on the alliance evolution process.

The reputation of partner firms is first tested during the formation stage. As Ring and Van de Ven (1994) suggest, when partners negotiate and actually commit to an alliance (alliance formation), they rely much on informal sense making and psychological contract. These mechanisms emphasize that alliance making is a relational contracting process and that this process depends on a certain level of interfirm trust and even interpersonal trust among managers (Borch, 1994; Dodgson, 1993). The formation stage is critical in assessing the trustworthiness of partners because partners begin to interact and familiarize themselves with each other. Trust may easily break down if one or more partner firms are found to behave opportunistically. It is also possible that initial interactions strengthen interfirm and interpersonal trust. The result is a heightened perception of each other's trustworthiness. Furthermore, since an alliance will tend to have its own reputation, alliance formation is likely to transfer such alliance reputation to the reputation of its partners.

Operation Stage

As compared with the formation stage, the operation stage will affect firm characteristics more widely. Except for competitive positions, all the other characteristics are likely to change in this stage. Partner firms' competitive positions will remain unchanged because the alliance is yet to generate results in the operation stage. In contrast, market commonality between the partner firms will continue to rise in this stage because the alliance is likely to grow in size and market share. In addition, the operating results may continue to help partners in assessing and reassessing each other's trustworthiness. Alliance managers rely on both role interactions and personal interactions to run the alliance. The partner firms will realize whether the other partner is interested in exploiting the relationship or investing in the relationship. Thus, a partner firm's perceived trustworthiness will evolve during the operation stage.

The resource profiles of the partner firms will begin to change as a result of alliance activities. Alliance operation will help partner firms in developing resources that they did not already own, contributing to "feedback effect on parent firms" in terms of resource similarity (Nakamura et al., 1996, p. 521). Also, during alliance operation, resources may develop convergently or divergently. A convergent operation emphasizes symmetrical interfirm learning, and the partner firms will acquire some knowledge and know-how from each other. The result is a higher level of resource overlap and a lower level of resource diversity. Contrariwise, a divergent resource development indicates further specialization in one's own area of strength. Learning is not important in this mode of development. Resource diversity will remain high or go even higher.

Also, strategic objectives of partner firms are likely to change in the operation stage. Oftentimes, partner firms enter alliances with a learning orientation, that is, with an intention to appropriate the other's tacit knowledge and know-how. Although learning takes time and may be accomplished during the outcome stage, it begins to take place during the operation stage. When this objective is largely accomplished, partner firms may demand a renegotiation of the deal. In such a situation, they will tend to have quite different objectives in the alliance, such as using the alliance as a cash cow or supporting their core businesses.

Outcome Stage

One key feature of the outcome stage is that it is tied with performance evaluation. Partner firms may use a benefit/cost framework or they may measure realized performance outcome with their expected outcome and judge whether the discrepancy is too great. A negative discrepancy will lead the partners to reevaluate the alliance and adjust their approaches. It may also change the strategic objectives of the partner firms in the alliance. When outcomes match expectations, partners become more committed to the alliance. However, a successful accomplishment of their mission may also change partners' strategic objectives in the alliance.

The competitive positions of partner firms will eventually be affected by alliance evolution at the outcome stage as well. They may not change before the outcome stage because the competitive positions of firms change only over the long haul. The partner firms may achieve stronger competitive positions via the alliance for a variety of reasons. They may acquire valuable resources from the alliance that can be used in the parent firm. Or they may enter a critical market through the alliance. Or, again, they may gain legitimacy from the prominence of a partner firm.

During the outcome stage, the resource profiles of partners will continue to evolve as the alliance evolves. As we discussed earlier, the resources that are acquired or developed through alliance operation serve to gradually alter each partner's resource profile. Besides, we believe that the other two variables—market commonality and firms' reputation—will not be greatly affected by alliance evolution at the outcome stage. The changes in the market commonality of the partner firms will have already been adjusted for prior to the outcome stage. Similar adjustments will have taken place regarding interfirm trust among the partners.

CONCLUSION

One of the key issues in understanding the developmental processes of strategic alliances is how the alliance conditions change over the different stages of development. A related question involves the nature of the co-evolutionary dynamics of alliances in terms of their constituent partner firms.

In this chapter, we proposed a process model of alliance development that is based on the ideas of alliance conditions and an alliance system comprising co-evolutionary elements. We suggested that alliance conditions differentially impact the alliance developmental processes across three commonly accepted stages, namely, formation, operation, and outcome stages. We defined alliance conditions as consisting of collective strengths, interpartner conflicts, and interdependencies. Alliance conditions, we noted, are impacted by the alliance environment, comprising specific partner firm characteristics. Alliance conditions also cause certain changes in the partner firms of the alliance, and these partner firm changes, in turn, affect the developmental processes. We further examined the co-evolution of the alliance and its constituent partners along the developmental stages in relation to the complex role of the alliance conditions.

We first discussed, in some detail, the construct of alliance conditions, identifying both its antecedents and its constituent factors. We suggested three alliance condition variables that adequately capture the character of an alliance at any given moment, namely, collective strengths, interpartner conflicts, and interdependencies. These conditions are determined by the alliance environment, which comprises the characteristics of the partner firms. Thus, changes in the alliance environment (with or without the impact of the alliance) alter alliance conditions.

Second, we suggested that alliance conditions serve as a link between the alliance environment and the alliance developmental process. We contended that the three alliance condition variables, in specific combinations, constitute the prerequisites for alliances to be formed, operated, reformed, and terminated.

Third, we argued for a new approach to understanding the alliance developmental process and discussed at some length how the three developmental stages are differentially impacted by the three alliance condition variables. We suggested that different kinds of alliance outcome, for example, progress, reformation, decline, and termination, can be postulated by examining the changing patterns of alliance conditions.

Fourth, we proposed a co-evolutionary model of the alliance process. So far as we know, no existing framework has clearly delineated such a co-evolutionary process. We focused our attention on the co-evolutionary interactions between the alliance and its constituent partner firms, exploring, in particular, the changes in the alliance conditions and partner firm characteristics in the three developmental stages. We believe our examination of alliance co-evolutionary dynamics helps in better understanding the complexities of alliance developmental processes.

Finally, from an overarching perspective, we integrated the three alliance process approaches found in the literature, namely, that of alliance developmental stages, alliance conditions, and alliance co-evolution, and also, thereby, addressed the specific limitations of the individual approaches.

In regard to possible empirical research on alliance development and alliance co-evolution reflected in our model, we have provided the basis for deriving the necessary test propositions; these are implicit in the contents of the cells in Table 4.3. We believe that a listing of explicit statements of all these propositions—a considerable number in total—would needlessly clutter the chapter.

The managerial implications of our model of alliance development are valuable. By understanding and thinking critically about the import of Table 4.3, a manager of a strategic alliance should be in a position to determine the specific actions needed for effective performance. Depending on how the manager assesses the alliance conditions, and given the developmental stage under consideration, the model suggests clear prescriptions for handling various situations arising in alliances. An added benefit is that the courses of action indicated on this basis is buttressed by a comprehensive understanding of the interactive dynamics of alliance conditions and partner firm characteristics and activities. Such conceptual insights should afford significant advantage to managers while making choices about effective strategies in alliances.

For example, we may use the framework to analyze the development process of the alliance between Northwest Airlines and KLM Royal Dutch Airlines (Tully, 1996). In 1992, Northwest was in deep trouble and almost went bankrupt. KLM came to its rescue by acquiring 25% of Northwest. The equity-based alliance allowed the two airlines to link their hubs in Detroit and Amsterdam and offer transatlantic traveling under one brand name through code-sharing. In this case, Northwest's weak financial position and KLM's weak competitive position in the United States (a firm characteristic) led to a high degree of interdependencies (an alliance condition). Besides, since the two had low market commonality, there was a low level of interfirm conflicts (another alliance condition). As a result, the alliance was formed and quickly entered the operation stage. The initial performance of the alliance was very impressive: the combined transatlantic market share jumped from 7% to 11% in two years. Clearly, the alliance experienced rapid growth and proceeded successfully from the operation stage to the outcome stage under favorable alliance conditions.

During the initial period, Northwest's financial situation improved remarkably, and the firm became profitable again. In terms of firm characteristics, a weak competitive position became a strong one, and the level of interdependencies went down. Meanwhile, KLM profited much from its initial investment and went on to exert even more control over Northwest. The attempt created interfirm conflicts in the alliance. Since two out of three alliance conditions were deteriorating, the alliance ran into trouble and faced a possible reformation in the outcome stage. As this case suggests, the insights from our framework include a recognition that the levels of interdependencies and interpartner conflicts in the alliance will change when partners' situation and objectives evolve over time. Prior agreements on possible ways to modify and terminate the alliance may help contain the uncertainties engendered by changing alliance conditions.

As another example, we may apply the framework to examine the high-profile alliance between US West (a major local telephone company headquartered in Denver, Colorado) and Time Warner (Cauley, 1996). In 1993, US West invested $2.55 billion for a 25.5% share in a joint venture with Time Warner. The joint venture—Time Warner Entertainment—comprised most of Time Warner's cable systems, the HBO channel, and Warner Brothers Studios. At the beginning of the partnership (formation stage), the two firms had low market commonality (telephones and entertainment) and diverse resource profiles (US West's financial resources vs. Time Warner's physical resources and reputation). Thus, our framework would suggest a low level of interpartner conflicts and a high level of interdependencies in their joint venture. A couple of years later (operation stage), the relationship started to show signs of strain. US West vetoed several deals proposed by Time Warner Entertainment to form alliances with telecom firms such as AT&T, apprehensive that such alliances would eventually compete against US West's own local telephone business. Furthermore, when Time Warner proceeded to acquire Turner Broadcasting System in 1996, US West took its partner to court, arguing that the acquired Turner assets would effectively compete against those of the joint venture (Time Warner Entertainment). The court eventually dismissed the case and the two firms were on the verge of a divorce (McCarthy, 1996). In the meantime, US West completed an acquisition of Continental Cablevision, further reducing its reliance on the joint venture.

Clearly, the relationship went sour as the two firms were heading for greater market commonality (in telephone and cable business) and more similar resource profiles (through acquisitions). The alliance conditions deteriorated quickly, as reflected in a high level of conflicts and a low level of interdependencies. The two firms began negotiations for ending the alliance. One plan was to give back to Time Warner the HBO channel and Warner Brothers, while granting US West a majority ownership of the cable business. However, the two parties could not agree on the financial terms. Meanwhile, there was a stock market boom and the value of the cable business went up substantially. To some extent, the good fortune alleviated the conflicts. In July 1997, the two firms announced that they were basically satisfied with the condition of the joint venture and would continue with the existing relationship (Fabrikant, 1997). Thus, we may say that at this point of the outcome stage the alliance stabilized.

There are several limitations in our proposal that should be addressed in future research. First, the key construct of alliance conditions needs to be examined further in terms of other relevant factors beyond the three that we have discussed here. For instance, the optimal degrees of competition and cooperation between partner firms may be explored in the different developmental stages. The dominance of competition over cooperation, or vice versa, could well be detrimental to continued alliance stability in different stages (Das & Teng, 2000a). Second, we examined the alliance environment only in terms of partner firm characteristics. The industry and general environments have been left out in order to keep our analysis within manageable limits. Clearly, future research should include other important alliance environment factors, such as industry characteristics and the institutional environment, and also attend to a more extensive list of firm characteristics. And finally, our discussion of the alliance co-evolutionary system has not explicitly taken the temporal dimension into account. Although time is an implied dimension in our model, its fundamental role in co-evolution has not been fully examined. For example, future research should focus on the differing planning horizons of partner firms and explore how these may affect the co-evolutionary dynamics of alliances and the requisite alliance conditions for effectiveness in the different developmental stages.

ACKNOWLEDGMENT

This chapter, save some minor changes, was earlier published as Das, T. K., & Teng, B. (2002). The dynamics of alliance conditions in the alliance development process. *Journal of Management Studies, 39*, 725–746.

REFERENCES

Ariño, A., & de la Torre, J. (1998). Learning from failure: Towards an evolutionary model of collaborative ventures. *Organization Science, 9*, 306–325.

Borch, O. J. (1994). The process of relational contracting: Developing trust-based strategic alliances among small business enterprises. *Advances in Strategic Management, 10B,* 113–135.

Brouthers, K. D., Brouthers, L. E., & Harris, P. C. (1997). The five stages of the co-operative venture strategy process. *Journal of General Management, 23*(1), 39–52.

Cauley, L. (1996, March 12). Time Warner, US West go to court this week in bitter partnership feud. *Wall Street Journal,* p. B7.

Chen, M.-J. (1996). Competitor analysis and interfirm rivalry: Toward a theoretical integration. *Academy of Management Review, 21,* 100–134.

Das, S., Sen, P. K., & Sengupta, S. (1998). Impact of strategic alliances on firm valuation. *Academy of Management Journal, 41,* 27–41.

Das, T. K., & Rahman, N. (2001). Partner misbehavior in strategic alliances: Guidelines for effective deterrence. *Journal of General Management, 27*(1), 43–70.

Das, T. K., & Teng, B. (1996). Risk types and inter-firm alliance structures. *Journal of Management Studies, 33,* 827–843.

Das, T. K., & Teng, B. (1997). Sustaining strategic alliances: Options and guidelines. *Journal of General Management, 22*(4), 49–64.

Das, T. K., & Teng, B. (1998). Between trust and control: Developing confidence in partner cooperation in alliances. *Academy of Management Review, 23,* 491–512.

Das, T. K., & Teng, B. (2000a). Instabilities of strategic alliances: An internal tensions perspective. *Organization Science, 11,* 77–101.

Das, T. K., & Teng, B. (2000b). A resource-based theory of strategic alliances. *Journal of Management, 26,* 31–61.

Das, T. K., & Teng, B. (2001a). A risk perception model of alliance structuring. *Journal of International Management, 7,* 1–29.

Das, T. K., & Teng, B. (2001b). Trust, control, and risk in strategic alliances: An integrated framework. *Organization Studies, 22,* 251–283.

D'Aunno, T. A., & Zuckerman, H. S. (1987). A life-cycle model of organizational federations: The case of hospitals. *Academy of Management Review, 12,* 534–545.

Dodgson, M. J. (1993). Learning, trust, and technological collaboration. *Human Relations, 46,* 77–95.

Doz, Y. L. (1996, Summer). The evolution of cooperation in strategic alliances: Initial conditions or learning processes? *Strategic Management Journal, 17* [Special Issue], 55–83.

Eisenhardt, K. M., & Schoonhoven, C. B. (1996). Resource-based view of strategic alliance formation: Strategic and social effects of entrepreneurial firms. *Organization Science, 7,* 136–150.

Fabrikant, G. (1997, July 17). Time Warner to remain in venture with US West. *New York Times,* p. D6.

Greiner, L. E. (1972). Evolution and revolution as organizations grow. *Harvard Business Review, 50*(4), 37–46.

Gulati, R. (1995). Does familiarity breed trust? The implication of repeated ties for contractual choice in alliances. *Academy of Management Journal, 38,* 85–112.

Gulati, R. (1998). Alliances and networks. *Strategic Management Journal, 19,* 293–317.

Hannan, M. T., & Freeman, J. (1977). The population ecology of organizations. *American Journal of Sociology, 82,* 929–964.

Harbison, J. R., & Pekar, P., Jr. (1998). *Smart alliances: A practical guide to repeatable success.* San Francisco, CA: Jossey-Bass.

Hardy, C., & Phillips, N. (1998). Strategies of engagement: Lessons from the critical examination of collaboration and conflict in an interorganizational domain. *Organization Science, 9,* 217–230.

Inkpen, A. C., & Beamish, P. W. (1997). Knowledge, bargaining power, and the instability of international joint ventures. *Academy of Management Review, 22,* 177–202.

Jarillo, J. C. (1988). On strategic networks. *Strategic Management Journal, 9,* 31–41.

Jones, C., Hesterly, W. S., & Borgatti, S. P. (1997). A general theory of network governance: Exchange conditions and social mechanisms. *Academy of Management Review, 22,* 911–945.

Kanter, R. M. (1994). Collaborative advantage: The art of alliances. *Harvard Business Review, 72*(4), 96–108.

Kogut, B. (1988). Joint ventures: Theoretical and empirical perspectives. *Strategic Management Journal, 9,* 319–332.

Kogut, B. (1989). The stability of joint ventures: Reciprocity and competitive rivalry. *Journal of Industrial Economics, 38*(2), 183–198.

Koza, M. P., & Lewin, A. Y. (1998). The co-evolution of strategic alliances. *Organization Science, 9,* 255–264.

Kumar, R., & Nti, K. O. (1998). Differential learning and interaction in alliance dynamics: A process and outcome discrepancy model. *Organization Science, 9,* 356–367.

Larson, A. (1992). Network dyads in entrepreneurial settings: A study of the governance of exchange relationships. *Administrative Science Quarterly, 37,* 76–104.

Levine, S., & White, P. E. (1961). Exchange as a conceptual framework for the study of interorganizational relations. *Administrative Science Quarterly, 5,* 583–601.

Levinthal, D., & Myatt, J. (1994). Co-evolution of capabilities and industry: The evolution of mutual fund processing. *Strategic Management Journal, 5,* 45–62.

McCarthy, S. (1996). US West loses Time Warner suit. *Telephony, 230*(24), 3.

McKelvey, B. (1982). *Organizational systematics: Taxonomy, evolution, classification.* Berkeley: University of California Press.

Medcof, J. W. (1997). Why too many alliances end in divorce. *Long Range Planning, 30,* 718–732.

Nakamura, M., Shaver, J. M., & Yeung, B. (1996). An empirical investigation of joint venture dynamics: Evidence from U.S.-Japan joint ventures. *International Journal of Industrial Organization, 14,* 521–541.

Niederkofler, M. (1991). The evolution of strategic alliances: Opportunities for managerial influence. *Journal of Business Venturing, 6,* 237–257.

Olk, P. (1997). The effect of partner differences on the performance of R&D consortia. In P. W. Beamish & J. P. Killing (Eds.), *Cooperative strategies* (Vol. 1) *North American perspectives* (pp. 133–159). San Francisco, CA: New Lexington.

Oliver, C. (1990). Determinants of interorganizational relationships: Integration and future directions. *Academy of Management Review, 15,* 241–265.

Powell, W. W. (1987). Hybrid organizational arrangements: New form or transitional development? *California Management Review, 30,* 67–87.

Ring, P. S., & Van de Ven, A. H. (1994). Developmental processes of cooperative interorganizational relationships. *Academy of Management Review, 19,* 90–118.

Spekman, R. E., Isabella, L. A., MacAvoy, T. C., & Forbes, T., III. (1996). Creating strategic alliances which endure. *Long Range Planning, 29,* 346–357.

Stafford, E. R. (1994). Using co-operative strategies to make alliances work. *Long Range Planning, 27*(3), 64–74.

Steensma, H. K., & Corley, K. G. (2000). On the performance of technology-sourcing partnerships: The interaction between partner independence and technology attributes. *Academy of Management Journal, 43,* 1045–1067.

Thorelli, H. B. (1986). Networks: Between markets and hierarchies. *Strategic Management Journal, 7,* 37–51.

Tully, S. (1996, June 24). Northwest and KLM: The alliance from hell. *Fortune, 133*(12), 64–68, 70, 72.

Van de Ven, A. H. (1992, Summer). Suggestions for studying strategy process: A research note. *Strategic Management Journal, 13*[Special Issue], 169–188.

Weitzel, W., & Jonsson, E. (1989). Decline in organizations: A literature integration and extension. *Administrative Science Quarterly, 34,* 91–109.

Zaheer, A., McEvily, B., & Perrone, V. (1998). Does trust matter? Exploring the effects of interorganizational and interpersonal trust on performance. *Organization Science, 9,* 141–159.

CHAPTER 5

INSULAR STAGES OF ALLIANCES AND COUNTERINTUITIVE COMMUNICATION NEEDS

Varghese P. George

ABSTRACT

Stages of alliances permit greater focus on the immediate job at hand. However, such partitions also usually lead to excessive detachment between stages.
Alliances are replete with boundaries of various other kinds as well. The ones
you face in a partner firm can be more difficult to surmount than the ones in
your own firm. Difficult boundaries feed the insularity of stages to the detriment of the performance of alliances, which in the best of circumstances is
never high. Borrowing from the research on innovation, I present a typology
of essential purposes for communication, consisting of coordination, information exchange, and synergy. It will be the foundation for a framework to overcome the insularity of stages of alliances. Practical suggestions include design
of structures and processes based on anticipated interdependence, bridging
techniques using overlapping individuals and stages, design of information
systems, and selective *direct* interactions among participants. While partitions
and boundaries implacably encourage insularity, the way out is counterintuitive. That can happen only through careful anticipation of interdependence

Management Dynamics in Strategic Alliances, pages 101–116

and early design and set up of structures and processes. There also are no shortcuts for tapping tacit knowledge and for unlocking individual and group synergies. For these, face-to-face communication is essential. It is also somewhat ironic that, as a general form, alliances tap benefits from distant sources, and yet, their greatest benefits accrue from selectively bridging that distance.

INTRODUCTION

A manager described the previous job at the parent organization as finding alignment among many elements analogous to solving a single Rubik's Cube. The new job at an alliance, the manager claimed, was more like solving a *Double* Rubik's Cube, immensely more difficult and complex. Such characterizations arise from imperfectly intermeshing organizational strategies, cultures, structures, and procedures. Yet, in the backdrop of inexorable technological innovations and relentless market pressures, firms find it nearly impossible to depend just on being able to exploit some capabilities internally and to buy others in the markets. To make up the difference, forms of mutually beneficial and less than permanent arrangements in the form of alliances across firm boundaries have become the norm. Despite their wide prevalence, managing alliances still poses severe challenges. In this chapter, I use a combination of stages of alliances and a typology of requisite communication from the innovation literature to arrive at a framework for designing and managing effectively the various processes in an alliance.

ALLIANCES AS COMPLEX AND DYNAMIC ENTITIES

Alliances help organizations exploit complementary capabilities. However, they are immensely more complex than the regular projects of their respective parent organizations. Alliances, therefore, demand a much higher level of ingeniousness and effort for success. Dissatisfaction with the performance of alliances began to appear quite early both in anecdotes and in the literature (Chowdhury, 1992; Harrigan, 1985; Park & Russo, 1996; Sherman & Sookdeo, 1992). A large set of studies that examined the problem in depth, although influential in the literature, was not very helpful in improving the performance of alliances. Few issues stood out. *First,* the *causal* variables were formulated at the partner level, for example, partner influence (Killing, 1982, 1983), asymmetry (Beamish & Banks, 1987; Harrigan, 1988), and such, or at a higher level, for example, competitive structure (Baum, Calabrese, & Silverman, 2000; Park & Russo, 1996). These certainly are not easily amenable to managerial intervention at the alliance level. *Second,* the *performance* of alliances was cast either at the firm level, for example, innovation (Kotabe & Swan, 1995; Pennings & Harianto, 1992), and as stock market response (Koh & Venkatraman, 1991; McConnell & Nantell, 1985; Woolridge & Snow, 1990). Both are quite removed temporally from the management of an alliance. *Third,* when the performance measures are at the alliance level, for example, survival, longevity (Harrigan, 1988), and managerial perceptions (Draulans, deMan, & Volberda, 2003), they are usually *ex post facto* measures correlated more often with the coarser higher-level constructs than to crucial issues of context, structure, or process at the alliance level itself.

We should keep in mind, however, that the task of defining and measuring performance of alliances is very complex and difficult. Unlike the performance measures of firms, no simple, comprehensive, and widely agreed-upon criteria exist for alliances (Geringer & Hebert, 1991; Harrigan, 1985; Lorange & Roos, 1992). If we are to make any serious dent in solving the problems related to performance of alliances, our conceptualizations should be such as to enable managerial manipulations of both designs and processes at the level of an alliance itself. They should not just be primarily around pre- or postconditions to alliances. Such a genre of inquiry has been ascendant. They highlight, for example, the importance of trust (Krishnan, Martin, & Noorderhaven, 2006; Zaheer, Lofstrom, & George, 2002; Zoller, 1999), of conflict resolution (Lin & Germain, 1998; Ring & Van de Ven, 1994), of balance between under- and overstructuring (Dussauge & Garrette, 1995), of efficiencies shaped mostly by *internal* factors (Oliver, 1990), and of the extraordinary importance of communication (Hedlund, 1994; Kogut & Zander, 1996; Kotabe, Martin, & Domoto, 2003).

A common thread in the inquiries about the facilitative processes of alliances, though not always clearly visible, is the notion of *life cycle* or *developmental stages* of an alliance. Das and Teng (2002, p. 725) proposed "an integrated process model of alliances that is based on alliance conditions, alliance developmental stages, and an alliance system comprising co-evolutionary elements." They argued that all alliances proceed through a formation stage, an operation stage, and an outcome stage, and that the sequential stages have interdependencies among them. They pointed out that it is especially important to consider the dynamic aspects of the evolution of alliances, without which it would be difficult to understand the inherent tensions (Das & Teng, 2000) and to manage the dynamic learning requirements (Das & Kumar, 2007). Similar lifecycle approaches have been used extensively elsewhere in the management literature (Abernathy & Utterback, 1978).

Ring and Van de Ven (1994, p. 90), in that vein, offered a formal process framework that "focuses on formal, legal, and informal social-psychological processes by which organizational parties jointly negotiate, commit to, and execute their relationship." They use this framework to describe and explain the temporal stages in a cooperative relationship: emergence, evolution, and dissolution. These have been helpful in organizing causes and effects related to a phenomenon in a neat temporal order. Such order also aids both in identifying direct pathways of influence of antecedents and in delineating prescriptive interventions. Das and Teng (2002) reported a large number of inquiries proposing stages of alliances including one of their own earlier ones. They suggested in that earlier inquiry (Das & Teng, 1997) that the process of alliance management can be divided into seven major stages: considering strategic alliances, selecting alliance partners, negotiating the alliance agreement, setting-up of the alliance, operating the alliance, evaluating alliance performance, and modifying the alliance. While that framework is more detailed than the later ones, its reach extends to elements exogenous to the prospective alliance. Some of these exogenous elements will have influence only until the start of an alliance, and some others will have continuing influence on the alliance. Our particular interest here is in the latter. The more parsimonious framework in the later literature, with just three stages of formation, operation, and outcome, however, is a bit too abstract and tightly packed to easily highlight and deal with the plausible bottlenecks and the breakdowns. George and Farris (1999) investigated performance of alliances and, based on structured interviews, inductively developed a set of five perceptual stages of the managers to identify the unique characteristics of these stages, the difficulties they observed in handing-off across the stages, and the influence of each stage on the eventual performance of the alliance. I will use that model, broadly commensurable with others we discussed (neither too compact nor too elaborate) to build the framework for this chapter.

Bottlenecks and Breakdowns Leading to Insularity of Stages of Alliances

As shown in Table 5.1 and in Figure 5.1, George and Farris (1999) conceptualize four formative stages and one postformative stage of an alliance. The early formative stages are labeled Recognition, Research, Relationship Set-up, and Ramp Up. During the Recognition stage, a company recognizes the need and the promise of a potential alliance. Such recognition takes place at any level of the hierarchy or the value chain of the company. Recognition is usually followed by the Research stage, when the company engages in research into the prospects of the potential alliance. This could include analyses to ensure technological and market appropriateness, as well as early planning for resource allocation. The Relationship Set-up stage follows next. During this stage, the partners in the alliance negotiate and arrive at a plan for implementing the collaborative project. The final formative stage

TABLE 5.1   Descriptions of the Formative Stages

Formative Stages of Alliances	Description
Recognition	A company recognizes the need and the promise of a potential alliance. Such recognition takes place at any level of the hierarchy or the value chain of the company.
Research	The company engages in research into the prospects of the potential alliance. This could include analyses to ensure technological and market appropriateness as well as early planning for resource allocation.
Relationship set-up	During this stage, the partners in the alliance negotiate and arrive at a plan for implementing the collaborative project.
Ramp up	This is the implementation stage for the set-up plan.
Ongoing management	The collaborative project may still be growing. However, at this stage it is largely beyond the special vulnerabilities of the formative stages. It now will start going through the normal vicissitudes of any business project.

Source: George & Farris, 1999

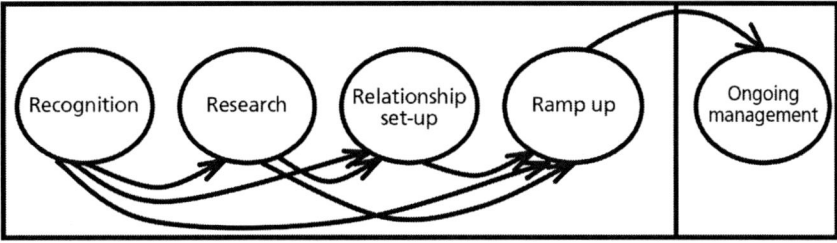

Figure 5.1   Formative stages of an alliance. *Source:* George & Farris, 1999.

is labeled Ramp Up, and it is during this stage that the implementation of the set-up plan takes place.

The postformative stage is labeled as Ongoing Management. It is intended as a placeholder of sorts in this framework. During this stage, the collaborative project may still be growing. However, it is largely beyond the special vulnerabilities of the formative stages. Once the Ramp Up stage is successfully completed, we assume that the project is well beyond prototyping any product or service, and that the viability of the project is well-established. The venture now will go through the normal vicissitudes of any business project.

The reasons for the Double Rubik's Cube syndrome that we saw at the beginning of the chapter become more obvious from the study. Different actors from the partnering companies dominate each of the different stages. The issues they have to deal with are entirely different too. For example, the people leading the Recognition stage more often than not worried entirely about strategic implications, while the people managing the Ramp Up stage struggled with operations even when they sought, often without success, strategic clarifications. The organizational processes were different for the different stages too. The Research stage usually had mostly the lawyers doing due diligence and staff people completing market and technology research as needed.

One of the most important findings of the study was that the better performing alliances had better integrations across stages. Such integration was achieved either by designed systems that simply worked or by a fortuitous combination of circumstances. The latter included a technology that was ready enough for the market so that integrative overheads were minimal and the stages were completed rapidly with some overlaps. These overlaps meant that the information sequence was not broken. In contrast, as should be expected, information gaps in the alliances, wherever they existed, caused serious problems. One of the worst examples was of an operational manager seeking strategic clarity in the middle of a Ramp Up. He discovered that the people who set up the alliance had left the company, and the related documents were sent off to storage from where it was difficult to retrieve them. Channels of communication were not only broken, but potential sources of information were inaccessible.

Given that only a small fraction of the alliances were deemed a success, informational dysfunction was more the general rule than the exception. The stages, which are inevitable due to the dynamic transitions in an alliance, are remarkably and helplessly insular. The finding calls out unambiguously for a comprehensive communication strategy across and within stages in alliances. The study by George and Farris (1999) also called for anticipatory and contingent designs of processes for earliest anticipation of problems, preparation, and quickest problem solving, as envisaged in the bidirectional arrows in Figure 5.2. Adapted from the innovation literature, this chapter puts forward a scheme for the same.

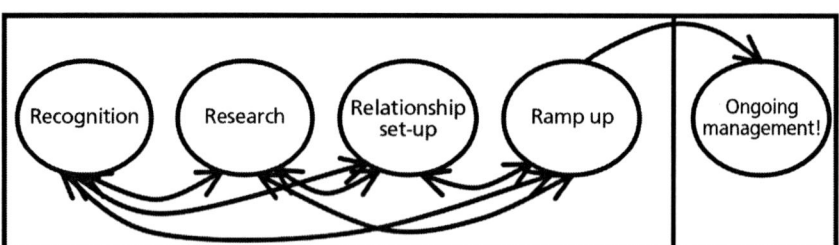

Figure 5.2 Using formative stages for improving performance—earliest anticipation of problems, preparation, and quickest problem solving. *Source:* George & Farris, 1999.

Communication

For all the multifaceted nature of organizations, some elemental claims are now nearly axiomatic. Structure influences processes. Communications are the carrying media for processes. Optimal processes lead to improved performance. We saw in the discussion in the last section that stages of alliances sometimes become the bottleneck and cause breakdown in communication flows. This should not be a surprise because a long tradition of research on organizational communication confirms that their networks fragment along structural fissures (Allen, 1977, 1986; Allen & Cohen, 1969; Allen & Fusfeld, 1976; Allen & George, 1989; Katz & Allen, 1982). The same research also shows that "structure" need not be limited to the organizational kind. Almost any structure has the propensity to splinter communication networks. The physical boundaries of buildings and geographical separations are dramatic examples.

Since boundaries and partitions of many structures—organizational, geographic, functional, cultural, and so on—abound in alliances, it is only natural that we observe highly fragmented communication networks. These, in turn, thwart process flows to the great detriment of final performance. Scholars to date have handled the role of communication in alliances only rather modestly or indirectly (e.g., Kale, Dyer, & Singh, 2002; Monczka, Petersen, Handfield, & Ragatz, 1998; Monge et al., 1998). The extensive work done to shape and design communication networks for innovation has great relevance for alliances as well.

Classifying Communication by Purpose

We can improve considerably the design and the management of an environment if we can clearly understand the purposes of the requisite communicational transactions. With this in mind, three types of communication have been put forward (Allen, 1986, 2007): for the *coordination* of activities, for exchanging *information,* and for creating *synergy.* Although this typology has provided much support for conceptualizations around the research on innovation and communications, and has broad acceptance from practitioners in the context of organizational and architectural designs, the three types of communication have not appeared all together much in the literature. However, it would be safe to state that *each* type has had a long, storied, and somewhat independent scholarly tradition. Coordination, for example, has been studied extensively in organizations (e.g., Gulati & Singh, 1998; Kogut & Zander, 1996; Malone, 1987; Van de Ven, Delbecq, & Koenig, 1976) and elsewhere.

Information also continues to have vigorous scholarly attention from diverse points of view (Alchian & Demsetz, 1972; Argyris, 1977; Daft & Lengel, 1986; Maier, 2007; Shapiro & Varian, 2000). In an attempt to sharpen the syntax around the use of the term "information," scholars have been using a hierarchy consisting of, in order of increasing value, data, information, knowledge, understanding, and wisdom (Ackoff, 1989). While acknowledging some mutual interdependence among the constructs in the hierarchy around information, it would behoove us to sidestep that debate. The typology here is intended to characterize communication. If the act of communication is "to inform," we would label it as communication for information. In other words, this type of information is intended to represent the active exchange or transmission of the full gamut of constructs related to information through communication.

Synergy, the motivation behind the third type of communication, also has multifarious presence in the literature, all of which represent the idea that a combination of entities may have the capacity to produce results they independently cannot. Examples of synergy abound in many areas of everyday human activities, ranging from the music of orchestras to the partnerships of couples to raise children. Considerable scholarly efforts have been brought to bear on inquiries into synergy and therefore, improved performance, in organizational groups (Cattell, 1951; Hackman, 1987; Hall, 1971; Hall & Watson, 1970; Lasker, Weiss, & Miller, 2001; Tattersall, 1984). Synergy captures the positive difference between what is separately and individually possible when things work out, which is its usual meaning, and the negative difference, if things go awry.

If you were to ask what *else* might be expected from communication, the answers, in all likelihood, can be subsumed in one of these three types. They are, therefore, collectively exhaustive. There is no claim that they are mutually exclusive; communication for coordination may include significant information collaterally provided, which may also lead to synergistic effects. The elements of the communication typology also are not exactly orthogonal. Nonetheless, as we saw above in their separate bodies of literature, the underlying constructs of coordination, information, and synergy are remarkably unique and thus have sufficient contrast among them. Table 5.2 has the listing of the typology, and we will henceforth refer to it as the C/I/S (Coordination/Information/Synergy) typology.

TABLE 5.2   Different Types of Communication Needed for Innovation

Purpose	Description
Coordination	Communication to coordinate the learning process
Information	Communication to send and acquire knowledge
Synergy	Communication to promote interpersonal creativity

Source: Allen, 1986, 2007

Benefits of the Typology for Alliances

We might explore how the three types of communication might be adapted specifically to alliances. Recall that complimentary capabilities of separate firms are brought together to create something new in alliances. It is only natural that considerable coordination will be required to align the complementary capabilities and exploit them across organizational, physical, and other boundaries. Most alliances also are set up with technology or knowledge-intensive goals. Such goals put at premium the value of appropriate information exchange. Even where the technology or the knowledge is not all that extraordinarily complex or sophisticated, the need for information exchange remains rather high because both sides should have access to each other's tacit knowledge. Finally, the most essential purpose of any alliance is the accomplishment of something each could not have independently done; that is a synergistic goal by definition. Therefore, the processes that were the target for improvement via the three communication types developed in the context of managing innovation are equally or more relevant for alliances.

OPTIMIZING COORDINATION, INFORMATION, AND SYNERGY

The fundamental challenge in any alliance in optimally coordinating, sharing information, and creating synergies comes from the natural human tendency to divide to conquer large or complex entities. We partition everything ranging from living spaces (Alexander, 1964) to organizations (Aiken & Hage, 1968; Blau & Schoenherr, 1971; Blau & Scott, 1962; John Child, 1972; Hall, 1977; Lawrence & Lorsch, 1967) to tasks (Von Hippel, 1990) to recipes (Julia Child, 1968). Most of these examples benefit, though some less and others more, from at least a semblance of what Alexander (1964), an architect, refers to as "synthesis."

Partitioning of living spaces, Alexander's (1964) example, is usually easy. Putting them back together, or synthesizing, as a well-mated whole, is the work of true inspiration. The multidivisional organizational structure with its elaborate partitions is another example. It is a consequence of the natural evolution of organizations. The eroded linkages from partitioning are partially rebuilt temporarily through project teams and matrix structures. Von Hippel (1990) shows that partitioned innovation tasks can be better managed by utilizing the predictability of interdependence, shifting the boundaries of partitions, and reducing the barriers to interactions. Alliances have more than their share of Double Rubik's partitions from all the boundaries *within* and *across* at the least two parental organizations. They usually do not seem to benefit from any systematic synthesis.

The major counterforces to integration arise in an alliance from well-known sources. The principal players usually change for each stage. Although interdependent, the functional focus at each stage is dramatically different, resulting in cultural and linguistic distance. The gestation periods for each stage can be substantial in some cases, leading to temporal isolation and consequent organizational dementia. All these come on top of myriad organizational, geographic, and cultural partitions of the two or more parents. Some partitions may be more permeable than others. One manager, having been frustrated in getting access to one's own company's earlier strategic reviews, simply approached the partner company and readily obtained all the information needed.

The challenge is to find the right bridges across multifunctional actors distanced by partitional boundaries of some nefarious kinds, whose impact is compounded severely by inevitable temporal separations. This certainly is not an insurmountable problem. A simpler version of this problem is successfully solved in the day-to-day activities in every organization and even in kitchens. It is just that additional layers in an alliance, which add exponential complexity, need to be more nonreflexively handled than such things usually are.

Reflexive handling would make partitions *less* permeable. Each stage might become a bit more focused, easier, and even more effective, but their sequential combination would be a disaster. *Anticipatory* designs and *reflective* executions can go a long way in mitigating the problem. While that is counterintuitive while dealing with the immediate tasks of a given stage, it is essential that preceding stages are considered *not* as stand-alone isolates, but as tributaries leading to a final common goal.

Consider the nature of coordinational burdens at each stage. The *levels* of coordination required during Relationship Set-up and Ramp Up stages are clearly more intense than during Recognition and Research stages. Further, the type of tasks to be coordinated, and the people who manage them during the more intensive Relationship Set-up and Ramp Up stages, are usually very different. The former would consist of tasks with more cognitive elements dealing with negotiations and formulations, which are predominantly strategic in nature. The latter would consist of tasks with more cooperative action elements dealing with implementation, which are predominantly operational in nature. During the former, self-interest would dominate, with the partners posturing for the best deal each can get. Common interests come to the fore during the latter, whether self-interest abates or not.

When we examine alliances closely, we hardly ever find the preceding stages providing proper support to the Ramp Up stage. The Recognition stage generally basks in the glow of the final potential of the alliance, which is usually very attractive, and in the hope of realizing the "thrill of the deal." The Research stage is more about intellectual property protection, market research, and modestly about overall feasibility. During the Relationship Set-up stage, the focal firm is more interested in protecting its own interests than in streamlining the forthcoming operation. When the Ramp Up stage begins, sometimes the best help the operational people can get comes from using the residual relationships from the not-too-uncommon introductory retreat. It is more often the case that the operational managers bitterly complain that they do not even know who to call in the alter firm to solve a problem that is not within the sphere of influence of their direct counterparts. This need not be.

Every stage of an alliance can be anticipated, even if the outcome may not be. From the very early stages, especially with the Research stage, structures and processes can be put in place and set in motion so that coordination appropriate to the stage takes place effectively, and preparation for the subsequent stage also takes place. This would also mean *organizational* and *process* planning should be part of the Research and Relationship Set-up stages, which usually gets crowded out by market research and legalistic intellectual property protection efforts. Earliest identification and modest participation of representatives from later stages will go a long way in smoothing channels of communication. Designing adequate overlaps across stages would be another technique to assure continuity. Given that interorganizational boundaries are inevitably less permeable than intraorganizational ones, transparent, compatible features among partners too will make the differential burdens of stages for coordination a bit lower. Much can be done with anticipatory planning to assuredly improve coordination in an alliance.

Strengthening the interdependent processes *across* stages, as we just discussed, is one way to improve coordination. *Within* each stage, improving coordination can be more of a conventional effort of streamlining information processing (Galbraith, 1974) and managing the process of interaction among players engaged in interdependent work (Malone, 1987; Malone & Crowston, 1994). It is important, however, to set up mechanisms to ease coordination across challenging boundaries instead of preempting with structures and controls that exact larger compensation for potentially higher coordination costs (Gulati & Singh, 1998), which would be the intuitive, but self-defeating, reaction.

The information needed for coordination is just one of the many types of this genre needed for successfully carrying out the work in an alliance. In knowledge-intensive environments, considerable technical information also will need to get exchanged for the successful completion of tasks. A comprehensive information management system that securely manages, stores, and transmits all the codifiable information, both technical and organizational, would be a relatively easy solution. There cannot be any excuse not to implement such a system. However, that can only be the starting point and would take care of only a small part of the information needed in an alliance.

There is universal agreement that people know more than they can explain. Such personal knowledge (Polanyi, 1958, 1966) is more valuable, and perhaps also more crucial, for an alliance. Personal knowledge consists of not only matters of technical nature but also covers organizational routines and cultures. Techniques to tap these are quite straightforward. People should have the opportunity to interact directly at close quarters to be able to extrapolate the meaning of the tacit knowledge available with their counterparts.

It is essential to create sufficient opportunities for face-to-face interactions, but the benefits extend beyond gleaning new information. The C/I/S typology's purpose that is most elusive is synergy. An alliance itself is the pursuit of a distinct, higher-level, targeted institutional synergy. Within that pursuit, it is possible that many finer strands of individual and group synergies can emerge. However, their likelihood of emergence is highly dependent on proximal, face-to-face interactions, without which there is no chance of them seeing the light of day. So to both tap into tacit knowledge and to unlock individual and group synergies, sufficient opportunities for direct interactions must be made possible at every stage in the alliance. Given the right opportunities, the inside kernels of tacit knowledge can grease the skids of an alliance a lot better, and the unlocked synergies can make its promise much bigger. It is somewhat ironic that, as a general form, alliances are intended to tap benefits from distant sources, and yet, the greatest benefits from them accrue by selectively removing that distance.

CONCLUSION

We examined in depth some of the implications of stages in alliances. While such partitioning allows for greater focus on the job at hand, the stages also become highly insular. That, of course, is seriously detrimental to the performance of alliances. Borrowing from the research on innovation, we used a typology of essential communication purposes, consisting of coordination, information exchange, and synergy, to develop a framework to overcome the insularity of the stages of an alliance. We marshaled design of structures and processes based on anticipated interdependence, bridging techniques using overlapping individuals and stages, design of information systems, and selective direct interactions among participants. However, these efforts need to be even more robust and vigorous than for intraorganizational projects because the interorganizational boundaries in an alliance are even more difficult to penetrate.

ACKNOWLEDGMENTS

I want to place on record my sincere appreciation for Colin Capelle, my indefatigable graduate assistant. Special thanks to Renee Tolchinsky for reading my drafts and giving valuable suggestions.

REFERENCES

Abernathy, W. J., & Utterback, J. M. (1978). Patterns of industrial innovation. *Technology Review, 80*(7), 40–47.

Ackoff, R. L. (1989). From data to wisdom. *Journal of Applied Systems Analysis, 16*(1), 3–9.

Aiken, M., & Hage, J. (1968). Organizational interdependence and intra-organizational structure. *American Sociological Review, 33,* 912–930.

Alchian, A. A., & Demsetz, H. (1972). Production, information costs, and economic organization. *American Economic Review, 62,* 777–795.

Alexander, C. (1964). *Notes on the synthesis of form.* Cambridge, MA: Harvard University Press.

Allen, T. J. (1977). Managing the flow of technology: Technology transfer and the dissemination of technological information within the R&D organization. Cambridge, MA: MIT Press.

Allen, T. J. (1986). Organizational structure, information technology, and R&D productivity. *IEEE Transactions on Engineering Management, 33,* 212–217.

Allen, T. J. (2007). Architecture and communication among product development engineers. *California Management Review, 49*(2), 23–41.

Allen, T. J., & Cohen, S. I. (1969). Information flows in research and development laboratories. *Administrative Science Quarterly, 14,* 12–19.

Allen, T. J., & Fusfeld, A. R. (1976). Design for communication in the research and development lab. *Technology Review, 78*(6), 64–71.

Allen, T. J., & George, V. P. (1989). Changes in the field of R&D management over the past 20 years. *R&D Management, 19*(2), 103–113.

Argyris, C. (1977). Organizational learning and management information systems. *Accounting, Organizations and Society, 2,* 113–123.

Baum, J. A. C., Calabrese, T., & Silverman, B. S. (2000). Don't go it alone: Alliance network composition and startups' performance in Canadian biotechnology. *Strategic Management Journal, 21,* 267–294.

Beamish, P. W., & Banks, J. C. (1987). Equity joint ventures and the theory of the multinational enterprise. *Journal of International Business Studies, 18,* 1–16.

Blau, P. M., & Schoenherr, R. A. (1971). *The structure of organizations.* New York, NY: Basic Books.

Blau, P. M., & Scott, W. R. (1962). *Formal organizations.* San Francisco, CA: Chandler.

Cattell, R. B. (1951). New concepts for measuring leadership, in terms of group syntality. *Human Relations, 4,* 161.

Child, J. (1968). *The French chef cookbook* (1st ed.). New York, NY: Knopf.

Child, J. (1972). Organizational structure, environment and performance: The role of strategic choice. *Sociology, 6*(1), 1–22.

Chowdhury, J. (1992). Performance of international joint ventures and wholly owned foreign subsidiaries: A comparative perspective. *Management International Review, 32*(2), 115–133.

Daft, R. L., & Lengel, R. H. (1986). Organizational information requirements, media richness and structural design. *Management Science, 32,* 554–571.

Das, T. K., & Kumar, R. (2007). Learning dynamics in the alliance development process. *Management Decision, 45,* 684–707.

Das, T. K., & Teng, B. (1997). Sustaining strategic alliances: Options and guidelines. *Journal of General Management, 22*(4), 49–64.

Das, T. K., & Teng, B. (2000). Instabilities of strategic alliances. An internal tensions perspective. *Organization Science, 11,* 77–101.

Das, T. K., & Teng, B. (2002). The dynamics of alliance conditions in the alliance development process. *Journal of Management Studies, 39,* 725–746.

Draulans, J., de Man, A. P., & Volberda, H. W. (2003). Building alliance capability: Management techniques for superior alliance performance. *Long Range Planning, 36,* 151–166.

Dussauge, P., & Garrette, B. (1995). Determinants of success in international strategic alliances: Evidence from the global aerospace industry. *Journal of International Business Studies, 26,* 505–530.

Galbraith, J. R. (1974). Organization design: An information processing view. *Interfaces, 4*(3), 28–36.

George, V. P., & Farris, G. (1999). Performance of alliances: Formative stages and changing organizational and environmental influences. *R&D Management, 29,* 379–389.

Geringer, J. M., & Hebert, L. (1991). Measuring performance of international joint ventures. *Journal of International Business Studies, 22,* 249–263.

Gulati, R., & Singh, H. (1998). The architecture of cooperation: Managing coordination costs and appropriation concerns in strategic alliances. *Administrative Science Quarterly, 43,* 781–814.

Hackman, J. R. (1987). The design of work teams. In J. W. Lorsch (Ed.), *Handbook of organizational behavior* (pp. 315–342). Englewood Cliffs, NJ: Prentice-Hall.

Hall, J. (1971, November). Decisions, decisions, decisions. *Psychology Today, 5,* 51–54.

Hall, J., & Watson, W. H. (1970). The effects of a normative intervention on group decision-making performance. *Human Relations, 23,* 299–317.

Hall, R. H. (1977). *Organizations: Structure and process.* Englewood Cliffs, NJ: Prentice-Hall.

Harrigan, K. R. (1985). *Strategies for joint ventures.* Lexington, MA: Lexington Books.

Harrigan, K. R. (1988). Strategic alliances and partner asymmetries. *Management International Review, 28,* 53–72.

Hedlund, G. (1994). A model of knowledge management and the N-form corporation. *Strategic Management Journal, 15,* 73–90.

Kale, P., Dyer, J., & Singh, H. (2002). Alliance capability, stock market response, and long term alliance success: The role of the alliance function. *Strategic Management Journal, 23,* 747–767.

Katz, R., & Allen, T. J. (1982). Investigating the Not Invented Here (NIH) syndrome—A look at the performance, tenure, and communication patterns of 50 R&D project groups. *R&D Management, 12*(1), 7–19.

Killing, J. P. (1982). How to make a global joint venture work. *Harvard Business Review, 60*(3), 120–127.

Killing, J. P. (1983). *Strategies for joint venture success.* New York, NY: Praeger.

Kogut, B., & Zander, U. (1996). What firms do? Coordination, identity, and learning. *Organization Science, 7,* 502–518.

Koh, J., & Venkatraman, N. (1991). Joint venture formations and stock market reactions: An assessment in the information technology sector. *Academy of Management Journal, 34,* 869–892.

Kotabe, M., Martin, X., & Domoto, H. (2003). Gaining from vertical partnerships: Knowledge transfer, relationship duration, and supplier performance improvement in the US and Japanese automotive industries. *Strategic Management Journal, 24,* 293–316.

Kotabe, M., & Swan, K. S. (1995). The role of strategic alliances in high-technology new product development. *Strategic Management Journal, 16,* 621–636.

Krishnan, R., Martin, X., & Noorderhaven, N. G. (2006). When does trust matter to alliance performance? *Academy of Management Journal, 49,* 894–917.

Lasker, R. D., Weiss, E. S., & Miller, R. (2001). Partnership synergy: A practical framework for studying and strengthening the collaborative advantage. *Milbank Quarterly, 79*(2), 179–205.

Lawrence, P. R., & Lorsch, J. W. (1967). *Organizational environment: Managing differentiation and integration.* Homewood, IL: Richard D. Irwin.

Lin, X., & Germain, R. (1998). Sustaining satisfactory joint venture relationships: The role of conflict resolution strategy. *Journal of International Business Studies, 29,* 179–196.

Lorange, P., & Roos, J. (1992). Strategic alliances: Formation, implementation, and evolution. Cambridge, MA: Blackwell.

Maier, R. (2007). Knowledge management systems: Information and communication technologies for knowledge management. New York, NY: Springer Verlag.

Malone, T. W. (1987). Modeling coordination in organizations and markets. *Management Science, 33,* 1317–1332.

Malone, T. W., & Crowston, K. (1994). The interdisciplinary study of coordination. *ACM Computing Surveys, 26*(1), 87–119.

McConnell, J. J., & Nantell, T. J. (1985). Corporate combinations and common stock returns: The case of joint ventures. *Journal of Finance, XL,* 519–536.

Monczka, R., Petersen, K., Handfield, R., & Ragatz, G. (1998). Success factors in strategic supplier alliances: The buying company perspective. *Decision Sciences, 29,* 553–577.

Monge, P., Fulk, J., Kalman, M., Flanagin, A., Parnassa, C., & Rumsey, S. (1998). Production of collective action in alliance-based interorganizational communication and information systems. *Organization Science, 9,* 411–433.

Oliver, C. (1990). Determinants of interorganizational relationships: Integration and future directions. *Academy of Management Review, 15,* 241–265.

Park, S. H., & Russo, M. V. (1996). When competition eclipses cooperation: An event history analysis of joint venture failure. *Management Science, 42,* 875–890.

Pennings, J. M., & Harianto, F. (1992). Technological networking and innovation implementation. *Organization Science, 3,* 356–381.

Polanyi, M. (1958). *Personal knowledge: Towards a postcritical philosophy.* Chicago, IL: University of Chicago Press.

Polanyi, M. (1966). *The tacit dimension* (1st ed.). Garden City, NY: Doubleday.

Ring, P. S., & Van de Ven, A. H. (1994). Developmental processes of cooperative interorganizational relationships. *Academy of Management Review, 19,* 90–118.

Shapiro, C., & Varian, H. R. (2000). *Information rules.* Boston, MA: Harvard Business School Press.

Sherman, S., & Sookdeo, R. (1992). Are strategic alliances working? *Fortune, 126*(6), 77–78.

Tattersall, R. (1984). In defense of the consensus decision. *Financial Analysts Journal, 40*(1), 55–57.

Van de Ven, A. H., Delbecq, A. L., & Koenig, R., Jr. (1976). Determinants of coordination modes within organizations. *American Sociological Review, 41,* 322–338.

Von Hippel, E. (1990). Task partitioning: An innovation process variable. *Research Policy, 19,* 407–418.

Woolridge, J. R., & Snow, C. C. (1990). Stock market reaction to strategic investment decisions. *Strategic Management Journal, 11,* 353–363.

Zaheer, A., Lofstrom, S., & George, V. P. (2002). Interpersonal and interorganizational trust in alliances. In F. J. Contractor & P. Lorange (Eds.), *Cooperative strategies and alliances* (pp. 347–377). London, England: Elsevier Science.

Zoller, S. A. (1999). Are you satisfied with your technology alliances? *Research-Technology Management, 42*(2), 10–12.

CHAPTER 6

BEYOND THE "IDEAL"

Exploring Controls in Interfirm Settings From a Combinatorial Perspective

Ariela Caglio
Angelo Ditillo

ABSTRACT

The aim of this chapter is to evaluate the "ideal" control archetypes proposed for interfirm alliances and to deepen our understanding of the potential control archetypes' coexistence and evolution. This purpose will be pursued by using a *combinatorial view*, which will provide new original insights into interorganizational control. First of all, it will contribute to elucidating the possible connections among control elements, rather than just one-to-one relations between control items and contextual variables, thus incorporating the notion of a *systemic fit*. Second, it will recognize that various control combinations may be effective at the same time, underlining, in this way, the principle of *equifinality*. Third, it will clarify that *complementarity* of controls is not only the result of consistency deriving from uniformity but can also result from dissimilarity of control mechanisms. By focusing on these principles, an approach for designing control configurations in interfirm alliances will be presented.

Management Dynamics in Strategic Alliances, pages 117–134

INTRODUCTION

The objective of this chapter is to question the validity of "ideal" control archetypes proposed for interfirm alliances. Their fine-grained description and comparison will emphasize their limitations, which depend on a static conception of the link between the characteristics of transactions and controls, assuming that once the nature of the relationship changes, controls change in a linear direct one-to-one way. As a consequence, ideal control archetypes offer only limited insights into the multifaceted reality of practice, and more complex and varied forms of control traits, empirically observed in reality, need to be explained. The extension of this static conception to a more nonlinear, dynamic view of control will be illustrated here through a process perspective that recognizes that different models may be present at the same time with reference to the same strategic alliance, and that these latter may jump between different ideal types over time, emphasizing the multiplicity and complexity of the trajectories that they can take. Control patterns will be, therefore, described as the emergent, self-organized outcome of the interactions that occur in the interfirm relationships, affected by perturbations that push them to oscillate between different configurations of control and to undertake new areas of the interorganizational space. This process does not occur in a deterministic way and will be described as a progression of certain institutional factors that push the interfirm relationship toward a specific trajectory (Thrane, 2007).

This chapter will contribute to expanding our knowledge on the control archetypes' coexistence and evolution by using a *combinatorial perspective*, which will offer new powerful interpreting insights into interorganizational control (Malmi & Brown, 2008; Milgrom & Roberts, 1995). First, it will explain the potential interaction among control traits, rather than just pairwise links between control elements and environmental or other external variables, thus incorporating the notion of a *systemic fit* (Grandori & Furnari, 2008). Second, it will illustrate the possibility that more than one combination of controls is effective in the same context, emphasizing the concept of *equifinality* (Sandelin, 2008). Third, it will clarify that *complementarity* of control mechanisms is not only the result of consistency by "similarity in kind" but can also stem from differences of control mechanisms (Caglio & Ditillo, 2008; Grandori & Furnari, 2008). By using these principles, an approach for designing control forms in interfirm relationships will be illustrated.

DEFINING THE "IDEAL" INTERFIRM CONTROL ARCHETYPES

The management literature suggests that alliances have generally tended to fail and be terminated at an excessively high rate (Das & Teng, 2000). Many contributors maintain that the instability rate of alliances is between 30% and 50% (Beamish, 1985; Das & Teng, 2001; Killing, 1983; Kogut, 1988; Park & Ungson, 2001). In the field of joint ventures, Gordon Redding estimated that "About 50% of joint ventures fail" (as cited in Young, 1994, p. 35). Kogut (1988) showed that 32% of joint ventures failed within their first 10 years, and Gomes-Casseres (1987) found that while 16% of wholly owned subsidiaries were "unstable," this percentage was higher—31%—for joint ventures. In addition, estimates of unsatisfactory international joint venture performance have ranged from 37% to over 70% (Geringer & Hebert, 1991). Many collaborating partners face problems in coping with a partner's conflicting interests, an inevitable loss of operating autonomy, differing cultures and/ or management styles. And a lack of trust between partners sometimes generates a more complex and hence, destructively slow decision-making processes (Groot & Merchant, 2000). Some writings suggest strongly that many alliances suffer from poor control practices and conclude that this is one of the prime determinants of alliance failure (Amigoni, Caglio, & Ditillo, 2003; Caglio & Ditillo, 2008; Geringer & Hebert, 1989; Groot & Merchant, 2000).

In the last 2 decades, there has been a variety of research contributions in which the analysis of the use of control practices in alliances has been stressed (Caglio & Ditillo, 2008; Cristofoli, Ditillo, Liguori, Sicilia, & Steccolini, 2010; Das & Teng, 1998; 2000; Grandori, 2004; Håkansson, Kraus, & Lind, 2010; Hopwood, 1996; Van der Meer-Kooistra & Scapens, 2008). In particular, using a transaction cost economics background, a relevant amount of knowledge has been developed with reference to the different control forms that can sustain and regulate transactions in alliances. Starting from the 1990s, a high number of contributions were published on the topic, originally in noneconomic journals, and then progressively in the management literature. In an influential paper published in 1999, Ghosh and John maintained that transaction cost economics has become "the dominant paradigm for analysing issues in several areas" (p. 131), including interfirm control.

Some authors have investigated the role of management controls in interorganizational relationships by using a configurational approach (Håkansson & Lind, 2004; Langfield-Smith & Smith, 2003; Sartorious & Kirsten, 2005; Speklé, 2001; van den Bogaard & Speklé, 2003; Van der Meer-Kooistra & Vosselman, 2000; Vosselman, 2002). On the basis of this logic, some ideal control configurations are identified, and deviations from these ideals are assumed to result in lower performance (Grandori & Furnari, 2008).

Market-Based Archetypes of Control

Speklé (2001) proposed a theoretical framework that distinguishes between different modes of control. One of these archetypes is market based and assumes a straightforward regulation of alliances' transactions based on competition. According to the author, this is a suitable form in contexts characterized by high programmability and low asset specificity. A similar model was proposed also by Van der Meer-Kooistra and Vosselman (2000), who describe the market-based archetype where all information is included in prices; the contracts are not detailed; there are no specific investments; and if one party of the relation behaves opportunistically, alternative parties can be chosen without incurring relevant switching costs. In this context, the only control mechanism concerns the regular measurement and evaluation of the performance of the partners. This archetype suits a context characterized by high task programmability, high measurability of output, low asset specificity and high task repetition. It fits a transaction environment with low uncertainty and in which many parties are able to compete for the same transactions. Also, Håkansson and Lind (2004), through the analysis of a business relationship between two firms in the telecom industry, presented an ideal market-based control archetype. This latter was defined as a form of control where the interface between the two coordinated activities is standardized to ensure that several customers' demands are matched with the supply of several producers of similar products. This is proper when activities are complementary, dissimilar, and performed independently of each other in any specific sense, but dependent on their common standardized product. If an assumption is made of the existence of imperfections in the market, then there will be a specific need of information concerning the prices of the standardized product from different suppliers. Furthermore, it will be necessary to have information about the "consuming" activities of other buyers. This latter information is required as each partner must develop its own "consumption" in accordance with the others in order to demand the same solution to retain the standardization of its products.

Hierarchical Archetypes of Control

An alternative archetype has been described in the literature, emphasizing the bureaucratic nature of controls used to monitor the counterpart in an alliance. Van der Meer-Kooistra & Vosselman (2000) proposed a bureaucracy-based pattern, characterized by long-term detailed contracts to monitor the performance of the partners and by control mechanisms made up of specified norms, standards, detailed rules, and rigid performance targets. Their objective is to foster continuous supervision, performance measurement, and evaluation through a regular process of information supply. It should be applied in the presence of high task programmability, high output measurability, moderate asset specificity, and medium repetitiveness of transactions. Furthermore, it matches an environment where low uncertainty and a medium level of predictability prevail. Similarly, Håkansson and Lind (2004) presented a hierarchical form of control. In a hierarchy, two activities are directly coordinated. In principal, they become one activity and can be perfectly adapted to each other, but they can only be jointly related to other activities. The adaptation is based on information about the two activities and their closely complementary relationship. This includes information about the resources needed to perform the activities. If some of these resources are heterogeneous, it is possible to develop and thereby learn about their interplay. To take advantage of this, the company needs a continuous supply of very detailed accounting and nonaccounting information concerning technical and economic aspects of the activities performed and the use of resources. This control archetype is useful when two activities are closely complementary and similar. In this case, being closely complementary is defined as representing a situation where different phases of a production process require some coordination. Similar activities are defined as those activities that require the same capability for them to be undertaken.

Within the realm of the same hierarchical archetype, some other authors have specifically concentrated on the control practices of one specific form of alliances, that is, joint ventures (JVs). These alliances were the object of specific analysis because, as reported by Geringer and Hebert (1989), "The issue of control has received only fragmented and unsystematic attention in the JV literature" (p. 237), and "managers have received minimal guidance about when and how to use [the various control options], as well as about the potential trade-offs between alternative control options" (p. 250). In addition, the strategic alliance literature has suggested that these interorganizational forms have specific features that make them a separate category of alliances in terms of controls (Das & Teng, 2001). In line with these considerations, several contributions have been published on the contextual variables potentially implicated in the use of management controls in joint ventures. Yan and Gray (1994) analyzed the relationship between the bargaining power of potential partners and the structure of management control in U.S.-Chinese joint ventures. Data from the four case studies analyzed (in the electronic office equipment, industrial process control, personal hygiene products, and pharmaceuticals industries) confirmed a positive relationship between the relative bargaining power of a venture partner and the management control it exercises. Groot and Merchant (2000) enlarged the spectrum of the contextual variables and identified three primary dimensions to study control in international joint ventures (IJVs): control mechanisms, control focus, and control tightness. In their analysis of three international joint ventures (in the automotive, chemical, and electronic components industries), they found that when partners have a broad set of objectives for an IJV, their control focus is broad; and when partners use an IJV to diversify their product offerings (rather than extending the geographical coverage of their existing product lines), they tend to use relatively loose controls. In addition, the analysis of data indicated that all partners monitored their IJV's overall financial results and that the partners' more in-depth involvement in the IJV's management was not in areas where they had the greatest control concerns, but where they thought their superior knowledge and capabilities provided them the greatest potential for contribution.

Trust-Based Archetypes of Control

The management literature has suggested that trust is a key element and a source of confidence in alliances (Das & Teng, 1998; Ring & Van de Ven, 1992; Sydow & Windeler, 1998). Researchers have identified a multidimensional nature of trust. There are various classifications of trust types. Rousseau, Sitkin, Burt, & Camerer (1998) distinguish between calculus-based trust, relational trust, and institution-based trust. Calculus-based trust is related to utilitarian considerations and is based on credible information, such as reputations and information from network relationships about another's goodwill and competencies. In addition, it refers to opportunities for deterrence whenever malfeasance may occur, such as withdrawing future business opportunities and the spreading of information about one's behavior among networked partners, affecting other current and future relationships the partner is and may get involved in. Relational trust derives from continuous interaction between trustor and trustee, and related to information available to the trustor from within the relationship itself. Finally, institution-based trust concerns institutional controls the relationship is subject to, such as the ability to rely on legal forms and societal norms and values, which may as well undermine trust. Alternatively, another classification of trust refers to the distinction between contractual trust, competence trust, and goodwill trust. Contractual trust is based on the moral standard of honesty and relies on assumptions that the other party will honor the agreement, whether the agreement is written or not (Van der Meer-Kooistra & Vosselman, 2000). Competence trust emphasizes perceptions of ability and expertise, and concerns "the expectation of technically competent role performance" (Barber, 1983, p. 14). Goodwill trust refers to expectations about an open commitment of the parties. It concerns the partners' intentions to perform according to agreements (Noteboom, 1996). In the management accounting literature, Langfield-Smith and Smith (2003) proposed the use of various control mechanisms for engendering different types of trust in alliances: proactive information collection for building competence trust; and regular meetings and communications for establishing mutual interests, clarifying expectations, and resolving joint disputes. With reference to trust, some authors theorized the existence of a specific archetype. Van der Meer-Kooistra and Vosselman (2000) proposed a trust-based model consisting of broad frameworks contracts, sustained by personal consultation and intensive communication, to generate confidence that the other party will not behave opportunistically. Behavior controls are not suited in these situations and are replaced by social controls, and formal controls tend to emphasize output controls that develop over time through the sharing of private information. This pattern is suitable when task programmability is low, output measurability is low, asset specificity is high, transactions are not highly repetitive, and when the transactions environment is characterized by high uncertainty and risk. These characteristics make the trust-based pattern of control resemble the clan form introduced by Ouchi (1979).

This archetype assumes that trust cannot be combined with other types of control and that there is, therefore, a substitutive relationship between trust and formal control. This has been supported by many authors. Ring and Van de Ven (1994), for example, maintained that there is a substitutive relationship by analyzing the contrast between formal legal contracts (control) and psychological contracts (trust), where psychological contracts represent unwritten and largely nonverbalized combinations of consistent expectations possessed by interacting parties about each others' rights and dues. Other authors that focused on international joint ventures confirmed this substitutive relationship by considering the level of trust as an independent variable for explaining the level and form of control: mutual trust among partners leads to their loosening the control (Yan & Gray, 1994); "when trust between (or among) international joint ventures partners is relatively low, the partners' controls over the international joint venture will be relatively tight; and the partners' control focus will be relatively broad" (Groot & Merchant, 2000, p. 584). Yet they also concluded that

> while trust between IJV partners is probably an important variable that explains a significant proportion of the variance in partners' control tightness and breadth of control focus, it is not a dominant factor. The effects of trust (or lack of trust) seem to be overshadowed by the effects of other factors. (Groot & Merchant, 2000, p. 602)

WHY "IDEALS" FAIL TO EXPLAIN REALITY

One of the reasons why ideals fail to explain the complexity of alliances' control is related to the fact that control archetypes have been developed often without distinguishing between economic institutions (markets and firms) and methods of organizing and control (the price system and the hierarchy) (Hennart, 1993). This distinction is relevant because while markets and firms can be defined precisely with reference to their strong juridical and economic dimensions and recognition, prices and what can be called "hierarchies" are methods used to organize and control economic activities (Coase, 1937; Demsetz, 1991; Grandori, 2004; Hennart, 1993). Markets and firms use one or both methods to control transactions. Although markets predominantly use prices as methods of organizing and control, and firms rely primarily on hierarchical controls, there is not a one-to-one correspondence between price-based mechanisms and markets, and hierarchical mechanisms and firms. Therefore, firms may develop internal pricing systems, and markets may use behavioral constraints (Hennart, 1993). This overlap between economic institutions and control forms has been adopted, for example, by Van der Meer-Kooistra and Vosselman (2000) when distinguishing between market-based, bureaucracy-based, and trust-based patterns of control for controlling alliances, or in the work of Håkansson and Lind (2004), when describing market, hierarchy, and cooperation forms of control.

This overlap between institutional forms and control methods has often led to the reification of control archetypes and the development of the various control patterns as polar governance choices on the basis of which "a syndrome of attributes that bear a supporting relation to one another" (Williamson, 1991, p. 271) is applied. The underlying principle in this area has been that "selective intervention," in which a single mechanism is transplanted from one institutional form to another, is considered to be inefficient or "impossible" (Zenger & Hesterly, 1997). This may clarify, for example, the opposite view between the theoretical expectations of Speklè (2001), in the case of moderate asset specificity and high programmability, and the empirical conclusions achieved by Van der Meer-Kooistra and Vosselman (2000) in similar situations. In fact, the former refers to an ideal archetype, while the latter to an empirical form that is found in practice. By assuming the possibility of transplanting one mechanism from one form to another—for example, the use of some bureaucratic mechanisms in a market-based relationship—it would be possible to reconcile this contradiction found in the literature (Caglio & Ditillo, 2008).

One of the main consequences of this coincidence between institutional forms and control patterns is that in the literature, only "frequent" and "simple" archetypes of control have been investigated; but what about "rare" and "more complex" combinations of control traits, which can be more efficient and effective? When attempts to describe more articulated forms of control have been made, the number of archetypes introduced has proliferated to an unmanageable number; for example, nine in the framework proposed by Speklé (2001). And what about "potential" combinations, not experienced yet, but which can show their superior nature? The principles of how to construct these combinations of control mechanisms in a consistent way has not been specifically addressed by the literature. If these principles had been developed and control forms had been arrayed along a continuum from market-based to hierarchical forms, instead of identifying polar forms, some of the contradictions found in the contributions could have been resolved. In fact, the number of possible control forms and contexts in which they could be suitably applied would expand, avoiding in this manner the risk of assuming that all the different ways in which management control mechanisms can be complementarily associated are given, and of being forced to consider those empirical forms that diverge from ideal types as approximations of pure types or inefficient empirical solutions.[1]

In addition, the definition of these control typologies (e.g., market based, bureaucracy/hierarchy based or trust based) has also potentially resulted in the risk of a circular research design. This is because often, control typologies have been defined by recognizing patterns between many interrelated organizational and technological variables, leading to identification of associations between control and variables that constitute the basis for the control type. For example, the argument of using hierarchy as a form of control in a context where two activities are complementary, similar, and directly coordinated (Håkansson & Lind, 2004), which is the set of characteristics that define the use of the hierarchical organization, incorporates this risk.

Finally, the logic of ideal control archetypes has potentially led to an interpretation of the role of accounting-based mechanisms that is only marginal in controlling interfirm alliances (Caglio & Ditillo, 2008). In fact, management accounting contributors who have focused on control archetypes have included accounting in patterns, either supposedly theoretically sustainable or identified as empirically consistent with reference to their joint occurrence and positive association with performance.[2] As a consequence, accounting-based control mechanisms have been mainly associated with bureaucratic/hierarchical-like forms of organization and have assumed specific and fixed roles, which are different in each control pattern (Håkansson & Lind, 2004; Hopwood, 1996). For example, Van der Meer-Kooistra and Vosselman (2000) indicated the use of accounting rigid performance targets specifically with reference to bureaucratic patterns. In a similar way, Håkansson and Lind (2004) suggested that accounting is adopted to control and affect individuals' action in hierarchical coordination, to guarantee the normative requirement of reciprocity in market coordination and, finally, to contribute to developing shared values and beliefs and support the organizational tradition in business relationships. Seen in this way, the role that accounting-based control mechanisms can play, when analyzed in combination with other controls, seems to be highly constrained in interfirm alliances or limited to the presence of few contingency variables, therefore providing minimal and potentially biased understanding of the role of accounting-based mechanisms as one of the components of control combinations in interorganizational settings.

FROM THE IDEALS TO THE CONTROL PRACTICES

Some authors have tried to overcome the idea of polar types and pure archetypes of control and have proposed a discrete array of mixed control choices. Speklé (2001), for example, presented different discrete forms of an optimal mix of market and hierarchical control elements. He suggested that when activities are characterized by low levels of programmability and moderate asset specificity, a mixed form of market control—market-based boundary control—applies. In this case, the availability of sufficiently powerful reputation effects in the suppliers' environment implies the definition and enforcement of the boundaries, relegated to the market reputation of the firms, to assure that their behavior meets some minimum standard of professionalism. In a domain of high programmability and moderate asset specificity, combinatory forms of control, in which residual market discipline is joined with elements of administrative origins, are adopted (hierarchical arm's-length control). Finally, in a context of moderate asset specificity, governance structures that combine elements of both market and hierarchies at the same time may be used. More specifically, in case of high programmability, market elements are joined with hostage arrangements to correct asymmetric stakes in the contract (hybrid arm's-length control). In such arrangements, parties to the contract are required to make investments or to transfer valuable assets, the full cost of which can be recovered only in case of successful contract execution, thus curtailing the potential gains from opportunistic defection and compensating for the loss of market discipline that results from small numbers bidding. In case of low programmability, the hybrid form of exploratory control is in place. This form of control is akin to the hierarchical variant in its reliance on close interaction, joint responsibility, and the resultant information flows to achieve cooperation and behavior congruence, but it provides additional, higher-powered market incentives. This involves the establishment of outsourcing relationships with a limited number of suppliers, which allows a comparative assessment of their performance.

Some other authors have started to recognize that different control mechanisms and models may be present at the same time with reference to the same alliance, and that control solutions are arrayed on a vast continuum from markets to hierarchies with the high majority in the "swollen middle" that integrates control elements of both markets and hierarchies (Caglio & Ditillo, 2008; Grandori & Furnari, 2008; Vosselman & Van der Meer-Kooistra, 2009; Zenger & Hesterly, 1997). Dekker (2004) developed a framework including three forms of control: outcome control, behavior control, and social control. These forms of control are meant to solve co-ordination problems and appropriation concerns. The typical variables of transaction cost economics (asset specificity, environmental uncertainty, and frequency) are linked to appropriation concerns, intended as the need to safeguard each own part of the value generation. The distinctive variables of organizational theory (task uncertainty and interdependence) are associated to coordination problems, defined as the issues deriving from pooling resources and division of tasks to be performed. The main predictions of Dekker's framework are that control problems influence collaborating firms' need to invest effort in selecting a good partner to mitigate the problems and to design and implement formal control mechanisms to manage the problems. Investing more efforts in finding a good partner reduces the need for formal control. Increasing trust in goodwill and capabilities, after thresholds, are expected to reduce the strength of the association between respectively appropriation concerns and coordination requirements and the use of formal controls and partner selection efforts (Håkansson et al., 2010).

Håkansson and Lind (2004) have suggested that in the same alliance, different relationships are activated among different departments of the firms, and each of them can be characterized by the different controls, which coexist. In their own words,

> The overall coordination in a relationship like the one in the case study is based on a rather complicated structure involving hierarchies, relationships between sub-units and even market characteristics. The relationship exists in terms of something "total," which is spoken about and for which there are managers responsible. But this totality is not uniform but includes all the three classical coordination mechanisms. It involves a mix of relationships whereby the hierarchically governed sub-units have some very close relationships with some sub-units, but more market-like relationships with others. This is clearly a form of multi-dimensional coordination where issues related to different activities are dealt with in quite different ways. Thus, it is not a uniform coordination form. Individual units within each of the two companies have quite distinct and clearly defined goals. Thus, as a coordination form, hierarchy is vital within the relationship. These units have several types of relationships with other units within their own company, as well as with units within the counterpart. Some of these relationships are clearly emphasized by the close cooperation—having obvious relationship features—while others are of a more competitive or hostile type. (p. 68)

In the joint venture literature, Chalos and O'Connor (2004) have introduced three significant contingent variables potentially explaining the use of mixed patterns in the control of joint ventures. In their survey of U.S.-Chinese joint ventures, they found that equity ownership was associated only with expatriate staffing, a cultural control, while partner knowledge influenced a broad set of controls. More specifically, the partner perceived socialization practices, foreign manager decision responsibilities, parent company communications, and manager performance incentives (some of which are accounting based) to be effective control mechanisms that were positively related to the diffusion of knowledge. In addition, the other contingent variable that was considered and that could potentially affect the adoption of specific control mechanisms was represented by asset specificity, which was found to be associated with socialization practices, decision-making responsibility, parent company communications, and manager performance incentives.

Some alternative contributors have stressed more the evolution of ideals, suggesting that alliances may jump between different ideal archetypes over time. For example, Thrane (2007), using a nonfunctionalist theoretical perspective, analyzed the multiplicity and complexity of trajectories that an interorganizational alliance may take. The data showed that the control pattern that the interorganizational relationship assumes is the evolving, self-organized result of the connections in the network and the perturbations that push the relationship to move across different patterns and enter new areas of the interorganizational space. The relevant conclusion was that this process does not take place in a mechanistic way or erratically, but is activated by certain institutional elements, which leads the relationship into specific directions (Caglio & Ditillo, 2008).

Finally, some other authors have proposed some arguments that overcome the idea that trust and control are in a substitutive relationship and have suggested that therefore the trust-based archetype can be combined with the other forms of control. They propose that a simple inverse relationship between trust and control is not in place. In fact, on the one hand, a substitutive relationship between trust and control has always been maintained by assuming that control mechanisms simply play the role of reconciling the goals of the collaborating firms, being therefore potentially replaceable by trust. However, control mechanisms may also be used to coordinate the activities of the different subjects of an alliance and, with this objective, it is very difficult to replace them by trust (Dekker, 2004). On the other hand, trust can be introduced for reasons other than integrating partners' objectives, such as to increase the ability of partners to manage the process of learning (Kale, Singh, & Perlmutter, 2000), and therefore, for this objective, it cannot be replaced by control. With these different roles, the levels of trust and control cannot be explained in relative terms, one with reference to the other (Caglio & Ditillo, 2008).

In addition, the analysis of the relationship between trust and control has always been conducted without considering the explicit relative cost burdens implied by these two solutions, and the inclusion of this variable into the framework could contribute to explaining different choices of trust-control combinations. In fact, partners may decide to adopt trust as a lower-cost solution whenever a sufficient level of control is achieved to safeguard the transactions and avoid the use of unnecessary expensive formal control mechanisms and the risk of damaging the quality of their relationships (Dekker, 2004).

Das and Teng (1998) have suggested a complementary relationship between trust and control in alliances; an increase in the level of either trust or formal control simply results in a higher level of control. They argued that trust and control are instrumental in achieving a high level of confidence, so they jointly contribute to the total level of reliance one partner has in partner cooperation. They also noticed that to have effective control over a partner in an interorganizational relationship, a certain level of trust is needed. Trust helps in reducing the level of resistance and in building harmony in the "controller-controlled" relationship. The use of formal control mechanisms may actually enhance a trusting relationship, by narrowing the domain of risk and by providing more objective performance measures.

Tomkins (2001) has maintained that such relationships do not take into account that trust between partners is built through a dynamic process, based on expectations of continuity and repeated interaction. Rather than defining a linear association between trust and control, the author described an interactive relationship between the two as evolving over the relationship life cycle. Such association can be characterized by an inverted U-shape, with a positive relationship between trust and control at earlier stages of the relationship and a negative association between the two in later stages of the relationship, once trust intensity becomes established at high levels.

THE COMBINATORIAL LOGIC TO DESIGN CONTROL FORMS IN INTERFIRM RELATIONSHIPS

One of the remedies to the limitations presented in the previous sections is represented by the adoption a complementarity-based approach, developed in organizational economics (Milgrom & Roberts, 1995). According to this approach, control is seen as a set of practices that may include different elements such as planning, cybernetic, reward and compensation, administrative and cultural controls (Malmi & Brown, 2008). Complementarity is a principle on the basis of which the adoption of one of these elements increases the value of using another control element (Grandori & Furnari, 2008; Milgrom & Roberts, 1995). This logic has many potential advantages: first of all, it incorporates the relation among many control attributes (systemic fit), and not their pairwise fit with external contextual variables; second, it clarifies the notion of "consistency": it is more comprehensive than "similarity in kind" and includes also complementarities that derive from differences (Grandori & Furnari, 2008). In addition, it recognizes that two control configurations may possess the characteristics of equifinality, which means that while the control packages may look quite different, they both produce an equally good outcome. Two packages may have contrasting elements, yet do the same job as a result of internal consistency between the chosen elements in each of the packages (Malmi & Brown, 2008; Sandelin, 2008).

A possible way to achieve such complementarity would be to refocus attention on control problems rather than on control solutions. For example, Hennart (1993) suggests to concentrate on the problems of cheating and shirking and their corresponding costs in order to decide the combinations of controls. The cost of using price-control mechanisms (cheating costs) is related to the cost of measuring output as well as the losses deriving from the fraud when measurement is imperfect. The cost of using hierarchical control mechanisms (shirking costs) is related to the cost of introducing boundaries to behavior together with the residual amount of shirking due to imperfect behavior constraints. Price-based controls minimize shirking but determine cheating; behavior controls minimize cheating but lead to shirking. The choice of control combinations would, thus, be based on the relative costs of measuring output plus that of tolerating the residual amount of cheating as compared to those of constraining behavior and of bearing the residual account of shirking.

An alternative view would be to concentrate on the specific roles that control mechanisms may play in achieving cooperation (Baiman & Rajan, 2002; Cooper & Slagmulder, 2004; Dekker, 2003), maintaining coordination (Dekker, 2004; Tomkins, 2001), and solving appropriation concerns (Baiman & Rajan, 2002; Caglio & Ditillo, 2008; Dekker, 2003, 2004; Seal, Cullen, Dunlop, Berry, & Mirghani, 1999). The focus on control problems, as Dekker (2004) has partially done, would allow analyzing the fungibilities between control solutions. In addition, it would allow dealing with the following issues: Which control solutions can be integrated to deal with a certain problem? In which amount? Can combinations of controls change in relative weight depending on the intensity of adoption? Can alternative control packages be effective in the same contexts? Is there any maximum limit in the use of different control solutions to face the same control issues? In this way, a "combinative view" of control solutions with various breadths could be developed, and a "grammar" for distinguishing to what problems the different mechanisms can be selectively applied could be identified (Grandori & Furnari, 2008). According to this logic, the rationale for constructing control alternatives, rather than merely evaluating them, would be fostered. This would help in predicting what combinations of control archetypes, rather than simply to consider them individually and separately, and learn them empirically and post hoc as has mainly been done so far in the literature. The exploration of the potential blending of controls would also contribute to designing new or unusual combinations without being forced to interpret them as "bad proxies" of superior theoretical models (Caglio & Ditillo, 2008; Grandori, 2004; Milgrom & Roberts, 1990).

NOTES

1. For a similar discussion applied to organizational mechanisms, see Grandori (2004).
2. For this kind of criticism of traditional contingency contributions, see Grandori (2004).

REFERENCES

Amigoni, F., Caglio, A., & Ditillo, A. (2003). Dis-integration through integration: The emergence of accounting information networks. In A. Bhimani (Ed.), *Management accounting in the digital economy* (pp. 17–35). New York, NY: Oxford University Press.

Baiman, S., & Rajan, M. V. (2002). Incentive issues in inter-firm relationships. *Accounting, Organizations and Society, 27,* 213–238.

Barber, B. (1983). *The logic and limits of trust.* New Brunswick, NJ: Rutgers University Press.

Beamish, P. W. (1985). The characteristics of joint ventures in developed and developing countries. *Columbia Journal of World Business, 20*(3), 13–19.

Caglio, A., & Ditillo, A. (2008). A review and discussion of management control in inter-firm relationships: Achievements and future directions. *Accounting, Organizations and Society, 33,* 865–898.

Chalos, P., & O'Connor, N. G. (2004). Determinants of the use of various control mechanisms in US-Chinese joint ventures. *Accounting, Organizations and Society, 29,* 591–608.

Coase, R. (1937). The nature of the firm. *Economica, 4,* 386–405.

Cooper, R., & Slagmulder, R. (2004). Interorganizational cost management and relational context. *Accounting, Organizations and Society, 29,* 1–26.

Cristofoli, D., Ditillo, A., Liguori, M., Sicilia, M., & Steccolini, I. (2010). Do environmental and task characteristics matter in the control of externalized local public services? *Accounting, Auditing & Accountability Journal, 23,* 350–372.

Das, T. K., & Teng, B. (1998). Between trust and control: Developing confidence in partner cooperation in alliances. *Academy of Management Review, 23,* 491–512.

Das, T. K., & Teng, B. (2000). Instabilities of strategic alliances: An internal tensions perspective. *Organization Science, 11,* 77–101.

Das, T. K., & Teng, B. (2001). Trust, control, and risk in strategic alliances: An integrated framework. *Organization Studies, 22,* 251–283.

Dekker, H. C. (2003). Value chain analysis in interfirm relationships: A field study. *Management Accounting Research, 14,* 1–23.

Dekker, H. C. (2004). Control of inter-organizational relationships: Evidence on appropriation concerns and coordination requirements. *Accounting, Organizations and Society, 29,* 27–49.

Demsetz, H. (1991). The theory of the firm revisited. In O. E. Williamson & S. G. Winter (Eds.), *The nature of the firm: Origins, evolution, and development* (pp. 159–178). Oxford, England: Blackwell.

Geringer, J. M., & Hebert, L. (1989). Control and performance of international joint ventures. *Journal of International Business Studies, 20*(2), 235–254.

Geringer, J. M., & Hebert, L. (1991). Measuring performance of international joint ventures. *Journal of International Business Studies, 22,* 249–264.

Ghosh, M., & John, G. (1999). Governance value analysis and marketing strategy. *Journal of Marketing, 63* [Special Issue], 131–145.

Gomes-Casseres, B. (1987). Joint venture instability: Is it a problem? *Columbia Journal of World Business, 22*(2), 97–107.

Grandori, A. (2004, January-February). The changing core of organization and organization theory: From contingency to combinative. *Rivista di Politica Economica,* 49–62.

Grandori, A., & Furnari, S. (2008). A chemistry of organization: Combinatory analysis and design. *Organization Studies, 29,* 459–485.

Groot, T. L. C. M., & Merchant, K. A. (2000). Control of international joint ventures. *Accounting, Organizations and Society, 25,* 579–607.

Håkansson, H., Kraus, K., & Lind, J. (2010). Accounting in networks as a new research field. In H. Håkansson, K. Kraus, & J. Lind (Eds.), *Accounting in networks* (pp. 1–13). New York, NY: Taylor & Francis.

Håkansson, H., & Lind, J. (2004). Accounting and network coordination. *Accounting, Organizations and Society, 29,* 51–72.

Hennart, J.-F. (1993). Explaining the swollen middle: Why most transactions are a mix of "market" and "hierarchy." *Organization Science, 4,* 529–547.

Hopwood, A. G. (1996). Looking across rather than up and down: On the need to explore the lateral processing of information. *Accounting, Organizations and Society, 21,* 589–590.

Kale, P., Singh, H., & Perlmutter, H. (2000). Learning and protection of proprietary assets in strategic alliances: Building relational capital. *Strategic Management Journal, 21,* 217–237.

Killing, J. P. (1983). *Strategies for joint venture success.* New York, NY: Praeger.

Kogut, B. (1988). Joint ventures: Theoretical and empirical perspectives. *Strategic Management Journal, 9,* 319–332.

Langfield-Smith, K., & Smith, D. (2003). Management control systems and trust in outsourcing relationships. *Management Accounting Research, 14,* 281–307.

Malmi, T., & Brown, D. (2008). Management control systems as a package—Opportunities, challenges and research directions. *Management Accounting Research, 19,* 287–300.

Milgrom, P., & Roberts, J. (1990). The economics of modern manufacturing, technology, strategy and organization. *American Economic Review, 80,* 511–528.

Milgrom, P., & Roberts, J. (1995). Complementarities and fit: Strategy, structure and organizational change in manufacturing. *Journal of Accounting and Economics, 19,* 179–208.

Noteboom, B. (1996). Trust, opportunism and governance: A process and control model. *Organization Studies, 17,* 985–1010.

Park, S. H., & Ungson, G. R. (2001). Inter-firm rivalry and managerial complexity: A conceptual framework of alliance failure. *Organization Science, 12,* 37–53.

Ouchi, W. G. (1979). A conceptual framework for the design of organizational control mechanisms. *Management Science, 25,* 833–848.

Ring, P. S., & Van de Ven, A. (1992). Structuring cooperative relationships between organizations. *Strategic Management Journal, 13,* 483–498.

Ring, P. S., & Van de Ven, A. (1994). Developmental processes of cooperative interorganizational relationships. *Academy of Management Review, 19,* 90–118.

Rousseau, D. M., Sitkin, S., Burt, R. S., & Camerer, C. (1998). Not so different after all: A cross-discipline view of trust. *Academy of Management Journal, 38,* 7–23.

Sandelin, M. (2008). Operation of management control practices as a package—A case study on control system variety in a growth firm context. *Management Accounting Research, 19,* 324–343.

Sartorius, K., & Kirsten, J. (2005). The boundaries of the firm: Why do sugar producers outsource sugarcane production? *Management Accounting Research, 16,* 81–99.

Seal, W. B., Cullen, J., Dunlop, A., Berry, A., & Mirghani A. (1999). Enacting a European supply chain: The role of management accounting. *Management Accounting Research, 10,* 303–322.

Speklé, R. F. (2001). Explaining management control structure variety: A transaction cost economics perspective. *Accounting, Organizations and Society, 26,* 419–441.

Sydow, J., & Windeler, A. (1998). Organizing and evaluating interfirm networks: A structurationist perspective on the network processes and effectiveness. *Organization Science, 9,* 265–268.

Thrane, S. (2007). The complexity of management accounting change: Bifurcation and oscillation in schizophrenic inter-organisational systems. *Management Accounting Research, 18,* 248–272.

Tomkins, C. (2001). Interdependencies, trust and information in relationships, alliances and networks. *Accounting, Organizations and Society, 26,* 161–191.

van den Bogaard, M. A., & Speklé, R. F. (2003). Reinventing the hierarchy: Strategy and control in the Shell Chemicals carve-out. *Management Accounting Research, 14,* 79–93.

Van der Meer-Kooistra, J., & Scapens, R. W. (2008). The governance of lateral relations between and within organizations. *Management Accounting Research, 19,* 131–148.

Van der Meer-Kooistra, J., & Vosselman, E. G. J. (2000). Management control of interfirm transactional relationships: The case of industrial renovation and maintenance. *Accounting, Organizations and Society, 25,* 51–77.

Vosselman, E. G. J. (2002). Toward horizontal archetypes of management control: A transaction cost economics perspective. *Management Accounting Research, 13,* 131–148.

Vosselman, E., & Van der Meer-Kooistra, J. (2009). Accounting for control and trust building in interfirm transactional relationships. *Accounting, Organizations and Society, 34,* 267–283.

Williamson, O. E. (1991). Comparative economic organization: The analysis of discrete structural alternatives. *Administrative Science Quarterly, 36,* 269–296.

Yan, A., & Gray, B. (1994). Bargaining power, management control, and performance in United States-China joint ventures: A comparative case study. *Academy of Management Journal, 37,* 1478–1517.

Young, I. (1994, March). Asia/Pacific joint ventures: Risks and rewards. *Chemical Week, 15.*

Zenger, T. R., & Hesterly W. S. (1997). The disaggregation of corporations: Selective intervention, high-powered incentives, and molecular units. *Organization Science, 8,* 209–222.

CHAPTER 7

EFFECTIVE MANAGEMENT OF STRATEGIC ALLIANCES IN INTERNATIONAL CONSTRUCTION

Beliz Ozorhon
David Arditi

ABSTRACT

Interfirm collaboration has become an important component of creating competitive advantage in many sectors. Strategic alliances are of particular importance in international construction since local regulations and cultural differences preclude foreign companies from conducting business profitably, hence encouraging foreign companies to establish joint ventures with local companies. However, managing such strategic alliances is difficult because of the complex structure of such alliances that entails diverse organizational and managerial styles, and competing objectives and strategies. In this chapter, the key drivers governing the effective management of strategic alliances in international construction will be explored. In this respect, motives, risks, and advantages of establishing and operating such alliances will be discussed; performance issues will be addressed with particular emphasis on the indicators and drivers that govern the success of strategic alliances; and a framework for

Management Dynamics in Strategic Alliances, pages 135–160
Copyright © 2012 by Information Age Publishing
135

analyzing the performance of such alliances will be presented. This research builds upon the findings of a questionnaire survey administered to 28 Turkish contractors who entered into a total of 68 strategic alliances with non-Turkish partners. Based on the findings of this survey and the analysis of the data using structural equation modeling, the success factors associated with the evolutionary stages of a strategic alliance, namely, partner selection, formation, and operation will be discussed, and recommendations will be provided. The role of partner-fit, the quality of partner relations, the effectiveness of the control structure, and the impact of project management skills for deriving long-term alliance benefits will be discussed. It is expected that the information in this chapter will help construction professionals during the planning process of strategic alliances.

INTRODUCTION

International collaborative arrangements such as international strategic alliances (SAs) are very complex to manage successfully, mainly because of the difficulty of matching the goals and attitudes of self-directed organizations (Ozorhon, Arditi, Dikmen, & Birgonul, 2010). Moreover, the rational motives behind these alliances are not congruent with the strategic direction of the individual firms participating in the SA. Consequently, despite their increasing importance, SAs are frequently plagued with high degrees of instability and poor performance (Parkhe, 1993). SAs are reported to have performed poorly with high rates of instability ranging from 37% to over 70% (Geringer, 1991; Park & Ungson, 1997). It is therefore not surprising that performance of SAs has been a prominent theme of research over the past two decades (Beamish, 1988; Geringer & Hebert, 1989, 1991; Glaister & Buckley, 1998; Killing, 1983).

The majority of the current literature on SAs concentrates on manufacturing industries, while SA theories have not been investigated empirically in the construction industry. Like in other industries, achieving high levels of performance is difficult in the construction industry as performance is greatly impacted by partner compatibility, interworking relationships, SA structure, host country conditions, and project-specific characteristics. A review of the literature suggests that only an adequate combination of criteria should allow addressing the multidimensionality of performance, which requires a better understanding of the links between its different indicators.

The performance of SAs in construction was modeled in Ozorhon's (2007) research based on the experiences of Turkish contractors and their foreign partners. The aim of this research was twofold: to develop a complete/multidimensional performance metric for SAs in construction, and to explore the direct and indirect impact of internal and external drivers on SA performance by investigating the impact of interpartner fit, interpartner relations, the structural characteristics of the SA organization, host country factors, and project-related factors on SA performance. Based on the findings of this study, key strategies are provided in this chapter, relative to partner selection, formation, and operation of SAs in international construction.

STRATEGIC ALLIANCES IN INTERNATIONAL CONSTRUCTION

Motives for Establishing Strategic Alliances in International Construction

There are a number of overriding economic and political reasons for the rise in the popularity of SAs. A number of researchers (Beamish & Inkpen, 1995; Blodgett, 1992; Tallman & Shenkar, 1994) have identified a variety of reasons behind multinational enterprises' decisions to enter into SA agreements. These include the characteristics of foreign markets, such as access to suitable distribution channels, sharing heightened economic and political risks in new business ventures, government pressure, and technology transfer (Makino & Delios, 1996). The literature concerning alliance formation can be categorized into four major theoretical streams, namely the transaction cost approach (Williamson, 1975), the competitive strategy approach (Porter, 1980), the organizational knowledge and learning approach (Hamel, 1991), and the resource dependence (Pfeffer & Salancik, 1978, as cited in Demirbag & Mirza, 2000) or organization theory approach (Kogut, 1988). All of the theories deal with firms trying to achieve certain strategic objectives, although each has a different focus and should be seen as complementary rather than competing. Transaction cost theory focuses on cost minimization; resource dependency theory on obtaining resources; organizational learning on acquiring knowledge; and strategic behavior theory on maximizing profits.

The increasing magnitudes, complexities, and risks associated with major construction projects have brought together organizations with diverse strengths and weaknesses to form SAs to collectively bid for and execute projects (Kumaraswamy, Palaneeswaran, & Humphreys, 2000). Construction organizations have extensively used SAs as a vehicle to enter new construction markets around the world. The use of SAs basically stems from theories on how strategic behavior influences the competitive positioning of a construction organization. According to Kwok, Then, and Skitmore (2000), SAs can be in one of three legal forms, such as corporation, partnership, or contractual/consortium. According to Norwood and Mansfield (1999), some motives for forming SAs are to participate in overseas projects; to maintain an overseas presence, particularly when the market is low in the home country; to spread financial risk; to bring in outside expertise; to make use of an existing geographical or regional base; and to access greater manpower from a local partner.

Alliances improve the strategic position of firms in competitive markets by providing resources from other firms that enable them to share costs and risks in product design, production, marketing, or distribution. Forging an alliance enables a firm to focus resources on its core skills and competencies while acquiring other components or capabilities it lacks from the marketplace (Zaman & Mavondo, 2002). According to Nielsen (2002), there are several advantages obtained through SAs such as risk/cost sharing, transfer of knowledge-related capabilities, improved competition, access to new markets, and easier adaptation to internationalization. Benefits of an alliance with a company active in a host country include faster and easier access to the local market and local distribution systems, improved knowledge of the local economy, improved access to local human resources, preferential treatment from the host country relative to issues like the repatriation of dividends, the registering of investment to increase the capital base, and the securing of government contracts and work permits (Beamish, 1988).

International construction projects are just one of the activities that involve multinational participants from different political, legal, economic, and cultural backgrounds (Chan & Tse, 2003). There are risks associated with an SA in international construction due to partner and host country-related factors. Partner-related risks include but are not limited to inheriting a partner's financial problems, having disagreements about accounting standards, distrust between partner employees, policy changes in parent companies affecting the project, lack of management competence, disagreements about staff allocation and positions in the project team hierarchy, disagreements on allocation of work to be done, and technology-transfer disputes (Bing, Tiong, Fan, & Chew, 1999). Ostler (1998) identifies major host government-related risks encountered by construction organizations operating in the international arena. These include political, economic, structural, policy, environmental, market, and production factors.

Life Cycle of Strategic Alliances in International Construction

Prior research has indicated that SAs are transitional organizations with a dynamic nature (Franko, 1971; Harrigan, 1986). The process of an SA in this study is distinguished in three stages: partner selection, formation, and operation.

Partner Selection

The selection of the appropriate partner constitutes one of the major drivers of success for the SA. Geringer (1991) posits that the partner selection process is considered to be of crucial importance to the formation and operation of SAs. Partner selection determines an SA's mix of skills, knowledge, and resources; its operating policies and procedures; and its vulnerability to indigenous conditions, structures, and institutional changes (Geringer, 1991). Killing (1983) states that it is impossible to identify an exhaustive list of criteria that an organization should meet when attempting to assess a potential *complementary* partner. Geringer (1991) discusses the strategic drivers of partner selection criteria distinguishing between partner-related and task-related indicators (operational skills and resources). Those criteria will be discussed in detail in following sections.

Formation

Firms select strategies to improve their competitive postures and to gain an advantage over one or more competitors (Harrigan, 1986). SAs are formed based on strategies of how to manage environmental uncertainties, how to overcome lack of resources, and in particular, how to manage the firm's range of interorganizational relations. During the formation stage, potential partners spend considerable time identifying their common compatible interests in the task-related areas. Foreign organizations that possess unique organization-specific advantages that are strongly desired by the local partner are usually in a position to negotiate an agreement from a position of strength (Sridharan, 1997). Kwok et al.'s (2000) study identified a number of critical factors including negotiation, profit and loss distribution, clarity of contribution among partners, control and decision-making policy, clarity of sharing of risks and liabilities, composition of decision-making body, and dispute-resolution procedures.

Operation

During the operation of a project, it is important to enter into a fair engineering contract, employ qualified subcontractors and suppliers, maintain a good relationship with the host government and other parties, and adopt renegotiation as a dispute resolution and problem-solving technique (Bing & Tiong, 1999). The partner selection and venture formation processes set the basis of the relationship between the partners during the operation of the SA (Gjerde, 1995, as cited in Mohamed, 2003). The smooth operation of the SA is dependent mainly upon the interaction between the partners in making strategic and operational decisions (Sridharan, 1997). For SAs to survive, their parents must find a way to work together, that is, they must be able to agree on goals and policies, and to renegotiate them in response to changes in the environment (Doz, 1996).

Performance of Strategic Alliances in International Construction

Previous studies have shown that SAs have a high failure record, reporting on the dissolution rate but also on the ineffectiveness and the inefficiency of the SA management. One might conclude that the problems are caused by the different goals of establishing the SA, disparate managerial styles and systems, different national cultures and management cultures, and incompatibility of structure (Beamish, 1988; Killing, 1983). Although there is a considerable amount of research in this area, the assessment of SA performance has been problematic, and efforts to identify variables associated with SA performance have been constrained by disagreements regarding the comparability and reliability of alternative performance measures and methods (Geringer & Hebert, 1991). Anderson (1990) argues that the major reason for the controversy stems from a lack of clarity about what an "indicator" of performance is and what a "driver" of performance is. The evaluation of SA performance can be achieved by using subjective or objective measures or both. Unfortunately, there is no consensus on the most appropriate criteria and methods for the evaluation of SA performance.

Performance Indicators

In their summary of prior empirical research, Geringer and Hebert (1991) categorized extant studies into three groups depending on a variety of indicators used to assess SA performance: financial indicators, objective measures, and subjective assessment of satisfaction.

Early studies relied on a variety of traditional financial indicators such as profitability, return on investment, growth, market share, and cost position (Dang, 1977; Lecraw, 1983; Tomlinson, 1970, as cited in Geringer & Hebert, 1991). Recently, financial performance has also been studied as a categorical variable on the basis of gains and losses. Despite their wide usage, financial measures may fail to reflect the extent to which an SA has achieved its short and long-term objectives (Anderson, 1990; Killing, 1983). For example, SAs formed in developing countries may not be able to generate financial profit for a long time.

Some studies use objective measures of performance such as the survival of the SA (Franko, 1971; Killing, 1983), its duration (Harrigan, 1986; Kogut, 1988), instability (Franko, 1971; Sim & Ali, 2000), renegotiation of the SA contract (Blodgett, 1992), and dissolution (Park & Ungson, 1997). However, instability is not always tantamount to collaborative failure as is widely assumed. The dissolution might be a result of success, that is, both the partners obtained their expected benefits and decided to discontinue. Thus, duration and survival appear to be unacceptable measures of performance because termination of an SA may be a result of success, failure, or simply an adaptation to changes in the environment.

A partner's satisfaction with the overall performance of the SA is one of the most frequently used subjective measures of SA performance (Beamish, 1988; Geringer & Hebert, 1991; Killing, 1983; Parkhe, 1993). It is neither a financial measure, such as profitability, market share, or rate of return nor an objective measure, such as survival, duration, stability, or number of contract renegotiations. According to Yan and Gray (2001), the achievement of the partners' original strategic objectives is the most appropriate measure of SA performance since the traditional measures such as profit, market share, and growth are relatively meaningless for new ventures in emerging markets.

Drivers of Performance

Many factors have been suggested in the literature as potentially important drivers of SA performance. These include partner- and task-related variables, firm- and industry-related factors, and managerial- and host country-related factors. Partner-related criteria relate to the efficiency and effectiveness of the partners' operations. These factors include firm size, previous SA experience, and type of SA partner. Task-related criteria relate to the operational skills and resources of the partner. The key resources that partner companies can provide to an SA include capital, plant, technology, know-how, technical support, human resources, and organizational capabilities. Both partner- and task-related indicators have been used in research on SAs (Geringer, 1991).

It has been noted in the SA literature that complementary needs create interpartner fit, which is expected to generate a synergistic effect on SA performance (Buckley & Casson, 1988). Most authors suggest that a mismatch in terms of alliance fit is the most important reason for alliance failure. Fit can arise in three main forms: strategic fit, organizational fit, and cultural fit (Luo, 1998).

Extant literature has focused on commitment, cooperation, collaboration, communication, trust, and conflict resolution as the important components of alliance relationships (Luo, 2002). This group constitutes the soft dimension of SAs labeled "interpartner relations" (Demirbag & Mirza, 2000). The managerial factors include ownership, SA decision-making structure, control exercised by partners, and operational autonomy (Geringer & Hebert, 1989; Killing, 1983), which may be labeled SA structural factors (Merchant, 2005). Factors such as cultural distance, political risk, and industry-specific conditions (Park & Ungson, 1997) can be labeled institutional factors.

FRAMEWORK TO MEASURE THE PERFORMANCE
OF STRATEGIC ALLIANCES IN INTERNATIONAL
CONSTRUCTION

This study is built upon the findings of research by Ozorhon et al. (2010), who proposed and tested a set of indicators and drivers for modeling SA performance in international construction. The following sections present the research methodology, the data collection process, and the components of the framework developed by Ozorhon et al. (2010).

Research Methodology

A questionnaire survey was administered to the Turkish partners of SAs. Almost half of the projects were undertaken in 18 foreign countries including Afghanistan, Bulgaria, Jordan, Russia, Iraq, India, and the United States, whereas the remaining projects were undertaken in Turkey. Considering the fact that medium-to-large companies are likely to undertake SAs with more frequency compared to smaller firms, the target population was set as the members of the Turkish Contractors Association (TCA). All of the respondents were upper-level managers of large contractors with an average age of 39 years, operating both in domestic and international markets, and having expertise mainly in general contracting and infrastructure construction. The number of SA projects completed by Turkish construction companies with foreign partners in the last ten years is around 110 (TCA, 2005). A total of 68 completed questionnaires were returned for data analysis, 48 of which were administered through face-to-face interviews and 20 via e-mail. Around 60% of the target population was covered in this study. Data were collected from 28 Turkish partners that undertook 68 international construction projects. The choice of only one partner in a joint venture as opposed to all partners was motivated by the difficulties in obtaining data from all partners due to logistical and cost barriers.

The data were analyzed using a software package called EQS 6.1, a structural equation modeling (SEM) tool. The general form of SEM consists of a measurement model that specifies how the hypothetical constructs are measured in terms of the observed variables, and that establishes the validity and reliability of the observed variables; and a structural model that explores the causal relationships between the validated constructs, and that tests the hypothesized causal effects (Bollen, 1989). In the first step, construct validity is tested through qualitative and empirical validity tests. Content validity is a qualitative test and refers to the degree to which the construct is represented by indicators that cover the domain of meaning of the construct (Dunn, Seaker, & Waller, 1994), whereas reliability, convergent, and discriminant validity tests comprise the empirical part of the construct validity. In the second step, SEM tests the hypotheses between the validated constructs.

Indicators of SA Performance

Anderson (1990) notes that given a minimum of three elements to an SA, at least two partner firms and the SA management, it may be difficult to decide which aspects of performance are to be measured because this decision may depend on whose perspective is considered. The model proposed by Ozorhon (2007) investigated parameters related to the indicators and drivers of SA performance. In this research, a four-dimensional construct was proposed to measure SA performance. It includes the performance of the project, the SA partner, the SA organization itself, and a partner's perceived satisfaction with the SA. While some of these components involve subjective measures, some others are objective assessments.

The indicators of each proposed construct were initially derived from the literature; they were then revised by professional and academic experts who participated in pilot studies to establish content validity for these constructs (Ozorhon et al., 2010). Reliability, which refers to the consistency of measurement, was measured by the Cronbach's alpha coefficients. The reliability values for all the indicators are satisfactory since the Cronbach's alpha coefficients are all above 0.70, the minimum value recommended by Nunnally (1978). According to Dunn et al. (1994), if the factor loadings are statistically significant, then convergent validity exists. In this study, the statistically significant (at 5%) and substantial factor loadings for "overall SA performance" are evidence of convergent validity. Besides, the correlation matrices calculated for all constructs show that all intercorrelations are below 0.90, suggesting that there is no multicollinearity (Hair, Anderson, Tatham, & Black, 1998), but indicating that the constructs have discriminant validity.

(a) Project Performance
Project performance is defined as the extent to which the predefined project objectives are realized. SAs in construction are essentially formed to execute project-based activities. Part of the operational success of an SA in the construction industry can be defined in terms of project success. The most commonly cited project goals are related to budget, schedule, and functionality/quality considerations (Handa & Adas, 1996) in addition to client satisfaction (Ashley, Lurie, & Jaselskis, 1987). In this research, "project performance" is defined as an objective measure of achieving project

targets including completion of the project on schedule, within budget, in good quality, and with maximum client satisfaction.

(b) Partner Performance

Besides fulfilling financial or operational objectives, a company may get involved in an SA for a number of additional motives, such as to enhance organizational learning (Kogut, 1988); to improve the strategic positioning of the company; to gain presence in new markets (Contractor & Lorange, 1988; Tatoglu & Glaister, 1998); to participate in overseas projects; to maintain an overseas presence, particularly when the market is low in the home country; to spread the financial risk; to bring in outside expertise; to make use of an existing geographical or regional base; and to access greater manpower from partners (Norwood & Mansfield, 1999). Partner performance measures the extent to which the preset organizational objectives of a company are realized as a result of a project undertaken through an SA. In this study, the performance of an SA partner is measured relative to sharing risks, sharing resources, reducing costs, learning managerial and technical skills from partners, facilitating entrance to international markets, enhancing competitiveness, creating long-term relationships, and making more profit. "Partner performance" is a subjective measure but is based on company policy, past history, and accumulated data.

(c) Performance of SA Management

While "project performance" measures the success of the SA operation at the project level, and "partner performance" at partner company level, "performance of SA management" measures the success of the SA operation at the centralized SA level. "Performance of SA management" is a subjective measure, and it can be defined by the effectiveness of control over the SA operation. Yan and Gray (1994) defined the scope of management control in terms of strategic, operational, and structural indicators. Adopting a similar approach, "performance of SA management" was measured in this study by the level of effectiveness of management control in terms of strategic control at the board of directors level; operational control at the general management level; and organizational control imposed by the partners in forming the venture's organizational structure, processes and operating routines.

(d) Perceived Satisfaction with SA

A partner's satisfaction with the overall performance of the SA is one of the most frequently used subjective measures of SA performance (Choi & Beamish, 2004; Demirbag & Mirza, 2000; Fey & Beamish, 2001; Geringer & Hebert, 1991; Killing, 1983; Parkhe, 1993). The main advantage of subjective indicators based on respondents' perceptions is their ability to provide information regarding the extent to which the SA has achieved its overall objectives (including financial, survival, or expansion objectives, or any objective, as the case may be). The perceived satisfaction of an SA partner with the SA is a purely subjective measure that was used in this study as one of the performance indicators.

Drivers of SA Performance

The drivers of SA performance were defined in terms of internal factors that include strategic fit, national culture fit, organizational culture fit between SA partners, the quality of interpartner relations, and structural SA characteristics; and external factors including host country conditions, familiarity with conditions in host country, and project-related factors (Ozorhon, 2007).

(1) Interpartner Fit in SAs
Partner fit determines the extent to which partner firms can get along and realize anticipated synergies from the SA (Buckley & Casson, 1988). Interpartner fit is a multidimensional concept that commonly includes strategic fit, resource fit, operational fit, organizational fit, and cultural fit (Das & Teng, 1998; Luo, 1998). Considering the overlap between these dimensions, "interpartner fit" is defined in this study by three indicators, namely, strategic fit, national culture fit, and organizational culture fit, but cover without overlap all factors mentioned in the literature (Ozorhon et al., 2010).

Strategic fit: This consists of the following indicators that are commonly cited in the literature and found to be effective in SA success: goal congruency between SA partners (Mohr & Spekman, 1994); previous experience in the host country (Beamish, 1988); previous experience with similar projects (Gunhan & Arditi, 2005); adequacy of management skills, technical skills, and human resources (Luo, 1998); quality of the relationship with the client; complementarity/compatibility of partners' financial capabilities; company size (Merchant, 2005); management systems (Sridharan, 1997); and national/international workload (Beamish, 1988).

National culture fit: Hofstede (1991) developed a pioneering and widely accepted classification scheme that breaks national culture into the following five indicators. *Power distance* focuses on the degree of equality or inequality between people in a country's society. *Individualism-collectivism* focuses on the degree the society reinforces individual or collective achievement and interpersonal relationship. *Masculinity-femininity* focuses on the degree the society reinforces the traditional masculine work role model of male achievement, control, and power. *Uncertainty avoidance* focuses on the level of tolerance for uncertainty and ambiguity within the society, the extent to which rules are obeyed and risks are avoided. *Long-term orientation* focuses on the degree the society embraces long-term devotion to traditional, forward-thinking values. These five factors identified by Hofstede are adopted in this study to measure national cultural fit. Several researchers reported that differences in national cultures are a source of poor communication, inadequate cooperation, lack of commitment, and ineffective conflict resolution between SA partners (Mohr & Spekman, 1994; Parkhe, 1991). These problems occur because of the dissimilarities of partners' interpretation of and responses to strategic and managerial issues.

Organizational culture fit: Hofstede, Neuijen, Ohayv, and Sanders (1990) asserted that organizational culture is best measured by organizational practices instead of more abstract assumptions and values. Hofstede et al. empirically found six independent indicators that describe the numerous organizational practices. *Process-oriented vs. results-oriented culture* is related to the risk attitude of organizations; *employee-oriented vs. job-oriented culture* is about how the employees are valued; *professional vs. parochial approach* is related to how employees are identified; *open vs. closed system* refers to the perceived communication climate within the organization; *loose vs. tight control* dimension refers to the degree of internal structuring in the organization; and *normative vs. pragmatic* dimension considers the popular notion of customer orientation. These six factors identified by Hofstede (1991) are adopted in this study to measure organizational cultural fit. Partners with dissimilar organizational cultures may expend time and energy to establish mutually agreeable managerial practices and routines to facilitate interaction (Park & Ungson, 1997), which can in turn lead to a significant negative influence on SA performance (Pothukuchi, Damanpour, Choi, Chen, & Park, 2002).

(2) Interpartner Relations in SAs

The nature of the relationship between SA partners is likely to affect SA operations (Buckley & Casson, 1988; Parkhe, 1993). In this study, "interpartner relations" is defined by the following six indicators (Ozorhon et al., 2010).

Commitment can be described as the willingness of SA partners to exert effort on behalf of the SA (Mohr & Spekman, 1994). Committed partners are likely to consider long-term gains rather than short-term advantages. Committed partners are interested in creating and maintaining a good relationship with the other partners and thus are less likely to let differences in functional approaches result in conflicts and negatively affect SA performance.

Effective *communication* between the SA partners is important for good interpartner relations since partners do not usually start an SA with a full understanding of each other's goals, capabilities, and behaviors; in many instances, these are revealed when the SA starts operating (Doz, 1996). Communication allows the partners to understand the goals of the alliance, and the roles and responsibilities of all the actors.

Cooperation is one of the key indicators of interpartner relations. Cooperation is required to overcome the potential misunderstandings and coordination difficulties that can arise from differences in managerial or organizational practices (Das & Teng, 1998). Cooperation is critical to avoid possible conflicts (Ozorhon et al., 2010).

Previous cooperation and experience earned from prior engagements between the partners allows the partners to justify subsequent risky steps (Das & Teng, 1998) and fosters a climate of openness that is essential for discussing behavioral problems that may be a barrier to learning (Doz, 1996). In addition, prior relationships indicate a history of repeated interaction, which may lead to relational advantages, stability, development of specialized skills and routines such as specific knowledge about the structure and operation of the partner organization (Shenkar & Zeira, 1992).

Conflict resolution refers to methods of resolving amicably the conflicts between partners. Fey and Beamish (1999) define SA conflict as the interaction between SA partners, where the actions of one partner prevent or compel some outcome against the resistance of another partner. Beginning with early SA research, scholars have suggested that extensive conflict negatively affects SA performance (e.g., Harrigan, 1986; Killing, 1983). It follows that the amicable resolution of disputes is essential for the continuity of an SA in harmony.

The degree of *trust* between the partners is one of the most critical indicators affecting interpartner relations, because trust provides for greater adaptability in an SA and enhances the exchange of knowledge, a key component of organizational learning and SA success (Bing et al., 1999; Das & Teng, 1998; Park & Ungson, 1997; Parkhe, 1993).

(3) Structural Characteristics of the SA

The structural characteristics related to the SA organization include the extent of management control imposed on the SA, ownership distribution, and the completeness of the contract (Ozorhon et al., 2010).

The *extent of management control* is one of the most tested drivers of performance in the research on SAs. Control is defined as the influence exercised by the SA partners over the management of the SA (Geringer & Hebert, 1989; Killing, 1983). The exercise of managerial control has been one of the most important subjects in the SA literature (Parkhe, 1993; Yan & Gray, 1994). In this study, adopting the approach of Choi and Beamish (2004), management control is divided into three categories: (a) shared management for all activities, (b) dominant management for all activities by one of the partners, and (c) split management of activities for which each partner has competence. To improve performance, Mjoen and Tallman (1997) proposed that the activities controlled by each partner should be matched with their respective firm-specific strengths.

Distribution of ownership involves an SA's equal or unequal division of ownership and has been found to affect its performance (Blodgett, 1992; Geringer & Hebert, 1989; Killing, 1983). The ownership of an SA may be dominated by the respondent company, by a foreign partner, or can be equally shared by the partners. According to Killing (1983), the dominance of one partner will increase stability avoiding the managerial costs inherent in an SA and potential conflicts between partners. However, Blodgett (1992) argued that roughly equal equity shares will result in greater stability because the partners are equally committed to the SA. It is proposed by Ozorhon (2007) that it is most advantageous when the partner from the host country has dominant ownership, and that the ownership structure has no effect on performance if the host is a third country.

The *completeness of the SA contract* is an essential success factor that can avoid a great deal of trouble and conflict in future SA operations (Bing & Tiong, 1999). Since there are many potential problems in construction projects, the contract between the SA partners should define the rights and responsibilities of each party clearly to ensure success (Luo, 2002).

(4) Host Country-Related Factors in SAs

Host country-related factors are investigated relative to host country conditions and a partner's familiarity with conditions in the host country.

Host country conditions consist of political risk, macroeconomic conditions, strength of the legal system, and relations of the host government with foreign entities. *Political risk* is defined as the occurrence of politically motivated events that affect the SA's ability to operate effectively in the host country (Ashley & Bonner, 1987). It includes inconsistency in policies, changes in laws and regulations, restrictions on fund repatriations, and import restrictions. *Macroeconomic conditions* such as fluctuations in economic conditions, inflation, and foreign exchange rates affect the overall performance of the construction industry and are also critical to the performance of SAs. The *strength of the legal system* in the host country is important in the formation and operation of an SA as it is the legal system that regulates the management of claims, disagreements, conflicts, disputes, and any and all contract-related problems. The *quality of the relations between SA partners and the host government* may be critical for the success of an SA, especially for government projects, since one of the principal market characteristics frequently cited as influencing SA performance is how policies are implemented by host country governments (Osland, 1994).

Familiarity with conditions in the host country: Psychic distance, used synonymously with cultural distance, is defined as "a firm's degree of uncertainty about a foreign market resulting from cultural differences and other business difficulties that present barriers to learning about the market and operating there" (O'Grady & Lane, 1996). The psychic distance may affect the performance of an SA adversely because the SA partner is not familiar with the local environment in terms of legal, political, and economic conditions. In this study, psychic distance has been renamed as "familiarity with conditions in the host country" and defined in terms of familiarity with the language, business practices, political and legal system, economic environment, industry structure, and national culture of the host country (Ozorhon et al., 2010).

(5) Project-Related Factors in SAs

Although some companies may cooperate with the same partner in several projects, SAs in the construction industry are considered to be project-based rather than continuous collaborations. In this study, project-related factors cover project risks that are frequently reported in the literature as significant (e.g., Bing et al., 1999), including completeness of payments by the client; tolerance/flexibility of the client; relations with other project parties; competence of other project parties; completeness of project definition; availability of resources; technical complexity of the project; impact of indicators such as weather and soil conditions; completeness of the design; completeness of the contract documents; handling the project requirements in terms of quality, environment, health, and safety; penalty sanctions concerning duration; and effectiveness of the project management functions such as planning, coordination, monitoring, and controlling (Ozorhon et al., 2010).

Findings

Figure 7.1 shows the hypothesized relations between the constructs of the model. The numbers on the arrows represent the path coefficients that are equivalent to regression weights. The analysis suggests that "interpartner relations" is the main driver of "SA performance" with a path coefficient of 0.585. "National culture fit" has a moderate effect on performance (path coefficient: 0.356), which is followed by "structural characteristics of the SA" (0.270), "project-related factors" (0.246), and "organizational culture fit" (0.221). On the other hand, no significant influence of "strategic fit," "host country conditions," and "familiarity with conditions in the host country" on "SA performance" was found. However, "strategic fit" had an indirect effect on performance through "interpartner relations,"

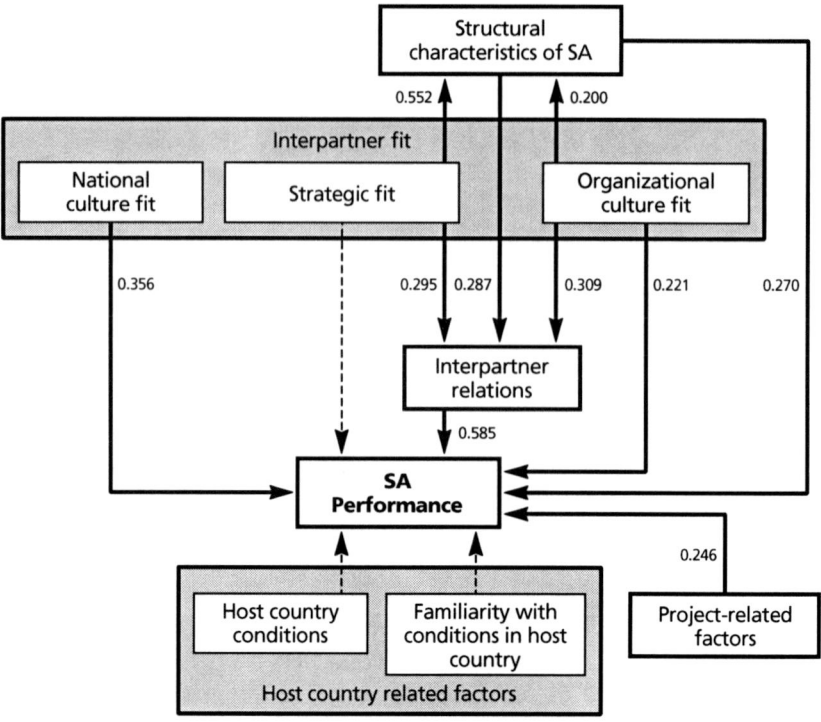

Figure 7.1 The structural equation model for SA performance (adapted from Ozorhon, 2007).

and "structural characteristics of the SA." The most interesting finding is that "host country conditions" and "familiarity with conditions in the host country" do not have significant interaction with any construct in the entire model. Links that are not statistically significant at $\alpha = 0.05$ were eliminated from the model (shown in dashed lines in Figure 7.1).

KEY STRATEGIES FOR MANAGING STRATEGIC ALLIANCES IN INTERNATIONAL CONSTRUCTION

Based on the findings of Ozorhon et al.'s (2010) study, it may be concluded that internal factors (i.e., strategic fit, national culture fit, organizational culture fit between SA partners, quality of interpartner relations, and structural SA characteristics) are the key drivers of performance, whereas external factors (i.e., host country conditions, familiarity with conditions in host country, and project-related factors) have no or little influence on "SA performance." In addition, indicators associated with the preformation stage of an SA, especially the strategic, organizational, and cultural fit between partners, are critical both for a well-functioning SA organization and achieving project and individual company objectives.

It is believed that research findings can help professionals during the strategic planning process of SAs. Figure 7.2 illustrates the steps of strategic planning of construction companies starting from market research and project selection toward completion of a project via an SA. Potential projects are *usually* evaluated by a team and/or the head of the business development department in a company. Strengths, weaknesses, opportunities, and threats (SWOT) analysis is performed for each possible project. Considering also the company's mission and strategies, a project/market selection decision is made. Based on the characteristics of the project/market, the company's related department assesses the benefits, advantages, and disadvantages of entering the market as a single investor or as an SA. If the resources and experience of the company are not sufficient to complete that specific project, or if the company does not have the necessary information related to practices in the host country, it may consider participating in an SA.

The following strategies provide recommendations for practitioners on partner selection and on the formation and operation of an SA based on Ozorhon et al.'s (2010) research findings.

Partner Selection

Partner selection is one of the most critical strategic decisions of a company and should be made carefully. The activities of a team that is responsible for partner search, including the creation of the profile of an ideal partner, list of potential partners, and selection of the most appropriate partner may enhance the performance of partnerships in the construction business. Such a team can benefit from the conclusions drawn in this study relative to strategic fit, national culture fit, and organizational culture fit. During partner search, the strengths and weaknesses of the company should be reviewed and potential partners that can complement the weaknesses with their competencies should be taken into consideration. The most appropriate partner should be selected after the expectations are defined. In addition, in the qualification process, strategic and organizational assets, and cultural similarities between companies should be considered in order to have smooth relations.

Differences in management styles and organizational cultures may hinder the success of SAs. A cultural integration process may be useful in avoiding conflicts among the partners. However, creation of a corporate/organizational culture for an SA is not easy due to the project-based nature of

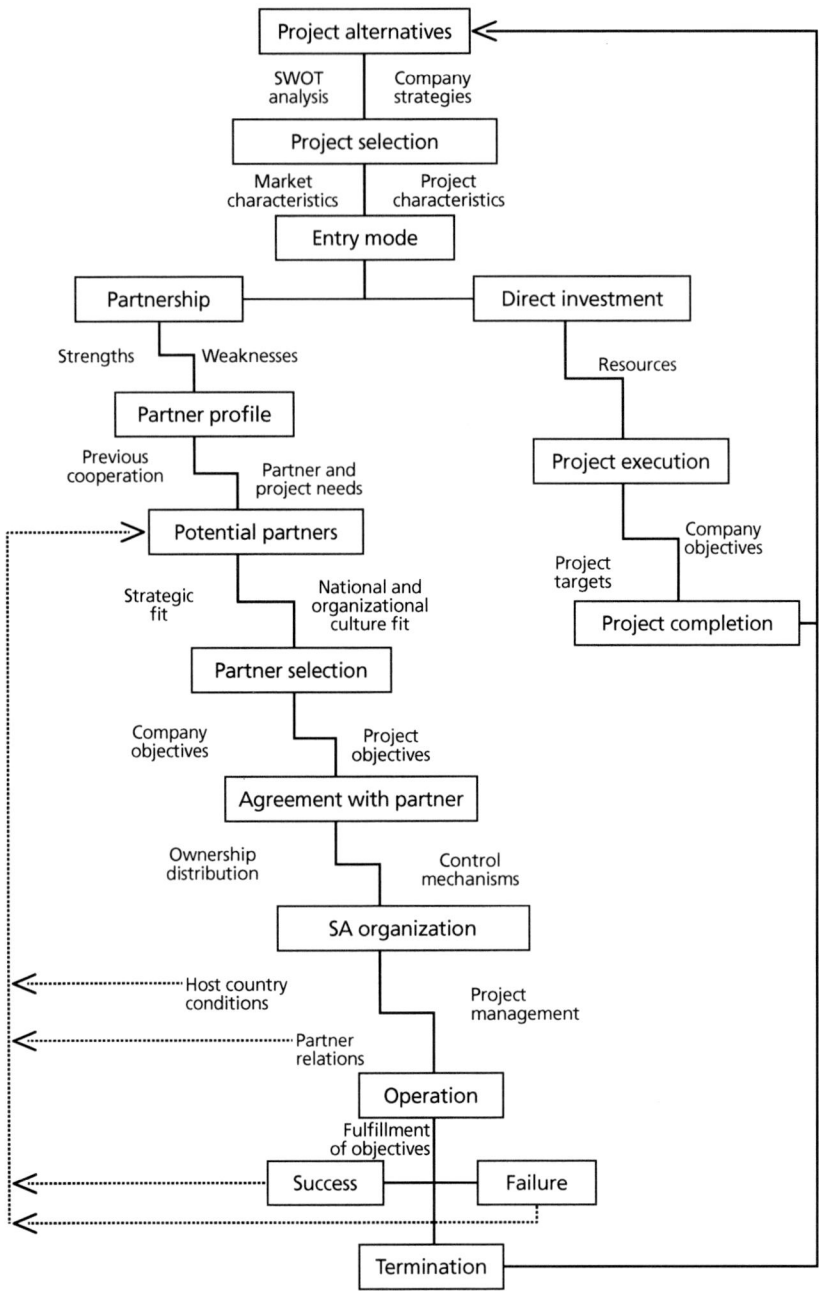

Figure 7.2 Steps in the strategic planning of a company in the SA process (from Ozorhon, 2007).

SAs in construction. The national and organizational cultures of partners cannot be integrated by force; rather, partners should be aware of the fact that culture is one of the uncontrollable parameters of the SA process; so mutual understanding is a better way to avoid future conflicts. According to Parkhe (1991), the process must start by trying to understand the partners' way of thinking and behaving, an effort in which the use of training programs for cultural understanding can provide a valuable help. For example, the joint use of rituals and ceremonies may be an effective way to create a corporate culture. Another way is to hire the services of a consultant that can provide recommendations and programs to sort out conflicts (Lajara, Lillo, & Sempere, 2003). As mentioned in previous sections, manager/personnel choice is critical for SA success. Swierczek (1994, as cited in Lajara et al., 2003) highlights the importance of multicultural skills in the managers working for SAs. Based on the findings of Ozorhon et al.'s (2010) research, it is recommended to select partner representatives considering their international/multinational experiences so that they can avoid conflicts due to cultural mismatches and can facilitate communication among partners.

Formation

As Trafford and Proctor (2006) state, many SAs lack alliance strategies. However partners should adopt coherent alliance strategies that have four main components including a business strategy to shape the logic and design of the alliance; a dynamic view to guide the management and evolution of the alliance; a portfolio approach to enable coordination among the alliance to enhance flexibility; and an internal infrastructure that supports and strives to maximize the value of external collaboration (Gomes-Casseres, 2000). As Ozorhon et al.'s (2010) findings suggest, structural SA characteristics, which involve development and implementation of SA strategies and objectives, impact both partner relations and performance. Therefore, establishment of coherent strategies will help partners to realize both company and project objectives successfully. This reveals the importance of ownership distribution, extent of management control, and the completeness of the SA contract. A home country partner that has majority ownership is likely to put into full use their familiarity with the conditions in the host country. Split management control is also suggested to increase the level of performance since the specific competencies of each partner could be utilized effectively. For a successful SA organization, a complete contract should be prepared in which company and project objectives are reflected, roles and responsibilities of each party are defined, and ownership distribution together with control mechanisms are arranged based on the specific needs of the project and contribution of partners. A complete and thorough SA contract leads to smooth operation and enhances inter-partner relations, as suggested by Ozorhon et al.'s (2010) findings.

Ozorhon et al.'s (2010) study also suggests that project-specific factors are highly associated with SA performance. This finding supports the view that each construction project is unique and that appropriate strategies should be developed to handle the particular risks and problems associated with each project. Given the variables that control project-related factors, this can be achieved by making sure that the owner has a clear idea of the expected product and issues clear instructions to designers, who in turn produce a complete set of design documents. The SA will benefit if the contract between the owner and the SA partners is unambiguous and the duties, responsibilities, and liabilities of the parties are clearly stated at the start of the project. Strong project management performance and availability of resources also help.

Operation

"Interpartner relations" appears to be the core construct of Ozorhon et al.'s (2010) model due to its strong linkages with "SA performance" and "strategic fit," "organizational culture fit," and "structural SA characteristics." This model indicates that previous cooperation between SA partners, commitment to the SA, cooperation of SA partners during strategic decision making, and communication are the major indicators of "interpartner relations" and consequently of "SA performance." "Strategic fit" and "organizational culture fit" appear to be the key factors that enhance "interpartner relations."

Implementation of coherent strategies basically depends on the commitment of SA management that necessitates a strong, honest, confident, powerful, and decisive *leadership*. Weak organizational leadership causes lack of clear vision and direction (Trafford & Proctor, 2006). The managers should personally take part in the cooperative management process and show their commitment and enthusiasm both to and in the operation of the SA. The managerial board may include a financial representative to better track the progress of the operations. The participation of senior managers must go beyond the formulation of a strategy based on alliances; they must personally take part in managing the cooperation and show their commitment and enthusiasm in the alliance (Hoffmann & Schlosser, 2001; Inkpen & Roos, 2001, as cited in Lajara et al., 2003). Trafford and Proctor (2006) reported that failure of an SA was governed by weaknesses in commitment and cooperation within the SA. Strong leadership is important in terms of achieving commitment that is the most important indicator of partner relations that has a dominant effect on SA performance.

Problems of commitment, cooperation, and communication can be resolved through a clear understanding of the SA organization; discussions around future financial planning; a full understanding of the contract; efficient mechanisms to discuss issues with the client; and an environment that encourages awareness of the objectives of the SA, the partners, and the client. This can be achieved through regular weekly and monthly meetings between the managerial board of the SA and the project manager. Predefined project targets and company objectives can be monitored through progress reports, and action can be taken to meet the goals. Effective communication tools improve cooperation among the partners, create a more collaborative environment, and lead to mutual trust and a painless decision-making process.

Effective and efficient participation of personnel on every level is a prerequisite for success. This may be achieved by proper human resource management that identifies each person's skills, motivates employees to use those skills, and places the appropriate individuals at key positions. Recruitment and selection, training, and performance appraisal are the important tasks of a human resource management team (Lajara et al., 2003). All staff in an SA should be informed and involved in new initiatives and strategies, and they should feel a part of a common identity. This will help partners create a cooperative culture and enhance interrelations. In addition, effective project management helps partners mitigate project risks that moderately influence the performance of the SA. Considering the uniqueness of each construction project, project managers have significant functions. The selection of the project manager is the most critical decision of the human resource management team. Therefore, the success of an SA is governed to a large extent by the effective actions of the Human Resource Management Department.

Since completeness of contract is significant for both a properly designed SA organization (control and ownership distribution) partner and client relations besides project management, contracts should be carefully managed. Partners should be particularly sensitive to contract and claims management issues since contractual issues play a major role in dispute resolution as well. A contract administrator and a claims manager should collaborate throughout the SA process, including the negotiation period between partners, contract preparation, operation, termination, and in case of disputes among partners or with the client.

SA projects are highly evolutionary and go through a sequence of interactive cycles of learning, reevaluation, and readjustment. Considering the dynamic nature of the SA, learning along environment, task, process, skills, and goals helps mediation between the initial conditions and the outcomes of the alliance (Doz, 1996). Effectiveness of organizational learning within the SA and adapting the organization to changing conditions enhances interpartner relations. Dynamic learning within the SA helps partners to communicate more frequently, increases their commitment to the SA, and creates a cooperative environment that significantly contributes to SA success.

Postproject evaluation is also an effective mechanism for the success of future partnerships. The extent to which the objectives of the partners and projects are fulfilled determines the performance of the SA. Based on the success/failure of the SA, companies become aware of the factors affecting the performance, and using the knowledge gained in each SA, they can evaluate future potential partners on a sounder basis.

CONCLUSION

Strategic alliances (SAs) are essential in improving performance in the construction industry. Forging an SA enables construction companies to share financial and human resources as well as managerial and technical skills that are critical for accomplishing a successful project, while the same success could not have been achieved had each company attempted to perform the project on their own.

Despite the dramatic growth in SAs in recent years, achieving high levels of SA performance has proven to be difficult in the construction industry. Although motives, partner selection strategies, structure, benefits, risks and critical success factors for SAs are extensively discussed in the literature, there is no agreed-upon way of measuring performance. Ozorhon et al. (2010) proposed a four-dimensional performance construct to measure SA performance in international construction and determined the drivers and their impacts on performance. The research used SEM to test the hypotheses regarding the drivers of SA performance. The analysis assessed the effect of partner fit, interpartner relations, structural SA characteristics, host country, and project-related factors on performance.

The findings of the analysis may be used to formulate a road map for construction companies that intend to form SAs with foreign partners. Key strategies are provided to effectively manage SAs during partner selection, and the formation and operation of SAs. Considering the key drivers of overall SA performance, first, companies should concentrate on finding compatible partners that could best complement their capabilities in terms of strategic, organizational, and cultural assets. Second, they should establish an appropriate structure for the SA organization in which each partner controls the activities related to its core competency, and they should prepare a complete and thorough agreement that defines each partner's roles and responsibilities clearly. Project-specific factors should be taken into account as well as managerial issues of the SA organization in order to achieve project objectives, which in turn determine the success of the SA.

REFERENCES

Anderson, E. (1990). Two firms, one frontier: On assessing joint venture performance. *Sloan Management Review, 31*(2), 19–30.

Ashley, D. B., & Bonner, J. J. (1987). Political risks in international construction. *Journal of Construction Engineering and Management, 113*, 447–467.

Ashley, D. B., Lurie, C. S., & Jaselskis, E. J. (1987). Determinants of construction project success. *Project Management Journal, 18*(2), 69–79.

Beamish, P. W. (1988). *Multinational joint ventures in developing countries.* London, England: Routledge.

Beamish, P. W., & Inkpen, A. C. (1995). Keeping international joint ventures stable and profitable. *Long Range Planning, 28*(3), 26–36.

Bing, L., & Tiong, R. L. K. (1999). Risk management model for international construction joint ventures. *Journal of Construction Engineering and Management, 125*, 377–384.

Bing, L., Tiong, R. L. K., Fan, W. W., & Chew, D. A. S. (1999). Risk management in international construction joint ventures. *Journal of Construction Engineering and Management, 125*, 277–284.

Blodgett, L. (1992). Factors in the instability of international joint ventures: An event history analysis. *Strategic Management Journal, 13*, 475–481.

Bollen, K. A. (1989). *Structural equations with latent variables.* New York, NY: Wiley.

Buckley, P. J., & Casson, M. (1988). A theory of co-operation in international business. In F. J. Contractor & P. Lorange (Eds.), *Cooperative strategies in international business.* Lexington, MA: Lexington Books.

Chan, E. H. W., & Tse, R. Y. C. (2003) Cultural considerations in international construction contracts. *Journal of Construction Engineering and Management, 129*, 375–381.

Choi, C. B., & Beamish, P. W. (2004). Split management control and international joint venture performance. *Journal of International Business Studies, 35*, 201–215.

Contractor, F. J., & Lorange, P. (1988). Why should firms cooperate? The strategy and economics basis for cooperative ventures. In F. J. Contractor & P. Lorange (Eds.), *Cooperative strategies in international business* (pp. 3–30). Lexington, MA: Lexington Books.

Das, T. K., & Teng, B. (1998). Between trust and control: Developing confidence in partner cooperation in alliances. *Academy of Management Review, 23*, 491–512.

Demirbag, M., & Mirza, H. (2000). Factors affecting international joint venture success: An empirical analysis of foreign-local partner relationships and performance in joint ventures in Turkey. *International Business Review, 9*(1), 1–35.

Doz, Y. L. (1996). The evolution of cooperation in strategic alliances: Initial conditions or learning processes? *Strategic Management Journal, 17*[Special Issue], 55–83.

Dunn, S. C., Seaker, R. F., & Waller, M. A. (1994). Latent variables in business logistics research: Scale development and validation. *Journal of Business Logistics, 15*(2), 145–172.

Fey, C. F., & Beamish, P. W. (1999). *Joint venture conflict: The case of Russian international joint ventures.* Working Paper #99-104, Stockholm School of Economics, St. Petersburg, Sweden.

Franko, L. G. (1971). *Joint venture survival in multinational corporations.* New York, NY: Praeger.

Geringer, J. M. (1991). Strategic determinants of partner selection criteria in international joint ventures. *Journal of International Business Studies, 22,* 41–62.

Geringer, J., & Hebert, L. (1989). Control and performance of international joint ventures. *Journal of International Business Studies, 20,* 235–254.

Geringer, J. M., & Hebert, L. (1991). Measuring performance of international joint ventures. *Journal of International Business Studies, 22,* 249–263.

Glaister, K. W., & Buckley, P. J. (1998). Measures of performance in the UK international alliances. *Organization Studies, 19,* 89–118.

Gomes-Casseres, B. (2000). Mastering management. *Financial Times, 16*(10), 14–15.

Gunhan, S., & Arditi, A. (2005). Factors affecting international construction. *Journal of Construction Engineering and Management, 131,* 273–282.

Hair, J. F., Jr., Anderson, R. E., Tatham, R. L., & Black, W. C. (1998). *Multivariate data analysis.* Englewood Cliffs, NJ: Prentice Hall.

Hamel, G. (1991). Competition for competence and interpartner learning within international strategic alliances. *Strategic Management Journal, 12,* 83–103.

Handa, V., & Adas, A. (1996). Predicting the level of organizational effectiveness: A methodology for the construction firm. *Construction Management and Economics, 14,* 341–352.

Harrigan, K. R. (1986). *Managing joint venture success.* Lexington, MA: Lexington Books.

Hofstede, G. (1991). *Cultures and organizations: Software of the mind, intercultural cooperation and its importance for survival.* New York, NY: McGraw-Hill.

Hofstede, G., Neuijen, B., Ohayv, D., & Sanders, G. (1990). Measuring organizational cultures: A qualitative and quantitative study across twenty cases. *Administrative Science Quarterly, 35,* 286–316.

Killing, J. P. (1983). *Strategies for joint venture success.* New York, NY: Routledge.

Kogut, B. (1988). Joint ventures: Theoretical and empirical perspectives. *Strategic Management Journal, 9,* 319–332.

Kwok, H. C. A., Then, D., & Skitmore, M. (2000). Risk management in Singapore construction joint ventures. *Journal of Construction Research, 1,* 139–149.

Kumaraswamy, M. M., Palaneeswaran, E., & Humphreys, P. (2000). Selection matters in construction supply chain optimization. *International Journal of Physical Distribution and Logistics Management, 30,* 661–680.

Lajara, B. M., Lillo, F. G., & Sempere, V. S. (2003). Human resources management: A success and failure factor in strategic alliances. *Employee Relations, 25*(1), 61–80.

Luo, Y. (1998). Joint venture success in China: How should we select a good partner? *Journal of World Business, 33,* 145–166.

Luo, Y. (2002). Contract, cooperation, and performance in international joint ventures. *Strategic Management Journal, 23,* 903–919.

Makino, S., & Delios, A. (1996) Local knowledge transfer and performance: Implications for alliance formation in Asia. *Journal of International Business Studies, 27*[Special Issue], 905–928.

Merchant, H. (2005). The structure-performance relationship in international joint ventures: A comparative analysis. *Journal of World Business, 40,* 41–56.

Mjoen, H., & Tallman, H. (1997). Control and performance in international joint ventures. *Organization Science, 8,* 257–274.

Mohamed, S. (2003). Performance in international construction joint ventures: Modeling perspective. *Journal of Construction Engineering and Management, 129,* 619–626.

Mohr, J., & Spekman, R. (1994). Characteristics of partnership success: Partnership attributes, communication behavior, and conflict resolution techniques. *Strategic Management Journal, 15,* 135–152.

Nielsen, B. B. (2002). *Determining international strategic alliance performance.* Working Paper-6, Department of International Economics and Management, Copenhagen Business School, Denmark.

Norwood, S. R., & Mansfield, N. R. (1999). Joint venture issues concerning European and Asian construction markets of the 1990s. *International Journal of Project Management, 17*(2), 89–93.

Nunnally, J. (1978). *Psychometric theory.* New York, NY: McGraw-Hill.

O'Grady, S., & Lane, H. W. (1996). The psychic distance paradox. *Journal of International Business Studies, 27,* 309–333.

Osland, G. E. (1994). Successful operating strategies in the performance of US-China joint ventures. *Journal of International Marketing, 2*(4), 53–78.

Ostler, C. H. (1998). *Country analysis, its role in the international construction industry's strategic planning procedure.* First International Construction Marketing Conference, Construction Management Group, School of Civil Engineering, University of Leeds, England.

Ozorhon, B. (2007). *Modeling the performance of international construction joint ventures.* Unpublished PhD dissertation, Middle East Technical University, Ankara, Turkey.

Ozorhon, B., Arditi, D., Dikmen, I., & Birgonul, M. T. (2010). The performance of international joint ventures in construction. *Journal of Management in Engineering, 26,* 209–222.

Park, S. H., & Ungson, G. R. (1997). The effect of national culture, organizational complementarity, and economic motivation on joint venture dissolution. *Academy of Management Journal, 40,* 279–307.

Parkhe, A. (1993). Messy research, methodological predispositions, and theory development in international joint ventures. *Academy of Management Review, 18,* 227–268.

Porter, M. (1980). *Competitive strategy: Techniques for analyzing industries and competitors.* New York, NY: Collier McMillan.

Pothukuchi V., Damanpour, F., Choi, J., Chen, C. C., & Park, S. H. (2002). National and organizational culture differences and international joint venture performance. *Journal of International Business Studies, 33,* 243–265.

Shenkar, O., & Zeira, Y. (1992). Role conflict and role ambiguity of chief executive officers in international joint ventures. *Journal of International Business Studies, 23,* 55–75.

Sim, A. B., & Ali, M. Y. (2000). Determinants of stability in international joint ventures: Evidence from a developing country context. *Asia-Pacific Journal of Management, 17,* 373–397.

Sridharan, G. (1997). *Factors affecting the performance of international joint ventures: A research model.* First International Conference on Construction Industry Development, National University of Singapore (Vol. 2, pp. 84–91).

Tallman, S. B., & Shenkar, O. (1994). A managerial decision model of international cooperative venture formation. *Journal of International Business Studies, 25,* 91–113.

Tatoglu, E., & Glaister, K. W. (1998). Performance of international joint ventures in Turkey: Perspectives of Western firms and Turkish firms. *International Business Review, 7,* 635–656.

TCA. (2005). *Turkish Contractors Association* [in Turkish]. Retrieved from http://www.tmb.org.tr/genel.php?ID=2

Trafford, S., & Proctor, T. (2006). Successful joint venture partnerships: Public-private partnerships. *International Journal of Public Sector Management, 19*(2), 117–129.

Williamson, O. (1975). *Markets and hierarchies.* New York, NY: Free Press.

Yan, A., & Gray, B. (1994). Bargaining power, management control, and performance in United States-China joint ventures: A comparative case study. *Academy of Management Journal, 37,* 1478–1517.

Yan, A., & Gray, B. (2001). Antecedents and effects of parent control in international joint ventures. *Journal of Management Studies, 38,* 393–416.

Zaman, M., & Mavondo, F. (2002) *Measuring strategic alliance success: A conceptual framework.* Retrieved from http://smib.vuw.ac.nz:8081/WWW/AN-ZMAC2001/anzmac/AUTHORS/pdfs/Zaman.pdf

CHAPTER 8

LEARNING DYNAMICS IN STRATEGIC ALLIANCES

T. K. Das
Rajesh Kumar

ABSTRACT

In this chapter, we propose a framework for examining the dynamics of learning in the various stages of alliance development. We describe three kinds of learning in alliances—content, partner-specific, and alliance management—and discuss the saliencies and implications of particular types of learning in different alliance stages. The framework makes clear that alliance learning varies according to the stages of the alliance developmental process (formation, operation, outcome), and that different types of learning have different strategic implications. Briefly, content learning augments the collective strengths of the alliance, partner-specific learning (i.e., learning about a partner as opposed to learning from a partner) is crucial in determining whether or not an alliance gets formed, and alliance management learning helps build the confidence of the alliance partners in managing alliances. The chapter responds to the need of managers with alliance responsibilities for a framework to help identify and exploit the most effective types of learning opportunities, vis-à-vis partners and the alliance as a whole, during the specific alliance development stages of formation, operation, and outcome.

Management Dynamics in Strategic Alliances, pages 161–191

INTRODUCTION

Interfirm alliances have become increasingly common due to globalization, deregulation, and the accelerating pace of technological change. These cooperative arrangements take many forms, ranging from joint marketing to equity-based joint ventures. Alliances allow the firms to share the costs of R&D, expedite the introduction of new products in the global marketplace, minimize costs, gain access to resources, and provide a means for accessing new technologies of partner firms. In particular, the idea that alliances are an important vehicle for learning has considerable intuitive appeal and perhaps, for this reason, continues to dominate the academic as well as the practitioner literature on alliances (e.g., Anand & Khanna, 2000; Hamel, 1991; Kumar & Nti, 1998). However, the focus of much of the existing research is on how alliances may be useful for learning purposes in the competitive business arena and not sufficiently on the internal learning dynamics of alliances. While the topic of learning by and through alliances is no doubt of relevance, the need for an adequate understanding of the learning dynamics within alliances is also clearly an important subject for examination for the effective management of alliances.

Furthermore, although there is by now a considerable amount of literature detailing the potential benefits and costs associated with learning in alliances, much remains to be investigated about the dynamics of learning in the alliance development process. As Das and Teng (2002) argue, the processual dynamics underlying the evolution of alliances are still a relatively unexplored phenomenon. In this chapter, we develop a framework for analyzing the learning dynamics in the various stages of strategic alliance development.

We divide the chapter into four parts. First, we discuss the different types of learning that are likely to occur when firms enter into alliances. Second, we review the literature for linkages between alliance process models and learning. We then elaborate on our framework for understanding the nature and dynamics of alliance learning in the different alliance stages. We conclude by noting the implications of this framework for studying and managing alliance learning.

THREE TYPES OF LEARNING IN ALLIANCES

We will attempt to identify here the basic themes in the vast literature on organizational learning that may have a bearing on our discussion of learning in alliances. Although learning is implicit in all social systems, the current emphasis on learning in the organizational literature has its roots in the intensification of the global competition in the late 1970s. Scholars have focused their attention on three central issues in the literature. The first issue is a definitional one, namely, the nature of organizational learning. The second focuses on the processes of learning, namely, how does learning occur? The third deals with the fundamental question of learning to learn effectively, that is, the factors that impede the reliability and validity of the learning.

Definitions of organizational learning abound in the literature. An influential one is that by Huber (1991), who notes, "*An entity learns if, through its processing of information, the range of its potential behaviors is changed*" (p. 89, emphasis in original). Levitt and March (1996) view organizational learning as reflecting a change in organizational routines. Changes in routine are products of experiential learning and get embedded in the organization's memory. Crossan, Lane, and White (1999) take a somewhat broader perspective on organizational learning, viewing it as a mechanism that is critical for an organization's strategic renewal. Although the specific foci of the different definitions vary, the underlying commonality is the recognition that organizational learning entails a change in the knowledge structures of the organization. These knowledge structures are embodied in an organization's routines and are stored in an organization's memory. When firms enter into alliances, the changes in knowledge structures may occur at different levels and in varying degrees. First, by gaining knowledge from the alliance, the partners may reshape their strategy and the means of implementation. Alternatively, they may create a new knowledge structure in the alliance that may help their performance. Finally, they may also develop skills for managing alliances effectively.

How does learning occur? It is important to note first, that organizational learning is both intraorganizational as well as interorganizational, and that an adequate framework of learning dynamics would need to encompass the interrelationships between these different levels (Argote, McEvily, & Reagans, 2003; Holmqvist, 2003). Intraorganizational learning, by itself, is a multilevel process that simultaneously and collectively involves the individual, the group, and the organization. Interorganizational learning is dependent on the learning strategies pursued by the different organizations. Integrative learning strategies will lead to collective knowledge development, whereas distributive learning strategies may prevent that from occurring. Second, learning intent does not imply that valid learning will occur. Third, learning is a costly process because, in order to be effective, it involves a degree of institutionalization—a multilevel process necessitating the integration of individual-, group-, and organizational-level perspectives. While the managerial school seems to suggest that this learning process can be managed (Bell, Whitwell, & Lukas, 1982), it would still be one that is unlikely to bear fruit overnight.

When learning is the primary motive for alliance formation, it is easier to gauge the strategic intentions of one's partner and to put in place safeguards to minimize the potential risks of opportunistic behavior of the partner (Das, 2005). However, it is important to remember that even when learning is not the primary objective, it is possible that learning-related goals may subsequently displace the original intentions as the alliance evolves over time.

It is also important to note that even in those alliances where learning is the primary motive, there may well be very different kinds of learning that are involved. Lubatkin, Florin, and Lane (2001) draw a distinction between interfirm collaborations that involve vicarious learning, knowledge absorption learning, knowledge grafting learning, and reciprocal learning. Vicarious learning alliances are alliances in which the knowledge to be transferred is easily accessible. Knowledge absorption alliances pose a slightly higher degree of difficulty, in that the ability to gain knowledge from one's partner is critically dependent on the focal firm's absorptive capacity. Knowledge grafting alliances are in the nature of mergers and acquisitions, whereas reciprocal learning alliances bring together partners working in different knowledge domains who are noncompetitors in the core businesses. The key implication of these distinctions is that the focal firm has to discern and counter the strategic intentions of its partner accordingly as these intentions vary across different forms of learning alliances.

Generally speaking, scholars have identified three different kinds of learning that occur in strategic alliances: (a) content learning, (b) partner-specific learning, and (c) alliance management learning (Kale, Singh, & Perlmutter, 2000; Parise & Hendersen, 2001). We list in Table 8.1 some illustrative observations from the literature on these three kinds of learning in alliances. The purpose of this table is to provide the reader with an overview of the way in which scholars have looked at learning in alliances.

Content learning refers to the ability of an alliance firm to acquire and internalize knowledge from its partner. This type of learning may alter the bargaining power among the member firms if one of the partners outlearns the other (e.g., Hamel, 1991; Inkpen & Beamish, 1997; Reich & Mankin, 1986). The firm that outlearns its partner may apply the knowledge it has gained to other product domains, leading to superior economic performance. This will also afford the opportunity to either abandon its alliance partner or renegotiate for more favorable terms of collaboration. All this will have major strategic implications for the member firms as well as alliance evolution.

Partner-specific learning has two components: learning from a partner and learning about a partner. While learning from a partner is undoubtedly a significant issue in alliances, learning about a partner is no less important. Learning about one's partner is crucial because the motivation and ability

TABLE 8.1 Learning Types in Alliances

Authors	Learning Type	Illustrative Observations	Remarks
Alvarez Gil & Gonzalez de la Fe (1999)	Content	"Thus, while poor performance can lead to myopia that acts as a barrier to knowledge creation, the student partner may feel that the alliance does not yield satisfactory organizational performance because learning opportunities have been unexploited." (p. 403)	Content learning is limited both by the desire of the teacher to prevent the student from undertaking it and also by the performance of the alliance. Learning from a partner is very constraining inasmuch as opportunities for learning are constrained by the strategic motivations of the partner. Very much in contrast with the work of Dussauge, Garrette, & Mitchell (2000).
Anand & Khanna (2000)	Alliance Management	"Valuation of alliances cannot afford to ignore the dynamic, cross alliance benefits of entering into a particular relationship." (p. 313)	Study suggests that firms differ in their "alliance capabilities" with the implication that some firms are better than others at learning from alliances. As the authors themselves note, it is unclear if the enhanced learning capability reflects greater capability in either learning about a partner or learning from a partner. The ability to pick the right partner may avoid negative outcomes, but it does not guarantee positive outcomes per se.
Ariño (2001)	Partner specific	"Non cooperative behavior by omission has a lesser effect than cooperative behavior by commission on the firm's own non cooperative behavior." (p. 18)	Paper focuses on learning about a partner as opposed to learning from a partner. The fundamental idea is that learning about a partner entails attributions about intentionality with these attributions shaping subsequent behavior. Although attributions about intentionality shape behavior, partners may differ in their assessment as to what constitutes cooperative behavior by commission and what constitutes noncooperative behavior by omission.

(continued)

TABLE 8.1 (continued) Learning Types in Alliances

Authors	Learning Type	Illustrative Observations	Remarks
Ariño & de la Torre (1998)	Content	"The existence of procedural solutions for conflict resolution may be an important aspect of initial conditions." (p. 323)	An empirical study of a joint venture suggests that partner-specific learning is fostered by how partners deal with perceptions of equity/inequity in the relationship. A case study very consistent with Kale et al. (2000), in that it highlights the importance of relational capital in determining how partners deal with perceptions of equity/inequity in relationships.
Doz (1996)	Content Partner-specific	Content learning is more likely to occur in projects that are of moderate importance to alliance partners. "Early small events in an alliance have a disproportionate importance in establishing, or not, a self reinforcing cycle of heightened efficacy expectations, greater institutional trust and personal trust and commitment, joint sense making and learning, and greater flexibility and adaptability." (p. 77)	Partner-specific learning is based on the ability to develop cooperation at the onset of the relationship. This work is consistent with other work suggesting that partners seek to maintain control over their core competencies to prevent giving away the store. The implication of this is that collaboration processes are critically dependent on the emergence of relational capital among the partners.
Dussauge, Garrette, & Mitchell (2000)	Content	"Because firms set up link alliances in order to take advantage of the complementary skills of the partner firms, the fact that the firms reorganize many link alliances by changing the allocation of activities among the partners suggests that the complementarity between the allies tends to shift over time." (p. 120)	Learning is more likely to occur in link as opposed to scale alliances. The authors note that content learning is a function of complementary skills among partners. If partners are aware of this complementarity and recognize that they might lose out in the alliance, then why do they enter these alliances?

Dyer & Singh (1998)	Content	"Alliances generate competitive advantage only as they move the relationship away from the attributes of market relationships." (p. 662)	Alliance partners can maximize learning by investing in relationship-specific assets, knowledge-sharing routines, complementary resource endowments, and "effective governance." The theoretical argument in this study seems to go against the empirical evidence that suggests that joint value creation is problematical.
Edmondson & Moingeon (1996)	Content Partner specific	Content learning is fundamentally a question of learning "how." "Learning how is required for the many situations in which speed and quality matter; learning why is required for diagnosis and relationship building." (p. 34)	Partner-specific learning is based on learning "why." The only piece that seeks to draw an explicit distinction between different forms of content learning, namely, learning why and learning how. Learning how may foster a more competitive mode of interaction, whereas learning why may induce a different dynamic.
Hamel (1991)	Content	"Outlearning a partner simply means 'winning' a series of micro bargains." (p. 101)	Content learning is dependent on learning intent, transparency, and receptivity. One of the first empirical papers that explicitly takes a strategic view of the learning process, arguing that the learning processes and outcomes are critically influenced by the learning orientation of the partners.
Kale, Singh, & Perlmutter (2000)	Content	"Relational capital is linked not only to alliance success in general, but also to very specific and important objectives such as learning and limiting partner opportunism." (p. 232)	Content learning is dependent on the relational capital among the partners as well as their ability to manage conflicts integratively. The paper does not explicitly address the issue as to how relational capital gets established in the first place with partners that may be competitors.

(continued)

TABLE 8.1 (continued) Learning Types in Alliances

Authors	Learning Type	Illustrative Observations	Remarks
Khanna, Gulati, & Nohria (1998)	Content	"Our models suggest that if firms view their relationship with others in the alliance as either strictly competitive or strictly cooperative, this may give rise to suboptimal outcomes for one or more firms in the alliance." (p. 205)	Content learning is predicated on the ratio of private to common benefits in an alliance. The greater the ratio of private to common benefits, the more competitive the interaction and the less likelihood that one partner may learn from another. A conceptual paper highlighting the dynamic tension that exists between cooperation and competition in an alliance. Beyond the recognition that alliance partners may differ in their assessment of private and common benefits, the subjective determinants of these perceptions are not explicitly outlined.
Kumar & Nti (1998)	Partner specific	"Unfavorable discrepancies may affect the partners' feelings of psychological attachment to the relationship as well as the pattern of interaction." (p. 365)	A conceptual paper suggesting that partner-specific learning is crucially shaped by how partners deal with unfavorable process and outcome discrepancies. The idea that the attributions about the discrepancies made by the partners determines the strategy pursued by alliance partners is very similar to the arguments advanced by Ariño and de la Torre (1998) and Kale et al. (2000).
Lane & Lubatkin (1998)	Partner specific	"Simply put, while imitating one's peers may not always be an effective course of action, the high level of relative absorptive capacity a firm will tend to have with its peers may make them the most easily understood teachers." (p. 474)	The ability of one partner to learn from another is dependent on (a) similarity of firms' knowledge bases, (b) organization structure and compensation policies, and (c) dominant logics.

Makhija & Ganesh (1997)	Content	"The model indicates that only when the bargaining power is perceived to be more or less balanced will the chances for a successful relationship improve. A balance in bargaining power will enable both partners to institute controls appropriate for their own objectives in the learning related joint venture." (p. 524)	Content learning is based on the kind of knowledge sought by each partner. Dissimilar learning needs lead to unequal learning rates, which affect the bargaining power among partners. Consistent with other works in highlighting the dynamic instability of alliances due to the possibility of differential learning. The paper has more of an economic as opposed to a sociological focus inasmuch as it does not explicitly deal with the relationship among partners and how such a relationship may moderate the dynamics of the relationship.
Mowery, Oxley, & Silverman (1996)	Content	"The presence of some alliances in our sample in which the firms display 'divergent development,' i.e., declining technological overlap suggests that some alliances are vehicles accessing rather than 'acquiring capabilities.'" (p. 89)	An empirical paper highlighting the potential limitations of the "capabilities acquisitions" view of strategic alliances. An empirical piece suggesting that content-based learning may not be as prominent as has traditionally been suggested. The evidence offered here is in contrast to the work by Dussauge et al. (2000), suggesting that such learning does occur.
Nti & Kumar (2000)	Content	"Firms with extremely high or low absorptive capacities may have difficulty in finding compatible alliance partners and they may actually end up in unstable learning alliances because they are likely to link up with firms whose absorptive capacities are very different." (p. 130)	Content learning is dependent on similarities among partners' absorptive capacities. What impact does the instability of the alliance have on the reputation of the partners? In other words, is there any detrimental impact of alliances?

(continued)

TABLE 8.1 (continued) Learning Types in Alliances

Authors	Learning Type	Illustrative Observations	Remarks
Parkhe (1991)	Content	Content learning is impeded by interfirm diversity. "When Type I diversity (mutual interdependency) is larger than Type II diversity (interfirm differences), ceteris paribus, longevity will be high....But when Type II diversity is larger than Type I diversity, ceteris paribus, longevity will be low." (p. 596)	The paper highlights the interplay of differences at the strategic and the organizational levels and their consequences for learning. A broad framework is developed and outlined here.
Stuart (2000)	Partner specific	"Particularly when one of the firms in an alliance is a young or a small organization, or more generally an organization of ambiguous quality, I believe that alliances convey endorsements." (p. 818)	An alliance with a reputable partner enhances the reputation of the focal firm. The effect is particularly strong when the focal firm is not that well-known. It is a little unclear if the impact on the reputation of a younger partner is temporary or long-lasting when the alliance is a failure.
Zajac & Olsen (1993)	Partner specific	"A focus on inter-organizational exchange processes suggests that exchanges in inter-organizational strategies are influenced by dynamic developmental processes with the processes themselves often subject to change." (p. 142)	Partner-specific learning is dependent on how interorganizational strategies evolve over time. Very similar to other process models reviewed earlier in stressing the fact that the learning processes are dynamically shaped by the strategies enacted by the different actors.

of a member firm to act in ways that will maximize joint value creation are clearly of some importance in sustaining and deepening commitment in the alliance. Partner-specific learning entails the use of the alliance as a mechanism for learning about the motivation and capability of the partner to maximize value creation. This type of learning is especially valuable as a prelude to acquiring or merging with another firm (e.g., Balakrishnan & Koza, 1993; Mody, 1993). In the short to medium term, this may well be the most important component of learning in alliances for several reasons. First, if a firm is learning from its partner, and second, if what it learns about its partner is positive, its motivation to continue with the alliance will be enhanced. Ahuja (2000) points out that if a partner firm has a high level of technical or commercial capital, its attractiveness as a potential partner increases. The same conditions will also reflect positively on the firm's capability to access and internalize knowledge from its partner (Grant & Baden-Fuller, 2004) and, in so doing, may enhance social capital. This has longer-term implications in that it may add to the propensity for partner collaboration. It will also give the alliancing firms a potential opportunity to establish routines that may facilitate their collaboration.

Finally, alliance management learning relates to a firm's ability to manage alliances effectively. Following Zollo and Winter (2002), one can conceive of alliance management learning as "a dynamic capability... through which the organization systematically generates and modifies its operating routines in pursuit of improved effectiveness" (p. 340). The authors suggest that the development of dynamic capability is dependent on the amount of learning investment that the member firms are willing to make.

Alliance management learning is significant because it is an essential ingredient for enhancing an organization's competitive ability over the long haul (Ireland, Hitt, & Vaidyanath, 2002). It also forms the basis for the concept of alliance capability that is gaining increasing research attention. The concept has two major components, namely, alliance experience and organizational processes that may allow the firms to profit from such experience (De Man, 2005). Although it is intuitively clear that prior experience may enhance a firm's alliance capability, some recent work has proposed boundary conditions on the transferability of this experience. For example, according to Hoang and Rothaermel (2005, p. 342), "It appears that to reap benefits from prior alliance experience, a firm needs to possess absorptive capacity, the potential capacity to acquire and assimilate new knowledge and the realized capacity to transform and exploit the new knowledge (Zahra & George, 2002)." We would surmise that firms with higher levels of alliance capability may be more effective in managing the learning process. They are also likely to have structured their alliance in a manner that mitigates any potential problems and are likely to have well-developed institutionalized mechanisms for managing conflict with their alliance partner. De Man (2005) points out that American companies have made greater efforts to develop their alliance capability in contrast to their European partners. Alliance management learning may also make a member firm more accepting of an exploratory intent in fashioning an alliance with a partner. Furthermore, the firm may become more adept at screening potential partners and in making certain that the alliance develops as intended.

LEARNING AND ALLIANCE PROCESS MODELS

When firms enter into alliances, they do so on the basis of certain native attributes that make it easier for them to engage in the process of value creation. Theorists have emphasized the importance of a firm's preexisting competitive position and the nature of its resource profile (Das & Teng, 2000a, 2003) in explaining the success of partner firms in value creation. Also, adopting a process perspective, a number of researchers have sought to explain how an alliance develops over time (e.g., Das & Teng, 2002; Doz, 1996; Kumar & Nti, 1998; Ring & Van de Ven, 1994).

While the notion of learning processes shaping alliance processes and outcomes is implicitly embedded in processual frameworks, only Doz (1996) and Kumar and Nti (1998) explicitly deal with the impact of learning on alliance evolution. In Doz's framework, a set of alliance conditions—task definition; partner routines; interface structure; and expectations of performance, behavior, and motives—determines how the learning process evolves in the alliance, prompting changes in conditions that in turn shape subsequent behavior. Kumar and Nti argue that learning-related discrepancies may pose a major problem for one or all of the partners because these cannot be evaluated objectively. As they note, "there is an ever-present hazard that a learning related discrepancy may be emerging locally, threatening to set in motion forces that can destroy commitment and trust in the relationship" (1998, p. 363). Both these frameworks stress content learning, noting that the differential ability of the partner firms in content learning may generate forces that may be detrimental to the relationship.

Alliance Development Stages

Although the frameworks noted above stress the importance of learning-related discrepancies in shaping alliance processes and outcomes, none of these are explicitly dynamic, that is, they do not explicate how the learning processes unfold through the different stages of alliance development (Das & Teng, 2002). A dynamic perspective is useful for not only understanding how the learning processes change over time, but also how the different types of learning (content, partner-specific, alliance management) may be differentially salient in these different developmental stages.

Das and Teng (2002) argue, for example, that all alliances proceed through a formation stage, an operation stage, and an outcome stage. During the formation stage, the alliance partners seek to negotiate the alliance and begin implementing the agreement that they have entered into. The formation stage is marked by the calculated expectation that the alliance partners will not experience inordinate degrees of relational risk and performance risk (Das & Teng, 1996) as well as inefficiency and inequity (Ring & Van de Ven, 1994). At the operation stage, the alliance partners implement the contractually binding commitments they have made. Implementing the agreements may be either a smooth or a conflict-prone affair. This stage enables member firms to solidify their perceptions (either positive or negative) about their partner. It also may lead one or both of the member firms to engage in content learning, while simultaneously promoting alliance management learning. The success or failure of an alliance is determined at the outcome stage, where it can either be stabilized, reformed, enter a state of progressive decline, or eventually be terminated (Das & Teng, 2002). The particular outcome would depend first, on whether the alliance has experienced a learning-related discrepancy and second, on the ability of the members to effectively cope with that discrepancy.

While these stages are sequential, there are also interdependencies among them. In other words, what transpires at the formation stage may affect what happens at the operation stage. Similarly, what happens at the outcome stage may induce the alliance partners to reinterpret their earlier experiences at the formation and operation stages. It may also initiate a process of renegotiation should one or the other partner consider it desirable at that juncture. Moreover, the time duration of these stages may also exhibit considerable variability. It may be the case, for example, that the formation stage takes a long time, but if a good and solid understanding has been achieved here, the operation stage may unfold rather smoothly. One might surmise, for example, that at the formation stage, partner-specific learning may be crucial, whereas at the operation stage, the relative importance of content learning increases, and at the outcome stage, alliance management learning may acquire decided salience.

We may also note that the unit of analysis in most of the existing work on explaining learning processes has been the individual member firms rather than the relationship between these firms and the strategic alliance. That current focus in the literature, once again, neglects the dynamic aspects of alliance evolution without which it would be difficult to understand how the alliancing firms deal with the inherent tensions in alliances (Das & Teng, 2000b).

Alliance Conditions

In our attempt to understand alliance learning, we need also to recognize that the different stages of alliance evolution (formation, operation, outcome) describe unique sets of alliance conditions (e.g., Doz 1996; Das & Teng, 2002). These alliance conditions are well-captured by three categories: (a) collective strengths of the alliance, (b) interpartner conflicts, and (c) the pattern of interdependencies among the alliance partners (Das & Teng, 2000a). Collective strengths define the extent of value creation by the alliance partners as they work together. This requires the willingness and the ability to learn from one's partner while also assisting the partner to learn. The alliancing firms may be able to maximize value creation through their interactions. The greater the difference in the absorptive capacities of the member firms, the lower would be the collective strengths of the alliance. However, if a focal firm with a higher absorptive capacity can provide the right incentives to the partner with a lower absorptive capacity, the collective strengths of the alliance may well be augmented (Nti & Kumar, 2000).

Interpartner conflicts stem from differences in strategic objectives among partner firms (e.g., Khanna et al., 1998), incompatibility in national and corporate cultures of the parent organizations (e.g., Ariño & de la Torre, 1998; Kumar & Nti, 2004; Parkhe, 1991), differing alliance horizons (Das, 2004, 2006), political activity among the alliance management team members (e.g., Pearce, 1997), and their experience in managing alliances. These conflicts generate process as well as outcome discrepancies (e.g., Kumar & Nti, 1998). Unfavorable process discrepancies reflect the fact that the member firms are dissatisfied with their pattern of interaction, whereas unfavorable outcome discrepancies reflect the inability of the alliance partners to achieve their learning-related objectives. Unfavorable process discrepancies reduce the psychological commitment of the partners to the alliance. While conflict resolution may well be the way to rebuild and reestablish trust among the members, it also increases the coordination costs in making an alliance function effectively.

Interdependencies define the extent to which the alliance members can benefit from their cooperation. The interdependencies may be either symmetric or asymmetric. When symmetric, there are benefits for both members in continuing with the alliance. In the symmetrical condition, the alliance members learn from each other in ways that are both equitable and efficient and hence, conducive to mutual value creation. However, over time, relationships among the members may become either symmetrical or less so and in the process, may either enhance or lessen the stability of the alliance.

THE DYNAMICS OF ALLIANCE LEARNING

In this section, we discuss the role and implications of the different types of learning as the alliance goes through its developmental stages, basing our discussion on the significant changes in the alliance conditions.

Formation Stage

In the formation stage, the prospective partners sound each other out about the possibility of entering into an alliance. If negotiations are successful, the partners proceed with the task of implementing the agreed-upon commitments. The formation stage is critical because the partners are usually unfamiliar with each other and, for that reason, are likely to scrutinize each other's behavior particularly carefully.

This stage of the alliance provides some opportunity for partner-specific learning. Partner-specific learning affects the judgments made by a firm about the relational risk and the performance risk inherent in entering into an alliance with the prospective partner. Relational risk focuses on the opportunistic behavior of one's partner, whereas performance risk focuses on the alliance's ability to achieve its objectives (Das & Teng, 1996, 1999). Although these judgments may not be made very explicitly at this stage, they are likely to subtly influence the subsequent pattern of interactions among the partners. A good example of this is in the sensemaking process that occurred in the alliance between Renault and Nissan. The partners acted in ways that strengthened the relationship between them. No attempt was made by either partner to act opportunistically or to withhold commitment. Both by acts of commission, as well as by acts of omission, the partners facilitated judgments that lowered the perception, both of performance and relational risk (Korine, Asakawa, & Gomez, 2002).

> **Proposition 1:** *The greater the ability of the partner firms to learn about each other at the formation stage of the alliance, the more confident they will be about the relational risk and performance risk inherent in the venture.*

Whether or not the partners form a positive or a negative assessment of these two kinds of risk at this stage is dependent on the negotiation strategies pursued by the partner firms. Integrative negotiation strategies (win-win) may promote information sharing and trust, while distributive negotiation strategies (win-lose) may prevent information from being shared and may heighten distrust among the parties.

Operation Stage

During the operation stage, the alliance partners begin to translate their contractual commitments into concrete reality. The alliance takes on the task of achieving its negotiated objectives. The operation stage of the alliance offers the opportunity to the partner firms to learn from each other as well as to mutually influence each other's perceptions about their desirability as a partner. Content learning will affect the competitive positioning of both firms, while partner-specific learning will affect their reputations.

A number of scholars have noted that content learning among alliance partners may significantly alter the competitive positions of the partner firms (e.g., Hamel, 1991; Nti & Kumar, 2000). Learning allows a partner firm to access critical technologies that can then be deployed effectively vis-à-vis competitors. Although learning undoubtedly has the potential for altering the competitive position of the firms, whether or not this potential is realized in practice depends on a number of factors. Lane and Lubatkin (1998) note, for example, that a focal firm's ability to learn from its partner is dependent on the similarity between the firms' knowledge bases, organizational structures, compensation policies, and dominant logics. The greater the similarity of the partners on these dimensions, the greater would be the likelihood of learning to occur. For Lane and Lubatkin, it is, therefore, the relative absorptive capacity, and not the absolute absorptive capacity *a la* Cohen and Levinthal (1990), that is the key determinant of learning. Anand and Khanna (2000) note that alliance capabilities are an important determinant of whether or not learning occurs. Alliance capability presupposes the existence of organizational mechanisms that systematize the learning from every alliance and allow for the dissemination of such knowledge within the organization.

Proposition 2: *The greater the content learning among the partner firms at the operation stage of the alliance, the more significantly will their competitive position shift vis-à-vis external competitors.*

When firms form an alliance, they do so on the basis of "resource alignment" among the partners (Das & Teng, 2000a, 2003) in order clearly to collectively utilize the resources that they contribute to the alliance. Das and Teng (2000a) note that there are four kinds of interpartner resource alignment: supplementary, surplus, complementary, and wasteful. Supplementary alignment implies that the firms are contributing similar resources that are being utilized effectively, whereas surplus alignment means that these similar resources are not fully utilized. Complementary alignment implies that the resources contributed by the partners are dissimilar and utilized well, while wasteful alignment occurs when the dissimilar resources of the partner firms cannot be effectively utilized.

The operation of the alliance may result in the resource profiles of the partners becoming progressively divergent. This may occur for a number of reasons. First, the partner firms may differ in their orientation toward the alliance. Partner firms that have an exploratory intent, as opposed to an exploitative intent, may be more motivated and capable of harnessing knowledge to enhance their own organizational capabilities. Hamel's (1991) study demonstrated that the alliance partners often differed in their strategic intent. Second, partner firms may differ in their ability to manage alliances, with the partner having the higher capability being more effective in utilizing the alliance for its own advantage. The partner firms may also differ in their organizational cultures and routines, some of which may be more conducive to acquiring and utilizing knowledge effectively. The divergence in the resource profiles of the partner firms may heighten alliance instability either due to a shift in the bargaining power of the partners or due to opportunistic behavior, as the weaker firm tries to acquire its partner's valuable resources, or due to the perception of inequity that may emerge when it becomes apparent that contributions are not commensurate with outcomes. At the very least, divergence in the resource profiles will lead the partner firms to renegotiate the terms of their cooperative agreement.

The operation stage is also marked by the emergence of interpartner conflicts. Interpartner conflicts may stem from factionalism and heightened political activity among members of the alliance management team, differences in cultures (corporate and national) among alliance partners, and the relative inexperience of the partner firms in managing alliances. Interpartner conflicts may also arise when the strategic directions of the partner firms are incongruent. Both Doz (1996) and Ariño and de la Torre (1998) provide illustrative cases of alliances that broke down when the strategic direction of the partner firms began to exhibit incongruencies. Disagreement over the allocation of benefits is yet another reason for conflicts among partner firms (Ring & Van de Ven, 1994).

Finally, Ariño (2001) notes that interpartner conflicts are likely to be exacerbated when a partner firm engages in noncooperative behavior by commission rather than by omission. A noncooperative behavior enacted through commission invites attributions of intentionality that shape the evolving relationship among the partner firms. Although our discussion suggests that interpartner conflicts are inevitable when partners engage in the process of joint value creation, the extent of dysfunctionality of the conflicts depends on how well the partners manage the conflict. For example, in the process of resolving interpartner conflicts, the partner firms may be able to use their latent knowledge to construct novel alternatives that may heighten the interdependencies among the partner firms and be beneficial for the alliance. As Hargadon and Fanelli (2002, p. 299) observe, "plurality provides members of knowledge-brokering firms with latent knowledge that may be more flexible in its abilities to interpret problematic situations and recognize useful combinations of past ideas." This is most likely to occur if the partner firms construe the conflict in positive rather than negative terms. Kale et al. (2000) note, for example, that integrative management of conflicts (a win-win approach) enhances the relational capital among the partners, while at the same time it lessens the motivation for the partners to behave opportunistically. An illustration of divergent resource profiles can be found in the alliance between Borden and Meiji Milk (Cauley de la Sierra, 1995). At the onset of the alliance, the resource profiles of the partner firms were complementary, in that the Japanese firm, Meiji Milk, was providing local market knowledge, while Borden was contributing critical competencies. Over time, as Meiji internalized these competencies, and Borden's learning declined or stagnated, the resource profiles of the partners began to diverge, and an intensification of conflict ensued.

Proposition 3: *The greater the divergence of the resource profiles among the partner firms during the operation stage of the alliance, the greater will be the potential for conflict and instability in the alliance.*

The operation stage of the alliance provides a basis for it to develop its collective strengths. As outlined earlier, the collective strength of an alliance describes its overall strategic capability. The strategic capability may manifest itself, for example, in a dominant market share, rapid pace of new product development, or entry into new markets. The collective strength of an alliance is very dependent on the partners' ability to jointly generate relational rents. Relational rent is defined by Dyer and Singh (1998) as "supernormal profit jointly generated in an exchange relationship that cannot be generated by either firm in isolation and can only be created through the joint idiosyncratic contributions of the specific alliance partners" (p. 662). The authors argue that the ability to maximize relational rents is dependent on the alliance partners' investment in relation-specific assets, their ability to develop interorganizational processes that would facilitate the access and transfer of knowledge among partner firms, the possession of complementary resources and capabilities, and effective governance. The development of interorganizational processes and governance mechanisms that enhance the collective strengths of an alliance are facilitated at moderate levels of cultural disparity and hindered when the disparity crosses a critical threshold (Phan & Peridis, 2000).

Proposition 4: *The greater the content and alliance management learning during the operation of the strategic alliance, the greater will be its collective strength.*

As a consequence of alliance operation, the competitive positioning of one or all of the partner firms may either strengthen or weaken their position relative to their competitors. Whether a positive or a negative outcome occurs depends, first, on the collective strength of the alliance and, second, on the ability of the partner firms to access that collective strength for their strategic positioning. The financial interdependencies between the partner firms refer to the degree to which the alliance enables the firms to strengthen their resource accumulation via the alliance. It may also be that the alliance provides little or no financial benefit, or even becomes a drain on the partner firms' resources.

Finally, technological interdependencies indicate the degree to which the alliance's technological capability becomes crucial for the partner firms in strengthening their own technological capability. Again, one can envisage two contrasting situations. In the first situation, the partner firms are not dependent on the technological strength of the alliance, whereas in the second there is a high level of dependence. A good example of a negative strategic interdependency between the partner firm and the alliance is the alliance between Borden and Meiji Milk that we mentioned earlier (Cauley de la Sierra, 1995). The partners in this case had entered into an alliance in Japan, with the Japanese partner marketing Borden's products in Japan. For a couple of decades the alliance performed reasonably well. However, over a period of time, Meiji was able to internalize critical competencies from the alliance, and once this internalization had occurred, the Japanese partner started introducing its own products that competed with those of Borden. Clearly, the Japanese partner was now no longer as dependent on the alliance, and for that reason could undertake strategic initiatives of its own. Borden, by contrast, was still very dependent on the alliance and reacted very negatively to Meiji's actions. Eventually, the 20-year old relationship between the partners broke down amidst considerable acrimony.

An example of a lack of positive financial interdependency between the alliance and the partner firm is the alliance between Rover and Honda (Alvarez Gil & Gonzalez de la Fe, 1999). Rover had entered into an alliance with Honda with the goal of learning Honda's manufacturing techniques. Honda, by contrast, wanted to use the alliance to expand its geographical coverage, gain economies of scale, and strengthen links with local suppliers. Alvarez Gil and Gonzalez de la Fe (1999) suggest that in this alliance, Rover failed to realize its objective of learning about Honda's manufacturing techniques. It only succeeded in "Roverizing Honda models," and while this had some learning effect, it failed to translate into adequate financial returns. One consequence of this was that Honda gained little positive financial synergy from the alliance, thereby lessening its commitment to the alliance.

Proposition 5: *During the operation stage of the alliance, the greater the degree of content learning among the partner firms, the greater will be the interdependency between the partner firms and the overall learning within the strategic alliance.*

Outcome Stage

In the outcome stage, the performance of an alliance can be evaluated with some clarity. We already noted that there are four possible outcomes at this stage: stability, reformation, decline, or termination (Das & Teng, 2002). If the alliance has met the expectations of its partners, it will be stable and may even expand. An alliance may need to be restructured or reformed if the expectations of the alliance partners are not met. Decline may well call for similar actions, although it may be a prelude to termination.

The outcome stage may affect both the partners' reputations and their competitive positions vis-à-vis external competitors. If the alliance generates positive outcomes for both partners, it would tend to reaffirm their trust and commitment to each other. However, as Selnes and Sallis (2003) note, this may not always happen, as trust has hidden costs that may impede the functioning of a partnership. These hidden costs take the form of relaxing of partner controls, loss of creativity due to groupthink, and the reluctance of the partners to convey negative information to each other. If the alliance does not produce positive outcomes for one or both of the partners, but the partners can handle their complaints in an amicable manner, no harm will be done to their reputation. Stuart (2000), in a study of alliances in the semiconductor industry, notes that a small or a relatively young partner benefited from an alliance with a partner that had a higher stature even though the alliance did not meet its objectives. The reputation of a smaller partner usually gets enhanced when it enters into an alliance with a more reputed partner. The troublesome scenario is where the outcomes are negative and the partners are not able to cope with such results effectively.

Competitive positions can be strengthened when one or both of the partners are able to gain access to new technologies and deploy them effectively. Perhaps the optimal situation is where there is reciprocal learning, because such a situation tends to reinforce the relationship among the partners. Since both the partners are learning from each other and maximizing value creation, there is the natural propensity to continue with the relationship. Relationships can become unstable when a partner outlearns its counterpart or where neither learns from the other. An alliance that was characterized by positive learning outcomes was the Renault-Nissan alliance mentioned earlier. At the time of the alliance formation, Nissan was on the verge of bankruptcy, while Renault was looking to strengthen its global position. Nissan's strengths lay in engineering, while Renault's strengths were in styling and design. This useful complementarity and the ability to translate it into positive synergies were unique aspects of the alliance (Yoshino & Fagan, 2003).

In sum, the learning dynamics of the partner firms is a process characterized by considerable ambiguity. This would be particularly true of firms with little prior experience in managing alliances, so that they would be essentially working with their expectations about the alliance. The challenges of drawing reliable and valid conclusions about learning are likely to be particularly acute if the expectations of the alliance partners are not met.

Proposition 6: *At the outcome stage of the alliance, the more positive the partner-specific learning, the greater will be the collective strength of the alliance.*

Also, during this outcome stage, the alliance partners evaluate how successful or unsuccessful the alliance has been. Conflicting perceptions at this stage may intensify interpartner conflicts. Indeed, at this stage, one or all of the partners may either decide to reevaluate the wisdom of continuing with the alliance or call for readjustments in the strategic direction and the governance mechanisms. The inclination to reevaluate and renegotiate the alliance is likely to be further intensified if there is "divergent development" among the alliance partners, that is, a situation where the technological overlap among the partner firms declines during the course of the alliance (Nakamura, Shaver, & Yeung, 1996). A study of alliances by Mowery, Oxley, and Silverman (1996) found that increased diversity in the partner firms' resource profiles characterized a substantial subset of alliances that they studied. The attempted renegotiation may not always be successful and for this reason may lead to termination of the alliance. This dynamic is evident, for example, in the alliance between Alpha motorized systems, a U.S.-based motorcycle and moped equipment manufacturer, and Kai Li Machine, a Chinese manufacturer of gearing systems (Everatt, 1999). Owing to a substantial gap in the strategic, organizational, and the cultural contexts of the partners, the partners not only failed to learn from each other, but more to the point, their relationship deteriorated substantially with the American company becoming increasingly skeptical of their Chinese counterpart's intentions. The relationship was eventually dissolved.

The learning evolution in the relationship between the partner firms may make the partners more cognizant of their abilities to jointly create value in an efficient manner and the extent to which their capabilities are complementary. This learning is crucial because the relationship among the partner firms is likely to determine their commitment to the alliance. While this is not the only determinant of alliance evolution, the learning that occurs here may play an important role in that evolution.

> **Proposition 7:** *At the outcome stage, the level of confidence among the member firms about the ability of the alliance to create value will be dependent on the content, partner-specific, and alliance management learning.*

Also, at the outcome stage, the collective strength of an alliance manifests itself in the ability of the alliance to compete effectively, accumulate financial resources in order to undertake new ventures, and enhance its managerial and technological capabilities. An alliance that possesses high collective strength will likely continue to prosper, whereas one whose collective strength is low may need to be restructured or may simply be terminated.

The critical question to be addressed here is whether an alliance has developed the collective strength that is essential for the alliance to survive and prosper. While the answer to this question has an important bearing on the strategies of the partner firms, it is also important for assessing the viability of the strategic alliance as an independent entity. And, as the collective strength of the alliance grows, it is more likely than not that the alliance will prosper.

It is during the outcome stage that the alliance partners may begin to rethink and reevaluate their alliance strategy, depending upon the pattern of interdependencies that come to characterize the relationship between the partner firms and the alliance. Positive strategic, financial, and technological interdependencies will enhance the commitment of the partner firms to the alliance, whereas negative interdependencies may lower their commitment. The critical issue here is whether there is a positive or a negative interdependence between the strategic alliance and the partner firms. This issue has the most fundamental bearing on whether the alliance partners will enhance their commitment to the alliance or will seek to exit from it.

> **Proposition 8:** *During the outcome stage of the alliance, the greater the degree of interdependence between the partner firms, the greater will be the degree of commitment of the partners to the alliance.*

DISCUSSION

We have highlighted the nature and the consequences of the three types of learning that get accomplished during the formation, operation, and outcome stages of an alliance. The formation stage marks the emergence of a possible relationship between potential partner firms. This is a phase marked by extensive sensemaking in which the intent is to enter into a contractual agreement, should that be feasible. An important decision variable in this context is the reputation of the potential partner. Learning about a partner is critical at this juncture. Given that a relationship is just being initiated at this stage, the other learning components are not relevant here.

The operation stage is where the alliance partners, having successfully completed negotiations, start translating the agreed-upon commitments into concrete reality. We have argued that at this stage, content learning initially becomes salient, both for the individual partner firms and the strategic alliance as a whole. When the alliance becomes operational, content learning may also become an important issue in shaping the interdependencies between the partner firms and the alliance.

The evolution of the relationship between the partner firms during the operation stage leads to further partner-specific learning that may encompass both learning from a partner and learning about a partner. We would argue that whether or not content learning occurs, and the degree to which it does occur, depends most critically on the preexisting reputations of the partner firms. If the partner firms enter into an alliance with positive reputations, they are likely to pursue integrative learning strategies, that is, strategies providing for "maximum transparency, receptivity, and thus interorganizational learning" (Larsson, Bengtsson, Henriksson, & Sparks, 1998, p. 292). Integrative learning strategies will maximize the collective strengths of the alliance while also allowing the individual partner firms to benefit in the process. The preexisting reputations with which the partner firms entered into the alliance may be further strengthened in the process. As the operations unfold over time, the first signs of positive interdependencies between the partner firms and the strategic alliance may begin to emerge if the partners have pursued integrative learning strategies. The initiation of positive interdependencies may also enhance the confidence of the partner firms in managing the alliance, with the consequence that the firms may be more willing to subsequently form additional alliances with the same or other partners. If, by contrast, the partners initiate the operation stage with somewhat negative perceptions of each other, they are likely to pursue competitive learning strategies that may, in turn, engender a self-destructive relationship.

In the outcome stage, the performance of the alliance and its implications for the partner firms become clear. The outcome stage is also likely to be influenced by the mode of interaction that transpired during the operation stage. If integrative learning strategies have been pursued in the operation stage, the competitive positions of the partner firms are likely to be strengthened vis-à-vis their external competitors. The impact of content learning on the partner firms may be most directly visible at this stage.

Although integrative learning strategies may change the competitive positions of the partner firms, it is conceivable that not all of the partner firms may benefit equally, and this may sow some seeds of distrust in the relationship between the partner firms. However, this potential negative outcome may not occur if the partners have a positive reputation and a long-term orientation, and are cognizant of the vantage point from which they entered the relationship.

Content learning is salient for the strategic alliance, and there is no denying that the collective strength of the alliance may increase, which in turn may accentuate the positive interdependencies between the partner firms and the alliance. Partner-specific learning is likely to be prominent in the interactions between the partner firms, as the partners are likely to learn much more about each other as they seek to develop shared routines to maximize relational rents. Integrative learning strategies will undoubtedly facilitate this process considerably. The emergence of positive interdependencies between the strategic alliance and the partner firms may further reinforce alliance management learning whose roots probably lie in the earlier stage. The interrelationships between the different coevolving components underscore the complexity of the learning dynamics in strategic alliances. Initial conditions matter, but the interplay between them is no less crucial. Thus, in summary, the formation stage of the alliance will be marked by the saliency of learning about a partner, the operation stage by the saliency of content learning, and the outcome stage by the saliency of the cumulative product of all three types of learning.

In this chapter, we have attempted to outline the dynamics of learning in the alliance development process. First, we have suggested that the different alliance conditions that impact upon the learning evolution are collective strengths, interpartner conflicts, and interdependencies. While collective strengths and interdependencies are associated with the strategic alliance and the relationship between the partner firms, interpartner conflicts are associated with the partner firms and the relationship between them.

Second, we have made a distinction between different types of learning and their associated strategic significance for the development of the alliance. In particular, we have underscored the fact that different types of learning are either more or less relevant for the different coevolving components in the alliance learning system. For the purposes of our analysis here, we have adopted three different types of learning that occur in strategic alliances: (a) content learning, (b) partner-specific learning, and (c) alliance management learning.

Third, we have noted that the different types of learning have different strategic implications. We have discussed how the strategic significance of the different types of learning may shift as the alliance progresses from the formation to the operation and the outcome stages. Briefly, partner-specific learning (learning about a partner) is crucial in determining whether or not an alliance gets formed; content learning determines the collective strengths of the alliance; and alliance management learning helps build the confidence of the partners to manage alliances.

Fourth, our framework draws attention to the fact that learning dynamics in alliances encompass both the level of the individual partner firms as well as the relationships with each other and the alliance. One implication is that the nature of the learning dynamics may not be consistent across all these different levels. For example, at the operation stage, an enhancement of the competitive position of a partner firm may be associated with heightened interpartner conflicts and lowered collective strengths of the alliance. Similarly, at the outcome stage, an increase in the divergence of the resource profiles of the partner firms may accentuate interpartner conflicts while simultaneously enhancing the potential for the collective strengths of the alliance to increase, if the conflicts can be reasonably contained.

And last, we have noted that a learning process occurs within a highly interdependent system. The existing work on alliances has focused primarily on the unique characteristics of the alliances in explaining how an alliance as an entity evolves over time (e.g., Das & Teng, 2002; Doz, 1996; Ring & Van de Ven, 1994). A crucial implication of the interactive system perspective discussed here is that whether an alliance prospers or falters depends significantly on what happens among the different learning components within the confines of that alliance. The specific outcome depends, importantly, on the evolution of the interdependencies between the partner firms and the strategic alliance. Thus, for instance, even though an alliance may be functioning smoothly for a time, it may not survive if the interdependencies wither between one or more of the partner firms and the alliance.

In sum, we have made the argument that appreciating the dynamics of learning in alliances, in terms of three types of learning, advances our understanding of the alliance developmental processes. This dynamic perspective brings to the fore the importance not just of the quality of managerial intervention, but also its timing in determining whether a troubled alliance can be rescued. In particular, our framework reveals that while learning is always elusive, drawing valid inferences about learning is quite complicated when there are multiple processes at play. Nevertheless, such learning is required for alliance management to be effective, even as one appreciates that drawing appropriate lessons from the proposed learning framework is likely to be at once a complicated and worthwhile endeavor.

Process-based frameworks for understanding alliance development are rare, and rarer still are frameworks that jointly incorporate dynamic interactive learning processes and alliance development processes. Thus, having both these kinds of processes in a framework offers distinct theoretical advantages, while also yielding practical insights for managers that may not be available otherwise.

Managerial Implications

The dynamic learning framework outlined here has important managerial implications. It has been noted that "very little research has been devoted to how interorganizational relationships are managed" (Barringer & Harrison, 2000, p. 396). While this is indeed a pertinent issue, our framework suggests that the management of alliance-based relationships is likely to be determined by how effectively the alliance partners manage the three types of learning—content, partner-specific, and alliance management learning. It is the ability to productively manage all the three types of learning that would impact on how the partners interact and determine how the alliance will evolve over time.

For instance, our framework suggests that the collective strengths of an alliance depend on the learning strategies (e.g., integrative vs. distributive, as in Larsson et al., 1998) pursued by partner firms and their ability to maximize relational rents (Dyer & Singh, 1998). We would also argue that integrative learning strategies and the maximization of relational rents are, in turn, dependent on learning about a partner. As we mentioned earlier, the literature has underemphasized learning about a partner as opposed to learning from a partner. If the alliance partner is perceived as having a positive reputation, it is likely that the focal firm will pursue integrative learning strategies that should enhance the collective strengths of the alliance. Also, a positive reputation will promote mutual responsiveness and adaptability among the member firms as well as a greater willingness to tolerate adverse performance during the operation of the alliance. The development of shared routines, critical to the maximization of relational rents, is a more likely outcome under these circumstances.

Second, the framework suggests that managers need to recognize the relative saliencies of the learning types in the different developmental stages. There are thus contingencies that managers must appreciate and incorporate in their thinking. Third, given the fluidity of the learning dynamics in a multi-actor system setting, managers involved in alliances must constantly monitor the ever-changing environment and be prepared to rapidly reorient their strategy and its implementation. This requires creative judgment, and while this judgment may not be preprogrammed in any deterministic fashion, it is vital for ensuring optimal adaptation in a changeful environment. There is also the simultaneous need to strengthen the capabilities of the partner firms, independent of the alliance. Thus, alliance managers need to optimally balance cooperation and competition, rigidity and flexibility, and short-term and long-term orientation (Das & Teng, 2000b).

The ability to manage the organizational learning process is becoming an important strategic asset, and this ability assumes an added level of complexity in the arena of alliances by virtue of the unique problems arising from having multiple organizations working together cooperatively for both individual and joint value creation. We have attempted to sketch the complex dynamics of learning in alliances against the backdrop of an increasingly competitive environment.

Future Research

Future research would obviously need to empirically assess the learning dynamics in strategic alliances. The propositions developed in this article should be of help in this endeavor. Research is also needed to study the intricacies of the coevolving learning components within an alliance, namely, the partner firms considered individually and the strategic alliance entity itself. That is, even as each component itself evolves in terms of learning, all of them also evolve simultaneously in the alliance, constituting the alliance learning system. As we noted earlier, the literature thus far has paid insufficient attention to the interactive character of the alliance learning process. One might also want to study the learning dynamics in alliances across industries and across different institutional environments. There are undoubtedly methodological issues that need to be addressed along the way, given the multidirectional causalities to contend with in this type of research. As a modest contribution toward that end, our attempt here has been to propose an initial framework for understanding the nature of the dynamics of learning in the alliance development process.

ACKNOWLEDGMENT

This chapter, save some minor changes, was earlier published as Das, T. K., & Kumar, R. (2007). Learning dynamics in the alliance development process. *Management Decision, 45,* 684–707.

REFERENCES

Ahuja, G. (2000). The duality of collaboration: Inducements and opportunities in the formation of interfirm linkages. *Strategic Management Journal, 21,* 317–343.

Alvarez Gil, M. J., & Gonzalez de la Fe, P. (1999). Strategic alliances, organizational learning, and new product development: The cases of Rover and Seat. *R&D Management, 29,* 391–404.

Anand, B. N., & Khanna, T. (2000). Do firms learn to create value: The case of alliances. *Strategic Management Journal, 21,* 295–315.

Argote, L., McEvily, B., & Reagans, R. (2003). Managing knowledge in organizations: An integrative framework and review of emerging themes. *Management Science, 49,* 571–582.

Ariño, A. (2001). To do or not to do: Noncooperative behavior by commission and omission in interfirm ventures. *Group & Organization Management, 26,* 4–23.

Ariño, A., & de la Torre, J. (1998). Learning from failure: Toward an evolutionary model of collaborative ventures. *Organization Science, 9,* 306–325.

Balakrishnan, S., & Koza, M. (1993). Information asymmetry, market failure, and joint ventures: Theory and evidence. *Journal of Economic Behavior and Organization, 20,* 99–117.

Barringer, B. R., & Harrison, J. S. (2000). Walking a tightrope: Creating value through interorganizational relationships. *Journal of Management, 26,* 367–403.

Bell, S. J., Whitwell, G. J., & Lukas, B. A. (2002). Schools of thought in organizational learning. *Journal of the Academy of Marketing Science, 30,* 70–86.

Cauley de la Sierra, M. (1995). *Managing global alliances: Key steps for successful collaboration.* Wokingham, England: Addison Wesley.

Cohen, W. M., & Levinthal, D. A. (1990). Absorptive capacity: A new perspective on learning and innovation. *Administrative Science Quarterly, 35,* 128–152.

Crossan, M. M., Lane, H. W., & White, R. E. (1999). An organizational learning framework: From intuition to institution. *Academy of Management Review, 24,* 522–537.

Das, T. K. (2004). Time-span and risk of partner opportunism in strategic alliances. *Journal of Managerial Psychology, 19,* 744–759.

Das, T. K. (2005). Deceitful behaviors of alliance partners: Potential and prevention. *Management Decision, 43,* 706–719.

Das, T. K. (2006). Strategic alliance temporalities and partner opportunism. *British Journal of Management, 17,* 1–21.

Das, T. K., & Teng, B. (1996). Risk types and inter-firm alliance structures. *Journal of Management Studies, 33,* 827–843.

Das, T. K., & Teng, B. (1999). Managing risks in strategic alliances. *Academy of Management Executive, 13*(4), 50–62.

Das, T. K., & Teng, B. (2000a). A resource-based theory of strategic alliances. *Journal of Management, 26,* 31–61.

Das, T. K., & Teng, B. (2000b). Instabilities of strategic alliances: An internal tensions perspective. *Organization Science, 11,* 77–101.

Das, T. K., & Teng, B. (2002). The dynamics of alliance conditions in the alliance development process. *Journal of Management Studies, 39,* 725–746.

Das, T. K., & Teng, B. (2003). Partner analysis and alliance performance. *Scandinavian Journal of Management, 19,* 279–308.

De Man, A.-P. (2005). Alliance capability: A comparison of the alliance strength of European and American companies. *European Management Journal, 23,* 315–323.

Doz, Y. L. (1996, Summer). The evolution of cooperation in strategic alliances: Initial conditions or learning processes? *Strategic Management Journal, 17*[Special Issue], 55–83.

Dussauge, P., Garrette, B., & Mitchell, W. (2000). Learning from competing partners: Outcomes and durations of scale and link alliances in Europe, North America and Asia. *Strategic Management Journal, 21,* 99–126.

Dyer, J. H., & Singh, H. (1998). The relational view: Cooperative strategy and sources of interorganizational competitive advantage. *Academy of Management Review, 23,* 660–679.

Edmondson, A., & Moingeon, B. (1996). When to learn how and when to learn why: Appropriate organizational learning as a source of competitive advantage. In B. Moingeon & A. Edmondson (Eds.), *Organizational learning and competitive advantage* (pp. 17–37). London, England: Sage.

Everatt, D. (1999), *Alpha Gearing Systems Shanghai Co., Ltd.* (Case # 99C014). Ontario, Canada: Ivey Management Services.

Grant, R. M., & Baden-Fuller, C. (2004). A knowledge accessing theory of strategic alliances. *Journal of Management Studies, 41,* 61–84.

Hamel, G. (1991). Competition for competence and inter-partner learning within strategic alliances. *Strategic Management Journal, 12,* 83–103.

Hargadon, A., & Fanelli, A. (2002). Action and possibility: Reconciling dual perspectives of knowledge in organizations. *Organization Science, 13,* 290–302.

Hoang, H., & Rothaermel, F. T. (2005). The effect of general and partner-specific alliance experience on joint R&D project performance. *Academy of Management Journal, 48,* 332–345.

Holmqvist, M. (2003). A dynamic model of intra- and interorganizational learning. *Organization Studies, 24,* 95–123.

Huber, G. P. (1991). Organizational learning: The contributing processes and the literatures. *Organization Science, 2,* 88–115.

Inkpen, A. C., & Beamish, P. W. (1997). Knowledge, bargaining power, and international joint venture stability. *Academy of Management Review, 22,* 177–202.

Ireland, R. D., Hitt, M. A., & Vaidyanath, D. (2002). Alliance management as a source of competitive advantage. *Journal of Management, 28,* 413–446.

Kale, P., Singh, H., & Perlmutter, H. (2000). Learning and protection of proprietary assets in strategic alliances: Building relational capital. *Strategic Management Journal, 21,* 217–237.

Khanna, T., Gulati, R., & Nohria, N. (1998). The dynamics of learning alliances: Competition, cooperation, and relative scope. *Strategic Management Journal, 19,* 193–210.

Korine, H., Asakawa, K., & Gomez, P.-Y. (2002). Partnering with the unfamiliar: Lessons from the case of Renault and Nissan. *Business Strategy Review, 13*(2), 41–50.

Kumar, R., & Nti, K. O. (1998). Differential learning and interaction in alliance dynamics: A process and outcome discrepancy model. *Organization Science, 9,* 356–367.

Kumar, R., & Nti, K. O. (2004). National cultural values and the evolution of process and outcome discrepancies in international strategic alliances. *Journal of Applied Behavioral Science, 40,* 344–361.

Lane, P., & Lubatkin, M. (1998). Relative absorptive capacity and interorganizational learning. *Strategic Management Journal, 19,* 461–477.

Larsson, R., Bengtsson, L., Henriksson, K., & Sparks, J. (1998). The interorganizational learning dilemma: Collective knowledge development in strategic alliances. *Organization Science, 9,* 285–305.

Levitt, B., & March, J. G. (1996). Organizational learning. In M. D. Cohen & L. S. Sproull (Eds.), *Organizational learning* (pp. 516–540). Thousand Oaks, CA: Sage.

Lubatkin, M., Florin, J., & Lane, P. (2001). Learning together and apart: A model of reciprocal interfirm learning. *Human Relations, 54,* 1353–1382.

Makhija, M. V., & Ganesh, U. (1997). The relationship between control and partner learning in learning-related joint ventures. *Organization Science, 5,* 508–520.

Mody, A. (1993). Learning through alliances. *Journal of Economic Behavior and Organization, 20,* 151–170.

Mowery, D. C., Oxley, J. E., & Silverman, B. S. (1996). Strategic alliances and interfirm knowledge transfer. *Strategic Management Journal, 17,* 77–91.

Nakamura, M., Shaver, J. M., & Yeung, B. (1996). An empirical investigation of joint venture dynamics: Evidence from US-Japan joint ventures. *International Journal of Industrial Organization, 14,* 521–541.

Nti, K. O., & Kumar, R. (2000). Differential learning in alliances. In D. O. Faulkner & M. de Rond (Eds.), *Cooperative strategy: Economic, business, and organizational issues* (pp. 119–134). Oxford, England: Oxford University Press.

Parise, S., & Henderson, J. C. (2001). Knowledge resource exchange in strategic alliances. *IBM Systems Journal, 40,* 908–924.

Parkhe, A. (1991). Interfirm diversity, organizational learning, and longevity in global strategic alliances. *Journal of International Business Studies, 22,* 579–601.

Pearce, R. J. (1997). Toward understanding joint venture performance and survival: A bargaining and influence approach to transaction cost theory. *Academy of Management Review, 22,* 203–225.

Phan, P. S., & Peridis, T. (2000). Knowledge creation in strategic alliances: Another look at organizational learning. *Asia Pacific Journal of Management, 17,* 201–222.

Reich, R. B., & Mankin, E. D. (1986). Joint ventures with Japan give away our future. *Harvard Business Review, 86*(2), 78–86.

Ring, P. S., & Van de Ven, A. H. (1994). Developmental processes of cooperative interorganizational relationships. *Academy of Management Review, 19,* 90–118.

Selnes, F., & Sallis, J. (2003). Promoting relationship learning. *Journal of Marketing, 67*(3), 80–95.

Stuart, T. E. (2000). Interorganizational alliances and the performance of firms: A study of growth and innovation rates in a high technology industry. *Strategic Management Journal, 21,* 791–811.

Yoshino, M. Y., & Fagan, P. L. (2003). *The Renault-Nissan alliance* (Case # 9-303-023). Boston, MA: Harvard Business School Publishing.

Zahra, S. A., & George, G. A. (2002). Absorptive capacity: A review, reconceptualization, and extension. *Academy of Management Review, 27,* 185–203.

Zajac, E. J., & Olsen, C. P. (1993). From transaction cost to transactional value analysis: Implications for the study of interorganizational strategies. *Journal of Management Studies, 30,* 131–145.

Zollo, M., & Winter, S. G. (2002). Deliberate learning and the evolution of dynamic capabilities. *Organization Science, 13,* 339–351.

CHAPTER 9

A TYPOLOGY OF INTERORGANIZATIONAL LEARNING

The Case of International Strategic Alliances in the Automobile Industry

Tsutomu Kobashi
Natsuko Fujikawa
Kazuyuki Kozawa

ABSTRACT

A typology-based approach to interorganizational learning (IOL), called the "multiple entities approach," incorporates a new concept called the "field for learning." Consideration of the physical and social distance between the field for learning and focal organizations demonstrates how distance determines whether the IOL is a loosely coupled system or a tightly coupled system. A comparison of two major strategic alliances in the automobile industry, the Renault–Nissan Alliance and NUMMI, a joint venture formed between General Motors (GM) and Toyota, shows that an imbalance in IOL occurred at NUMMI. The differences between these two cases in terms of IOL and the

Management Dynamics in Strategic Alliances, pages 193–211
Copyright © 2012 by Information Age Publishing
193

distance between the field for the learning and the parent organizations plays an important role in the success or failure of these alliances. The case studies of these alliances also demonstrate that there is no one best way to carry out IOL, and that different ways of learning management are necessary for different learning systems. Therefore, choosing an appropriate learning system is very important for organizational success.

INTRODUCTION

Organizations have to adapt to increasingly changing environments to attain profitable performance and success. Under recent circumstances, interorganizational relationships (IOR), such as international joint ventures (JV) and strategic alliances, are prospering. Many researchers have addressed such alliances (Faulkner & de Rond, 2000; Inkpen, 2002; Oliver & Ebers, 1998). In fact, IORs have received considerable attention from many scholars since the 1960s. The representative perspectives on IORs have focused on uncertainty and the reduction of uncertainty through the IORs. For example, in transaction cost economics, the transaction cost depends on environmental characteristics, including uncertainty, the number of transaction entities, and human characteristics, such as bounded rationality and opportunism (Williamson, 1975). If the cost is considered high, it is more efficient to carry out the transaction within the organization. From a resource dependence perspective, the organization is assumed to deal with or to avoid environmental uncertainty in order to create a stable and predictable environment (Pfeffer, 1987; Pfeffer & Salancik, 1978). If an exchange relationship or a competitive situation is uncertain, a focal organization tries to build relationships with factors in the environment and make use of them for access to resources, stabilization of results, and avoidance of control from the environment. From these perspectives, IORs are expected to stabilize the organizational environment.

Studies of IOL, on the other hand, have focused on the flexibility acquired through IORs. Each organization has its inertia, causing difficulty in organizational learning. An IOR, however, can help an organization to break free from inertia and cause the organization to acquire flexibility (Yoshida, 1991, 2004). In other words, IOL contributes to the creation of organizational values. Because many strategic alliances are expected to lead to new products or new technologies, IORs are deemed increasingly important in terms of value creation.

This tendency is evident in the automobile industry. Most automobile companies today have some kind of cooperative relationships with other rival companies as a response to the radically changing contemporary business environment. Although some IORs have succeeded in creating value through learning, some have not. Existing research clarifies which factors are important for IOL. For example, Child, Faulkner, and Tallman (2005) listed four factors affecting learning: the transferability of the knowledge, the receptivity of members to new knowledge, the possession of necessary competencies to understand and absorb the knowledge, and the extent to which the partner has incorporated the lessons of experience into the way it approaches the process of learning.

Research on this topic suggests two important needs: the identification of new factors affecting IOL and a theoretical consideration and integration of existing research findings.

Moreover, a typology of IOL, which incorporates the concept of the "field for learning," is most useful. In addition, a comparison of case studies of major strategic alliances in the automobile industry, that is, the Renault–Nissan alliance and NUMMI, an international joint venture (JV) between General Motors (GM) and Toyota, reveals differences in terms of IOL. Although both research fields are growing today, the relationship between them remains unclear.

TYPOLOGY OF INTERORGANZATIONAL LEARNING AND MULTIPLE ENTITIES

Developments of IOL Research

Although IOL research does not have a long history, there are, nevertheless, many focal points from which to examine this field. For example, Inkpen (2002) refers to the following topics as IOL research foci: motive, opportunities, measurement, antecedents, alliance outcome, bargaining power, impact on other organizational variables, processes, and protection of knowledge. In this case, learning through IOR is assumed to improve organizational capability. IOL is this kind of learning. Yoshida (2004) defines learning as the formation of knowledge by a single organization (organizational learning [OL]), unilateral and/or bilateral knowledge transfer between organizations, and formation and retention of knowledge specific to the interorganizational relationships.

He points out that each organization possesses a kind of inertia in that it makes it difficult for the organization to change itself in response to environmental changes. The inertia, which is reinforced through past successes, makes the organization's knowledge system outdated. For this reason, the organization needs new opportunities for learning. However, this inertia is actualized or recognized if the focal organization is able to gain knowledge, behavior, or resources that it cannot produce by itself and if such external resources have different characteristics from those of the focal organization. IOL clearly plays an important role in helping an organization to overcome a difficult situation, allowing an organization to learn.

One major issue in IOL research is to understand the effect of learning and to determine how to improve this effect of learning. Doz and Hamel (1998) pointed out three important factors for making learning effective in strategic alliances: learning will (motivation), opportunities for learning, and objective(s) of learning. Makhija and Ganesh (1997) described several learning processes, along with characteristics of knowledge. For example, legal contracts are suitable for the exchange of precise and explicit information, whereas team formation increases access to a variety of information for creative problem solving. While some studies deal with how to make learning effective, others look at an organization's ability to learn from partners. Furthermore, Lane and Lubatkin (1998) noted that there are few studies to identify with whom an organization should join in a partnership. They stated that IOL is enhanced when there are similarities in basic knowledge, organizational structure, and problems that are faced by both partners. According to Zhang (2004), however, the dilemma of IOL is that although it is important to learn as much as an organization can, opportunistic learning brings about a loss of trust and possible loss of profit for both organizations. That is, it is sometimes very difficult to foster trust between partners (Sasaki, 2004). Child, Faulkner, and Tallman (2005), on the other hand, noted that interpersonal relationships lead to interorganizational trust and development of IOR.

Typology of IOL

Varieties of management procedures to increase the effectiveness of IOL correspond to the various types of IOL. Two existing streams of research are useful to clarify the typology of IOL. First, Nonaka (1991) described two types of IOR, the interactive and the co-creative, as did Inkpen (2002). Inkpen referred to two types of IOL in terms of acquiring knowledge through an alliance: one involves learning from a partner, while the other involves learning with a partner. Das and Kumar (2007) pointed out the importance of the learning from a partner. Child et al. (2005) described the two types of IOL as bringing about changes in both cognition and behavior: received learning and integrative learning. With received learning, one partner willingly receives new insights from another, and with integrative learning, both parties endeavor to express and to share their knowledge and practices.

Both Nonaka (1991) and Inkpen (2002) offer research about the typology of IOL, while Child et al. (2005) look at the direction of IOL. A combination of all these concepts allows a classification of IOL into four types. Figure 9.1 and Table 9.1 show this typology. The vertical axis shows the di-

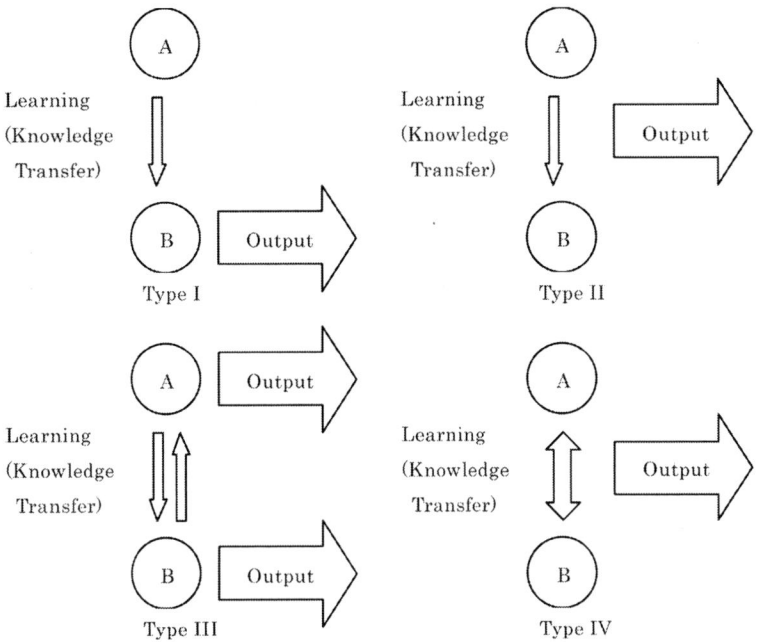

Figure 9.1 Typology of interorganizational learning.

TABLE 9.1 Typology of Interorganizational Learning

		Transfer of Knowledge Between Partners (Private benefit) or Creation of Innovation or New Knowledge (Common benefit)	
		Transfer (Private)	Innovation (Common)
Direction of Learning	Unilateral (Received)	Type I	Type II
	Bilateral (Integrative)	Type III	Type IV

rection of IOL, and the horizontal axis relates to whether or not IOL brings about common benefit.

In Type I, one partner willingly receives new insights from another. In Type II, one partner absorbs knowledge from another and makes use of it as common policy. This type is seen in IOL between a parent and a subsidiary company. In Type III, both partners learn from each other and obtain results based on the knowledge of both partners. In Type IV, the parties combine their knowledge to bring about common benefits. This type involves received learning as described by Child et al. (2005), while Types III and IV involve integrative learning. Types I and II involve learning from a partner as described in Inkpen's (2002) research, and Type IV involves the mutual learning of both parties. Altruism plays an important role in Types I and II, because one partner does not engage in learning at this stage.

The development of IOL has been widely studied. For example, Ring (1996) wrote that making repetitive transactions is a strategy for acquiring resources and promoting learning. Doz (1996) pointed out that a successful alliance is highly evolutionary and undergoes interactive cycles consisting of learning, reexamination, and recoordination. Khanna, Gulati, and Nohria (1998) noted that the ratio of a firm's private to common benefits affects its incentive for investment in learning; furthermore, as the ratio rises, the incentive to compete is high. Das and Teng (2002) stated that conflicts caused by opportunistic learning limit the development of alliances.

These studies promote our understanding of IOL, but they focus on how a given IOL develops. In other words, although the studies make clear how IOL in a given cell in Table 9.1 improves quality, they do not explain how and when one type of IOL becomes another type of IOL.

The "Field for Learning" and Organizations: Multiple Entities

While the typology herein presented is useful for identifying the situation of a given type of IOL, it is also necessary to address what may be called the "field for learning," the setting where learning or co-activity takes place. Since the 1990s, many studies have addressed this theme. For example, Nonaka and Konno (1998) introduced a concept called *ba*, which means place or field in Japanese. The *ba* provides a platform for advancing individual and collective knowledge, making it different from ordinary human interaction. Itami (1991) argued that *ba* comprises a bounded interaction field within which insiders develop their own "interpretation code," which gives meaning to information that might be conveyed by "information carriers," such as spoken language, documents, tone of voice, and the like. Because a well-formulated *ba* has good effects on organizational learning, it is an important consideration in IOL settings. The term "field for learning" is synonymous with *ba*.

The physical and social distance between the field for learning and focal organizations is another important consideration. If the distance between focal organizations and the field for learning is large, such as that which might occur with international joint ventures (JV), the result is a loosely coupled system (Orton & Weick, 1990). However, if the distance is

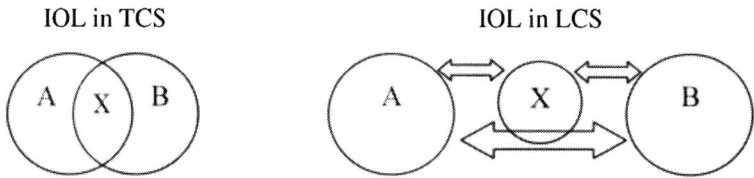

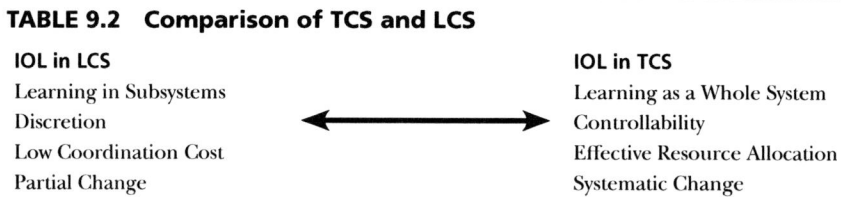

Figure 9.2 Systems of IOL.

TABLE 9.2 Comparison of TCS and LCS

IOL in LCS		IOL in TCS
Learning in Subsystems		Learning as a Whole System
Discretion	⟵————————————⟶	Controllability
Low Coordination Cost		Effective Resource Allocation
Partial Change		Systematic Change

short, the result is a tightly coupled system (see Figure 9.2 and Table 9.2). The letters A and B in Figure 9.2 indicate parent organizations; X indicates the field for learning; and each arrow represents learning. Table 9.2 shows exact contrasts between two systems.

The location of the field for learning is an important factor in IOL because it is likely to show its own behavior in an LCS (loosely coupled system). Therefore, an understanding of IOL requires an approach from the standpoint of multiple entities based on the relationships among focal organizations and the field for learning.

CASE STUDY: RENAULT–NISSAN ALLIANCE

The history of the Renault–Nissan alliance may be divided into three stages from the standpoint of the typology of IOL. Although the characteristics of more than one stage may coexist at some point, this overlap does not negate the typology.

Renault–Nissan Alliance: An Overview

Since the early 1990s, Nissan Motor Company, Ltd., faced a continuous downturn in business. This downturn made it difficult for Nissan to improve by itself, so eventually Nissan tied up with Renault, forming the Renault–Nissan alliance on March 27, 1999.

(1) First Stage: Salvation of Nissan by Renault (unilateral learning by Nissan)

When an alliance is formed, both sides bring merits to the alliance. Such was true in the case of the Renault–Nissan alliance. Table 9.3 shows the various merits of each company.

At this stage, existing learning is represented by the underlined items. Yoshikazu Hanawa, who was president of Nissan at the time the alliance was formed, sought to strike a balance between technology and cost, reorganization of *keiretsu* (transaction relationship), and the formulation of remedies through establishment of a cross-functional team. Hanawa thought that Nissan had much to learn from Renault because Renault's reorganization had been successful and its sales increased. His visits to Renault's plants allowed him to observe firsthand Renault's cost reduction plan. He said,

> One thing we have to learn from Renault is the way of cost reduction. Renault achieved results while reducing costs. Therefore, we will invite a person who possesses Renault's "know-how" to be our Deputy Chief Financial Officer. In addition, we will make up our deficit in marketing ability by consulting the vice president of product planning at Renault. First of all, we have to listen to them and follow their advice. (*Nikkei Business,* 1999, p. 12)

These statements indicate that Nissan was prepared to learn from Renault, an intention reflected in the Nissan Revival Plan (NRP), which was announced immediately after the formation of the Renault–Nissan alliance. Moreover, Renault's influence on Nissan is most clearly embodied in one person, Carlos Ghosn. Ghosn, who was the major influence in the rebuilding of Renault, took his ideas and methods with him when he came to Nissan, revised them, and applied them to rebuild Nissan. The NRP shares similarities with Renault's restructuring plan (see Table 9.4). Therefore, at this stage, Nissan was learning from Renault.

TABLE 9.3 Expected Advantages Through Alliance

Renault	Nissan
Asian market	Satisfaction for a debt
North American market	Renewal of management
	Restructure of production and marketing

Both

Full-lineup through complementarity of difference of car lineup between both companies

TABLE 9.4   Renault's Influence in the "Nissan Revival Plan"

	Renault (Restructuring since 1997)	Nissan Revival Plan (October 1999)
Factory shutdowns	France, Claire Plant Portugal, Setuval Plant Belgium, Vilvoorde Plant	Tokyo, Murayama Plant Kyoto, Nissan Shatai Kyoto Plant Nagoya, Aichi Machine Industry Minato Plant Fukuoka, Kyushu Engine Plant Yokosuka, Kurihama Plant
Personnel reduction	1984: 214,000 workers 1988: 182,000 workers (–32,000) 1998: 138,000 workers (–44,000)	1999: 148,000 workers 2002: 127,000 workers (–21,000)
Supplier reduction	Reduction of parts suppliers from 1,200 to 150	From 1,145 companies to 600
Cost reduction	1998: FF 9 billion 1999: FF 6 billion 2000: FF 6 billion	¥1 trillion by FY 2002 (¥600 billion through purchase only)

(2) Second Stage: Revival of Nissan and its Contribution to Renault (bilateral learning)

Although Nissan was learning from Renault during the first stage, learning in a reverse direction occurred as the alliance matured. First, Renault sent people such as Ghosn to Nissan and promoted Nissan's reformation. In this process, Renault benchmarked Nissan's factories in Europe, transferred knowledge through this benchmarking, and improved the productivity of Renault's factories (Heller, 2006). Renault and Nissan had no secrets between them and were open about everything with each other. What Nissan learned from Renault was a production system based on human engineering. Renault employed many aged laborers in its factories; the assessment system measured loads to labor in three grades. However, based on this system, many problems were revealed in Nissan factories. Dealing with these problems created a secondary effect: a decrease of 30% in the number of defective products. Jean-Louis Ricaud, vice president of Renault, said, "At first, not everything was open. This progress is the result of a continual effort to build trust" (*Nikkei Business,* 2006, p. 39).

Second, with Nissan's technical cooperation, Renault's JV in Korea started producing new cars in 2004 and 2005. Third, the influence of Nissan on Renault was seen in the structure of the supplier network. First Renault's purchase strategy was transferred to Nissan. The application of Renault's expertise allowed Nissan to reorganize its supplier network efficiently. Furthermore, Calsonic Kansei, a company belonging to the Nissan supplier network, was able to make use of its predominance at Nissan to become part of the Renault network (Kobashi, Konomi, & Kozawa, 2003).

These aspects indicate that Nissan was able to recover from the downturn through its alliance with Renault and also began to contribute knowledge to Renault. On the other hand, Nissan continued to learn from Renault. Therefore, in this stage, Renault and Nissan learned from each other, a situation that may be described as "bilateral learning."

(3) Third Stage: The Development of Common Projects (common learning)

In the second stage, both Renault and Nissan learned from each other. Throughout this stage, the number of activities bringing about common benefits increased. Therefore, learning in this stage may be considered to be common learning. At this third stage, research and development (R&D) activities, purchasing organization, information organization, and strategic organization were related.

(a) Joint development. At first, Renault and Nissan were cooperating on the development of new cars. At the beginning of the alliance, a complementary relationship existed between Renault and Nissan regarding the variety of cars. Subsequently, they started to work together to develop new cars jointly as the alliance matured, especially in the distribution of electric vehicles (EV) in various regions around the world. In developing EVs, Renault's technical expertise with compact cars was combined with Nissan's technical expertise with batteries to create value. As well, the predominant market positions of both companies were utilized to improve the infrastructure throughout the world.

The two companies also worked on the joint development of engines and transmissions in 2-litre cars because both organizations were already producing overlapping models. These results were achieved through joint development; that is, Renault staff members were transferred to the Nissan Technical Center and worked together with Nissan's engineers.

(b) Information organization. From 2001, both organizations worked on the formulation of a common system for management of information, plans of the basement, budget compilation, and cost reduction through benchmarking. Notably, Nissan decreased its system costs by 30%, and this effort was subsequently introduced to Renault. The two companies are now formulating a common system. This case illustrates how knowledge within both organizations was brought together to achieve common goals.

(c) Development of Renault–Nissan purchasing organization (RNPO). Carlos Ghosn, speaking of the foundation of Renault–Nissan BV (Besloten *vennootschap*), stated,

> The timing of this next step of the Alliance has been moved forward as a re-
> sult of the fast and strong success of the Nissan Revival Plan. Nissan is now in a

position to fully play its role in the Alliance with the goal of improved mutual performance. (*Nissan Press Release,* 2001)

The development of RNPO allowed both organizations to share the best practices of cost management, quality management, and transportation and to implement them jointly.

(d) Development of strategic organization. We can see the progress of IOL in the strategy formulation of the alliance. Renault–Nissan BV would have sole responsibility for decisions on mid- and long-term planning (3-, 5-, and 10-year plans), on commonalities in products and power trains, and on principles of financial policy. It would also make proposals to Renault and Nissan on issues such as the creation of joint companies, significant changes in market or product coverage, major investments, and third-party strategic cooperation. Existing Cross Company Teams, which had been building the alliance over the previous two and a half years, would report to Renault–Nissan BV, which would replace the Global Alliance Committee (G.A.C.), the current governing body of the Alliance. Although foci of the G.A.C. were formulating strategies and consideration of suggestions from project teams, Renault–Nissan BV covered a wider range of affairs.

CASE STUDY: NUMMI

The Renault–Nissan alliance shows the development of IOL and the proliferation of common projects. Likewise, NUMMI, a JV between General Motors (GM) and Toyota, illustrates many other aspects of IOL.

Expected Learning

According to Nti and Kumar (2000), the learning objectives of GM and Toyota appeared to be complementary. GM wanted to learn Toyota's lean production methods so that GM could become more successful in producing high-quality subcompact cars. Apparently, GM went into NUMMI, "expecting to find some secret technology, proprietary information'" when, in fact, the key to Toyota's success was the integration of "the people systems with the technology systems" (*Wall Street Journal,* 1986, p. 3). Toyota, on the other hand, wanted to learn how to adapt its manufacturing and human relations system to produce high-quality cars in the United States using American workers and suppliers, including how to deal with an American labor union. Ahmadjian and Lincoln (2000) described the same situation.

Many other studies described how GM and Toyota learned from each other at NUMMI. According to our model, however, there are two aspects of the learning: learning through NUMMI and learning from NUMMI. The former refers to learning from a partner, with NUMMI as mediator. On the other hand, the latter refers to NUMMI as the entity itself, which improved performance through learning. If this is the case, the learning process must be viewed from the standpoint of multiple entities.

The model herein allows a tracing of the learning at NUMMI by focusing on the relationship among GM, NUMMI, and Toyota and what each of the three organizations learned from the other two organizations.

GM's Learning

(1) Toyota to GM

GM is said to have learned the Toyota production system (TPS) to some extent (Zhang, 2004). As a result, GM significantly improved labor productivity from 31.98 hours per vehicle (HPVs) in 1998 to 23.61 HPVs by 2003. The productivity is close to that of Toyota (21.78 HPVs; Inkpen, 2005). GM also narrowed the gap between its quality ranking and those of Honda and Toyota, evidence of GM's having learned how to improve productivity.

(2) NUMMI to GM

Rubinstein and Kochan (2001) noted that the leaders of the United Auto Workers union (UAW) and senior managers in labor affairs recognized that teaching GM about the labor and management relations at NUMMI would clearly bring about some positive changes for GM. However, Shimokawa (2004) predicted that the penetration of NUMMI practices into GM would take a long time—the replacement of one generation of laborers by the next.

(3) General Evaluation

According to Buckland, Hatcher, and Birkinshaw (2003), when GM tried to transfer what it learned from NUMMI to its own factories, it failed. There were many factors at work, but a key problem was that the managers responsible for transferring their learning were spread too thin; they could not overcome the inertia and the "not invented here" suspicions of the people running GM's traditional factories. Singh and Zollo (2004) also noted that GM was less successful in transferring the cutting-edge practices tested at NUMMI to its other existing plants in spite of heavy investment to that end. The criteria examined by researchers—easibility, flexibility, digestibility, time horizon, cognitive, and cultural traits in particular—all pointed to the use of targeted alliances to achieve globalization objectives.

From the standpoint of systems, Nti and Kumar (2000) stated that GM was unable to embody the NUMMI "systems" as part of its operations, and GM did not develop a learning infrastructure that would enable it to utilize the skill of GM managers who were involved with NUMMI in its other operation. Although opportunities to learn from NUMMI were exhausted, the alliance provided an interesting example of an outsourcing relationship between two flagship firms in the automobile industry. In short, although GM learned about new ways to proceed, the learning was inadequate.

Toyota's Learning

(1) GM to Toyota

Toyota was able to gain access to the competitive strategies of its partner and to monitor developments within the U.S. auto industry rather easily (Doz & Hamel, 1998).

(2) NUMMI to Toyota

Toyota established a new $800 million automobile plant in Georgetown, Kentucky, in 1988. Toyota integrated NUMMI into its North American operations, transferring seasoned NUMMI managers to other plants and using common suppliers (Nti & Kumar, 2000). Ahmadjian and Lincoln (2000) reported that foreign production taught Japanese auto assemblers, including Toyota, two lessons: first, it was possible to conduct business with suppliers situated at a considerable distance; and second, it was possible to develop relationships with local suppliers without the benefit of decades of shared experience. However, as Martin, Mitchell, and Swaminathan (1995) show, some preference for the familiar remained.

(3) General Evaluation

In order to learn how to transfer their lean production process to the United States, Toyota entered into a joint venture to produce cars in California and used the learning generated at NUMMI to set up its wholly owned production facilities in Kentucky a few years later (Ahmadjian & Lincoln, 2000). Purchasing practices at NUMMI were put to practical use at the Kentucky factory. Those practices, mentioned later, are suited for the geographical and automobile industrial situation in the United States. Toyota's development in North America after that shows that experiences at NUMMI played a very important role in Toyota's success.

NUMMI's Learning

(1) Toyota to NUMMI

Toyota successfully transplanted its human relations practices and materials management system to the United States and also gained new experience in ocean freight logistics and environmental rules for U.S.-based plants (Nti & Kumar, 2000). Many of Toyota's practices in Japan were introduced to NUMMI, such as the Toyota Production system (TPS), *kaizen* activities (continuous improvement), Toyota's plan and inspection system, elaborated education and training, simple job structure, job rotation, team or group system, cooperative labor-management relationship, and their system of promotion based on long experience plus skill (Oshima, 1989). Since production at NUMMI was based on the Toyota system, many other practices were introduced to NUMMI.

(2) GM to NUMMI

Some factors and practices were introduced to NUMMI from GM too, including the factory layout, information network for production technology and procurement, lack of worker rotation between day shifts and night shifts, wage negotiation every 3 years, and community activities (Oshima, 1989). Because NUMMI initially used the site of the demolished GM Fremont, California, factory and employed workers laid off from GM, practices relating to GM were adopted by NUMMI.

(3) In General

In addition to the practices mentioned above, NUMMI had formulated its own original practices, including a repair process in each production line, an elaborated selection system at the time of employment, rotation aimed at justice with regard to job type, and parking lot and cafeteria benefits not based on seniority or position. In particular, formulating a good procurement system was an urgent problem for NUMMI. Although many suppliers were located near the Toyota factory in Japan, and Toyota had constructed a well-known supplier system, the situation in the United States was completely different. Therefore, NUMMI decided both to import supplies from a Toyota factory in Japan and to procure supplies from component makers in Chicago and Detroit, using the railroad for transportation. Thus, this kind of procurement system required a production control at NUMMI that was very different from that in Japan.

Overall Result

Toyota's ability to run its business in the United States effectively, based on experience at NUMMI, validates Toyota's success in learning. On the other hand, there are various opinions regarding GM's success. For example, Inkpen (2005, 2008) insists that GM was successful in learning. However, Kan Higashi, former senior managing director at NUMMI, says that although Toyota has systemwide discipline, GM failed because of only partial learning (Higashi, 2006).

Differences in the evaluation of GM's success may derive from differences in measuring the extent of learning and the scope of learning. Many authors point out Toyota's superiority to GM in quality. For example, Barney (2005) says that although there is no major difference in quality among all automobile makers when cars are new, Toyota's cars maintain their good quality for much longer, even after 15 years. Toyota's advantage is its ability to make such cars at a low cost. Higashi (2006) points out that the insufficient introduction of the Toyota production system (TPS) to GM brought about differences in quality between GM and Toyota. Even NUMMI was not able to achieve the same high quality as Toyota. For instance, the defect rate at NUMMI was about twice that of Toyota's factory in Brazil (*Nikkei Business*, 2007, p. 38). These studies show that GM's learning from Toyota and NUMMI was somehow limited to aspects such as productivity and cost, while there was still a gap with regard to quality.

As to the scope of learning, GM surely introduced the TPS to GM factories. As an example, Inkpen (2005) points to the important role of NUMMI in the development of the Opel plant in Eisenach, Germany. NUMMI alumni were involved in the startup, and GM achieved lean manufacturing. This experience was introduced to GM plants in other countries, such as Argentina, China, Poland, and Thailand. However, this introduction was not adequate for all GM factories, including those in the United States.

DISCUSSION

Comparison in Typology

An examination of the Renault–Nissan alliance from the point of IOL reveals that the characteristics of IOL changed from the formation of the alliance. At the formation of the alliance, the type of IOL shifted eventually through Type III to Type IV. For example, with regard to purchasing, Nissan first acquired Renault's knowledge. Then Renault began to learn from Nissan, and the two companies worked together as the Renault Nissan Purchasing Organization (RNPO).

During the first years of the formation of NUMMI, the type of IOL shifted eventually from Type I to Type III. Although many cars were produced at NUMMI, the learning situation was different.

Differences in IOL: The Role of the Field for Learning

There is a major difference in IOL between the two IORs, the Renault–Nissan alliance and NUMMI. In the case of NUMMI's, an imbalance of learning existed. Many researchers have studied this imbalance from various points, such as organizational settings, characteristics of knowledge, motivation, and absorptive capacity.

In addition to these factors, our case studies showed the importance of relationships among parent organizations and the field for learning for IOL. There are several effects of the relationships. The first relates to management of learning. The Renault–Nissan alliance is a tightly coupled one, with interlocking directorates, so there is no social distance between the two partners. NUMMI, however, was socially and geographically separate from both GM and Toyota. Therefore, mechanisms for knowledge transfer were much more necessary. In other words, an imbalance of learning was likely to occur because of the relatively loose relationships.

Second, another aspect is the development of the field for learning. If there is a long distance, the field for learning is likely to develop differently from that of the parent organizations. In that case, it is also important to learn from the field for learning itself because it comprises its own idiosyncratic knowledge and/or skills. As Inkpen (2005) so aptly stated, "The learning value of most alliances is usually greater than managers understand and appreciate when alliances are new and recently formed" (p. 133). Thus, knowledge and skill should be evaluated in terms of partners, as well as the fields for learning.

Third, the employment of knowledge is particularly important when the distance is long. In the Renault–Nissan alliance, knowledge brought about as a result of IOL was likely to be dispersed to the entire organization. On the other hand, knowledge generated far away could be used in several ways because it does not penetrate an organization directly. With NUMMI, Toyota made use of knowledge for the development of businesses in North America, not for Japan. Consequently, Toyota did not require a radical systematic change of the whole organization. On the other hand, GM did need to make a radical systematic change, but inertia and resistance prevented sufficient change.

CONCLUDING REMARKS

The typology presented herein, which is more detailed than those given in previous studies, comprises four types of IOL, as well as the possibility of shifts among them. It offers the benefit of allowing an understanding of the ramifications of IOL more precisely than previous models.

As viewed from the point of multiple entities, this typology uses the concept of "field for learning" to illustrate the importance of relationships between the field for learning and the parent organizations in IOL.

Case studies revealed a difference between the Renault–Nissan alliance and NUMMI in terms of IOL. On the one hand, there were similarities in familiar factors, such as organizational settings and motivation. On the other hand, however, if there is a long distance between the field for learning and the parent organization, as in the case of NUMMI, other problems and possibilities occurred. Whenever distance makes the management of learning more difficult, the field for learning would be expected to show idiosyncratic development and become a new source of learning. At the same time, the use of knowledge is also an important factor affecting IOL. Nonetheless, some aspects of IOL require further analysis. For example, more cases will be necessary to confirm the findings presented herein, which are based on only two case studies.

REFERENCES

Ahmadjian, C. A., & Lincoln, J. (2000). *Keiretsu, governance, and learning: Case studies in change from the Japanese automotive industry*. Working Paper No.76, Institute for Research on Labor and Employment, University of California, Berkeley.

Barney, J. B. (2005). Imitation won't make you a winner. *Nikkei BizTech, 5,* 24–31.

Buckland, W., Hatcher, A., & Birkinshaw, B. (2003). *Inventuring: Why big companies must think small.* Berkshire: McGraw-Hill.

Child, J., Faulkner, D., & Tallman, S. (2005). *Cooperative strategy* (2nd ed.). Oxford, England: Oxford University Press.

Das, T. K., & Kumar, R. (2007). Learning dynamics in the alliance development process. *Management Decision, 45,* 684–707.

Das, T. K., & Teng, B. (2002). The dynamics of alliance conditions in the alliance development process. *Journal of Management Studies, 39,* 725–745.

Doz, Y. L. (1996). The evolution of cooperation in strategic alliances: Initial conditions or learning processes? *Strategic Management Journal, 17,* 55–83.

Doz, Y. L., & Hamel, G. (1998). *Alliance advantage.* Boston, MA: Harvard Business School Press.

Faulkner, D., & de Rond, M. (2000). *Cooperative strategy: Economic, business, and organizational issues.* Oxford, England: Oxford University Press.

Heller, D. A., (2006, February-March). Inter-organizational learning determines whether M&A succeeds or not. *Works,* 28–30.

Higashi, K. (2006, October 16). Toyota way is a system wide discipline, GM failed because of partial learning. *Nikkei Business,* p. 1.

Inkpen, A. C. (2002). Learning, knowledge management, and strategic alliances: So many studies, so many unanswered questions. In F. J. Contractor & P. Lorange (Eds.), *Cooperative strategies and alliances* (pp. 267–289). Oxford, England: Pergamon.

Inkpen, A. C. (2005). Learning through alliances: General Motors and NUMMI. *California Management Review, 47*(4), 114–136.

Inkpen, A. C. (2008). Knowledge transfer and international joint ventures: The case of NUMMI and General Motors. *Strategic Management Review, 29,* 447–453.

Itami, H. (1991). *Firm as an informational "ba" (interactive field).* Working Paper, Hitotsubashi University, Tokyo, Japan.

Khanna, T., Gulati, R., & Nohria, N. (1998). The dynamics of learning alliances: Competition, cooperation, and relative scope. *Strategic Management Journal, 19,* 193–210.

Kobashi, T., Konomi, N., & Kozawa, K. (2003). A research on the co-evolution of multiple networks. In P. Hibbert (Ed.), *Co-creating emergent insight* (pp. 189–197). Glasgow, Scotland: University of Strathclyde.

Lane, P., & Lubatkin, M. (1998). Relative absorptive capacity and interorganizational learning. *Strategic Management Journal, 19,* 461–477.

Makhija, M. V., & Ganesh, U. (1997). The relationship between control and partner learning in learning-related joint ventures. *Organization Science, 8,* 508–527.

Martin, X., Mitchell, W., & Swaminathan, A. (1995). Recreating and extending Japanese automobile buyer-supplier links in North America. *Strategic Management Journal, 16,* 589–619.

Nikkei Business. (1999). Inside the Nissan–Renault alliance. *Nikkei Business,* March 22, pp. 6–15.

Nikkei Business. (2006). A crucial moment of Carlos Ghosn. *Nikkei Business,* October 16, pp. 36–41

Nikkei Business. (2007). Distressed Toyota. *Nikkei Business,* February 26, pp. 37–39.

Nissan Press Release. (2001, October 30). Renault and Nissan plan to step up development of the alliance.

Nonaka, I. (1991). Introduction to strategic alliances. *Business Review, 38*(4), 1–14.

Nonaka, I., & Konno, N. (1998). The concept of "ba": Building a foundation for knowledge creation. *California Management Review, 40*(3), 40–54.

Nti, K. O., & Kumar, R. (2000). Differential learning in alliances. In D. Faulkner & M. DeRond (Eds.), *Cooperative strategy: Economic, business, and organizational issues* (pp. 119–134). New York, NY: Oxford University Press.

Oliver, A. L., & Ebers, M. (1998). Networking network studies: An analysis of conceptual configurations in the study of inter-organizational relationships. *Organization Studies, 19,* 549–583.

Orton, J. D., & Weick, K. E. (1990). Loosely coupled system: A reconceptualization. *Academy of Management Review, 15,* 203–223.

Oshima, T. (1989). Technology transfer strategy of Japanese automakers in the United States: Case study of New United Motor Mfg., Inc. *The Quarterly Journal of Economic Studies, 12*(2), 39–56.

Pfeffer, J. (1987). A resource dependence perspective on intercorporate relations. In M. S. Mizruchi & M. Schwartz (Eds.), *Intercorporate relations: The structural analysis of business* (pp. 25–55). New York, NY: Cambridge University Press.

Pfeffer, J., & Salancik, G. R. (1978). *The external control of organizations.* New York, NY: Harper & Row.

Ring, P. S. (1996). *Networked organization: A resource based perspective.* Uppsala, Norway: Acta Universitatis Upsaliensis.

Rubinstein, S. A., & Kochan, T. A. (2001). *Learning from Saturn.* New York, NY: Cornell University Press.

Sasaki, T. (2004). Development of inter-organizational researches. In T. Saito, T. Waragai, & A. Aihara (Eds.) *The frontiers of management theories* (pp. 117–127). Tokyo, Japan: Gakubunsya.

Shimokawa, K. (2004). *Management history of global automobile industry.* Tokyo, Japan: Yuhikaku.

Singh, H., & Zollo, M. (2004). Globalization through acquisitions and alliances: An evolutionary perspective. In H. Gatignon & J. R. Kimberly (Eds.), *The Insead-Wharton alliance on globalizing: Strategies for building successful global businesses* (pp. 129–158). Cambridge, England: University of Cambridge Press.

Wall Street Journal. (1986). Nummi auto venture is termed success. *Wall Street Journal,* May 20, p. 3.

Williamson, O. E. (1975). *Markets and hierarchies.* New York, NY: Free Press.

Yoshida, T. (1991). Inter-organizational learning and organizational inertia [in Japanese]. *Organizational Science, 25*(1), 47–57.

Yoshida, T. (2004). *Organizational change and inter-organizational relationship.* Tokyo, Japan: Hakuto Syobo.

Zhang, S. (2004). *Management of inter-firm partnership.* Tokyo, Japan: Chuo Keizaisha.

CHAPTER 10

SURVIVAL OF THE FITTEST OR SURVIVAL OF THE GROUP?

Coevolutionary Dynamics in Strategic Alliances

Niki Hynes
Juliette Wilson

ABSTRACT

This study examines the theories of evolution and coevolution within the context of two industries at different stages of the industry life cycle. It examines some of the essential underlying assumptions of these theories including the unit of change, the unit of selection, and the outcome of these. These issues are explored and developed through the use of a qualitative case-study approach using empirical evidence from SMEs in the UK and Australia. Findings are that there seem to be multiple *simultaneous* units of change and of selection at these stages of the industry life cycle. Therefore neither evolution nor coevolution is sufficient in explaining this change, although coevolution appears to provide a better explanation for the intense formation of strategic alliances in both of these industries.

Management Dynamics in Strategic Alliances, pages 213–235

213

INTRODUCTION

Industry dynamics impacts both firm strategy and survival, and understanding which firms will succeed and *how* firms should compete or cooperate at different stages of the industry life cycle is important both to managers and to theorists. Most literature about firm strategy and performance approaches this issue by examining the strategy and performance of *single* firms. Yet with the increasing reliance on strategic alliances and networks, firms are also increasingly dependent on other firms for their own performance; a better understanding of how firms behave and change simultaneously is therefore crucial. Coevolution (where species change at the same time to mutual advantage) has long been documented and argued within the scientific academic community and has recently been applied to industry (Das & Teng, 2002; Volberda & Lewin, 2003; Wilkinson, Young, & Ladley, 2007).

This study reviews the current research on coevolution in industry and examines the application of the theories of evolution and coevolution to the way in which firms form, perform, and change within alliance relationships. The issues of the *unit of selection* in addition to the *unit of change* are examined in depth. The importance of the industry life cycle is examined to explore whether coevolution is a better explanation of evolution at certain stages of the industry life cycle. These issues are explored and developed through the use of a qualitative case-study approach using empirical evidence from SMEs in the UK and Australia in two different industries.

BACKGROUND

Interfirm alliances include a wide range of cooperative relationships (Grant & Baden-Fuller, 2004) covering a variety of contractual forms from joint equity ventures to contracts and less formal working agreements. Over the last 2 decades, there has been unprecedented growth in the number of these alliances, collectively termed "strategic alliances" (Das & Teng, 2000; Gulati, Nohria, & Zaheer, 2000). Some of this change toward cooperative structures has been stimulated by increased globalization of markets, decreasing product life cycles, and technological development. This proliferation of strategic alliances has been accompanied by an increasing stream of research by scholars who have examined many of the causes and consequences of alliance formations (e.g., Kogut, 1988; Varadarajan & Cunningham, 1995). The traditional models of firm behavior are difficult to apply to this cooperative behavior (Grant & Baden-Fuller, 2004; Parkhe, 1998), although theoretical approaches used include transaction cost economics (Hennart, 1998; Williamson, 1985), strategic or resource needs of firms

(Barney, 1991; Garcia-Pont & Nohria, 1999), and social structural explanations (Gulati, 1999; Gulati & Gargiulo, 1999).

Although there has been increasing research attention focused on alliance developmental processes, the understanding of these remains quite limited (Das & Teng, 2002; Koza & Lewin, 1988; Supphellen, Haugland, & Korneliussen, 2002). For example, although alliances are known to be highly evolutionary and unstable (Das & Teng, 2002), it is still relatively unclear how and why change within alliances occurs. A useful approach to this is the coevolutionary perspective, where coevolution refers to the simultaneous development of organizations and their environment, independently as well as interactively.

Theories of Evolution and Coevolution

To better explain the analogies of evolution and coevolution within a business sense, it is useful to briefly review the use, and occasional misuse, of these terms within the managerial literature. Evolution is based on the implicit notion of *inherited individual characteristics* within an overall group. The managerial literature has tended to focus on the implied assumption of *survival of the fittest,* which is not *necessarily* an element of evolution, but an associated idea concerned with selection. However, evolution does not always imply survival of the fittest, and selection could also occur by *random genetic drift.* The managerial literature has also traditionally dealt with the individual firm as the *unit of selection,* yet the unit of selection might not always be the individual firm.

Historically, the earliest work utilizing a coevolutionary approach includes Chandler (1962) and Weber (1978); but these early studies focused solely on the interaction between firm and environment (Huyens, Baden-Fuller, van den Bosch, & Volberda, 2001; Lewin, Long, & Carroll, 1999; Lewin & Volberda, 1999). Volberda and Lewin (2003) suggest that to do this, the population must consist of heterogeneous firms that have adaptive/learning capability that is able to interact and mutually influence each other. Both Das and Teng (2000) and Rodrigues and Child (2003) further developed this idea and suggested that the units of change in coevolution could be firms, alliances, or combinations of these.

While coevolution as a theory has implications for strategy setting, it is also interesting to examine the way in which firms are judged to be succeeding or failing. Do firms survive because they change together or do they survive because of individual characteristics? Furthermore, do firms that coevolve influence the "selection criteria" within an industry? Is the population at various times of its life cycle subject to such upheaval that coevolution is a better adaptive mechanism than evolution?

Process of Selection

In biology, evolution refers to the change in the inherited traits of a population from one generation to the next. These traits are the expression of genes that are copied and passed on to offspring during reproduction. Mutations (i.e., changes) in these genes occur naturally and can produce new or altered traits (phenotypes), resulting in potentially heritable differences between organisms. *Evolution* occurs when these heritable differences become more common or rare in a population, either nonrandomly through natural selection or randomly through genetic drift. *Natural selection* refers to the process by which favorable inherited traits (those that incur some form of advantage) become more common in successive generations of a population, and unfavorable heritable traits become less common. *Genetic drift* refers to a more random process of change within a population that happens by chance. Thus, evolution does not always result in the best individual unit being selected and is *not always* the same as survival of the fittest. The debate between the balance of natural drift and selection by fitness has been recognized since Haldane noted as long ago as 1949 that "the slowness of the rate of change makes it clear that agencies other than natural selection cannot be neglected" (as cited in Lande, 1976; Wilson & Hynes, 2009).

The evolutionary process has implicitly been integrated into management theory, and the phrase "survival of the fittest" has been popularized in both everyday life and business. Survival of the fittest refers to the selection of those most suited to a situation. It has been widely criticized as both an inaccurate term in biology and for being a tautological statement. Fitness is not explicitly described within this theory, although in biological terms it is also confused by its alternate meaning of ability to reproduce, which has little meaning in industry dynamics. The assumption is that firms that are best adapted to their situation or that are the "fittest" succeed or perform better than others. This assumption is so wide-reaching in management and economic theory that it is difficult to challenge, given especially its tautological meaning. However, by examining the underlying assumptions of evolution to industry dynamics, further issues arise; if the underlying assumptions are challenged, that is, the *unit* of change or evolution and the *unit* of survival, more questions are raised.

An alternative perspective is provided by the term "coevolution," which is used to describe cases where two (or more) species reciprocally affect each other's evolution. A common example of this is the acacia tree, which has hollow thorns to allow ants to live inside them. The tree produces food for the ants, and the ants defend the tree from animals that would eat it by stinging them. The two species have co-evolved to be mutually advantageous and in so doing, they have changed the unit of selection from a single organism (plant) to a pair of organisms. This means that if natural selection occurs, for example, a drought affects the acacia population, both the ant and the acacia will simultaneously be disadvantaged and likely die. Coevolution generally considers that natural selection takes place, but that the simultaneous change in both organisms results in favorable inherited traits, which confer advantage both at an individual level and simultaneously at a dyadic level as well.

Unit of Selection

Coevolution can lead to paired advantage where the coevolved organisms perform better than non-coevolved pairs of organisms. While the unit of selection in biological coevolution is usually considered to be the individual, the mutual adaptation that has occurred usually means that the partner is also advantaged. This can result in *pairs* of organisms being selected for simultaneously, as explained in the example of the acacia and the ant. The idea of advantage conferred in dyadic units is implied, but not well-developed within the management literature. Units of selection could therefore be individuals, pairs, or may in fact be whole groups.

Group selection implies that advantage is gained at a group level rather than at an individual level and has been rarely examined (Wilkinson, 2006). Group selection in a biological sense can be illustrated by the example of poultry (egg) farmers. Hen breeders have been able to increase overall egg production by breeding from groups of laying hens rather than selecting those that are the best individual layers, that is, the fittest individuals (Muir, 1996; Muir & Craig, 1997). If chickens are selectively bred for only one characteristic (egg production), the chickens become aggressive and cannibalistic, and as a result, total group egg production decreases. By selecting on the basis of group laying (taking the best groups of laying hens and interbreeding these), rather than individual laying capabilities, the resulting offspring group also lays more eggs and allows farmers to maximize efficiency (Muir, 2005; Wilkinson et al., 2007). The underlying accepted rationale behind these results is that within any group, different animals fulfill different group needs.

Within management theory, the idea of group selection is implicit at many levels. At the level of firm with individual employees, resource dependency theory suggests that advantage is gained from maximization of resources (Barney, 1991; Penrose, 1959). Thus, a firm's competitive position is seen as dependent on the mix of individuals in it. There are roles for leaders, followers, team players, creative people, and so on. Each of these individuals has different attributes that they bring to the firm, and the firm as a whole is greater than the sum of these individual attributes because of the symbiosis between these individual actors.

Group selection can also occur for groups of firms, as in the eclectic paradigm, also known as the OLI paradigm (Dunning, 1988, 2001). This has been mostly applied to theories of internationalization and also within the theory of comparative advantage (Ricardo, 1976) and later adapted into Porter's theory on competitive advantage of nations (Porter, 1990). For example, if country A had a "fitter" group of firms producing computers for country B, then country A would be the fittest and therefore more likely to survive. This may occur at a national level but more commonly occurs in regional clusters (Keeble & Wilkinson, 1998). Comparative advantage appears to be formed through agglomeration effects in regional clusters and may result in selection occurring at group rather than individual level (Pouder & St. John, 1996).

Potentially, a more useful application of the notion of group selection is within industries. Group selection could therefore apply to supply chains, networks of firms, or a mixture of these, as in regional clusters.

A simplistic example can illustrate the idea of different units of selection within industries; for example, a firm may coevolve and also be subject to individual and/or group selection. Firm A cooperates with firm B to produce a new product. Firm A has the licensing rights for the product in North America and firm B has the rights in Europe. Within Europe, the regulations then change, which opens up competition, and the new product has a much shorter European life span than in North America. The production of the new product is an example of coevolution; however, in this scenario, individual selection is taking place. However, if a technological breakthrough occurs in this market, which replaces the need for the recently developed product, then firms A and B would be disadvantaged simultaneously, and if this breakthrough technology was successful, firms A and B would be selected against simultaneously and fail. This example, although simplistic, shows that firms can coevolve, but selection can be at the individual or at the dyadic level. These ideas are summarized in Figure 10.1, which shows a supply chain with varying units of selection.

In reality, firms compete simultaneously in many ways: as part of alliances, as part of a supply chain or network, and as individuals. They may therefore be subject to simultaneous individual, dyadic, and group selection (see Figure 10.1). The development of strategic alliances and networks by firms is arguably a coevolutionary adaptation to the simultaneous selection of individuals, dyads, and groups. However the alliances or agreements reached through forming networks can also evolve and change, and this introduces the idea that an abstract entity such as the strategic alliance can also be a unit of change.

The above discussion has gone some way toward delineating the issues involved in applying the analogy of coevolution to a business setting, and in doing so, three main issues arise. The first is the *unit of change* being

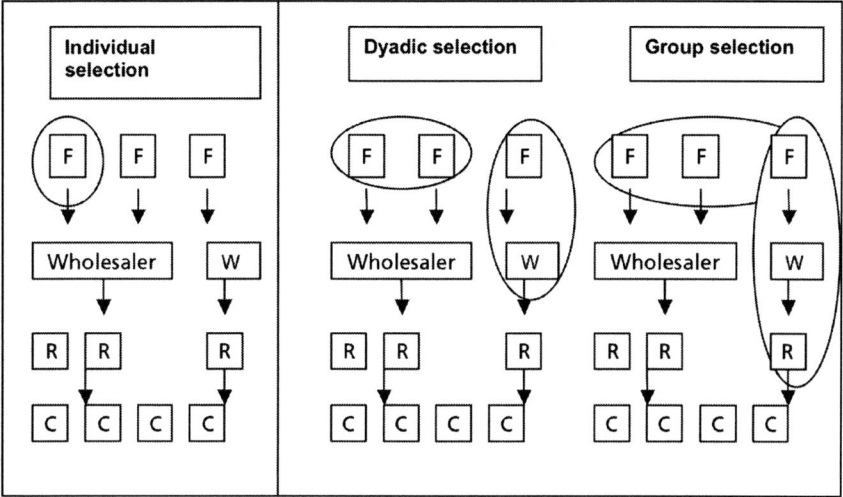

Figure 10.1 Units of selection within a supply chain or industry (Wilson & Hynes, 2009).

considered; whether change occurs at an individual (firm) level or whether it occurs concurrently at dyadic or group (supply chain or network) level. Evolution suggests change initially occurs at individual level, whereas co-evolution considers simultaneous changes with firms and their environment or dyadic pairs of firms. The second issue is the *unit of selection*, which may be at individual level, dyadic or group level, or a combination of these. Third, there is the *mechanism for selection*; is this a result of the "best" being selected, or through a more random process similar to genetic drift? Within the business context, other important issues arise. These include the "consciousness of change": businesses can proactively change themselves and often their environment, whereas in both evolutionary and coevolutionary theory this happens by chance. Another issue is the measure of success or survival: in biological terms, this is strictly the ability to reproduce, whereas in a business context, there may be multiple measures of success. These ideas are summarized in Table 10.1.

The shaded areas in Table 10.1 illustrate the focus of most extant literature, which is concerned with the setting of strategy at a firm level, based on the assumption of individual firm selection through a selective mechanism. However, despite this theoretical development, nearly all empirical work has still been largely firm based, and the unit of selection, or survival, has been the individual firm (Rodrigues & Child, 2003; Wilson & Hynes, 2009). The focus of nearly all previous research has been the basis of the firm's advantage as being brought about by simultaneously changing with the environment or interacting with other firms. This is not inconsistent with

TABLE 10.1 Issues Arising in the Application of Coevolutionary Theory to Business

Theory	Unit of change	Selective Unit	Means of selection
Evolution	Individual (firm)	Individual	Random genetic drift
Evolution	Individual (firm)	Individual	Survival of the fittest
Coevolution	Pairs or more (dyads or chains)	Firm	Random genetic drift
Coevolution	Pairs or more (dyads or chains)	Firm	Survival of the fittest
Coevolution	Pairs or more (dyads or chains)	Dyad or Group/Chain	Random genetic drift
Coevolution	Pairs or more (dyads or chains)	Dyad or Group/Chain	Survival of the fittest

the difference in selection mechanisms hinted at by Volberda and Lewin (2003), where they suggest a cyclical motion through micro- and macroevolutionary measures, which lead to coevolutionary journeys.

Das and Teng (2002, p. 728) further developed this by examining coevolution throughout different stages of alliance development, arguing that there may be "underlying factors that may affect the entire developmental processes that are not examined." This adaptive response to the changing environment can be framed within the industrial life cycle framework. This framework describes the evolution of an industry, including progressive stages of growth, maturity, and decline. Proponents of the framework argue that industry characteristics at each stage require an appropriate organizational structure, decision-making process, and strategy. This context influences the nature and extent of a firm's external resource needs and resource acquisition behavior (Winter, 1995). These resource needs and the characteristics of the industry can be largely influenced by the stage of life cycle that the industry is in and the stage of life cycle that the firm is in. The life cycle literature has focused predominantly on firms entering or exiting an industry (Janovic & McDonald, 1994; Klepper, 1996), and largely on the assumption that firms enter the market alone, compete alone, and are selected alone. Williamson (1985) built on Schumpeter's (1934) early work, which described the industry life cycle as several stages, including the early or exploratory stage, an intermediate development stage, and a mature stage (see Table 10.2). The early stage typically has a high degree of uncertainty, and the primary focus of this stage is the growth of the firm; the intermediate stage is the time at which marketing and manufacturing techniques are sharpened, and finally, a mature industry is one where marketing, manufacturing, and management all reach a relatively advanced degree of refinement. Klepper (1996) suggests that innovation is higher in the initial phase, followed by a period of "shakeout." These studies helped to examine the outcomes of different stages of the industry life cycle. This

TABLE 10.2   Industry Life Cycle with Relevance to Coevolution and Selection

Introduction	Growth	Maturity	Decline
Population unstable; Many small firms with high need for venture capital.	Population remains unstable and growing rapidly, but rules of competition beginning to be established; Shakeout of firms.	Firms compete intensively as market stabilizes. Several dominant firms dominate the market.	Population unstable.
No established supply chain, so many options possible.		Changes in supply chain population ecology have massive impact on producers and consumers; can lead to multilevel coevolution and changes in entire populations.	Changes in supply chain population ecology have massive impact on producers and consumers; can lead to multilevel coevolution and changes in entire populations.
No established standards; many competing technologies.	Establishment of a dominant standard or architecture	One dominant technology with suppliers mostly offering this.	Discontinuous change might mean market is replaced.
Coevolution occurring through strategic alliances; alliances essential to establish industry positions.	Less need for alliances.	A growing need for alliances.	Coevolution occurring through strategic alliances; alliances essential to maintain viability.
Unit of selection is variable.	Unit of selection more focused on individual firms.	Growing trend for selection to involve more than one firm.	As industry declines, group selection becomes more dominant as whole supply chains are affected.

period of shakeout is often when many firms fail. We argue that the importance of the key themes of coevolutionary research differs according to different stages in the industry life cycle (Table 10.2). As illustrated below, this covers the levels and type of cooperation, the stability of the population, the industry structure, and the dominant technology.

Work on emerging industries tends to confirm the idea that there is a high number of small firms at the early stages of industry development, and that after some time of technological and market adjustment, the industry reaches some degree of legitimacy (Mazzucato, 2002; McGahan, Argyres, & Baum, 2004). The adoption of a technology or technological standard by a market can lead to the selection of firms (Hill, 1997). This "shaking out" of firms occurs in the growth stage of an industry. Strategic alliances in this scenario are seen as a way to "keep a foot in the door" for new technologies and has been considered to be a motivating factor for large incumbent technology firms to form many strategic alliances with small firms. By doing so, these large firms hope to retain options in each of the new emerging technologies and therefore be coselected for the winning technology (Hill, 1997; Rice & Galvin, 2006). Thus, it would seem that at emerging stages of an industry, where many small players enter the field, along with a small number of larger firms, coevolution may be a better explanation for change, and coselection is a better explanatory variable than evolution and individual selection. Firms often work codependently at this stage, often as a result of resource deficiency, and the process of working together in a rapidly changing environment can result in concurrent change within the organizations. Much of the mainstream strategy literature (Bowman & Faulkner, 1996; Porter, 1985) focuses on firm strategy, monitoring the environment leading to strategic change and success or failure (Ansoff, 1957); and the theory of evolution has been commonly applied to these middle stages of the industry life cycle.

Finally, for industries in decline, the number of firms is shrinking, and demand is relatively static or declining for a product. In this scenario, complete supply chains are selected for together; companies supplying the wrong downstream buyer may fail at the same time and because of the downstream seller. There is little chance for these companies to find other market opportunities as market supply chains are established and mature. Many small companies need to work together through strategic alliances at this stage to ensure that the group is selected for, rather than the individual firm; the overall market size does not increase, so the only strategy for growth is increasing or retaining market share (Klepper, 1996).

METHODOLOGY

This study examined the application of the coevolution literature to strategic alliance formation in the UK fresh produce industry, and to the Australian biotechnology industry; two very differing industries, at distinct stages of their life cycle. The issues discussed above were explored and developed through the use of a qualitative approach, allowing an understanding of a "complex, holistic picture" (Cresswell, 1998). Data was collected from secondary sources, extensive semistructured interviews with one or more members of the senior management team of the UK and Australian businesses on-site, participant observation in meetings with overseas partners in three European countries, and the use of records and follow-ups with one or more senior members of each business over a period of 8 months. This is an area where little empirical research has been conducted. The use of in-depth interviews allowed the researcher to gain an insight into these factors in a way that could not be achieved through a quantitative survey, building up a picture of interconnection rather than a list of single key factors. The interviews were conducted at the respondent's place of work. Given the sensitive nature of the contents of the interview, most interviews were conducted in a private office with only the researcher and the interviewee present. The information obtained from all respondents was obtained only after guarantees about the confidentiality of any disclosures. Immediately after the interview, the taped transcripts were checked and the interview notes were read to ensure there were no areas of ambiguity or uncertainty. Each interview varied in length, lasting between 1 and 3 hours.

The samples for the UK and Australian interviews were chosen on a nonprobability judgement basis. The UK data was stratified in terms of geographical area and produce type to obtain a spread of producers across the country and covering the main produce types. A range of firm size and ownership profiles was chosen. In total, 33 UK producers were contacted and 20 interviewed. The Australian sample was selected after inviting all listed biotechnology firms within Queensland. Many declined to be interviewed; the final sample included 13 organizations, which all gave interviews together with industry associations. Although a relatively small sample, this is consistent with other qualitative research samples, which are often very small, even a single case. Indeed, Patton (2002) argues that the validity, meaningfulness, and insights generated from qualitative inquiry has more to do with the information richness of the cases selected and the observational/analytical capabilities of the researcher than with sample size. Patterns and themes were identified in the data following a variation on content analysis outlined by Miles and Huberman (1984) and Easterby-Smith, Thorpe, and Lowe (1991). Patterns of data were assigned into categories and judged according to internal homogeneity and external heterogeneity, and links between constructs were examined.

ANALYSIS AND DISCUSSION

In this study, all the alliances were originally driven by needs from one or both firms for the partners' critical resources, supporting a resource-based view (Barney, 2001; Varadarajan & Cunningham, 1995). However, these resources varied from products, money, access to networks, and/or endorsement. All the alliances reported on had been operational for more than 1 year and in most cases, much longer than that.

The Australian Biotechnology Industry: An Emerging Industry?

The Queensland Government is committed to establishing the State as the center of excellence in biotechnology in the Asia Pacific and by 2025 will employ over 16,000 people and generate $4 billion in revenues to an industry worth $20 billion. Queensland's biotechnology industry currently comprises around 88 companies and 68 biotechnology-related research institutes. Combined, these organizations employed over 5,200 people and generated an estimated $690 million in revenues in 2004/2005 (Thorburn, Parbeen, & Rallapalli, 2006).

In addition, the "smart state" strategy encourages particular types of biotechnology industry, primarily those focused on human health; and several strategies have been put in place to encourage start-ups including cooperative networks. The source of financing for most biotechnology companies in this region remains commercial venture capitalists. Many start-ups are single product or service companies, and since the commercialization of biotechnology, products can be marketed between 5 and 20 years after discovery; many small companies are found in these early development stages. The companies included in this study largely fell into this category.

Most companies interviewed were small start-ups with fewer than 10 employees; some were still incubator firms, but others had been around longer. All had formed strategic alliances. These ranged from R&D projects, licensing in/out agreements, clinical trials of varying degrees, and upscaling to commercial production of new materials. Some alliances spanned marketing and finance as well, although these were less common. These small biotechnology firms did not have enough resources and actively sought out a range of strategic alliances, including suppliers, collaborators, and large companies who could act as guarantors of reputation/quality that would then lead them to better outcomes in different ways: producing products, testing drugs, and raising venture capital. These firms all confirmed that they could not survive on their own. Examples of this are "In Australia, they [other companies] don't have the resources to set up their own labs in general; they are one-man operations or two at best, so they have to outsource everything, so therefore, we are very good partners to work with," and "It [the alliance] ... is a mechanism by which we can leverage our finance needs if you like and be able to roll over the grant into the next option period."

Every firm interviewed had multiple alliances, and these had, by the nature of being involved in these alliances, changed the firms. In some instances, they led to new alliance opportunities, showing evidence of co-evolution at several levels: between firms; between firms and the alliance; and between alliances, firms, and the environment. Some showed evidence of changing with their alliance partners over time, but others used alliances sparingly and for fixed portions of time to help with resource needs.

> **Q:** And do you think that relationship with X has led to other opportunities that you maybe would not have had without it?
>
> **A:** Well it is interesting. They have actually brought some clients to [Firm A] and now that we are doing the bioanalyticals for [Firm A], we are actually now working more closely with [X], so we had an alliance with them, and another alliance with them, and now we have got the three-way thing happening and it is interesting. [Firm A] have a consultant who brings a lot of clients to them, and now we are starting to work with their consultant as well, so it is interesting how things evolve. It starts off here, but then it mushrooms.

The need for survival was also expressed in other ways; some firms saw alliances as ways to increase their survival changes by "hedging their bets" on new emerging technologies:

> Because you cannot pick the winners on early-stage stuff, you are better off actually having a very large portfolio [of alliances]. So we have found that by working with them, they don't want to invest in building a small team of their own because that is as much as their resource could be.

For other firms, being part of the "right" strategic alliance gave credibility to the company, and they believed this would lead to increased venture capital (VC) funding opportunities. A slightly surprising driving force behind the structure of the firms, and the way in which they worked together or coevolved, was the pressure from VCs to exit the industry.

> One of the other reasons for it is the venture capital industry here, and they are very, very focused on exits, and they want exits within a five-year time-frame usually and at the very outside, somewhere between five and ten. And if you are doing pharmaceutical development, then you are not going to get all that far in five years. . . . It does not create large companies. . . . It is just all about money; it is all about investment. It is really not about long-term economic development at all.

Given that evolution and coevolution are about mechanisms of change and adapting to the environment, the analogy given by these two theories fails to explain a common phenomenon in this industry; that is, of having an exit strategy at a fairly early age of the company. However, even when early exit was seen as the end point for a company, alliances were seen as a mechanism to achieve this, showing that in this industry, coevolving to form alliances and coevolving to make these alliances work ended in the end of one company through a merger to another:

> The exit strategy for X is a trade sale, and that will either happen in the next two years or X will disappear. It is a finite end to the whole thing, and we have the technology. We have driven it about as far as it needs to go. We don't do much in the way of R&D, we just try to sell the product, and we either do or we don't. I mean, if we don't, then we will file the patent, so to speak, and keep it going for the moment, but there are enough candles to keep the patents alive, because the technology may not be seen as desirable this year, but it may be seen as desirable in a couple of years' time.

This dependence on venture capital was significant, but perhaps more so in this particular industry, was the difficulty in scaling up from discovery to testing (clinical trials) and then scaling up once more before commercialization. These growth stages appeared to be the impetus for exiting the industry and selling off the intellectual property. Another company said,

> But I think, you know, there are lots and lots of small companies for whom $1 million/$2 million gets them a prototype and a proof of concept, and another $5 million gets them convincingly close to the market, and then they suddenly realize, you know what, to get manufacturing going and things like that, we need $20/$30/$80 million. Where are we going to find that? Particularly in the last six to nine months, and I suspect for the next six months, you would not turn to the public markets for raising that money. You really have to try to find a big company that is going, you know, they are going to eat your lunch, but you know that is part of the deal you have gotta do.

This worked both for small biotechnology firms and the larger pharmaceutical firms that they partnered with; however, it was clear that the respondent felt that the two firms did not "need" each other anymore, perhaps implying that there were stages of development that clearly showed coselection, but that this period was now passed. This company cited the case of an alliance that had been used to help with successful product development in clinical trials and how that very success had nullified the need for the alliance to be ongoing:

> That is an interesting question. I suppose it is because we probably don't need them now as much as we did. I mean, they still don't need us in the sense that they can survive without us, their product would stand on its own, it is not on the market yet, but it probably will be in the not-too-distant future. Our product does not need theirs anymore either, but we would still prefer to go with them. In other words, of the options available now, there are more than there

were then, but as it still happens, that is the best plan for us, I suspect, to do it, not least because they are now with really big pharmas now, which suits us because that is eventually where we see our product as targeted.

In summary, this is an industry in an emerging state; most of the companies are young and heavily into product development. The biotechnology industry within Queensland is determined very much by its environment—the ability to seek funding and local government initiatives—and these external factors played a large role in determining which alliances were entered into. All firms sought out alliances initially for resource needs, and most alliances showed coevolutionary change over a period of time between the firms, the firm and the alliance, and the environment. Sometimes this extended to locating and entering new alliances. Moreover, some firms hinted that the relationships they had formed through alliances increased the likelihood of gaining funding, and this suggested a change from individual selection to dyadic selection.

The UK Fresh Produce Industry: A Mature/Declining Industry

Changes in the UK retail food industry over the last 20 years have had an important effect on the fresh produce sector in the UK with the emergence of a few key firms in the industry. The wholesale markets, traditionally the most important outlet for agricultural produce, have decreased numerically and in relative importance (Mintel Market Intelligence, 2005), and in the past few years, the few major food retailing chains have become the dominant force in food retailing. By 2005, these chains accounted for 84% of all fresh fruit and vegetables sold in the UK (Mintel Market Intelligence, 2005).

Firms who are not supplying these retailers have come under significant competitive pressure, and many have exited the industry. Only 13% of fruit growers and 7% of vegetable growers had sales of £1 million or more in 2007, and only 5 fruit and 60 vegetable growers had sales of more than £5 million (DEFRA, 2008). Yet the majority of farm holdings in horticulture are small, specialist businesses, often operating on a regional basis for production and often specializing in particular areas of the market.

In common with the biotechnology industry, there were recurring themes in this dataset of resource-driven needs for strategic alliance on both sides of the alliance dyad. UK growers sought partners who could work with them to supply the UK market outside the UK growing season and to develop new product ranges. The key objective and strategic value of all the alliances was to find partners to provide consistent high quality product when the UK firms could not provide it themselves as demanded by the UK retailers. For partner firms, the major motivating force to form strategic alliances was gaining access to the UK market. This market was seen as highly lucrative, with high barriers to entry. The motivation to form an alliance for the UK firm can be seen as an attempt to change the unit of selection from an individual firm to a dyad. All the firms interviewed had chosen to form alliances rather than expand abroad through vertical integration. This choice, which is central to transactions cost theory, was influenced by two factors: relative costs and risk. Most firms did not have the financial resources to even consider expansion. This view was encapsulated by a number of growers.

> The costs of getting a partnership up and going are much lower than expanding abroad as a firm. . . . If we wanted to have as much land under cultivation as in the UK, it would require an investment of £50 million. The only thing you can do is find a willing partner.

The alliances in this study showed a high degree of integration between the partner firms. Partners inputed resources and worked together on a continuing basis, evolving at both the alliance level, which often changed from its initial objectives and also resulting in changes within the originating firms. This shows simultaneous coevolution between the firm and the alliance, and the firm and partner firm, supporting Das and Teng's (2002) definition of coevolution as different parts of a system evolving simultaneously and interacting with each other so that one partner's evolution is affected by another partner's evolution. In common with the biotechnology industry, there is evidence of these alliances evolving out of other relationships and these alliances themselves evolving both in terms of structure and of scope over time. In total, 14 (40%) of the alliances were between firms who had had prior trading relationships, which then developed into an alliance. Another 12 included firms learning about their potential existing partners through other existing trading relationships, such as wholesalers, suppliers of equipment and seed, agents, and importers. Four firms learned about their partners through informal networks in the industry, and only two had no prior knowledge of their partner. None of the firms had had previous alliances with their partner, although this has largely to do with the fact that most firms had little alliance activity before these current alliances. The alliance itself also became a new organizational form. So while the firms still saw themselves as disparate entities in terms of their identity, they regarded the alliance as a form in its own right, as noted, "Our partnership is an entity in its own right, separate from both ours and our partner's business" and "There is great symbiosis. Both parties are as dependent on each other for things to work."

Flexibility of the alliance to change with the changing objectives, resources, and relative power of the partners was also a significant determinant of alliance success, as cited by others (Bleeke & Ernst 1991; Doz, 1996; Dyer & Singh, 1998): "The best alliances are unstructured, loose, not written down, but based on mutual trust and acceptance of each others' position, point of view, and efforts. That is what we have," and "Our supplier has a business now that is worth four times what it was three years ago, and it is still growing. Both of us are now very dependent on each other."

In three alliances, the partners were looking for a significant increase in integration between the partner firms through investigating the options for a joint venture, and one firm was actually in the process of setting up a joint venture. This can be explained as either an evolutionary process for the alliance or a coevolutionary process of the two firms. In these cases, this change in structural form was driven by a need for increased control over the day-to-day running of the relationship.

> We have decided that we need to be growing in Spain. We are not seeing the improvements in cultural practices coming through as quickly as we would like. The reason we are doing it with [partner firm] is in part a hand-holding exercise. [Partner firm] have experience of what is going down in Spain and for the first few years it will be much better if we have them showing us the ropes...there are things that happen in Spain that wouldn't happen in other countries.

The performance of the alliances was important to the UK growers because without alliances, the key relationships with UK multiple retailers were jeopardized. But equally, there were risks: switching to other partner firms might take a year until the next growing season, and there was a risk that by that time, other growers might have taken the "best" partners. Additional key benefits included new product development, development of technical skills, market information, technological interchange, interchange of academic knowledge, expansion of potential markets, and networking opportunities. In general, the more integrated the alliance was in the firm, and the more open the alliance, the more additional benefits the firms got from the alliance. Thus firms who saw the alliances as a key part of their supply network where both parties were working toward the development of the business tended to have alliances wherein partners were involved in all areas of each others' business such as new product development, and no part of the business was out of bounds. These alliances all brought with them a number of additional benefits other than those that were the key drivers for alliance formation themselves.

Where there were changes in the environment, alliances could falter. An example of this was changing requirements during supply seasons. For most of the year, the source of product was clearly defined by the growing conditions in the countries concerned. Therefore the period when the UK partner needed their alliance partner to supply product was clearly demarcated. However, technological improvements in growing and storage techniques have meant that the crossover periods from end of season in one country and beginning of season in another are becoming increasingly blurred and longer in duration. This has meant that at these times, alliance partners were both growing product that they wanted to supply to their end customer, and therefore the dependence on each other changed. The alliance between the two firms needed to change or coevolve in this instance with changes in the environment:

> The key factor that is likely to affect our relationship is the ever-lengthening seasons. We [Firm B] want to grow longer into the autumn and start earlier, and our partners want to continue longer into the traditional UK summer season and start earlier in the autumn. This is likely to become a bigger issue.

The balance of needs was also affected when the focal firm was no longer necessary to provide the key resource driver for the partner firm, notably access to the UK market. Two firms had had experience of their partners trying to cut them out of the supply chain. For both of them, this had led to the end of the alliance relationships: "Partnerships can go wrong. We have had lots of experience of suppliers sending product to a more profitable customer or claiming not to have a crop. Trust is crucial."

In summary, a large proportion of alliances in this industry grew out of relationships with firms that they had already been involved with on a trading basis or known through third parties. The strongest driving force was environmental, and firms reacted to environmental change by forming alliances, thus showing a degree of coevolution. The alliance relationships also coevolved in terms of scope and operations and in some instances in terms of new emerging structures, quite separate from those of the two firms. In this mature/declining industry, coevolution through alliance formation and during the alliance life span was seen as a survival mechanism, and the unit of selection was therefore changed to be the dyad rather than the single firm.

CONCLUSIONS

This study has examined the application of coevolutionary theory and applied this to Das and Teng's (2002) framework of formation, operation, and outcome of strategic alliances. The use and misuse of the terms evolution and coevolution have been explored by returning to the original biological context. In doing so, the issues involved in applying these theories to business have become more explicit. First, there is the issue of the mechanism of selection. Second is the issue of what is being selected: is this at the firm level, or is there a more complex mixture of dyadic or group selection occurring? This study extended this work by examining the coevolutionary process within the context of the industry life cycle, at times where selection is most intense. At least at the early and very late stages of industry change, coevolution appears to provide a better explanation for the success or failure of individual firms and of dyads and groups of firms.

The empirical evidence suggested that firms sometimes *chose* to coevolve into dyadic forms as a means of consciously trying to alter the unit of selection (Barney, 2001). Strategic alliances are formed by firms wishing to compete together either in dyadic form or as supply chains. Firms actively tried to move from competing on an individual basis to competing as a group/supply chain, while simultaneously recognizing the requirement for competitiveness at firm, alliance, dyad, and supply chain levels. Where this happens early in the life stage of a firm, this is often seen as a conscious mechanism to avoid selection as a single unit; instead, opting to be selected at a group level along with the dominant firm in the strategic alliance.

Second, the alliances themselves sometimes caused change within the individual firms, dyads, and supply chains, and firms seemed to view alliances as discrete forms in their own right. This supports to some degree the idea of the unit of change being simultaneously single, dyadic, and group in nature in a coevolutionary manner. In addition, it suggests that coevolution occurs not just between the firm and its environment, but that the alliance itself can also coevolve, and that firms change because of each other. At the latter stage of industry life cycle, this dyadic or group change is seen as essential to remaining in the market and to prevent selection against all levels of competition; individual firms see being in a reliable partnership as an essential mechanism to avoid being cut out of the supply chain.

A third factor is the outcome of change. The overwhelming positive outcomes of alliances in this study suggest firms that have made the coevolutionary change to alliances or chains succeeded. At the early stage of the biotechnology industry, few firms chose to operate in isolation, and government subsidies, incentives, and local action groups ensure that this is a high-visibility issue. Not being part of the club would be a hazardous move for a new small player. Within the mature and more disparate and fragmented industry of fresh produce, strategic alliances and the ability to coevolve have kept small players alive and forced the selection to be made at group level. In industries where little turbulence exists or where firms perceive little risk, less change may occur, and the formation of strategic alliances may be less. However, in this study, the emerging industry players and the mature industry players both sought out alliances with the view that they would enhance the success of the company, or at least ensure its survival.

There may also be implications for selection processes in different industries so that the balance between natural selection and random drift differs. The alliances themselves sometimes seemed to be subject to random drift and seeking satisfactory solutions rather than optimizing solutions. This has strong implications for managerial practice since it may be that in some environments, selection is not on "fitness" or may not even occur at all. Indeed, in new industries where many small companies start up, there may be a period of random drift. This remains an issue worthy of future research.

In a declining industry, firms also viewed themselves as succeeding because they were part of an alliance relationship. In this industry, there was a great deal of change at this time, with the balance of power in the supply chain held by the dominant multiple retail customers. This supply chain structure acted as the catalyst for this coevolutionary change.

Within the emerging industry of biotechnology, the industry norms appear to have predefined life cycles for this industry sector: instead of building companies that commercialize one product and then move onto the next, the structure seems to define that companies establish, form alliances, coevolve for a period of time, leverage the alliances, and then find an exit strategy. This, in some ways, contradicts the underpinnings of the industry life cycle, which suggests there is a shakeout based on market effectiveness and efficiencies. It would appear that firms, in fact, are established only to exist through this emerging industry period. During this time, they are dependent on the coevolution of alliances and are indeed selected by the results of their alliance participation. The need to use strategic alliances to survive the first emerging stage of product, market, or company growth was clear. The companies worked closely with multiple alliance partners, and this was clear evidence of coevolution. The unit of selection is less clear; without the alliances, the companies would have failed immediately as they lacked resources, yet it is unclear in this study whether the dependence on any one firm resulted in coselection.

There are, of course, limitations with this study; the two industries in this chapter came from differing countries and were both relatively small sample sizes. Biotechnology is not a clear-cut example because there are few direct competitors in the start-up stage. Until an industry has reached a level of legitimacy, this is common among emerging industries (Aldrich & Fiol, 1994). The UK fresh produce industry is one that has gone through unprecedented change as the supermarkets converge and dominate the supply chain. Further research should look at more industries to see if the patterns here were, in large, determined by the environment that these firms operated in, or perhaps whether the life stage of the industry is, in fact, a significant factor in evolutionary and coevolutionary behavior.

REFERENCES

Aldrich, H. E., & Fiol, C. M. (1994). Fools rush in? The institutional context of industry creation. *Academy of Management Review, 19,* 645–670.

Ansoff, H. (1957). Strategies for diversification. *Harvard Business Review, 35*(5), 113–124.

Barney, J. B. (1991). Firm resources and sustained competitive advantage. *Journal of Management, 17,* 99–120.

Barney, J. B. (2001). Resource-based theories of competitive advantage: A ten-year retrospective on the resource-based view. *Journal of Management, 27,* 643–650.

Bowman C., & Faulkner, D. (1996). Competitive and corporate strategy. London, England: Irwin Professional Publishing.

Bleeke, J., & Ernst, D. (1991). The way to win in cross-border alliances. *Harvard Business Review, 69*(6), 127–135.

Chandler, A. (1962). *Strategy and structure.* Cambridge, MA: MIT Press.

Cresswell, J. W. (1998). *Qualitative inquiry and research design: Choosing among five traditions.* Thousand Oaks, CA: Sage.

Das, T. K., & Teng, B. (2000). A resource-based theory of strategic alliances. *Journal of Management, 26,* 31–61.

Das, T. K., & Teng, B. (2002). The dynamics of alliance conditions in the alliance development process. *Journal of Management Studies, 39,* 725–746.

DEFRA. (2008). *Farm incomes in the UK.* London, England: Department for the Environment Food and Rural Affairs (DEFRA).

Doz, Y. (1996). The evolution of cooperation in strategic alliances: Initial conditions or learning processes? *Strategic Management Journal, 17*(S1), 55–84.

Dyer, J., & Singh, H. (1998). The relational view: Co-operative strategy and sources of inter-organizational competitive advantage. *Academy of Management Review, 23,* 660–679.

Dunning, J. H. (1988). Explaining international production. London, England: Unwin Hyman.

Dunning, J. H. (2001). The eclectic (OLI) paradigm of international production: Past, present and future. *International Journal of the Economics of Business, 8*(2), 173–190.

Easterby-Smith, M., Thorpe R., & Lowe, A. (1991). *Management research: An introduction.* Newbury Park, CA: Sage.

Garcia-Pont, C., & Nohria. N. (1999). Local versus global mimetism: The dynamics of alliance formation in the automobile industry. *Strategic Management Journal, 23,* 307–321.

Grant, R. M., & Baden-Fuller, C. (2004). A knowledge accessing theory of strategic alliances. *Journal of Management Studies, 41,* 61–84.

Gulati, R. (1999). Network location and learning: The influence of network resources and firm capabilities on alliance formation. *Strategic Management Journal, 20,* 397–420.

Gulati, R., & Gargiulo. M. (1999). Where do interorganizational networks come from? *American Journal of Sociology, 104,* 1439–1438.

Gulati, R., Nohria, N., & Zaheer, A. (2000). Strategic networks. *Strategic Management Journal, 21,* 203–215.

Hennart, J.-F. (1998). A transaction costs theory of equity joint ventures. *Strategic Management Journal, 9,* 361–374.

Hill, C. E. (1997). Establishing a standard: Competitive strategy and technological standards in winner takes all industries. *Academy of Management Executive, 11*(2), 7–22.

Huyens, M., Baden-Fuller, C., van den Bosch, F. A. J., & Volberda, H. W. (2001). Co-evolution of firm capabilities and industry. *Organization Studies, 22,* 971–1012.

Janovic, B., & MacDonald, G. M. (1994). The life cycle of a competitive industry. *Journal of Political Economy, 102*(2), 322–347.

Keeble, D., & Wilkinson, F. (1998). Collective learning and knowledge development in the evolution of regional clusters of high technology SMEs in Europe. *Regional Studies, 33*(4), 295–303.

Klepper, S. (1996). Entry, exit, growth, and innovation over the product life cycle. *American Economic Review, 86,* 562–583.

Kogut, B. (1988). Joint ventures: Theoretical and empirical perspectives. *Strategic Management Journal, 9,* 319–332.

Koza, M. P., & Lewin, A. Y. (1988). The co-evolution of strategic alliances. *Organization Science, 9,* 255–264.

Lande, R. (1976). Natural selection and random genetic drift in phenotypic evolution. *Evolution, 30,* 314–334.

Lewin, A. Y., Long, C. P., & Carroll, T. N. (1999). The co-evolution of new organizational forms. *Organization Science, 10,* 535–550.

Lewin, A. Y., & Volberda, H. W. (1999). Prolegomena on co-evolution: A framework for research on strategy and new organizational forms. *Organization Science, 10,* 519–534.

Mazzucato, M. (2002). The PC industry: New economy or early life-cycle? *Review of Economic Dynamics, 5,* 318–345.

McGahan, A. M., Argyres, N., & Baum, J. A. C. (2004). Context, technology and strategy: Forging new perspectives on the industry life cycle. *Advances in Strategic Management, 21,* 1–21.

Miles, M. B., & Huberman, A. M. (1984). *Qualitative data analysis: A sourcebook of new methods.* London, England: Sage.

Mintel Market Intelligence. (2005). *Fresh fruit and vegetables–U.K.* London, England: Mintel International Group.

Muir, W. M. (1996). Group selection for adaptation to multiple-hen cages: Selection program and direct responses. *Poultry Science, 75,* 447–458.

Muir, W. M. (2005). Incorporation of competitive effects in forest tree or animal breeding programs. *Genetics, 170,* 1247–1259.

Muir, W. M., & Craig, J. V. (1997). Improving animal well-being through genetic selection. *Poultry Science, 77,* 1781–1788.

Parkhe, A. (1998). Understanding trust in international alliances. *Journal of World Business, 33,* 219–239.

Patton, M. Q. (2002). *Qualitative research and evaluation methods.* Thousand Oaks, CA: Sage.

Penrose, E. T. (1959). *The theory of the growth of the firm.* New York, NY: John Wiley.

Porter, M. E. (1985). *Competitive advantage.* New York, NY: Free Press.

Porter, M. E. (1990). *The competitive advantage of nations.* New York, NY: Free Press.

Pouder, R., & St. John, C. H. (1996). Hot spots and blind spots: Geographical clusters of firms and innovations. *Academy of Management Review, 21,* 1192–1226.

Ricardo, D. (1976). *The principles of political economy and taxation* [1817 reprint]. London, England: Dent.

Rice, J., & Galvin, P. (2006). Alliance patterns during industry life cycle emergence: The case of Ericsson and Nokia. *Technovation, 26,* 384–395.

Rodrigues, S., & Child, J. (2003). Co-evolution in an institutionalized environment. *Journal of Management Studies, 40,* 2137–2162.

Schumpeter, J. (1934). *The theory of economic development.* Cambridge, MA: Harvard University Press.

Supphellen, M., Haugland, S. A., & Korneliussen, T. (2002). SMEs in search of international strategic alliances: Perceived importance of personal information sources. *Journal of Business Research, 55,* 785–795.

Thorburn, L., Parbeen, S., & Rallapalli, S., (2006). *Queensland biotechnology report.* Canberra, Australia: Innovation Dynamics Pty Ltd.

Varadarajan, P. R., & Cunningham, M. H. (1995). Strategic alliances: A synthesis of conceptual foundations. *Journal of the Academy of Marketing Science, 23,* 282–296.

Volberda H. W., & Lewin, A. Y. (2003). Co-evolutionary dynamics within and between firms: From evolution to co-evolution. *Journal of Management Studies, 40,* 2111–2136.

Weber, M. (1978). *Economy and society: An outline of interpretive sociology* (G. Roth & C. Wittich, Trans.). Berkeley: University of California Press.

Wilkinson I. F. (2006). The evolution of an evolutionary perspective on B2B business. *Journal of Business and Industrial Marketing, 21,* 458–465.

Wilkinson, I., Young, L., & Ladley, D. (2007, August 30–September 1). *Group selection versus individual selection and the evolution of cooperation in business networks.* Proceedings of the conference on Industrial Marketing and Purchasing, Manchester, England.

Williamson, O. E. (1985). *The economic institutions of capitalism: Firms, markets, relational contracting.* New York, NY: Free Press.

Wilson, J., & Hynes, N. (2009). Co-evolution of firms and strategic alliances: Theory and empirical evidence. *Journal of Technological Forecasting and Social Change, 76,* 620–628.

Winter, S. (1995). Four R's of profitability: Rents, resources, routines, and replication. In C. A. Montgomery (Ed.), *Resource-based and evolutionary theories of the firm* (pp. 147–178). Boston, MA: Kluwer.

CHAPTER 11

SOCIAL TECHNOLOGY AND STABILITY/TRANSFORMATION OF ALLIANCE NETWORKS

Dilemmas and Paradoxes of Cooperation

Sof Thrane
Jan Mouritsen

ABSTRACT

This chapter analyzes and develops the concept of social technologies in alliance networks. The literature has pointed to the importance of several elements of social technologies such as shared values, trust, and cooperative behavior in sustaining and developing networks. This chapter adds to the literature through showing how the mobilization of the social technology of cooperative behavior is a nonlinear and fragile accomplishment. The mobilization of social technologies is uncertain because alliance networks are formed to exploit complementarity and diversity. Diversity, however, separates the network into groups around faultlines demarcating contradictory social structures. The utilization and mobilization of social technologies in alliance networks are therefore paradoxical. On the one hand, alliances and networks thrive on diversity and, on the other hand, diversity and faultlines

Management Dynamics in Strategic Alliances, pages 237–266
Copyright © 2012 by Information Age Publishing

237

make collective decision making difficult. Alliance networks are therefore highly unstable and complex since conformity is necessary for social technology to work, yet diversity is necessary to make complementarity productive. This chapter suggests that alliances are especially prone to conflict and disintegration when collective decisions are made in the alliance, whereas bilateral or dyadic interactions flow more smoothly. These findings are based on a longitudinal study of two alliance networks. The alliance networks consist of potential competitors who ally in order to exploit complementarities based on differences in technological competencies and geographic scope as well as to enhance credibility to efforts at diversification, their businesses, and winning large contracts.

INTRODUCTION

Research on interorganizational networks identifies the importance of social technologies such as trust and shared valued in sustaining, developing, and controlling interfirm networks and alliances. Shared values and trust can replace formal types of controls and safeguards as these are more effective in building relational advantages. Dyer and Singh hypothesize that "The greater the alliance partners' ability is to employ *informal* self-enforcing safeguards (e.g., trust) rather than *formal* self-enforcing safeguards (e.g., financial hostages), the greater the potential will be for relational rent, owing to (1) lower marginal costs and (2) difficulty of imitation" (Dyer & Singh, 1998, p. 671; emphasis in original).

Shared values and trust are thus control mechanisms. They are a governance structure capable of increasing rents to interfirm cooperation. Social control is portrayed as increasing with time: "Several theories suggest that cooperative behavior between firms increases with the length of the relationship" (Inkpen & Currall, 2004, p. 593; Tomkins, 2001). Trust is said to be part of a virtuous circle in which initial trust lowers cost and feeds into a greater reliance on social controls: "The greater the initial level of trust between joint venture partners, the lower the initial joint venture monitoring and control costs by the partners and the greater the initial reliance on social controls" (Inkpen & Currall, 2004, p. 590). Faems, Janssens, Madhok, and van Looy (2008) study the relationship between structural (contracts) and relational (trust) perspectives, arguing that contractual flexibility feeds into alliance dynamics with increasing trust and returns to the relationship. Cooperative behavior and trust are thus a potentially powerful social technology capable of lowering cost and developing the relationship. Trust is "the magic in alliance success" (Koza, as cited in Young-Ybarra & Wiersema, 1999, p. 439).

Despite the promises of social technologies in developing a network or relationship, it has been suggested that the effects of social technologies diminish over time. If a joint venture leads to the transfer of skills, the relative bargaining power of each party may change and provide incentives for opportunistic behavior leading to an increase in formal controls (Inkpen & Currall, 2004; Khanna, Gulati & Nohria, 1998). Yet the literature generally lacks longitudinal studies of the ways in which social technologies emerge and develop (Adler & Kwon, 2002; Ariño & de la Torre, 1998; Koza & Lewin, 1998). Furthermore, withdrawal from alliances is a neglected subject within the literature (Greve, Baum, Mitsuhashi, & Rowley, 2010).

This chapter employs longitudinal analysis to study two alliance networks, which are "multiparty alliances, in which multilateral transactions among the network members are facilitated by the network...network members are co-specialized, bringing a unique value adding capability, such as knowledge resources or market access, to the network" (Koza & Lewin, 1999, p. 639). Such alliances are instable (Das & Teng, 2000), operating far from equilibrium. This is why it is interesting to study the complexities and emergence of social structures and technologies. The chapter draws on structuration theory (Giddens, 1984) and research on group dynamics (Pelled, Eisenhardt, & Xin, 1999), and argues that social technologies are paradoxical in a collective network mode, such as when joint decisions are made, where they may actualize contradictions and transform them into conflicts.

DEVELOPMENT OF THEORY

The Social Technology of Networks

The literature on interfirm alliances and networks indicates that formal governance mechanisms such as contracts and hostages should be supplanted by informal social mechanisms such as trust and norms of cooperative behavior (Dyer & Chu, 2003; Dyer & Singh, 1998; Husted & Folger, 2004; Inkpen & Currall, 2004; Young-Ybarra & Wiersema, 1999; Zollo, Reuer & Singh, 2002). Social technologies are said to be more effective than formal governance mechanisms in generating relational advantages and capabilities (Dyer & Chu, 2003; Dyer & Singh, 1998) and in minimizing transaction and production cost. Dyer and Chu found that trust lowered ex post transaction cost (negotiation cost) and concluded that "trust [is] unique as a governance mechanism because the investments that trading partners make to build trust often simultaneously create economic value (beyond minimizing transaction costs) in the exchange relationship" (Dyer & Chu, 2003, p. 66).

The social technology of networks has been proposed to stand for many elements such as justice (Husted & Folger, 2004), social capital (Bolino, 2002; Frank & Yasumoto, 1998; Gargiulo & Benassi, 2000; Leenders &

Gabbay, 1999; Nahapiet & Ghoshal, 1998; Portes, 1998; Tsai, 2000; Walker, Kogut, & Shan, 1997; Yli-Renko, Autio, & Sapienza, 2001), trust (Inkpen & Currall, 2004; Young-Ybarra & Wiersema, 1999), interorganizational routines (Zollo et al., 2002), cooperation vs. competition (Das & Teng, 2000), short-term vs. long-term orientation (Das & Teng, 2000), shared values (Young-Ybarra & Wiersema, 1999), and network identity and learning routines (Dyer & Nobeoka, 2000).

Despite these different emphases, social technologies are generally understood as generalized factors that shape practices and improve performance linearly and directly (for an exception, see Das & Teng, 2000). Social technology has been defined as concerned "with what exists as a revelation of what ought to be, and of the method of realizing what ought to be" (Henderson, 1901, p. 468). They identify an ideal and methods of reaching these ideals. Social technologies reflect "a system or mechanism adapted to further in the best possible way all the interests...of the entire community (Henderson, 1901, p. 471). The social technology of networks thus entails a vision of how the network should function, what the goals of the network should be, and methods of realizing its intended functioning, and it is supposed to further the interest of all the members of the network. A network "must agree on a policy because they must live together, and must find a practicable method of realizing the covenanted end. Thus they are social technologist" (Henderson, 1912, p. 216).

Social technologies are mobilized in concrete settings by actors in a network. The social technology of networks entails, as stated above, elements such as shared values, trust, common identity and learning, and interorganizational routines, which participants must agree on in order to further the goals of the network. Yet this position seems to neglect a fundamental feature of social life: social systems are differentiated in terms of values, trust, and acceptance of the use of power (Giddens, 1984).

The evolution and change of social technology is, furthermore, a process. Whether this evolution is effective is a much more difficult question, since it is an open question if shared values are always beneficial (Young-Ybarra & Wiersema, 1999). If network partners have less-than-fully common interests and values, it may not be likely that common goals evolve without problems.

In an alliance network that consists of multiple partners and focuses on the exploitation of complementary resources, homogeneity in firm values is unlikely. Diversity, which is understood as differences in firms' or partners' normative orientations (e.g., risk aversion, view of what effective network structures are) and that may be related to demographic variables (e.g., firm size and technology), is a basis for complementarity and can, as such, create positive economic effects, but also ambiguities and contradictions (Dyer & Singh, 1998; Pelled, 1996)[1] Diversity may create faultlines (Lau & Murnighan, 1998) along dimensions such as race, sex, and age (Pelled, 1996); functional background; education and tenure (Pelled, Eisenhardt, & Xin, 1999; Peters & Karren, 2009); and personal diversity (Harrison, Price, & Myrtle, 1998), which may challenge social technologies. Hence, contradictions and conflicts related to diversity and faultlines (Brickson, 2000; Chatman & Flynn, 2001; Watson, Kumar & Michaelsen, 1993) may hamper the use of the social technology. The proposed effects of implementation of social technologies may not materialize because interaction and alliance dynamics may impede such a linear relationship.

Mobilization of Social Technologies and Structuration Theory

Giddens' (1984) structuration theory proposes that structure—which social technologies seek to change—both enable and constrain behavior in an alliance network. The relationship between the social technology and behavior form a duality. "According to the notion of duality of structure, the structural properties of social systems are both medium and outcome of the practices they recursively organize" (Giddens, 1984, p. 25). Structure consists of the "rules and resources, recursively implicated in the reproduction of social systems" (Giddens, 1984, p. 377). In this perspective, social elements such as trust, norms of cooperative behavior and shared values are fragile, and social structures can be *drawn on* in specific episodes to condition outcomes, but they are not reified as social structures that lay firm foundations for social practices.

Structuration theory is a complex body of propositions that has been debated elsewhere (e.g., Held & Thompson, 1989). For our purposes, it suffices to point out the three central elements of the duality of structure: signification (language), domination (power), and legitimation (norms and sanctions) (Giddens, 1984, p. 29). Signification allows actors to make sense of the world and to uphold communication through commonly understood interpretative schemes, which are the "modes of typification incorporated within actors' stocks of knowledge, applied reflexively in the sustaining of communication" (Giddens, 1984, p. 29). Social technologies promote certain discourses and sense-making patterns, which may motivate but not determine interactions. Domination is related to power over people or nature through the use of various kinds of facilities that help to command people or objects (Giddens, 1984, p. 33). Domination and power are related to (control) mechanisms that make certain kinds of social practices strong and other forms weak. Last, legitimation informs sanctions through norms, which "center upon relations between the rights and obligations expected of those participating in a range of interaction contexts" (Giddens,

1984, p. 30). These analytical distinctions help us to understand how social technologies are involved in interorganizational processes, specifically how social technologies evolve and disintegrate. Such studies are lacking (Ariño & de la Torre, 1998; Koza & Lewin, 1998).

There is active mobilization of social technologies because in principle, all actors could decide to "act otherwise," reject them, and make them superfluous. This makes the actual use and emergence of social technologies important. Structuration theory also helps to understand change through contradiction and conflict: "A structurationist perspective, rather than defining relationships in networks as trusted, fair, reciprocal, and mutually committed, it would be more fruitful to conceptualize social processes in general and network processes in particular as full of tension and contradiction" (Sydow & Windeler, 1998, p. 280).

Contradiction—disjunction of principles of system organization—may lead to conflict, because it supplies faultlines (Giddens, 1981, p. 237). Hence "conflict and contradiction tend to coincide because contradiction expresses the main faultlines in the structural constitution of societal systems. The reason for this coincidence is that contradiction tends to involve divisions of interest between different groupings or categories of people" (Giddens, 1984, p. 198). Contradiction is based on differences and it may (or may not) translate into active conflict, for example, via tensions around shared goals and shared culture (Inkpen & Tsang, 2005; Tsai & Ghoshal, 1998). Through these lenses, it is possible to analyze carefully how social technologies are constructed, developed, and mobilized in action.

METHOD

Drawing on structuration theory, the study is grounded in theoretical assumptions that allowed us to develop categories and concepts through the empirical investigation. The approach is "interpretative with a critical flavor" (Gephardt, 2004, p. 456; Weber, 1922/1980). Figure 11.1 shows our research model.

Research Object and Selection of Cases

Structuration theory guided our reflections on how to study social technologies as a dynamic, nonfixed phenomenon (Lee, 1999) in a "real life" context (Yin, 1994, p. 6). The case-study approach can help to theorize the multiplicity of linkages and relations between existing, potential, and abandoned entities in the network.

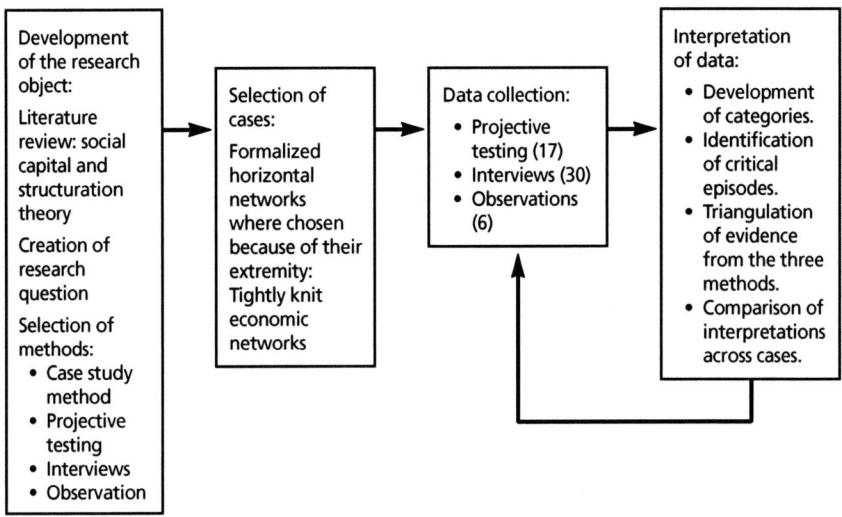

Figure 11.1   The research model.

Two commercial networks that wished to cooperate about branding, knowledge development, and sharing of customers were enrolled in the study. They were formalized alliance networks rather than value chains (Ahuja, 2000, p. 318; Inkpen & Tsang, 2005; Koza & Lewin, 1999) with explicit membership rules, decision rules, common IT systems, as well as quality controls. This type of network is interesting because it has sufficient closure to enable the formation of shared values (Coleman, 1988), trust, and norms of justice. Cases were thus chosen based on their extremity as tightly knit formalized networks (Pratt & Rosa, 2003) and theoretical relevance (Dutton & Dukerich, 1991; Eisenhardt, 1989).

Data Collection

First, we applied what Alvesson (2003) calls reflexive interviewing and developed a dialogue with respondents. We explored their concerns and preoccupations by continually following their lines of reasoning rather than merely keeping to our predetermined interview guide. The interview situation was an exploration of respondents' perspectives on their participation in the network.

Second, the interview explored the following themes and questions: (a) What is the business idea of the network? (b) What are the valued characteristics of network partners? (c) How is cooperation within the network organized? (d) What is management in and of the network? (e) What is leadership in the network? (f) How is knowledge managed in the network?

Our interest in social technologies and structuration theory motivated these questions (see also Koza & Lewin, 1999, p. 639) The first item of the interview guide concerned motives for entering the network and expected social and economic benefits from network participation, and it addressed signification through attention to perceived effects and logic of the network. The second item covered legitimate behaviors and practices in the network. The third, fourth, fifth, and sixth items concerned power and domination in various ways: partners' relations, facilities, technologies, and tools.

The categories of the interview guide were complemented with case-specific issues. Like Dutton and Dukerich (1991) and Ariño and de la Torre (1998), we focused on key events, issues, and themes such as, for example, the attempt to set up a sales function in one of the networks. This issue emerged in the interviews just before the decision was taken and was fiercely discussed in the network. These events were moments during which social technologies should prove their worth, and they were incorporated into the interview guide. The guide thus developed over time, although the structure of six items was kept intact. In total, 30 interviews were conducted, and they were transcribed verbatim.

We also employed *projective interview techniques*[2] in order to investigate interpretive schemes (signification) and norms (legitimation) more carefully because by making the respondent talk about another person, he or she presents arguments about what is important for the network (signification) and what legitimate behavior is (legitimation). The projective interview technique identifies values and norms unobtrusively (Hechter, 1992, p. 215). This data collection method complies with the demand that "the crucial point is that the relevant deep-level variables in any situation are those that bear directly on the fundamental purposes of the group" (Harrison et al., 1998, p. 105). The use of implicit interview techniques enabled categorization of norms and interpretive schemes in the network. Concepts and elements of the social technology like "cooperative behavior" were developed in the analysis phase. An example of how this has been written up in our research manuals is provided in Table 11.1 from the network that will subsequently be called Elec.net.

Table 11.1 shows what respondents consider good and bad norms and behavior, and it shows our notes about the encounters reported in the projective interview. It will be used in the empirical section of the chapter. In addition to interviewing and projective testing, network interactions at board meetings and general assemblies were observed on six occasions. In two instances, we were allowed to tape-record the meeting, and twice we were not allowed to do so. At two other occasions, we deemed it inappropriate. Observation of the network was important because we could experience interaction around issues discussed in interviews and projective testing. Also, observing network interaction gave rise to new questions in

TABLE 11.1   Projective Interview Data from Elec.net (abbreviated examples)

Respondent number	Quotations about the perfect member	Quotations about the inadequate member	Comments/interpretation
1	"He is thoughtful and has an eye for the financial side, he has got control of his organization and if you control your organization, then you are also a good partner that keeps appointments and makes sure that his employees have the competence that they need."	"He is eerie. He looks to the side. He is not trustworthy."	Thoughtfulness develops control or command of own operations and competence. This is related to trustworthiness.
2	"Dynamism, sporty, power. He will not be stopped by the first hindrance and if he was a salesman, then if he is thrown out of the front door, he crawls in by the back door."	"A stupid grinning and laidback, withdrawn. It is good to be visionary and he is not. We should drive fast forward."	Movement is positive; the business should be driven fast forward.
3	"Fresh, open, not afraid to use himself to go forward, he has got drive."	None	Openness and drive are important; the network should progress.
4	"Trustworthy and in control of the things that he works with as well as in relation to the people that he works with."	"He is not open; he looks distant, maybe calculating. He is the type that says 'first my own gain and then I will contribute.'"	Trustworthiness is positive and free-riding is negative.
5	"He has got the open trustful face. Honest. Honesty is important."	"Hides himself, one who has no opinion."	Someone closed is valued negatively.
6	"Looks open and honest."	"This guy might be speculating how I can get something out of it."	The distinction is between open and honest people and people inclined to free-ride.
7	"Serious and is able to cut through the crap. He signals that he is in control and he is calm An active person in control. Calm. The other person is positive and has energy, and that is important. Everybody likes that. It drives things, it is important to have somebody who talks like waterfall, who can pull things with him, where the other guy might be holding things back."	"Don Juan. Not trustworthy, he is distant. He is spoiled. Things are not moving fast enough, he is probably more into selling clothes and stuff like that, cars where you do not have to go into details."	The serious person is in control and creates trust with the customer.
8	"He looks trustworthy; if you make a deal with him, then he keeps it. He would not run away with your customers."	"Some only think about themselves."	A good partner is trustworthy and does not steal your customers.

the interviews. This additional information allowed us to create a nuanced account of network interaction.

Interpretation

Interviews were transcribed and analyzed throughout the research period. Interpretation followed a three-stage process. First, each interview was interpreted to gain an understanding of the respondent's views generally. Second, key categories, events, and issues were developed through open coding (Strauss & Corbin, 1998). Third, interviews were reread, and comments and quotations pertaining to explanations of key issues (e.g., the central sales mentioned above) were then gathered in separate documents, that is, axial coding. Fourth, the case study was written around events and issues. Finally, two types of control were employed.

The first control was triangulation (Yin, 1994, p. 92). Two researchers were involved in collecting data, and several methods and data sources were used (interviews, projective testing, and direct observation). This approach may augment construct validity and the accuracy of the study. Triangulation may also enhance validity because it allows data collection to be reflexive. Generally, the different data sources corroborated each other. The set-up of central sales in one of the networks may serve as an example. Respondents in the implicit interviews distinguished between two types of partners—for example, progressives and skeptics—and these categories were corroborated by interviews and observation, for example, skeptical partners were opposed to central sales also in interviews and at a general assembly, we observed that the group of "skeptics" acted to oust a "progressive" on formal grounds rather than follow the custom of accommodating breaches of formalities. Triangulation of empirical evidence developed interpretations because it was possible to see the tensions in accounts since they could be checked against other materials. This was, for example, the case in which some respondents in interviews smoothed over conflicts and painted a brighter picture than observations produced.

A second control was to obtain feedback from respondents through workshops with network partners based on our findings. The purpose was to ensure validity of concepts through debating preliminary propositions, conclusions, and perspectives developed in the research.

EMPIRICAL FINDINGS: PATTERNS
OF NETWORK INTERACTION

The empirical findings about the two cases are structured according to our research problem. We start with a short introduction, which is followed by a description of the social technology/social structures sought and implemented as well as how the social structure is defined, followed by an analysis of how social technologies/structures are mobilized and transformed.

Advice.net

Advice.net was a network of independent consultants who aimed to sell "competencies" in contrast to the "big" consulting firms who were said to sell "systems." Three experienced consultants founded the network 2 years prior to the research. All partners had previously worked in larger companies in senior positions, but they did not enjoy life in the "big" companies. The partners prided themselves as independent, mature consultants who had worked as senior consultants and managers. The number of partners varied from a peak of 15 to 8 consultants when the research finished.

Advice.net had a *bilateral ownership structure*. First, it was an *egalitarian partnership* with shared liability, and second, the three founders owned a firm that had the rights to the *brand name*. These three founders therefore levied a fee on all transactions executed in the name of the network. To the individual consultant, Advice.net was a means to find resources and execute projects that could not be handled individually. It helped them to simultaneously be small and yet exploit the possibilities of a collectivity based on a brand name, and size based on cooperation with partners. The case analysis starts with developing the social technology of Advice.net, followed by an analysis of two distinct modes of mobilization—bilateral and collective mobilization.

The Efforts at Implementing Social Technologies in Advice.net
A group around the founders was explicit in the norms and practices that they wanted to govern the network. They sought to implement specific social structures, that is, to implement a social technology, and they presented norms as strength (self-confidence and extroversion), a culture of sharing, and flexibility. Strong behavior and self-confidence were mentioned in interviews and deemed necessary to share knowledge and to enable freedom, openness, and learning. The norms aspired to can be explained as follows by a respondent who was also founder:

> If you do not have high self-esteem and reflexivity, then I think you need to protect yourself more than what is otherwise necessary. One of the things that we have worked with in the network—where I think we have accomplished a lot—is to share knowledge and ideas without having to own the knowledge and the ideas and without payment.

These rules encouraged knowledge sharing and defined values, action patterns, and learning aspirations accordingly. Another partner had parallel thoughts: "What makes a network exist? It is that we as persons are open, we can use ourselves and each other not just as professional colleagues, but also as persons, as humans." Through its focus on openness, Advice.net had traits of a learning organization:

> We have, for the first time in our lives, such teamwork that you read about. You know how when you read about these fantastic teams, then you say "yeah all right, that's all very well, but how do you get it?" We have experienced this.

Second, a cooperative attitude by which consultants were willing to share customers and knowledge where deemed necessary for the functioning of the network. One of the partners suggested,

> I have become very aware that networks are based on giving and not primarily on getting. Because a network in itself is nothing, the network exists only through what you give to it.... The network exists because you give assignments to it. It is when you bring somebody from the network with you on your projects, which then creates new projects.

Sharing—a cooperative attitude as opposed to a competitive attitude (Das & Teng, 2000; Jorde & Teece, 1989; Zeng & Chen, 2003)—was therefore a crucial norm. Without a cooperative attitude, there would be no network, since it was carried only by common projects and shared customers. The value of sharing was therefore the main asset and social technology to be implemented.

A third espoused norm was extroversion and independence. Independence was closely related to sharing, because a consultant was only able to give when he had secured projects and could invite others to join. Selling projects involved contact with customers and required extroversion and directness:

> We do not want to get partners that are unable to sell actively. There are many of these consultants that do not sell actively. We are not interested in these persons if they are of no use. You have to be able to get in contact with the customers, and you have to be able to acquire projects.

The interviewees argued that introverted consultants could not sell since they could not persuade customers. Therefore, independence, extroversion, and sharing were interrelated.

A fourth norm concerned creativity and flexibility. Most of the consultants chose to be independent, because they were tired of the hierarchies of the modern enterprise. "I don't want to manage or to be managed" was a general slogan. This value had an effect on the structuring of the network, as a new partner explained,

> It is funny. These people have fled from hierarchical positions in industry, with all the control and role-playing and a lot of other stuff. They say, "Now I want to be creative, I will develop myself, I want to create something on the basis of all the experience I have. Both in relation to all the positive things I have not been able to implement because I have been locked up in the role I was playing. And in relation to all the negative experiences I have had with this bureaucratic inflexibility." We want something that is directly opposite. They are afraid of defining the things [e.g., vision, marketing, strategy] that "smell" like a normal business.

Organizational structure, hierarchy, and procedures were problematical, and freedom was praised. The founders thus aspired to have low levels of structural rigidity (Das & Teng, 2000; Faems et al., 2008). Networking entailed positive energies and development. A partner who had left the network suggested, "They wanted this uncontrollability because somewhere there is an anxiety that it [referring to procedures] hinders creativity." Creativity and flexibility were norms and values in opposition to hierarchy.

However, the norms (legitimation) and interpretative schemes (signification) were fragile and not uniformly shared. Some partners questioned the practicability of the values of strength and independence because not all were able to attract customers equally well. It was suggested that if the network developed a division of labor under which some consultants were responsible for selling and others, for example, for producing internal services, everybody would be able to participate. This approach was in conflict with the values of independence and flexibility since designated roles would create organizational procedures, which the partners of the network tried to avoid when starting their own firm. A partner who had left the network explained the problem as follows:

> We should have done it much more systematically. I had difficulty convincing the three founders about it. They do not like systems and structures. That does not belong in a network. A network is a symbiosis, an amoeba and stuff like that. That is all fine, but things do not necessarily happen if you do not agree how they are to happen. Then things happen unsatisfactorily, and some things fall out that did not have to fall out if we had been a bit more considerate.

A partner agreed: "Network does not mean that everybody has to take care of him or herself. It means that we should help each other." The values of the network were not uniformly shared, because sharing and flexibility often ran contrary to solidarity with partners who were not as strong and independent as others. Two versions of social technology, with differing goals,

TABLE 11.2   Social Technologies in Advice.net

	The Amorphous Network	The Hierarchial Network
Preferred network type	Loose couplings and strong, open, and independent partners.	Functional specialization so all can participate.
Values	Openness and strength, independence, sharing, flexibility	Solidarity, sharing, structured approach to interaction.
Desired node characteristics	High self-esteem, extroversion, strength, no role-playing, and altruistic orientation to work.	Specialized consultant who excels in certain roles. Altruistic attitude to work life.
Anticipated effects and goals	Amorphous, chaotic, learning network of strong consultants able to generate projects.	Functionally specialized network. A strongly orchestrated network where some sell and others produce.

means, and values thus competed in Advice.net (see Table 11.2, which is developed on the basis of projective testing, interviews, and observation).

There was tension between two sets of *interpretive schemes* and *norms*. This was problematic because the interpretive schemes and norms were also social technologies which, through a specific mode of functioning for the network as a whole, were supposed to translate network interaction into desirable economic effects. This would preclude tension and conflict. The contradiction between norms of sharing and nonhierarchical attention to each other on the one hand and some partners' hope of a network based on functional specialization on the other was fundamental.

Bilateral and Collective Mobilizing of Social Technologies in Advice.net

Table 11.2 characterizes the contradiction between the two types of partners in relation to the type of network that they preferred and the means to achieve these goals—their views on social technology. The bilateral mobilization was about the joint projects that partners implemented and was when partners were excluded from the network. The introvert and less strong partners could not deliver, and increasingly they were not invited to participate in activities. Gradually, their activities in the network were reduced, and they gradually withdrew; they were silently excluded (domination). One of the partners explained as follows:

> If you do not contribute, but only want to receive, then this network that we are creating is not the right thing for you. You have to find a new network and that's it. I mean to select, to exclude the partners that show no contribution. This is a necessary process.

Participation literally just stopped if a partner did not fit in; no decision had to be made. For example, the network had developed a big contract with a newspaper about joint marketing of seminars for business professionals. The contract was made with the founders and consequently "they [the founders] have the power over the assignment with the newspaper," as the dilemma was presented to us. Also, the telephone number posted in newspaper ads was that of one of the founders' secretaries, prompting the following speculation:

> On the basis of the campaign in the newspaper, there were a lot calls, and I said if they go to one of the founder's numbers, who hands out the requests? Then I was told, "there are no requests on the basis the marketing campaign in the newspaper; it is all from somebody that we know." I got the impression that the founders took first and that there was nothing left for the rest of us.

Access to customers created centrality in the network, and this was related to power (domination), even to the point where espoused aspirations were rejected (abandoning legitimation). The perception was that norms were tradable if economic gains were possible, and these perceptions questioned the extent to which members in the network could be trusted. The customer base was "your power base; this is your customers; if you have customers to trade with, then they ask you to participate in projects. If you do not have customers, then you are out." Such facilities make a partner powerful and a central person in the network.

Ten partners had left or had been asked to leave the network over the course of the 2 years of the research. The partners still in the network were the "strong" consultants, who paradoxically did not really "need the network," a partner said. A partner who had left the network explained how it worked:

> They might think that I wanted something else than what I wanted. I just wanted to participate. If just one of them had taken me on an assignment, then it would have been fine for me; this was all I asked for. ... They might have thought that I wanted to take over their customers.

The dilemmas of a cooperative attitude (sharing) and the power of external ties (Burt, 1992) conflicted and motivated the transformation of the network toward one with less trust among members. In the collective mobilization, the network functioned, at times, as the group around the founders had envisioned, as trusting cooperation between strong individuals. This showed in partner meetings that were oriented to affirm norms through socializing because they "usually revolve around values and culture." Some partners felt very emotionally attached to the network. A founder explains,

> I experience that Advice.net had become more like a family, an equal family. I think we do have something very special, which I will go a long way to keep. We have a family structure in some way, without there being a mom,

dad, or children. It is closely related. Just like I can be with close friends. This is just a working community, but there is the whole of me in it. I can talk about having pains in my back, that I am sad, I can tell about my kids, my husband, and about my life. It matters to me.

Norms and joint decision making were difficult to reconcile, however, which can be illustrated by the episode of signing a required partner agreement:

> What I experienced [at this meeting] was that we were looking at the holes in the cheese instead of trying to see what would be the best for us if we get in this situation. What I experienced here was that we were devil's advocates for each other, including myself, and I experienced that all the energy was taken out of the room, and then I thought that I don't want to do this—that was not the idea. So when we had tried two or three times, I said I don't want to do it. And then I went from fear and feeling insecure about not having signed this paper, so that we complied with the legal requirements. And I changed from wanting to sign to saying, "I don't want to sign that paper because it contained exactly the opposite of the idea behind the network."

The legal contract symbolized governance and hierarchy and was a challenge to the founders' espoused norms and legitimation because it was about power (domination). Others characterized these discussions as "tiring" and "tough" because they contrasted with norms of trust-based behavior and a concern for sharing and flexibility. Instead of focusing on the positive actions the network could take, discussions focused on negative discussions of what could go wrong. Hence, in the collective mobilization, the contradictory values and social technologies turned into conflict. This change from "silent" contradiction to open conflict was triggered by discussions, which necessitated joint decision making along the faultlines of the network. For instance, the partnership agreement could both be interpreted from "a trust-based" perspective and a "functional specialization" perspective, and the joint decision making regarding the contract therefore transformed contradiction into conflict. The network could function without conflict as long as sensitive issues were avoided.

Elec.net

Elec.net was a network of electrical installation companies that considered ICT an important business option, and it was founded with the aim to develop and exploit the then-emerging information and communication technology (ICT) business. Previously, the telecom industry was a government monopoly, and the network founders worked here. They formed the network in the aftermath of the liberalization of the industry some 12 years prior to the research.

The network partners were small- and medium-sized companies ranging in size from 10 to 100 employees. At the time of the research, the network had 13 partner firms owning the shares of the network and 20 associated partners who did not own any stock in the network. The expectation was that their number would increase to around 50. The size of Elec.net varied over the years and ranged from 26 to now 13 partner firms. More than *40 partner firms* had entered and left the network.

Elec.net had a formal management apex with a full-time manager (network CEO) who had a database showing what technologies partners could operate and their experience and competence with these technologies. The management apex provided procedures for training and education, and it was a nexus for strategic discussions. It also observed developments in markets and technology, and lastly, it carried out network administration and external relations, for example, home page maintenance. Elec. net was a closed network, and partners were *interrelated and interdependent.* Interdependence was underscored by the network brand name, which discouraged partners from discontinuing their membership. They "are afraid to lose their customers if they cannot use the Elec.net brand name," as it was suggested to us. To step out of the network could be very costly. Interdependence was thus based on *shared brand assets,* and it was induced by *administrative procedures* and information systems that were part of the infrastructure of the network and the individual firm: "All our systems are constructed around Elec.net; perhaps particularly our competency development systems," a partner explained.

Generally, three reasons to join the network were mentioned by respondents. One was access to markets. The partners were dispersed geographically and depended on each other to deliver the same quality of service to large customers who wanted their installations to work all over the country. They wished to cooperate in relation to customers as several partners would have to coordinate efforts to match the geographical spread of customer's offices. They thus pursued residual referral income (Koza & Lewin, 1999). The second was access to technological resources of partners and network. The network, for example, made courses in ICT for partner firms. Finally, partners wanted increased trustworthiness of a brand name, which was important because many customers doubted that electrical installation companies could posses the competencies needed in the ICT business.

Social Technology in Elec.net

In Elec.net, there were differing views on what should constitute the values and behaviors of the network. Entering the network in itself entailed long-term investments in ICT competencies for each partner and hence, to some extent, a long-term perspective on the cooperation. It further was built on the notion of cooperative behavior—partners were expected to share customers. Despite these basic elements of the social technology in Elec.net, partners disagreed on emphasis in values and orientations:

> It will always be so when that many people have gathered who have known each other for so many years. There will always be somebody "with whom you dance better than with others." You clear your opinions with them in order to see if they are aligned, so that you do not stand alone with the opinion of the day. So it functions like a small parliament.

Social bonds were *not equally distributed,* and cliques had formed over the years. According to the words of respondents, Elec.net was divided in two cliques. One group called itself the "progressives" and differentiated itself from the "skeptics." Their traits were different, as a progressive explained:

> The progressives are those that in my eyes are competent enough to see the trend in the market and what the customers want. It has something to do with age, company culture, and your employees. If you have a firm where all employees are of the type that comes in at 8 am and leaves at 4 pm and who does not think about his job anymore when he has come home, then it is difficult to be in this market, because it requires another culture than just to be a traditional electrical installation guy. So you need visionary coworkers that want something more than just that.

The division was also based on personal traits of the partners, to which another progressive gave details:

> If the customer has a need and another partner has the competencies to fulfill that need, then he should get the assignment because the more business we generate in total, the better. The progressive sees it like that—as opportunities. The other says, "You cannot come in and work in my geographical area, we will handle it ourselves." Then it does not matter if another competitor gets it.

According to this progressive, the skeptics were more self-centered and to some extent did not understand the network culture. For the progressives, the interpretive scheme (signification) concerned the enhancement of Elec.net through common investments to create growth in the ICT business, while for the skeptics, the ICT business was not to incur too high investments and risk. It should not replace the traditional electrical installation business, but just be an addition. And the progressive norms (legitimation) focused on mastering the future through intervention that would alter the course of affairs, while the skeptic norms reflected a conservative continuity between the past and the future. The two groups of skeptics and

TABLE 11.3   Social Technologies in Elec.net

	The Risk Taking Network	The Conservative Network
Preferred type of network	A fast-developing, high-investment and high-risk network. "Progressives."	A consolidating network, which develops competencies slowly and systematically. "Skeptics."
Value	Forward-looking approach to developing the network as an entity.	Cautious approach to maintain the past benefits of the existing network focusing on the individuality of the partner firms.
Desired node characteristics	Speed and risk. Competition through aggressive investment and explicit management of the market beyond the interest of any particular partner firm.	Safety and prudence. Competition through safeguarding money flows and reduced risk, and decentralized relations between partner firms.
Anticipated effects and goals	Efficiency and growth of the network enhanced via sharing of customers and common investments.	Network through voluntary growth of relations between partner firms. Risk reduced and growth manageable by decentralized means.

progressives were based on diversity. The two groups are characterized in Table 11.3 (see Table 11.1 in the Methods section for how projective testing was used and the Appendix for quotations).

Mobilization and construction of social technology in Elec.net: Strategy and organization.

The contradiction between the two views (the conservative vs. the risk-taking approach) on the network was silent between meetings and decisions in the network. Skeptics would routinely call on progressives to carry out jobs in other parts of the country where they were not represented or when they had relevant competencies. So at times, the differences had no consequences and even the fiercest of skeptics used the most progressive firms to carry out assignments. In the bilateral mobilization of network ties, the network had no problems, and unlike the consultancy network, no apparent exclusion of specific types of partners was noticed.

However, as the network partners were interdependent, sometimes decisions had to be coordinated and made collectively, and in the collective mobilization of the network, contradictions sometimes turned into conflicts. One example is as follows:

> At a point in time it was decided that we need to have this organized as a real company. It is not good enough to control by meetings in various parts of the country. Yet this is a voluntary organization, so it cannot be controlled like a real company. But because of this decision, we appointed managers and

what-do-I-know functions of the network. Then we had to appoint section managers in all partner firms who were to attend section manager meetings. In reality, it was the network CEO or a board member that made the decisions about adding central sales. . . . So now we suddenly have to pay a monthly fee of $1,500 for marketing staff without any real discussion of it.

The changes toward more rigid structures (Das & Teng, 2000) enabled the progressives to move their agenda of higher levels of investment forward, particularly in relation to the development of a sales function for the entire network. The investment was a challenge to a prior praxis of egalitarian decision making because the skeptics did not think they had approved the decision. One of the skeptics explained his feelings as follows:

An example is the "central sales" that was decided without really asking us. It is bad and annoying because I was at that meeting we had in April last year, and I think we had the first discussion of it then. But the people present were employed [i.e., managers in a partner firm, not partners], and they were told bluntly that this is how it is.

Many of the partners were unaware of the decision and "just received it in the mailbox." The skeptics responded by setting up an unofficial meeting between the owners without the network CEO.

The 15th of August we held an unofficial board meeting in order to determine the frame of mind of the owners and to try and influence the board, and we did it without our CEO, not because he was not allowed to be there, but because I think that there are people who do not say much when the CEO is present, because he may intimidate them.

At a later board meeting in August, skeptics agreed prior to the meeting to use a formal, rarely practiced, internal network rule about financial solidity to exclude a progressive from the meeting in order to enhance their chances of rejecting central sales. At the meeting, it was decided to close central sales. However, because of the execution of the decision—the decision was executed after a trial period where it could have been closed within a month— central sales was to be closed 4 months later and not 1 month later, as envisaged by the skeptics. This gave extra time to secure funding within or outside the network.

These developments increased withdrawal from the network. One skeptic explained, "There have been some progressive forces on the board that would like things to move faster than the majority of firms in Elec.net." A consequence was that some skeptics left the network and others were contemplating leaving:

I had hoped that we could bring Elec.net down to another more reasonable level of ambition, where more of us could join, and where we also could participate in the future, but that is not the way things turned out.

DISCUSSION: MOBILIZING AND CHANGING SOCIAL STRUCTURES

The detailed empirical material presented above suggests that the social technology of the network is a surprising set of rules and resources. Not only will it reinforce a community held together by values, sympathy, and trust, it also, and more importantly, carves out lines of contradiction and conflict.

Advice.net was intended as a community based on sharing, trust, openness, and flexibility, and it was a platform to team up for temporary projects. Partners had to be strong and self-organized. This norm was contradicted by partners who did not have these qualities, and they would gradually become marginalized because they were not assets in project work. The implementation of social technology entailed marginalization and exclusion and a return to a more "pure" network organization.

Elec.net illustrates that conflict arose when joint decisions were made and groups defined themselves by differences in signification and legitimation. Collective decision making was a clash between social structures, and the effect was that certain types of partners (the skeptics) tended to leave the network, making it a more "pure" progressive one.

Social Technology as Process

Focusing on the details of social interaction, it is possible to theorize social technologies as a fragile set of rules and resources, which can be initiated, transformed, and destroyed. Figure 11.2 illustrates how this is done.

Figure 11.2 models network dynamics with a social technology of shared values and trust. Diversity influences group formation when partners with values and norms join in order to advance their agenda. Diversity is necessary, however, because to survive, a commercial network needs partners with complementary competencies (Dyer & Singh, 1998). It also models how processes develop around this state, and four possible paths can be identified, two of which are about continuation and stabilization of network activities (Paths 1 and 2) and the two other ones are about change and transformation (Paths 3 and 4).

Path 1 at the bottom of Figure 11. 2 shows how the network works as a collectivity so that heterogeneity is a resource, and the normative aspirations of the collectivity are not disputed. For example, Elec.net worked by inte-

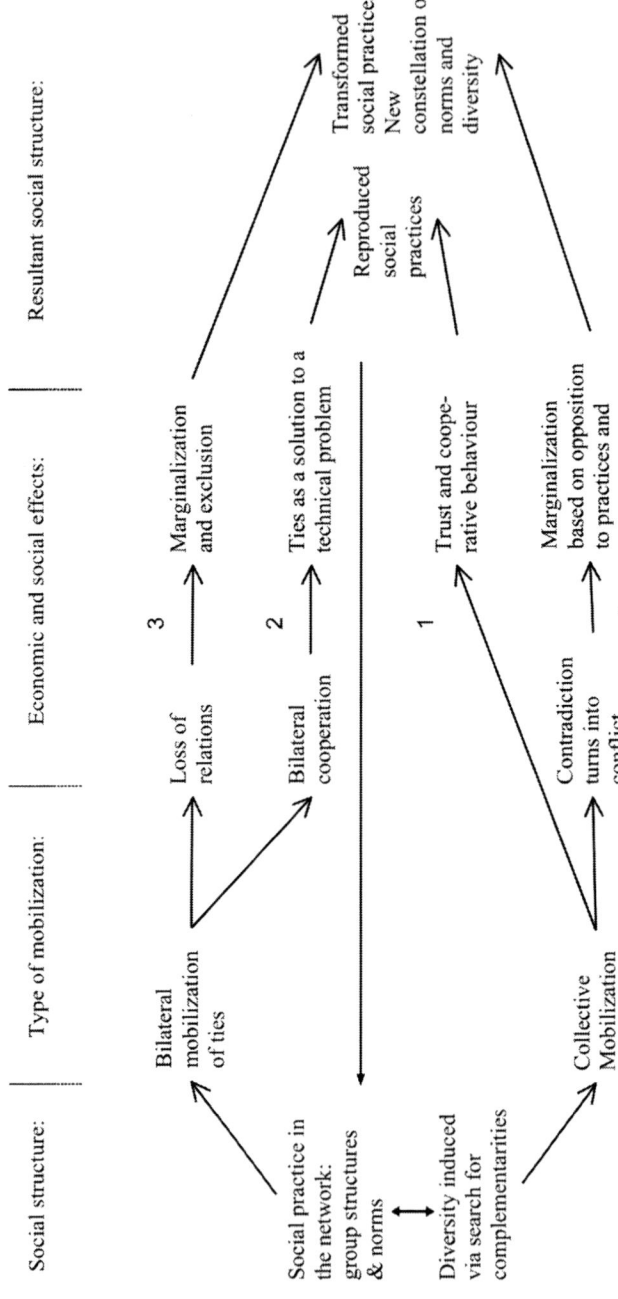

Figure 11.2 Mobilization and transformation of social technologies.

grating different competencies toward the customer, and they advertised their network on the home page illustrating solutions. They got quantity discounts through combining their purchases. Path 2 shows individual ties between actors in the network. In path 2, individuals draw on each other in specific business ventures by mutual agreement. For example, Elec.net partners located in different parts of the country call on each other to meet the needs of large customers who needed more manpower than they could offer individually. And if a customer having locations at several places in the country needed a job performed in another part of the country far away, the partner could ask a partner in that part of the country to perform the job, thereby substantially decreasing transportation costs and enabled through a profit sharing regime. The purpose is to solve an economic/ technical problem rather than a social problem.

Figure 11.2 also shows two types of transformations through conflict. Path 3's conflict marginalizes an actor when a relationship simply stops; no one calls on the partner anymore, and this partner is then expelled, with the consequence that the network has been transformed by a change in membership. Path 4, in contrast, is dramatic because this is the path by which social technology and structure of the networks are overtly at stake and whose content is articulated. Path 4 shows the network seeking to function as a coherent unit making joint decisions, and this is when contradictions between systems of signification, domination, and legitimation challenge existing practices. The resulting conflict is not about a single tie, but about the system of ties, and the conflict transpires as one system of rules and resources versus another. This conflict puts pressure on partners, and it is resolved when partners choose to leave or when partners are ousted because they do not share the rules and resources of the group turning out to be dominant. Conflict expels actors directly or through pressure from collective investments and arrangements that make life difficult for these actors. When the conflict eases again, social practices are more purely informed by the resulting social order and technology.

Contradiction does not necessarily produce conflict. Conflict is actualized only when the network seeks to mobilize social technology acting as coherent unity. It happens when the ambitions of the network as a totality are at stake, for example, in relation to decisions about strategy and structures in the network, when marginalization of members is a collective process.

In Paths 1 and 2, diversity and contradiction are resources for value creation because they allow complementarity to develop. Paths 2 and 3 show continuity and change without strong mobilization of social technology apart from norms about sharing customers. These findings contrast with and yet extend Gargiulo and Bernassi's (2000) conclusion that a network is either closed and cohesive or sparsely connected through multiple structural holes. Their cross-sectional approach can be transcended by our longitudinal and process approach so that the network and its social technologies are potentialities that need to be mobilized in order to have effects. In this mobilization process, it is always possible to marginalize a member or to include another member. Social technologies can be mobilized in a variety of ways through Paths 3 and 4.

The Paradox and Dilemma of Interfirm Networks

Commercial networks require diversity. Competencies, personality traits, and strategic hopes and aspirations are complementarities potentially important for relational advantages (Dyer & Singh, 1998). Complementarities require differences and diversity between partners. In Advice.net, degrees of strength, extroversion, and personal flexibility separated participants and created distinctions. In Elec.net, diversity in age, business focus, and perspectives regarding cooperation differed between skeptics and progressives. Such diversity influenced the structuring of the network; it mobilized differing interpretive schemes (signification) and norms (legitimation).

Inkpen and Tsang (2005, p. 158) argue that "the overall effect of cultural diversity should be beneficial to knowledge transfer." However, this view misses the point that social structures are then heterogeneous because of different accounts of effective behavior, it mobilizes normative questions about what the network should accomplish, and it expresses contradictions and faultlines. These contradictions and faultlines are not operative in the network continuously, but are mobilized in relation to situations in which the network is compelled to act strategically as a coherent unit or in which members begin to informally and bilaterally exclude partners. In the Elec. net case, for example, we saw how the division between progressives and skeptics was mobilized when the network discussed adding a central sales unit to the network. In other situations, progressives and skeptics were able to work together without any overt problems.

This dual functioning of the network points to a paradox in the management of alliance networks. They are formed in order to help orchestration and management of a diverse collection of partners acting in unity. They develop joint marketing, technology, strategy, and so on, but exactly in situations where the alliance network seeks to function as a unity—as a community—contradictions can be transformed into conflicts. When striving to act as a unit with strategies and joint goals, conflicts can emerge transforming the network and destroying, or changing, the intended functioning of the social technology.

This paradox has three implications. First, cultural and technological diversity are related to fragmentation that inhibits the mobilization and stabilization of social technologies (Pelled, 1996; Pelled & Eisenhardt, 1999).

Second, network economics require competencies/technologies to be nonredundant and thereby require diversity; but this also creates interdependencies and increases contradiction. Third, when diversity and complementarity are maximal, alliance networks may have to avoid or postpone joint decision making and mobilization of the entire network, or they may engage in strong coordination primarily when diversity is minimal. Otherwise, conflict may rip them apart.

Koza and Lewin (1999) suggest that alliance networks over time evolve into being more rationalized as well as utilizing more formalized modes of functioning. Institutional pressures direct isomorphic processes, especially in stable industries. Our findings seem to question this finding. Elec.net was a 14-year-old network, and despite the possibility of a slightly increasing formalization, the network did not evolve into a more rationalized and uniform mode of functioning. Rather, the steady influx of new partners (45 over the past 14 years) enabled the network to maintain its fragile balance between different groups of partners poised at edge of chaos (Prigogine & Stengers, 1984). This complex, unstable functioning of the network may be the only way that a network can both build relational advantages through complementarities and achieve joint goals through the implementation of social technologies. The social order, instabilities, and contradictions should be upheld by an influx of new partners that maintains diversity and the balance between different groups. An alliance network achieving order, stability, and equilibrium through social technologies may effectively be undermining its justification—its business model.

CONCLUSION

Drawing on longitudinal evidence about the operation of two small commercial networks, this chapter has analyzed the way in which social technologies impact alliance networks. Trust and shared values are not the magic ingredients that would ensure effective cooperation. When social technologies are analyzed and studied as processes, it becomes clear that they are fragile accomplishments, because they can be changed in any interaction and because diversity and faultlines separate groups with contradictory norms and interpretative schemes. Social technologies are constantly mobilized in interaction and therefore are potentially questioned and transformed all the time.

When social technology is related to a set of bilateral ties, it is substituted by economic and technical affairs in ongoing business relations. Ties can be developed by merely adding or dropping interactions, as can be done by any individual. This changes the constellation of ties and thereby the social technology as an effect of the structure of participants. When social technology is related to the collectivity, it works differently. In networks, differences in competences are necessary because otherwise there would be no complementarity. But complementarity also produces differences in outlook between groups regarding the business of the network. Faultlines thus accumulate, and when they are problematized, they create conflict associated with differences in social technology. Often the network membership is changed through such processes, and the result is a reconstitution of the social technology of the network; it has become more "pure" and less differentiated. Such a network undermines its own business proposition, and it therefore needs an influx of new members in order to maintain its complex, fragile order.

NOTES

1. Here, diversity focuses first on firm diversity as opposed to personal diversity. Second, diversity is measured as the values of owners view on corporation (Harrison et al., 1998, p. 105) rather than on their demographic variables such as firm size and technological specialization. These are interrelated but not directly and automatically.
2. The implicit system (IMP-SYS) has been developed by Heylen and licensed by NFO (www.nfoeurope.com) and is usually used for testing brand names. One of the researchers has been formally trained in the method. The projective technique consists of a photo set of eight men and woman displaying eight validated, behavioral positions. We showed the respondents the photos and asked them to choose one or more that typified a person with whom they would like to cooperate.

APPENDIX: Projective Interview Data from Advice.net (Brief Examples)

Respondent number	Quotations regarding the perfect network member	Quotations regarding inadequate network members	Comments/Interpretation
1	"He has got a high level of self reflection, high self-esteem. It is necessary to have high self-esteem because then you can protect yourself and you can share."	"Too independent . . . Does not listen to what others say."	Links self-esteem and knowledge sharing.
2	"She has self-confidence and signals that 'I will deal with this.' Self-confidence is important because what we sell is clearly the conviction of what we say, and if we are not self-confident, then we do not enter this market."	"Cold, withdrawn, shy."	Self-confidence is a necessary condition for the ability to sell their services.
3	"She has got a look in her eye and a real smile. A receiving smile—here I am. Looks me direct in the eyes and smiles directly; she is a girl that shows her soul and her personality, She is not afraid to show her personality, she is proud . . . She is a person of surplus."	"I do not know where I have got her. I cannot look her in the eyes. She is closed . . . not open, I cannot even see if she is angry. I cannot find her."	Openness is a desired trait, as it makes interaction fun.
4	"She is self-confident. She has got style, and she is not afraid to say anything; she believes in the competence she has got, does not oversell herself, but she is strong. She is constructive."	"Would expect help; is not strong enough; networks require that you trust yourself. Know yourself and do not have to tie up tightly with others. We need to have a foundation each and everyone, and I am not certain that she has got a foundation that will make her feel equal."	Strength is positive and necessary for equality.
5	"Open, visionary. He may need help to structure things . . . A good player, a tactician. He is not strategic."	"The more conservative type . . . He wants to be like the father at the end of the table. He is too anonymous; plays his own game, is not a network player."	Openness and honesty are valued to support cooperation.

REFERENCES

Adler, P. S., & Kwon, S. W. (2002). Social capital: Prospects for a new concept. *Academy of Management* Review, *27*, 17–40.

Ahuja, G. (2000). The duality of collaboration: Inducements and opportunities in the formation of interfirm linkages. *Strategic Management Journal, 21*, 317–343.

Alvesson, M. (2003). Beyond neopositivists, romantics, and localists: A reflexive approach to interviews in organizational research. *Academy of Management Review, 28*, 13–33.

Ariño, A., & de la Torre, J. (1998). Learning from failure: Toward an evolutionary model of collaborative venture. *Organization Science, 9*, 306–325.

Bolino, M. C. (2002). Citizenship behavior and the creation of social capital in organizations. *Academy of Management Review, 27*, 505–523.

Brickson, S. (2000). The impact of identity orientation on individual and organizational outcomes in demographically diverse settings. *Academy of Management Review, 25*, 82–102.

Burt, R. S. (1992). *Structural holes: The social structure of competition.* Cambridge, MA: Harvard University Press.

Chatman, J., & Flynn, F. J. (2001). The influence of demographic heterogeneity on the emergence and consequences of cooperative norms in teams. *Academy of Management Journal, 44*, 956–975.

Coleman, J. S. (1988). Social capital in the creation of human capital. *American Journal of Sociology, 94*, 95–120.

Das, T. K., & Teng, B. (2000). Instabilities of strategic alliances: An internal tensions perspective. *Organization Science, 11*, 77–101.

Dutton, J. E., & Dukerich, J. M. (1991). Keeping an eye on the mirror: Image and identity in organizational adaptation. *Academy of Management Journal, 34*, 517–554.

Dyer, J. H., & Chu, W. (2003). The role of trustworthiness in reducing transaction cost and improving performance: Empirical evidence from the United States, Japan, and Korea. *Organization Science, 14*, 57–68.

Dyer, J. H., & Nobeoka, K. (2000). Creating and managing a high performance knowledge-sharing network: The Toyota case. *Strategic Management Journal, 21*, 345–367.

Dyer, J. H., & Singh, H. (1998). The relational view: Cooperative strategy and sources of interorganizational competitive advantage. *Academy of Management Review, 23*, 660–679.

Eisenhardt, K. M. (1989). Building theories from case study research. *Academy of Management Review, 14*, 532–550.

Faems, D., Janssens, M., Madhok, A., & van Looy, B. (2008). Toward an integrative perspective on alliance governance: Connecting contract design, trust dynamics, and contract application. *Academy of Management Journal, 51*, 1053–1078.

Frank, K. A., & Yasumoto, J. Y. (1998). Linking action to social structure within a system: Social capital within and between groups. *The American Journal of Sociology, 104*, 642–686.

Gargiulo, M., & Bernassi, M. (2000). Trapped in your own net? Network cohesion, structural holes, and the adaptation of social capital. *Organization Science, 11,* 183–196.

Gephardt, R. P., Jr. (2004). From the editors. *Academy of Management Journal, 47,* 454–463.

Giddens, A. G. (1981). *A contemporary critique of historical materialism.* London, England: Macmillan Press.

Giddens, A. G. (1984). *The constitution of society.* Cambridge, England: Polity Press.

Greve, H. R., Baum, J. A. C., Mitsuhashi, H., & Rowley, T. J. (2010). Built to last but falling apart: Cohesion, friction, and withdrawal from interfirm alliances. *Academy of Management Journal, 53,* 302–322.

Harrison, D. A., Price, K. H., & Myrtle P. B. (1998). Beyond relational demography: Time and the effects of surface- and deep-level diversity on work group cohesion. *Academy of Management Journal, 41,* 96–107.

Hechter, M. (1992). Should values be written out of the social scientist's lexicon? *Sociological Theory, 10,* 214–230.

Held, D., & Thompson, J. B. (1989). *Social theory of modern societies – Anthony Giddens and his critics.* Cambridge, England: Cambridge University Press.

Henderson, C. R. (1901). The scope of social technology. *American Journal of Sociology, 6,* 465–486.

Henderson, C. R. (1912). Applied sociology (or social technology). *American Journal of Sociology, 18,* 215–221.

Husted, B. W., & Folger, R. (2004). Fairness and transaction costs: The contribution of organizational justice theory to an integrative model of economic organization. *Organization Science, 15,* 719–729.

Inkpen, A. C., & Currall, S. C. (2004). The coevolution of trust, control, and learning in joint ventures. *Organization Science, 15,* 586–599.

Inkpen, A. C., & Tsang, E. W. K. (2005). Social capital, networks, and knowledge transfer. *Academy of Management Review, 30,* 146–165.

Jorde, T. M., & Teece, D. J. (1989, Spring). Competition and cooperation: Striking the right balance. *California Management Review,* 25–37.

Khanna, T., Gulati, R., & Nohria, N. (1998). The dynamics of learning alliances: Competition, cooperation, and relative scope. *Strategic Management Journal, 19,* 193–210.

Koza, M. P., & Lewin, A. Y. (1999). The coevolution of network alliances: A longitudinal analysis of an international professional service network. *Organization Science, 10,* 638–653.

Lau, C. D., & Murnighan, J. K. (1998). Demographic diversity and faultlines: The compositional dynamics of organizational groups. *Academy of Management Review, 23,* 325–340.

Lee, T. (1999). *Using qualitative methods in organizational research.* Thousand Oaks, CA: Sage.

Leenders, R. T. A. J., & Gabbay, S. M. (1999). *Corporate social capital and liability.* Norwell, MA: Kluwer Academic.

Nahapiet, J., & Ghoshal, S. (1998). Social capital, intellectual capital, and the organizational advantage. *Academy of Management Review, 23,* 242–266.

Pelled, L. H. (1996). Demographic diversity, conflict and work group outcomes: An intervening process theory. *Organization Science, 7,* 615–632.

Pelled L. H., Eisenhardt, K. M., & Xin, K. R. (1999). Exploring the black box: An analysis of work group diversity, conflict, and performance. *Administrative Science Quarterly, 44,* 1–29.

Peters, L., & Karren, R. J. (2009). An examination of the roles of trust and functional diversity on virtual team performance ratings. *Group & Organization Management, 34,* 479–504.

Portes, A. (1998). Social capital: Its origins and applications in modern sociology. *Annual Review of Sociology, 24,* 1–24.

Pratt, M. G., & Rosa, J. A. (2003). Transforming work-family conflict into commitment in network marketing organizations. *Academy of Management Journal, 46,* 395–418.

Prigogine, I., & Stengers, I. (1984). *Order out of chaos.* New York, NY: Bantam Books.

Strauss, A., & Corbin, J. (1998). *Basics of qualitative research: Techniques and procedures for developing grounded theory* (2nd ed.). London, England: Sage.

Sydow, J., & Windeler, A. (1998). Organizing and evaluating interfirm networks: A structurationist perspective on network processes and effectiveness. *Organization Science, 9,* 265–284.

Tomkins, C. (2001). Interdependencies, trust and information in relationships, alliances and networks. *Accounting, Organizations and Society, 26,* 161–191.

Tsai, W. (2000). Social capital, strategic relatedness and the formation of intraorganizational linkages. *Strategic Management Journal, 21,* 925–939.

Tsai, W., & Ghoshal, S. (1998). Social capital and value creation: The role of interfirm networks. *Academy of Management Journal, 41,* 464–476.

Walker, G., Kogut, B., & Shan, W. (1997). Social capital, structural holes and the formation of an industry network. *Organization Science, 8,* 109–125.

Watson, W. E., Kumar, K., & Michaelsen, L. K. (1993). Cultural diversity's impact on interaction process and performance: Comparing homogenous and diverse task groups. *Academy of Management Journal, 36,* 590–603.

Weber, M. (1922/1980). *Wirtschaft und Gesellschaft.* Tübingen, Germany: Mohr.

Yin, R. K. (1994). *Case study research: Design and methods* (2nd ed.). Thousand Oaks, CA: Sage.

Yli-Renko, H., Autio, E., & Sapienza, H. J. (2001). Social capital, knowledge capital, knowledge acquisition and knowledge exploitation in young technology-based firms. *Strategic Management Journal, 22,* 587–613.

Young-Ybarra, C., & Wiersema, M. (1999). Strategic flexibility in information technology alliances: The influence of transaction cost economics and social exchange theory. *Organization Science, 10,* 439–459.

Zeng, M., & Chen, X. (2003). Achieving cooperation in multiparty alliances: A social dilemma approach to partnership management. *Academy of Management Review, 28,* 587–605.

Zollo, M., Reuer, J. J., & Singh, H. (2002). Interorganizational routines and performance in strategic alliances. *Organization Science, 13,* 701–713.

CHAPTER 12

MANAGING INTERNAL TENSIONS IN STRATEGIC ALLIANCES

T. K. Das
Bing-Sheng Teng

ABSTRACT

The instabilities of strategic alliances have been examined in the literature through a number of theoretical approaches. Alliance instabilities refer to major changes or dissolutions of alliances that are unplanned from the perspective of one or more partners. Although the literature identifies certain characteristics of strategic alliances that may lead to their unplanned dissolution, the extent of our understanding of this subject appears to be fragmented and incomplete. In this chapter, we propose a comprehensive framework for adequately understanding alliance instabilities based on the notion of internal tensions. We suggest that strategic alliances are sites in which conflicting forces develop and which can be viewed as being constituted by three key pairs of competing forces, namely, cooperation versus competition, rigidity versus flexibility, and short-term versus long-term orientation. This tensions framework helps us in explaining the intrinsic vulnerability of alliances in terms of a wide range of internal contradictions and enables us to examine, in an integrated manner, the incidence, dynamics, and eventual dissipation

Management Dynamics in Strategic Alliances, pages 267–313
Copyright © 2012 by Information Age Publishing
267

of the inherent instabilities. We discuss the interrelationships among the different internal tensions and their impacts on different types of strategic alliances. We also examine the termination of alliances through mergers/ acquisitions and dissolution. Finally, we suggest ways to empirically test the various ideas and propositions developed here and indicate directions for further research.

INTRODUCTION

We have witnessed in recent years a spurt in the numbers of strategic alliances between firms pursuing various kinds of economic objectives. Broadly defined, strategic alliances refer to interfirm cooperative arrangements aimed at pursuing mutual strategic objectives. Popular forms of strategic alliances include joint ventures, direct equity investments, research and development (R&D) agreements, research consortia, joint marketing agreements, buyer-supplier relationships, and so on. Strategic alliances seem to be proliferating with increasing competition and globalization. However, notwithstanding this popularity, strategic alliances tend to have relatively high instability rates.

Our purpose in this chapter is to suggest that internal tensions account for the inherent instabilities of strategic alliances. *Alliance instabilities* refers to *major changes or dissolutions of alliances that are unplanned from the perspective of one or more partners* (Inkpen & Beamish, 1997). We should note that alliances whose terminations were planned from the outset should not be considered unstable. However, if an alliance is dissolved prematurely or a merger/acquisition ensues that was not intended originally, we will consider the incident as one resulting from inherent alliance instability. The idea of internal contradictions in alliances provides the theoretical depth needed to fully exemplify various competing forces within alliances.

Although a number of theories have been or could be used to explain alliance instability, our literature review shows that these explanations are either weak or incomplete. Thus, no existing theory adequately accounts for the phenomenon of high instability rates of alliances across the board. By comparison, the internal tensions framework has the advantage both of being comprehensive and integrative and of highlighting the difference between alliances and single or formal organizations. The difference is that whereas formal organizations are characterized by a more stable dominance of certain forces, there is a need in alliances to maintain a delicate balance of several pairs of competing forces. The internal tensions perspective supports this balancing view and provides us with a clear-cut accounting of the inordinate instabilities of alliances.

We divide the chapter into five parts. First, we discuss how the extant approaches to explaining the inherent instabilities of strategic alliances are inadequate in significant ways. Second, we propose a framework of internal tensions, comprising three key pairs of competing forces, namely, cooperation versus competition, rigidity versus flexibility, and short-term versus long-term orientation. We follow with a discussion of the likely outcomes triggered by imbalances among these internal tensions. Third, we examine the termination of alliances through mergers/acquisitions and dissolution. In the fourth part, we examine the impact of these tensions in different types of alliances. Finally, we suggest ways to empirically test the various propositions developed here, note the limitations and boundary conditions of the internal tensions framework, and indicate directions for further research.

EXPLAINING ALLIANCE INSTABILITIES

Various studies show that strategic alliance formation has increased significantly in recent times (see Beamish & Delios, 1997; Hagedoorn & Schakenraad, 1993, 1994; Harbison & Pekar, 1998; Pekar & Allio, 1994).[1] However, despite this increasing trend, strategic alliances have generally tended to fail and be terminated at excessively high rates. We summarize in Table 12.1 the major empirical findings on alliance performance and instability in the last few decades. It appears that less than half of the alliances studied can be said to have performed satisfactorily. Defining unstable alliances as liquidations, acquisitions, and reorganizations, most studies indicate that the instability rate is somewhere between 30% and 50% (Beamish, 1985; Killing, 1988; Kogut, 1988; Park & Ungson, 1997; Stuckey, 1983). Furthermore, the studies that compared strategic alliances with formal organizations—usually wholly owned subsidiaries—show that alliances are less successful and less stable (Bleeke & Ernst, 1991; Gomes-Casseres, 1987; Hennart, Kim, & Zeng, 1998; Kent, 1991; Li, 1995; Pennings, Barkema, & Douma, 1994; Yamawaki, 1997).

In brief, a review of the findings in Table 12.1 suggests that strategic alliances are particularly unstable and unsuccessful. Researchers have rightly pointed out that the termination of an alliance does not necessarily signal failure (e.g., Inkpen & Beamish, 1997). Strategic alliances can end after achieving specified objectives or after outliving their usefulness. In these cases, the termination of the alliances can be either natural or planned. Nevertheless, alliance instability is not desirable for alliance partners because, by our definition, changes to the alliance status quo are inimical to the plans of at least one of the partners. Unplanned and premature alliance terminations and restructurings take place often as a consequence of adverse developments. That is also why researchers have often used alliance instability as a proxy for poor alliance performance (Geringer & Woodcock, 1995; Kogut, 1989). We need to understand why such an apparently

TABLE 12.1 Strategic Alliance Outcomes and Instability

Study	Alliance Type	Time Period	Empirical Particulars	Performance	Instability
Beamish (1985)	Joint ventures	prior to 1984	66 JVs	61% unsatisfactory	45% unstable[a]
Bleeke & Ernst (1991)	Cross-border alliances	up to 1990	49 alliances vs. 28 acquisitions	51% success rate for alliances 57% success rate for acquisitions (success: both partners achieved their objectives and both recovered their financial costs of capital)	—
Economist (1995)	Strategic alliances	around 1995	citing Boston Consulting Group studies	fewer than 40% of regional and 30% of international alliances are successful	—
Franko (1971a)	Joint ventures	1961–1967	1100 JVs	—	28.5% unstable[b]
Gomes-Casseres (1987)	Joint ventures	1900–1975	2,378 JVs vs. 3,555 wholly owned subsidiaries	—	30.6% of JVs unstable[c] 15.7% of wholly owned subsidiaries unstable
Harrigan (1988)	Strategic alliances	1975–1986	895 strategic alliances	45.3% mutually assessed to be successful	42% lasted more than 4 years
Hennart, Kim, & Zeng (1998)	Japanese joint ventures	1980–1991	323 Japanese manufacturing plants in U.S.	—	JVs more likely to exit than wholly owned subsidiaries
Kent (1991)	Joint ventures	1954–1973	563 JVs vs. 479 non-JVs in the petroleum industry	Performance of JVs significantly lower than non-JVs (better performance defined as lower bids)	—

Killing (1983)	Joint ventures		36 JVs	—	30% unstable[a]
Kogut (1988)	Joint ventures	prior to 1988	149 JVs	—	51.7% unstable[a]
Li (1995)	Joint ventures	1974–1988	267 foreign entries in U.S. (Including JVs)	—	JVs more likely to exit than wholly owned subsidiaries
Park & Russo (1996)	Joint ventures	1979–1988	204 JVs	27.5% failure rate (failure defined as dissolution and third-party acquisitions)	—
Park & Ungson (1997)	U.S.–Japanese joint ventures	1979–1988	186 JVs	—	43% dissolution rate (liquidation or sale to a third party)
Pennings, Barkema, & Douma (1994)	Dutch joint ventures	1966–1988	462 expansion projects (including JVs)	—	JVs more likely to exit than wholly owned subsidiaries
Stuckey (1983)	Joint ventures	1955–1979	60 JVs in the aluminum industry	—	42% unstable[c]
Yamawaki (1997)	Japanese joint ventures	1980–1990	371 subsidiaries (including JVs)	—	JVs more likely to exit than wholly owned subsidiaries

[a] Includes liquidations, acquisitions, and major reorganizations (see Beamish, 1985, p. 14; Kogut, 1988, p. 328).
[b] Includes changing ownership shares crossing the 50% or 95% lines, selling the stake in the venture, or liquidating the venture (see Franko, 1971b, pp. 17–18).
[c] Includes liquidations and acquisitions.
Source: Table has been developed in part from Beamish (1985) and Kogut (1988).

pragmatic strategy of voluntary business cooperation has all too often resulted in instabilities.

Researchers have attempted to address the puzzle of unstable alliances with several suggestions regarding possible deficiencies in strategic alliances (Alexander, 1995; Kogut, 1988, 1989; Koot, 1988; Parkhe 1993a, 1993b; Pearce, 1997). Although these suggestions are not mutually exclusive, we can identify several major approaches. We list these approaches in Table 12.2 in terms of their tenets, key empirical studies, likely explanations for instability, and deficiencies and gaps.

One explanation for the pitfalls of strategic alliances has its foundation in relational contracting theory (Macneil, 1974, 1980) and transaction cost economics (Williamson, 1975, 1985). Relational contracting theory posits that a sense of trust between exchange partners is essential for smooth exchange relationships, including strategic alliances. Transaction cost economics also stresses the negative impact of opportunistic behavior in interorganizational relationships. Scholars argue that because a firm may pursue its self-interest at the expense its partners in an alliance, all partner firms oftentimes find it hard to rely on trust. The cost of deterring opportunism and developing interfirm trust will be very high because alliance partners will have to employ all kinds of devices—in both ex ante contracts and ex post monitoring. A lack of interfirm trust can, thus, seriously undermine the basis for successful alliances.

We should note that transaction cost theory does not usually consider the possibility that efficient markets discourage opportunistic behavior in the long run (Hill, 1990). Therefore, problems of opportunism may not be as serious as transaction cost theorists suggest (Ghoshal & Moran, 1996). Also, a focus only on interfirm trust does not give us an adequate understanding of alliance instability. After all, other factors, such as partner choice, structural arrangements, and temporal orientations of partners, are also critically relevant.

A second approach to explaining the inherent deficiencies of strategic alliances is in terms of game theory. Some scholars argue that the situation concerning strategic alliances is akin to that of prisoners' dilemma in game theory, in which the players are unsure of the intentions of their partners so that both choose not to cooperate. The premise for such an outcome is that the payoffs from noncooperation should be higher than those from cooperation. Because many alliances are structured in a way that the firms can expect more payoffs from cheating or exploiting the partner, it seems inevitable that those alliances will eventually fail. In fact, scholars have recognized that game theory needs to be complemented by other theories for a better understanding of alliances (Parkhe, 1993b). Whereas game theory traditionally deals with the single-game situation, recent studies with repeated games indicate that cooperation could be a likely outcome

TABLE 12.2   Theories Potentially Relevant for Explaining Strategic Alliance Instability

Name of Theory (With authoritative references)	Tenets of the Theory (With representative quotes)	Empirical Studies	Explanation for Alliance Instability	Deficiencies/Gaps
Relational Contracting (Macneil, 1974, 1980)	Relational exchanges, as opposed to discrete exchanges, take place on the basis of a historical and social context, such as trust. "Relational exchange . . . accounts explicitly for the historical and social context in which transactions take place and views enforcement of obligations as following from the mutuality of interest that exists between a set of parties" (Heide, 1994, p. 74).	Heide, 1994; Zaheer & Venkatraman, 1995	Alliances are essentially relational contracts that may run into trouble if there is a lack of interfirm trust.	A lack of interfirm trust may not explain most alliance instabilities. Partners with no historical involvement also succeed.
Transaction Cost (Williamson, 1975, 1985)	Assuming economic actors are boundedly rational and often opportunistic, there is a cost (e.g., of monitoring and safeguarding) involved in economic transactions. "The essence of economic activity is the transaction; hierarchies manage productive activity because transactions costs make spot market transactions more costly, and therefore less efficient under certain circumstances" (Ramanathan, Seth, & Thomas, 1997, p. 54). "Firms choose how to transact according to the criterion of minimizing the sum of production and transaction costs" (Kogut, 1988, p. 320).	Gulati, 1995; Joskow, 1991; Parkhe, 1993b	Opportunistic behavior of partner firms, which is costly and difficult to control, greatly undermines the stability of strategic alliances.	The possibility that efficient markets, with the establishment of firm reputation, discourage opportunistic behavior (see Hill, 1990).

(continued)

TABLE 12.2 (continued)   Theories Potentially Relevant for Explaining Strategic Alliance Instability

Name of Theory (With authoritative references)	Tenets of the Theory (With representative quotes)	Empirical Studies	Explanation for Alliance Instability	Deficiencies/Gaps
Game Theory (Axelrod, 1984)	This theory studies the choice situations in which the final outcome will depend on what each person involved chooses to do. "Each partner fears that the other will get the larger payoff by acting opportunistically while it cooperates in good faith" (Gulati, Khanna, & Nohria, 1994, p. 61).	Heide & Miner, 1992; Parkhe 1993b; Parkhe, Rosenthal, & Chandran, 1993	Alliances can be viewed as games in which payoffs from cheating may be greater than those from cooperating. Thus, partners may not cooperate fully.	Recent studies with repeated games suggest that cooperation could be a likely outcome.
Resource Dependence (Pfeffer & Salancik, 1978)	Because firms depend on resources of other firms, interfirm relationships constitute a strategic response for controlling this dependence and uncertainty. "Resource dependence theory views interfirm governance as a strategic response to conditions of uncertainty and dependence" (Heide, 1994, p. 72). "The focus is on minimizing interorganizational dependencies and preserving the organization's autonomy while recognizing that interorganizational relationships are necessary to acquire resources" (Gray & Wood, 1991, p. 7).	Pfeffer & Salancik, 1978; Pfeffer & Nowak, 1976; Provan & Skinner, 1989	After firms acquire the kind of resources they need from their partners, the alliance will be terminated, thus contributing to a high degree of instability.	Certain key resources are minimally mobile and imitable, so that a transfer of resources may not be possible.

Bargaining Power (Bacharach & Lawler, 1981)	Bargaining power is critical in negotiations. Thus, the bargaining process is a process in which each party's bargaining power is wielded and manipulated. "The relative bargaining power of each joint venture partner shapes the pattern of management control that a venture adopts" (Yan & Gray, 1994, p. 1478).	Blodgett, 1991; Yan & Gray, 1994	As partner firms' relative bargaining power shifts in the life of an alliance (due to changes in inter-dependencies), firms tend to renegotiate their agreement.	Alliance agreements have legal binding, and they may actually discourage partners who acquire more bargaining power from recasting the deal.
Agency Theory (Jensen & Meckling, 1976)	Economic activities performed by a group of people have the advantages of teamwork. However, because agents will pursue self-serving goals, there is a cost for structuring and monitoring contracts. "Instead, in agency theory the firm is viewed as merely a nexus of contracts...between owners of the factors of production and customers....according to agency theory firms come into existence to exploit the advantages of teamwork while controlling agency costs...Agency costs include 'the cost of structuring, monitoring, and bonding a set of contracts among agents with conflicting self-interests'" (Ramanathan, Seth, & Thomas, 1997, p. 68).	Geringer & Woodcock, 1995	Managerial decisions regarding alliances often serve the interests of managers. To reduce compensation/employment risk, managers often proceed to internalize alliances.	The theory explains managers' motives for internalizing alliances. However, when no partner is any more able to do so than other partners, an equilibrium is created and the alliance is sustained.

(continued)

TABLE 12.2 (continued) Theories Potentially Relevant for Explaining Strategic Alliance Instability

Name of Theory (With authoritative references)	Tenets of the Theory (With representative quotes)	Empirical Studies	Explanation for Alliance Instability	Deficiencies/Gaps
Strategic Behavior (or Strategic Management) (Porter, 1980, 1985)	This theory is concerned with gaining an advantageous position against rival firms. Strategies are intended to achieve various goals, such as capitalizing on opportunities and minimizing threats. "Strategic behavior posits that firms transact by the mode which maximizes profits through improving a firm's competitive position vis-à-vis rivals" (Kogut, 1988, p. 322). "Strategic management theory…depicts a focal organization charting independent courses of action to gain competitive advantage" (Gray & Wood, 1991, p. 9).	Glaister & Buckley, 1996; Hatfield & Pearce, 1994	Strategic alliances may serve several goals, including risk reduction, access to technology and market, and so on. Unrealistic goal expectations and goal disparities may lead to accelerated alliance dissolution.	It seems implausible that alliances are motivated by unrealistic goal expectations.
Transitional	Because of internal managerial difficulties, strategic alliances are unable to carry out long-term projects. They often become essentially transitional entities. Alliances are "transitional devices rather than stable arrangements," and "they always involve significant costs in terms of coordination, reconciling goals with an independent entity, creating a competitor, and giving up profits" (Porter, 1990, p. 613).	Franko, 1971b; Kogut, 1989	Because alliances have a tendency to evolve into other organizational forms, alliance instability is only to be expected.	This approach is highly descriptive and fragmented, without a theoretical framework that effectively integrates various difficulties.

(Axelrod, 1984; Oye, 1986). According to institutional theory, firms tend to follow fashions in their industries to gain legitimacy (DiMaggio & Powell, 1983). As such, strategic alliances are likely to resemble infinitely repeated games for partner firms. Accordingly, researchers suggest that those with a reputation of being cooperative could actually benefit in the long run (Dollinger, Golden, & Saxton, 1997; Hill, 1990; Saxton, 1997). However, whether strategic alliances could indeed become more stable over time still awaits empirical support. In any event, this extension of game-theoretic thinking does not seem very promising in accounting for the general instabilities of strategic alliances.

A third approach is based on a resource dependence and bargaining power perspective. The resource dependence model indicates that firms rely on certain resources owned by others and manage interorganizational relationships to control and minimize such dependence. Strategic alliances enable firms to procure others' resources and thus reduce the level of dependence on the environment. Of course, forging an alliance usually increases a firm's dependence on its partner firm. Power imbalance has been found to be inversely related to perceived effectiveness in comarketing alliances (Bucklin & Sengupta, 1993). Some scholars maintain that the value of resources possessed by each firm determines its bargaining power in negotiations as well as bargaining results (Yan & Gray, 1994). Extending this view to joint venture instabilities, Inkpen and Beamish (1997) argue that shifts in the balance of partner bargaining power are responsible for unplanned terminations of joint ventures. According to them, because firms enter joint ventures mostly to acquire knowledge and skills, it is inevitable that the need for cooperation will diminish once that acquisition is completed, hence, usually, unplanned terminations.

The merit of this approach is that resource dependence explains both the formation and termination of alliances by the same logic. Nevertheless, it seems to us somewhat implausible that most joint ventures—and, more generally, strategic alliances—are formed to acquire knowledge. Firms may enter into strategic alliances for resource considerations (Das & Teng, 2000) or for reasons as disparate as market access, advantages of scale economies, sharing of risks and costs in R&D, and so on. Clearly, knowledge acquisition cannot greatly undermine the foundation of those alliances. Certain key resources are minimally mobile and imitable, so that a shift in bargaining power may not take place easily. Even when the alliance is formed to gain knowledge, Beamish and Inkpen (1995) note that accessing rather than acquiring a partner's knowledge makes a joint venture stable. Moreover, Doz (1996) reports that learning actually contributes to alliance success, whereas nonlearning leads to alliance failure. Hallen, Johanson, and Seyed-Mohamed (1991) found that changes in partners' bargaining power prompt interfirm adaptation, not necessarily instability. Thus, knowledge acquisition and shifts in bargaining power alone may not adequately account for the general phenomenon of alliance instabilities.

A fourth approach, agency theory, has also been extended to strategic alliances (Geringer & Woodcock, 1995; Ramanathan, Seth, & Thomas, 1997). According to this theory, collective economic activities can be advantageous due to the benefits of teamwork. However, because agents in exchange relations may pursue self-serving goals, explicit contracts need to be structured and monitored. Agency theorists have examined how managers make decisions that benefit themselves rather than their firms. As to strategic alliances, scholars suggest that managers are often motivated to fold the alliances into their own firms to control their own compensation or employment risk. A consequence is that many alliances are terminated rather quickly, often being sold to one of the partners.

Although agency theory provides a motivational account for unplanned alliance termination, it does not explain why many firms are able to acquire an alliance even though their partner firms may simultaneously tend toward the same objective. It seems likely that an equilibrium will be created when more than one partner firm is interested in integrating an alliance into its own firm. The result could reasonably be, by this logic, a sustainable alliance. In this light, the particularly high instability rates in alliances cannot be explained by agency theory.

Fifth, according to strategic behavior theory, firms develop strategies that will enable them to obtain advantageous competitive positions against their competitors (Porter 1980, 1985). In this view, through strategic alliances, firms may attain a better competitive position vis-à-vis their rivals (Kogut, 1988). Sound, specific goals are thus particularly important for gaining and wielding one's competitive advantage through alliances. According to this theory, a number of goals can be potentially achieved through strategic alliances, such as gaining access to technologies or markets; economies of scale or scope in production, risk reduction and sharing in R&D; synergy; and jointly attacking industry leaders (Glaister & Buckley, 1996; Hagedoorn, 1993). Although these goals explain alliance formation, researchers also suggest that unrealistic goal expectations and a lack of overlap with the goals of partners may be the reason for alliance instability (Hatfield & Pearce, 1994). Stafford (1994) argues that partner firms are often not patient enough to achieve their goals in an alliance. Thus, alliance instability is the result of imperfect strategic planning and implementation. Although this is certainly the case with some alliances, it is difficult to argue that firms have particularly unrealistic goals in alliances but not so in their own subsidiaries. In fact, strategic goals that have been linked with alliances mostly seem reasonable and legitimate.

Other approaches consider strategic alliances as inherently unstable, with a tendency to evolve into more stable organizational forms (Williamson, 1985). Because many alliances are characterized by a high degree of flexibility, a low level of irreversible commitment, and incomplete contracts, they are unsuitable for carrying out long-term projects. Thus, the termination of alliances is a fairly likely eventuality. Porter notes that alliances are "transitional devices rather than stable arrangements," and "they always involve significant costs in terms of coordination, reconciling goals with an independent entity, creating a competitor, and giving up profits" (1990, p. 613). Koot (1988) observes that there are several underlying dilemmas in joint ventures that are obstacles to success. These dilemmas include delicate balances between exploiting and investing, molding and growing up, as well as fighting and cooperation. Hennart et al. (1998) propose that the two main reasons for joint venture instability are problems in shared management and easier spin-offs. Others (e.g., Franko, 1971a; Kogut, 1988) attribute the instability of joint ventures to the tensions between parent firms, and between parent firms and the ventures. According to Kogut (1989), because competitive incentives among the partners and a lack of reciprocity are at odds with interfirm cooperation, joint ventures tend to be highly unstable. In essence, many authors have noted sundry inherent inconsistencies and contradictions in strategic alliances, but a coherent framework explaining those contradictions has yet to emerge.

In summary, extensive research has been published on the subject of alliance instability, but with less than satisfactory explanations provided by any of the principal approaches identified above. One basic theme in these approaches is that partner conflict is responsible for alliance instability. As part of this theme, researchers have pointed to contributing factors such as equity structures of alliances (Blodgett, 1992; Kogut, 1988), stages of multinational growth (Franko, 1971b), and the competitive environment (Kogut, 1989). The weakness of this general theme is that it remains unclear why the common interests present in alliances do not temper and severely control potential conflict. If alliances are a profitable strategy, then it seems to make sense for partners to restrain conflicts, pursuing mutual interests. Emphasizing the singular role of competition does not afford a full picture of alliance functioning. A second basic theme in the major approaches discussed above is that, because alliances represent incomplete contracts open to renegotiation, they naturally invite substantial restructuring later on (Inkpen & Beamish, 1997; Pearce, 1997). This highlights the detrimental effects of flexibility in alliances. However, flexibility, as a key advantage of strategic alliances, may actually help partners by not compelling them to renegotiate alliances when flexible agreements can better accommodate evolving operational requirements. Thus, alliance instability and termination may indeed be avoided precisely because of the incompleteness of contracts.

Hence, although all these approaches have identified certain characteristics of strategic alliances that may lead to their undesired dissolution, the extent of our understanding of this subject appears to be fragmented and incomplete. Because each approach has focused on limited aspects of strategic alliances, there is as yet no general framework that explains why strategic alliances are inordinately unstable. In particular, these approaches have not adequately addressed the simultaneous existence of several inconsistencies and pitfalls of strategic alliances.

To address these inadequacies of the existing approaches, we present here a framework of strategic alliances based on internal tensions, which accounts for both the incidence and the dissipation of alliance instabilities. It suggests that strategic alliances are the sites in which conflicting forces develop. Thus, this tensions-based view attempts to explain the inherent vulnerability of alliances in terms of a wide range of internal contradictions.

FRAMEWORK OF INTERNAL TENSIONS

The notions of opposites, contradictions, dialectics, tensions, dilemmas, and paradoxes constitute an important basis for social science theorizing (Astley & Van de Ven, 1983; Das, 1984; Ford & Ford, 1994; Kuhn, 1977; Poole & Van de Ven, 1989; Quinn & Cameron, 1988). Some scholars have applied the logic of dialectics, which is rooted in the idea of contradiction, to organizational studies (Benson, 1977; Heydebrand, 1977; Lourenco & Glidewell, 1975; McGuire, 1988; Zeitz, 1980). According to the dialectical view, the world is a unity of opposites. Within any entity, including an organizational entity, there are "colliding events, forces, or contradictory values which compete with each other for domination and control" (Van de Ven, 1992, p. 178).

This contradiction-based paradigm has spurred much theory development in management. For example, Greiner (1972) used the idea of contradiction in explaining organizational revolution. Quinn and Rohrbaugh (1983) adopted a competing-values approach—comprising the three pairs: internal versus external focus, flexibility versus control (structurewise), and process orientation versus outcomeorientation—to understand organizational effectiveness. Barley and Kunda (1992) analyzed the historical evolution of American managerial discourse in terms of alternating long waves of rational and normative ideologies of control, the former reflected in scientific management and systems rationalism and the latter in industrial betterment, human relations, and organizational culture. Much the same logic of contradiction has been applied to organizational change and development (Ford & Ford, 1994; Van de Ven & Poole, 1995).

Paradox is another oft-used contradiction-based notion that is defined as "two contrary, or even contradictory, propositions to which we are led by apparently sound arguments" (van Heigenoort, 1967, p. 45). The key here is that "both of the contradictory elements in a paradox are accepted and present" (Cameron & Quinn, 1988, p. 2). For instance, difficult reconciliations are involved in group dynamics in terms of individual identity and collective action (Jones, Hesterly, Fladmoe-Lindquist, & Borgatti, 1998; Smith & Berg, 1987). Also, various paradoxes have been identified as affecting the process of organizational change and transformation (see Quinn & Cameron, 1988).

Tension results from the presence of contradictions and the attempts to resolve such contradictions. For example, the notion of loose coupling (Orton & Weick, 1990; Weick, 1976) can be viewed as a resolution of noncoupling versus tight coupling. Indeed, Das (1984) suggests that there is inherent tension in the very notion of loose coupling because it juxtaposes two opposing concepts, namely, the concept of looseness and the concept of coupling, which is tantamount to tightness. Overall, Poole and Van de Ven advocate theory building that moves away from "consistency" and toward "the resolution of tensions or oppositions" (1989, p. 563). Quinn also has called for "a dynamic theory that can handle both stability and change, that can consider the tensions and conflicts inherent in human systems" (1988, p. 27).

Poole and Van de Ven (1989) suggest four strategies for dealing with paradoxes. First, in the temporal segregation strategy, opposites are separated by different time periods so that each opposing force dominates in turn, as in our two-party politics or in the evolutionary swings, mentioned earlier, in rational and normative ideologies in managerial discourse (Barley & Kunda, 1992). Second, in the spatial segregation strategy, forces are allocated to separate realms or levels, as in the separate organizational analyses of upper echelons and line workers. Third, in the synthesizing strategy, a new, creative synthesis or solution to the contradictions is sought; for example, Greiner's (1972) theory of organizational revolution and growth. Finally, in the strategy of accepting the paradox with its oppositions and contradictions, we balance the opposite forces without resolving or synthesizing them. As Maybury-Lewis (1989, p. 10) put it, "two-part systems have elected to maintain that stability by means of institutionalized equilibrium."

In this chapter, we adopt the balancing strategy that recognizes inevitable tensions and attempts to balance two contradictory forces so that neither dominates over the other. By balance, we mean a condition in which the strengths of the competing forces are at similar levels. A balance situation may lie anywhere from both forces being of low strength (or level) to both being of high strength. For instance, in studying firm-level strategic similarities of commercial banks, Deephouse (1999) finds that a strategic balance lies at intermediate levels of both similarity and differentiation, thereby balancing the pressures of legitimation and competition and achieving the most effective performance. Lado, Boyd, and Hanlon (1997) argue for "syncretic rent-seeking behavior" that "describes a firm's strategic orientation to achieve a dynamic balance (or syncretism) between competitive and cooperative strategies" (p. 122). The idea of balance within strategic alliances pertains to the relative strengths of contradictory forces, so that an imbalance results when one force is of high strength at the same time that the opposite force is of comparatively low strength, and vice versa.

Our internal tensions perspective of strategic alliances comprises three pairs of competing forces, namely, cooperation versus competition, rigidity versus flexibility, and short-term versus long-term orientations. Competition is defined as pursuing one's own interest at the expense of others, while cooperation is the pursuit of mutual interests and common benefits in alliances. Rigidity refers to the characteristics of mutual dependence and connectedness, whereas flexibility enhances the ability of partners to adapt, unencumbered by rigid arrangements. Short-term orientation views strategic alliances as transitional in nature, with a demand for quick and tangible results, whereas long-term orientation regards alliances as at least semipermanent entities, so that more patience and commitment are exercised. An integrated treatment of the competing force-pairs is significant because, as Quinn and Rohrbaugh observe regarding their value dimensions, whereas these are recognized individually, "they have never before been identified as integrated elements of a single conceptual framework" (1983, p. 370).

The contradictions and tensions in these force-pairs may lead to an overthrow of the status quo, that is, the strategic alliance. Whenever one force gathers enough power to dominate over its competing force, the alliance will evolve into something new. In this sense, strategic alliances are internally fragile because these internal tensions will tend to sway an alliance off balance. Because these three pairs of internal contradictions are either uniquely present or more salient in strategic alliances than in traditional (single) organizations, strategic alliances are likely to have a much higher failure rate. Strategic alliances can nevertheless be sustained if a careful balance between these competing forces can be maintained.

Indeed, a number of studies on alliances have already hinted about the idea of contradictions and tensions. Miles and Snow (1991) suggest that one key reason many network organizations fail is that the firms tend to *unbalance* their relationship, usually by leaning toward too much control or modification. Along similar lines, Ring and Van de Ven (1994) propose a framework of alliance making that consists of successive stages propelled by interactive components such as efficiency and equity.

We suggest that the findings of many previous studies can be subsumed within a framework of conflicting forces. By embracing a full-fledged internal tensions approach to strategic alliances, we attempt here to provide a general theoretical framework for those fragmented pieces of research.

We assume that one of the objectives in a strategic alliance is to secure the original arrangement and prevent the alliance from an unplanned dissolution. To that end, the partners should balance the contradictory forces that may work to unsettle the status quo. This is the logic we will weave into our discussion of each pair of contradictory forces.

Cooperation vs. Competition

The simultaneous existence of cooperation and competition between the partners is an important characteristic of strategic alliances. Whereas competition can be defined as pursuing one's own interest at the expense of others, cooperation is the pursuit of mutual interests and common benefits in alliances. Along similar lines, Buckley and Casson (1988) note that cooperation is essentially about mutual forbearance. The fundamental difference between strategic alliances and other single-firm strategies is interfirm cooperation, which is intended to create collaborative advantage otherwise unavailable to single firms. Many scholars do emphasize cooperative behavior in strategic alliances and the role of interfirm trust in the process (Das & Teng, 1998b). However, the recognition of the importance of cooperation does not mean that strategic alliances are free from competition. Competition is the rule of the market, and there is no exception for strategic alliances. First, oftentimes the partners are either direct or indirect, current or potential competitors. Second, some strategic alliances are in the nature of a learning race—a competitive contest—and whoever leads in this race wins.

Cooperation and competition are opposing forces within strategic alliances. Koot (1988) identifies fight versus team cooperation as one dilemma in alliances. The force of cooperation emphasizes goodwill, collective interests, and common benefits, whereas the force of competition subscribes to opportunistic behavior, zero-sum game, and private benefits (Khanna, Gulati, & Nohria, 1998; Yoshino & Rangan, 1995). The two forces differ significantly in both philosophy and spirit and can be viewed in terms of a paradox (Lado et al., 1997). Our foregoing discussion reveals that both forces are salient in strategic alliances. Indeed, both cooperation and competition are indispensable for a sustainable and successful alliance. Cooperation ensures the smooth working relationship needed to carry out the project, and competition protects a partner from losing its firm-specific advantage through inattention. As Teece puts it, "the challenge to policy analysts and to managers is to find the right balance of competition and cooperation" (1992, p. 1). Thus, the tension between simultaneous cooperation and competition may be responsible for the high failure rate of strategic alliances.

This tension of cooperation versus competition is most salient in selecting alliance partners—the first of three major stages in the alliance making process, along with structuring and managing an alliance (Das & Teng, 1997). As many studies suggest (e.g., Brouthers, Brouthers, & Wilkinson, 1995), the most desirable alliance arrangement balancing the contending forces of cooperation and competition is with partners that are approximately equivalent (in terms of their size, profitability, and status in their own industry) and possess complementary know-how and resources. One telling example is the Universal Card alliance between AT&T and Total System Services (TSYS) (Sankar, Boulton, Davidson, Snyder, & Ussery, 1995). Because both partners are leaders in their own particular industry, they could successfully build the alliance on their distinctive strengths.

Clearly, only if the tensions between the conflicting pairs are in some kind of balance could the status quo be maintained. If cooperation is lacking, opportunistic behavior will become prevalent, and no satisfactory partnership can be continued. The result is likely to be a dissolution of the alliance. Recently, the partnership between Time Warner and US West—Time Warner Entertainment—was on the verge of collapse. The primary reason was that potential competition had dominated their relationship. US West had vetoed several deals that could have allied Time Warner Entertainment with a telephone and a cable company because the deals might have undermined US West's own local telephone franchise. Likewise, when Time Warner proposed purchasing Turner Broadcasting, US West perceived the move as intention to compete with Time Warner Entertainment. US West thus vowed to block the deal (Cauley, 1996). The lesson is that when an alliance moves toward too much competition among the partners, its days are numbered.

When firms are too cooperative, they are likely to transfer their know-how and competence to the partners carelessly. In such cases, the previous balance between the partners will be disturbed because one partner will learn enough from the alliance to feel strong by itself. The outcome will be either renegotiation or termination. Thus, a balance between cooperation and competition is what importantly contributes to an enduring alliance. Hence:

Proposition 1: *The stability of strategic alliances will be inversely related to the difference between the cooperation level and the competition level.*

Rigidity vs. Flexibility

Another contradictory pair uniquely salient in strategic alliances is rigidity versus flexibility. We define rigidity in terms of the degree of connectedness of members with each other in an ongoing relationship. In the literature, rigidity is viewed as the opposite of flexibility, whether it is about rigid decision behavior (Rosman, Lubatkin, & O'Neill, 1994; Sharfman & Dean, 1997) or rigidity of core capabilities (Leonard-Barton, 1992). Rigidity in this chapter is a structural concept and can be used to describe organizations in two ways: structural rigidity in linking elements within the organization, and structural rigidity in linking with other organizations in relevant social networks. Clearly, constituencies within formal organizations are rigidly linked with each other. However, the level of structural rigidity tends to be much lower among formal organizations, even though all of them are linked to some extent with others in structures of social relations.

Characterized by a high degree of structural rigidity inside and a low degree of rigidity outside, formal organizations are stable under conditions in which there is a dominance of rigidity within themselves and a dominance of flexibility with other organizations. Hence, the tension of rigidity versus flexibility is not salient for stability within formal organizations. The matter is much more complicated for strategic alliances. In new organizational forms, such as virtual organizations, loosely coupled systems, networks, and strategic alliances, the differences between internal and external rigidity are blurred. These organizational forms transcend traditional organizational boundaries. Taking a strategic alliance as the unit of analysis, structural rigidity among partner firms becomes internal to the alliance. Thus, in strategic alliances, the level of rigidity within the system (i.e., interfirm connections) tends to be intermediate—higher than the level of rigidity external to formal organizations, but lower than the level of rigidity internal to formal organizations. Strategic alliances can arise only when neither rigidity nor flexibility is dominant. In other words, the maintenance of a delicate balance is a prerequisite for an alliance to exist. In this sense, we suggest that strategic alliances are inherently less stable because this conflicting pair of forces, together with others, is more prominent in strategic alliances than in formal organizations.

A key advantage of strategic alliances is the flexibility afforded to partners to be involved at a fairly low level. Flexibility is the degree to which partner firms are able to modify the structural arrangements in the alliance in order to adapt to changing conditions. When the risks in developing new products or expanding into new territories are too high, a strategic alliance allows a flexible, and easy-to-exit, alternative. The structurally more flexible alliances are the nonequity alliances, or alliances with no equity change or equity creation between the partners. Equity alliances, which include joint ventures and minority equity investments, sacrifice flexibility. This is because joint ventures are separately incorporated entities, and therefore the relationships among the partners are more formally laid out. Generally speaking, the partners should permit enough flexibility in the way they run strategic alliances.

In contrast to flexibility, there are strong arguments for structural rigidity as well. Strategic alliances have been criticized for being too flexible, undermining the ability to exercise strong control. They often suffer from insufficient details on how to collaborate, little irreversible commitment, unclear property rights, and weak authority structure. All these point to a lack of binding mechanisms. Structural rigidity can be enhanced through more joint equity ownership, nonrecoverable investments, and contractual specifications. The advantages of a high level of rigidity, especially through equity investment, have been comprehensively spelled out in the literature (Parkhe, 1993b; Williamson, 1983). These advantages include increasing incentives and commitment, aligning the partners' interests, and deterring opportunistic behavior.

The two opposing tendencies in strategic alliances—being flexible and being rigid—constitute another pair of contradictory forces in our framework. Opposing each other, flexibility and rigidity compete for dominance. Applying the same logic as in our earlier discussion, we submit that a relative balance between the two factors is essential for a sustainable alliance. Strategic alliances are advantageous compared to other forms of organizations, partly because alliances are intrinsically more flexible. At the same time, rigidity allows the partners to overcome potential problems in purely contract-based transactions. Thus, to make strategic alliances durable, both characteristics should be nurtured. Because, however, flexibility and rigidity are in the nature of competing forces, a middle ground may serve the best interests of an alliance.

When flexibility is given too much emphasis—and thus overwhelms rigidity—the alliance will tend to evolve into a new system that will require very little control. Eventually, the bond between the partners will weaken and the alliance will become vulnerable. One telling example is that of the ACE (Advanced Computing Environment) alliance mentioned in Gomes-Casseres (1996). As more than 150 firms signed on in the alliance, ACE was highly flexible but lacked sufficient power to coordinate the partners. Consequently, when Compaq and DEC decided to reduce their commitment to ACE, the alliance broke down. On the other hand, a single-minded pursuit of rigidity could disturb the prospect of an alliance as well. A system that is dominated by rigidity will be characterized by financial and contractual rigidity, restraining the partners from adapting to environmental changes. As many strategic alliances are created to cope with uncertainties in the competitive environment, such an overemphasis on rigidity significantly reduces the chances for success and survival.

This internal tension is particularly relevant in the choice of the governance structure of an alliance. The rationale behind an appropriate alliance structure consists in minimizing transaction cost, deterring opportunistic behavior, reliance on interfirm trust, and the comparative salience of relational risk vis-à-vis performance risk (Das & Teng, 1996). The choice between equity and nonequity alliances allows a direct correspondence with the opposition in rigidity versus flexibility. Rigidity will be required to align partners' interests, discourage opportunism, and provide a mechanism for distributing residuals. Flexibility will be needed to control risk, commit limited resources, adapt to changing conditions, and exit easily. In general, an equity alliance is preferable when the need for rigidity is somewhat stronger than that for flexibility, and vice versa.

In sum, the internal tensions view helps us appreciate the idea that the dominance of either flexibility or rigidity may change the status quo and trigger the evolution of a new structure—essentially a nonalliance. Thus:

Proposition 2: *The stability of strategic alliances will be inversely related to the difference between the rigidity level and the flexibility level.*

Short-Term vs. Long-Term Orientation

A strategic alliance is in a constant state of conflict between short-term and long-term orientations (Joskow, 1985). This conflict is present in any organization and is an important element in strategy making (Das, 1987, 1991, 1993). However, temporal orientations are particularly salient in strategic alliances, not only because the partners may attach different time tables to an alliance, but also because the duration of a strategic alliance is often ambiguous (Kogut, 1991). Beamish (1987), for example, differentiates between the needs of short-term and long-term importance in alliances. The short-term orientation views strategic alliances as transitional in nature, with a demand for quick and tangible results. In contrast, the long-term orientation regards strategic alliances as at least semipermanent entities, so that more patience and commitment are exercised. These two orientations reflect completely different philosophies of what to expect from an alliance. As Koot (1988) points out, there is a dilemma in whether to exploit or to invest in strategic alliances. Exploitation goes with a short-term orientation, whereas investing allows a longer time horizon.

There are plenty of reasons for a short-term orientation in strategic alliances. First, strategic alliances are known to be risky adventures. Thus, to adopt an incremental approach often serves the best interest of the partners. Newman (1992) found that many successful joint ventures in transforming economies adopted a more focused strategy, aimed at achieving visible, prompt performance. Ring and Van de Ven (1992) suggest that recurrent contracts that could be repeated on the basis of satisfactory performance are to be preferred under certain circumstances. Second, an expedited exploitation of an alliance will prevent it from becoming a burden on the partners, precluding also the problems of escalating commitment.

Although successful management of alliances depends on a great number of factors (Das & Teng, 1998a, 1999), we submit that the tension in short-term versus long-term orientation is a critical one. A long-term orientation provides needed commitment to a good working relationship, whereas a short-term orientation stresses prompt results that vitalize the alliance. One crucial implication relates to the process of learning in strategic alliances. In our internal tensions view, because interfirm learning tends to balance the needs for short-term orientation and long-term orientation, it stabilizes an alliance. In contrast to the issue of learning, researchers suggest that the partners should develop interfirm trust and blend organizational cultures (Das & Teng, 1998b; Kanter, 1994); clearly, these are attainable only in the relatively distant future.

Just as strongly, a long-term orientation has a number of advantages. First, certain alliances demand a relatively long-term orientation. For example, Joskow (1985) found that relationship-specific investments in strategic alliances are only possible when contract durations are long enough to control uncertainty. Second, a long-term orientation helps align the incentives of the partners, as they know that they will be working together for a long time. Finally, a "shadow of the future" effect is likely to discourage opportunistic behavior among partners (Axelrod, 1984; Heide & Miner, 1992).

Because the short-term and long-term orientations directly compete with each other in strategic alliances, we regard them as forming another key contradictory pair. A desirable state of tension between these two competing forces is one that does not permit dominance by either one. Again, the status quo is stable only if these two orientations can be balanced, as an overemphasis of either orientation will lead to a dissolution of the existing system. Should a short-term orientation dominate the thinking of the partners, the alliance would soon become a gold rush, where nobody cares about the sustainability of the alliance. In this case, the resources of the alliance will be exploited quickly, and then the alliance will be either transformed or terminated. Conversely, if an alliance is preoccupied with only long-term objectives, then short-term, tangible performance is likely to be ignored. It is difficult in practice to plan for a distant future for strategic alliances when the environment evolves quickly. As a result, the dominance of a long-term orientation may lead an alliance to adversity. Thus, a strategy that reflects only one temporal orientation is not compatible with the foundation for a sustainable strategic alliance. Hence:

Proposition 3: *The stability of strategic alliances will be inversely related to the difference between the short-term orientation and the long-term orientation.*

As compared to formal organizations, strategic alliances are faced with the unusual tension between short-term and long-term orientations, and this tension may contribute to the instability of strategic alliances. Though all organizations experience the same conflict between these two orientations, formal organizations can withstand the dominance by either orientation. Either short-term or long-term orientation can serve an organization well under certain circumstances (Das, 1986). By comparison, strategic alliances need to walk a thin line by maintaining an uneasy balance. Whereas a dominance of short-term orientation encourages exploitation among the partners, a dominance of long-term orientation without ongoing periodic results undercuts the partners' motivation and commitment.

Interrelationships Among the Internal Tensions

We turn to a discussion of the interrelationships among the three pairs of contradictory forces delineated above. This would afford us a more detailed appreciation of the utility of the internal tensions framework in understanding alliance instabilities. In system terms, the various force-pairs are related to each other in one way or another. Thus, it is incorrect to assume that the three pairs of contradictory forces are completely independent. An examination of their relationships not only further clarifies these concepts, but also yields additional insights into their impact on strategic alliances, including (in the next section) the role played by the three internal tensions in the process leading to alliance termination.

Before we discuss the relationships among the three internal pairs, it is helpful to note the differences among them in the nature of contradiction. The nature of contradiction refers to the type of conflict that is manifested in the particular pair. The tension between cooperation and competition is mainly behavioral, that is, it is concerned with the way in which the partners handle the operations of the alliances. The tension between rigidity and flexibility represents a structural tension, as the two forces compete mostly on governance and control arrangements. Lastly, the tension between short-term and long-term orientation is psychological (Das, 1986). The issue is not about the expected duration of the alliance. Rather, it has to do with the intentions of the partners in terms of either exploiting the alliance or investing in the alliance. Thus, partners may be preoccupied with exploiting the alliance even though the alliance may be expected to last a long time. Conversely, in an alliance that is not expected to last long, partners may still pay more attention to the state of the alliance rather than to immediate results. Thus, the temporal orientation of the partners should be viewed as a psychological position that they adopt in an alliance. As we will see next, this initial temporal position moderates the relationship between the other two internal tensions.

According to the tensions view, the three internal pairs of contradictory forces are interrelated within an evolving system. Our earlier discussion revealed that the tension in short-term versus long-term orientation represents the partners' orientation toward the alliance, that is, whether they view the alliance as either transitional or semipermanent. This stance may well shift over time. Although one can argue that a balance between short-term and long-term orientation is more desirable, in reality, partners will sometimes tend to lean markedly toward one orientation or the other. Because the partner firms may not have equivalent temporal orientations in alliances, an overall tendency of the alliance's temporal orientation can be viewed as an integration of all partners' orientations. We suggest that the two pairs, namely, cooperation versus competition and rigidity versus flexibility, can be either positively or negatively related to each other, depending on the temporal orientation of the partners. In other words, the tension in short-term versus long-term orientation serves as the moderating variable between the other two tensions.

When the partners have a short-term orientation for the alliance, more rigidity will lead to a higher level of cooperation. That is, structural rigidity enhances cooperation when both partners have a short-term orientation. They tend to be less concerned with both the long-term prospects of the alliance and the possibility of repeated future alliances with the same partners. Of course, because the opposites of rigidity and cooperation are flexibility and competition, we can use the same logic and also say that structural flexibility enhances competition. Without some degree of structural rigidity the firms will take advantage of their partners, just as they will in the marketplace. Such opportunistic behavior leads to a high level of competition among the partners, as each becomes skeptical about the others' behavior and intention. Thus, although both competition and cooperation are needed in alliances, interfirm competition will be intensified and cooperation discouraged. In this case, structural rigidity becomes an effective mechanism for controlling opportunistic behavior, thereby boosting the level of interfirm cooperation. When the partners adopt a short-term orientation, a relatively concrete structural setup will not only assuage their concerns about opportunism, but will also remind them about imminent retaliation triggered by their own actions. Accordingly, the more the partners are structurally locked in the deal, via arrangements such as nonrecoverable investments, equity ownership, legal deterrents, and detailed monitoring clauses, the higher will be the level of cooperation. Thus:

Proposition 4a: *The levels of rigidity and cooperation (as well as the levels of flexibility and competition) will be positively related when the partners have a short-term orientation in strategic alliances.*

When the partners have a long-term orientation, the situation is likely to be different. The reason is that people who are oriented toward a distant future are subject to the "shadow of the future" effect mentioned earlier and thus will tend to value cooperation more. Even when the alliances are not endowed with much structural rigidity, partners that plan for an extended future will emphasize a satisfactory cooperative relationship because they are in for the long haul. However, if there is a high level of rigidity in the alliance, the partners will tend to emphasize the importance of competition. The reason is that the partners with a long-term orientation in the alliance will become more concerned with unintended transfers of proprietary resources should they be deeply committed to the alliance. Because the partners are afraid of losing their firm-specific identities over a long time period, competition between them, such as in a learning race or in the protection of proprietary interests, is likely to be intensified. As we noted earlier, this is not so in the case of those with a short-term orientation for the alliance. Short-termers view strategic alliances as transitional, so that the possibility of the partners becoming indistinguishable due to transfers of proprietary resources is perceived to be remote. Therefore:

Proposition 4b: *At a high level of rigidity, cooperation and rigidity (as well as competition and flexibility) will be negatively related when the partners have a long-term orientation in strategic alliances.*

We present in Table 12.3 a few recent cases that illustrate alliance terminations and alliance difficulties. These case developments can be reasonably accounted for by our framework of internal tensions. In some instances, competition had dominance over cooperation, whereas in others the flexibility-rigidity or the short-term/long-term orientation was off balance. In sum, this sampling of cases illustrates how internal tensions may contribute to alliance instability.

TOWARD ALLIANCE TERMINATIONS

Termination options, such as acquisition or dissolution, are often featured in strategic alliance arrangements. More often, however, the partners have to adjust their arrangements in an ad hoc manner as contingencies unfold. The identification of the three pairs of contradictory forces internal to strategic alliances enables us to examine what option is more likely to be adopted when there is a shift in the balance of these forces.

Termination of existing alliances can take several common forms: termination by merger or acquisition, by dissolution, and by redefinition of the alliance. Because a merger/acquisition results in one organization carrying out

TABLE 12.3   Illustrations of Unplanned Alliance Terminations and Alliance Difficulties

Alliance Partners	Key Reasons for Unplanned Alliance Terminations and Alliance Difficulties	Status of Alliance	Remarks on Internal Tensions
Advanced Computing Environment Alliance	There are more than 150 firms in this alliance around the Mips R4000 chips. Because of insufficient power to coordinate the partners, the alliance failed to adopt a common ACE Unix standard. In 1992, Compaq, Santa Cruz, DEC, and other major partners left the alliance (Gomes-Casseres, 1996, pp. 136–140).	Dissolved	Flexibility dominated rigidity
AT&T–Olivetti	"By moving into the end-user office equipment market in Europe, AT&T could not cope with the new demands on its organizations. Consequently, AT&T's organizational style, professional and bureaucratic, clashed severely with the very dynamic, entrepreneurial style demonstrated by Olivetti's marketing and design-driven management" (Gates, 1993, p. 12).	Dissolved	Competition dominated cooperation (competing for preferred management style)
Dunlop–Pirelli	The two companies have different emphases in the alliance (i.e., industrial vs. financial focus). Pirelli believed in new product development—a long-term undertaking—whereas Dunlop would rather reduce investments in R&D to improve short-term financial performance (Gates, 1993, p. 22).	Dissolved	Direct conflict in time orientation, with no balance between short- and long-term orientation
Honeywell–Yamatake-Honeywell	In 1989, Honeywell sold 16% of Yamatake-Honeywell, which undermined the mutual trust between the two companies. Despite signing an explicit alliance agreement, disputes emerged in gray areas. For instance, the two partners started to compete head-on in the Chinese market for industrial controls (Gomes-Casseres, 1996, pp. 64–69).	Soured relationship	Competition dominated cooperation

Alliance	Description	Outcome	Tension
Liz Claiborne–Avon	"Avon acquired Parfums Stern, an upscale fragrance and cosmetics manufacturer, to improve its market image. With that, Liz Claiborne saw Avon no longer as a partner, but as an outright competitor. The already fragile relationship ended in a conflict" (Stafford, 1994, p. 69).	Venture acquired by Liz Claiborne	Competition dominated cooperation
McDonnell Douglas–Shanghai Aviation Industrial Corp.	McDonnell Douglas poured considerable financial and technological resources into the production alliance. It hoped for a big payoff in the distant future. However, because MD was bonded with the manufacturer whereas Boeing had allied itself with the Chinese aviation administration, MD was losing much ground to the competition (Kahn, 1996).	Alliance in deep trouble	Rigidity and long-term orientation dominated flexibility and short-term orientation
Meiji Milk Products–Borden	The two companies jointly market "Lady Borden," an upscale ice cream, in Japan. Due to competition from imports, its market share went down significantly. However, the partners, especially Meiji, were reluctant and slow to renegotiate the existing agreement, until Borden bowed out of the alliance (Serapio & Cascio, 1996, p. 63).	Dissolved	Rigidity dominated flexibility
Time Warner–US West	Potential conflict of interests has dominated the relationship. US West vetoed several deals of the alliance, which could have undermined its own local telephone franchise, whereas Time Warner wanted to block US West's intended acquisition of Turner Broadcasting for fear of direct competition with the alliance (Cauley, 1996).	Lawsuits, on the verge of dissolution	Competition dominated cooperation

the activities of the alliance, this type of termination represents a clear movement toward hierarchies. A termination by dissolution, on the other hand, is a return to market transactions. And a termination by redefinition of the alliance can be viewed as a modified alliance. Here, we do not discuss termination by redefinition because the alliance continues in its existence as an alliance.

Researchers have long viewed strategic alliances as a mix of markets and hierarchies in terms of managing transactions. Gulati (1995) reasons that strategic alliances are the best choice "when the transaction costs associated with an exchange are intermediate and not high enough to justify vertical integration" (p. 87). Bradach and Eccles (1989) state that pure types of markets and hierarchies are nonexistent because all governance modes include elements of markets, hierarchies, and trust. Still, markets and hierarchies remain the two contrasting governance mechanisms for carrying out economic transactions.

Toward Hierarchies

Because the forces of cooperation, rigidity, and a long-term orientation are closely related to hierarchies, a shift in balance toward these forces tends to end up in a merger or acquisition. That is, the joint task continues to be carried out, but this time within a hierarchy rather than in an alliance. In these cases, strategic alliances do move toward a more stable governance structure—hierarchy. First, when the alliances exhibit high cooperation, with low competition, the partner firms may gradually lose their firm-specific resources and therefore become vulnerable to aggrandizement by their partners. An unanticipated sale, in the form of either merger or acquisition, will be a natural consequence.

Second, an increasingly rigid alliance will also tend to end up in a merger or acquisition. Rigidity sacrifices strategic flexibility so that the alliance becomes less capable of dealing with the uncertainties in the competitive environment. Because the partners can no longer bank on the degree of strategic flexibility they desire from the alliance, the chances of failure increase. To end an alliance in which the partners are rigidly bound, one or more partners must take the alliance over, that is, move to a merger or acquisition. In contrast, if the level of connectivity is low, such as in the case of licensing, the alliance can be terminated easily by dissolution.

Finally, an alliance dominated by a long-term orientation is likely to be merged or acquired too, owing to the following two possibilities. First, because a neglect of short-term performance may often result in the failure of the alliance, it would be difficult for one or more partners to continue in the alliance. Thus, a merger/acquisition provides an option to those who are willing to stick it out. The second possibility is concerned with a shift in time orientation. The partners may initially forge an alliance in an attempt to try out a risky project. Because the alliance is intended to share risks on a trial basis, the partners' initial temporal orientation will tend to be short-term. Eventually, as more information becomes available, the uncertainty about the project may be reduced, and the partners may adopt a longer-term orientation. In consequence, the partners will prefer more integration, and a merger or acquisition will serve as the eventual means toward a hierarchical governance structure.

Toward Markets

We need also to note that a movement toward the dominance of competition, flexibility, and a short-term orientation is likely to lead to dissolution of the alliance, because these forces have a lot in common with market transactions. In this case, transactions that were conducted within the alliances are now conducted in the marketplace. An excessive level of competition can disable the effective operation of the alliance, with the partners then having to pull themselves out of the alliance. Clearly, the best way to preserve competition between alliance partners is to conduct the relevant transactions in the market.

Similarly, just as our earlier example of ACE showed, excessive flexibility may render an alliance susceptible to random buffeting by environmental changes. A lack of adequate structural rigidity makes it difficult to align the interests of partners. When alliances are on the verge of failure, the partners can walk away from the alliance relatively easily because they are minimally locked into the alliance. Finally, as partners move toward a short-term orientation, dissolution becomes a likely outcome. Clearly, the exploiting of short-term opportunities, without investing for a long haul, undermines the sustainability of alliances. When partners fail to balance the alliance with an appropriate long-term orientation, the dissolution of the alliance would seem to be inevitable. Therefore:

> **Proposition 5a:** *An alliance will move toward a merger or acquisition, rather than dissolution, when there is a dominance of cooperation, rigidity, or long-term orientation.*

> **Proposition 5b:** *An alliance will move toward dissolution, rather than a merger or acquisition, when there is a dominance of competition, flexibility, or short-term orientation.*

We present in Figure 12.1 the proposed relationships of the competing forces in alliances and consequent alliance outcomes. To summarize, what

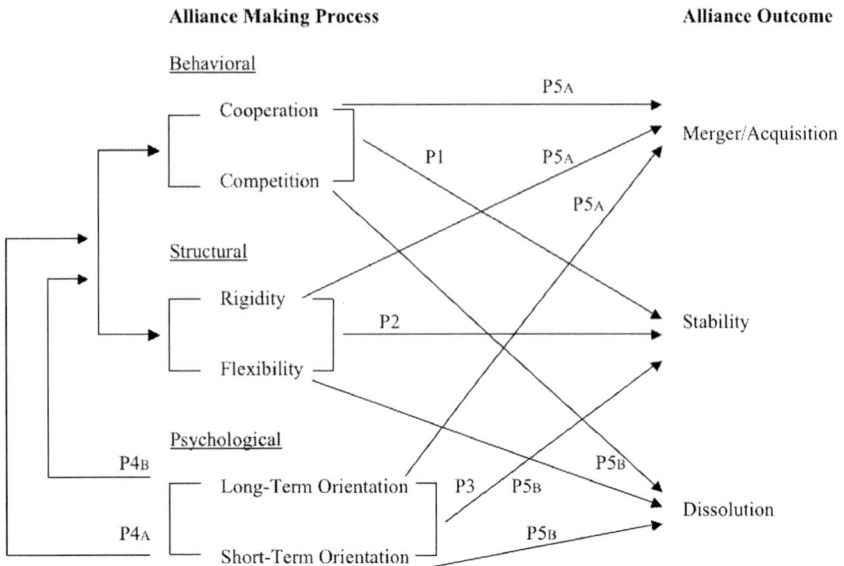

Figure 12.1 Hypothesized relationships in the internal tensions framework.

makes strategic alliances especially vulnerable is that they need to fashion and preserve a simultaneous balance between various internal tensions. And this challenge of maintaining a balance has contributed, and will continue to contribute, to their low rate of survival and success. To explore this dynamic further, we examine these internal tensions in different types of alliances.

INTERNAL TENSIONS IN DIFFERENT ALLIANCE TYPES

Alliances can be categorized in terms of their structural arrangements. Typical structural arrangements include joint ventures, minority equity alliances, equity swap, joint production, joint marketing, joint bidding, shared distribution, and licensing. Researchers have been interested in the rationale and implications of these various arrangements. The choice of alliance structure is closely related to alliance purposes (Glaister & Buckley, 1996), which restrain the structural options available to the partners. For example, if the purpose is acquiring a patented technology, then viable structures will include licensing, coproduction, and joint ventures. If the purpose is reducing R&D risk and cost, then joint R&D with/without minority equity stake will be the choice. Alliance purposes are inherently related to the competing forces. For instance, long-range objectives (e.g., setting industry standards and entering a foreign market) tend to encourage long-term orientation and cooperation. This connection between alliance purposes and the tensions is reflected in the relationship between the tensions and alliance structures, since structures are influenced by purposes. Based on our framework, we suggest that a particular alliance structure will have a distinctive role for each of the three tensions. That is, structural choices may predispose the alliance toward emphasizing certain tensions rather than others. Although a significant imbalance will lead to alliance termination, structural arrangements will affect the balance to some extent. Using the three tensions as three dimensions, we created an eight-cell table to examine such predispositions (see Table 12.4). We need to note that the same structure (e.g., JVs and joint R&D) may be placed at different extremes of the three dimensions. That is where management of alliances plays a role in balancing the internal tensions.

Competitive Alliances

When alliances lean more toward competition rather than cooperation, they may be called competitive alliances. Cells 1 to 4 represent four different conditions. Cell 1 is likely to be arm's-length contracts rather than alliances, as market transactions governed by contracts are characterized as competitive, flexible, and short-term oriented. In Cell 3, certain licensing and joint production agreements may be flexible and yet long-term oriented. These agreements are flexible enough to be revised as needed, although the alliance may be planned for a long period.

By comparison, alliance partners in Cells 2 and 4 are more rigid in their relationships. Short-term joint R&D and joint marketing agreements

TABLE 12.4   Alliance Structures and the Internal Tensions

	Short Term		Long Term	
	Flexible	Rigid	Flexible	Rigid
Competitive	(Arm's-length contracts)* Cell 1	Joint R&D Joint marketing Cell 2	Licensing Joint production Cell 3	JVs Minority equity alliances Cell 4
Cooperative	Funded research Shared distribution Product bundling Cell 5	Joint bidding Joint R&D Joint marketing Cell 6	Dealership Franchising Licensing Joint production Long-term sourcing Cell 7	JVs Minority equity alliances (Wholly owned subsidiaries)* Cell 8

* Not an alliance

would exemplify Cell 2, as the nature of collaboration requires partners to be deeply involved and their activities highly specified (rigidity). In addition, these partners compete hard to get ahead in their learning race (competition). Cell 4, however, has more long-term arrangements such as JVs and minority equity alliances. These equity-based alliances are not only designed for relatively long terms, but also embed partner firms deeply in the alliance through equity measures.

Cooperative Alliances

Alliances that are more cooperation oriented may be called cooperative alliances. In direct contrast to Cell 1, Cell 8 represents wholly owned subsidiaries, JVs, and minority equity alliances that are cooperative, rigid, and long-term oriented. Joint ventures and other equity-based alliances may be operated in a fairly cooperative manner, as the partners' interests are better aligned. On the other hand, the typical arrangements in Cell 6 may include joint bidding, joint R&D, and joint marketing. Because these arrangements require partners to cooperate in a project-specific manner, they tend to be more short-term oriented than JVs, and more rigid and cooperative than agreements such as licensing.

Cell 7 is defined as cooperative, flexible, and long-term oriented. Agreements such as dealership, franchising, licensing, joint production, and long-term sourcing tend to exhibit these characteristics. These arrangements are much more flexible than equity-based alliances and are not as competitive, because the partners often compete in different markets. Finally, Cell 5 appears to be the condition for funded research, shared distribution, and product bundling. These alliance arrangements are usually not for the long haul, and the mutually dependent relationship is relatively open for needed adjustments.

In sum, various structural arrangements may predispose alliances toward specific internal tensions. For example, JVs are likely to be on the long-term and rigid side, whereas funded research agreements tend to be on the short-term and flexible side. Although such predispositions do not suggest the dominance of any particular force, that is, the inclination is only to a limited degree, the possibility of imbalance in the competing forces is quite distinct.

In elaboration of our earlier Propositions 5a and 5b, we suggest that the slight imbalances inherent in the different alliance types will skew them toward predictable kinds of alliance terminations. In other words, those alliance types that are skewed toward competition, flexibility, and short-term orientation are more likely to be terminated through dissolution. Similarly, the alliance types that are characterized more by cooperation, rigidity, and long-term orientation are more likely to be terminated through mergers/

acquisitions. For example, because joint ventures, as we noted, tend to be comparatively rigid and long-term (and can be either cooperative or competitive; see Table 12.4), they will tend to culminate in mergers/acquisitions. In contrast, funded research and product bundling are short-term oriented and flexible, so that dissolution will tend to be the end result. Of course, most alliance types share a mix of small imbalances rather than a straightforward dominance of either competitive/flexible/short-term or cooperative/rigid/long-term combinations. Such mixes of slight imbalances work for maintaining the stability of alliances. In sum, because different alliance types suggest different kinds of small imbalances, they also induce the alliances toward specific types of alliance terminations.

DISCUSSION AND CONCLUSION

Theoretical Contributions

In this chapter, we developed a framework of strategic alliances in terms of their internal tensions as an attempt to address a theoretical deficiency in explaining the inherent instabilities of strategic alliances. Major theories of strategic alliances, such as transaction cost economics, do not succeed in adequately explaining the instabilities of strategic alliances. A general framework is needed that incorporates the many inconsistencies within alliances identified in various studies. Most studies concerning the reasons that strategic alliances have such a high rate of failure follow a piecemeal approach, in the sense that they explore limited, unrelated sources of instability. Other studies are merely descriptive and lack a theoretical framework for organizing the fragmented empirical observations. Our framework of internal tensions is intended to rectify both the shortcomings in the literature.

First, we argued that a strategic alliance itself can be viewed as a system of multiple tensions, namely, cooperation versus competition, rigidity versus flexibility, and short-term versus long-term orientation. Given that an entity should be studied as a system comprised of multiple subsystems, we examined strategic alliances as an aggregation of these three internal tensions. These subsystemic tensions are either created or intensified in strategic alliances. For example, the tension embodied in cooperation versus competition is not present in formal organizations. The tensions in rigidity versus flexibility and short-term versus long-term orientation, although observed in all organizations, are more salient in strategic alliances. The relationship among formal organizations with other organizations is dominated by flexibility, whereas strategic alliances have to maintain a balance between flexibility and rigidity. Similarly, whereas formal organizations may have a choice about either a short-term or a long-term orientation, in strategic alli-

ances, a dominance of either orientation tends to lead to unplanned terminations. The perspective proposed here implies that a system will continue
to evolve and be modified if internal factors are not in balance. As strategic
alliances are characterized by a number of contradictory forces, they can
easily be jeopardized by an imbalance among these forces. All in all, the
internal tensions perspective helps us understand that the inherent instabilities of strategic alliances spring from the difficult challenge of balancing
many competing forces simultaneously.

Second, this tensions view furnishes us with a general framework that integrates many previous studies. Other views, including ones that consider that
inherent dilemmas and imbalances are responsible for the failure of strategic
alliances, can also be easily subsumed under this perspective. The explanation provided by game theory and relational contracting theory—that cooperation failure is the principal reason for alliance instability—has been integrated into cooperation versus competition. We have argued that an alliance
is in trouble when the balance shifts toward too much competition but not
enough cooperation. In sum, previously fragmented pieces of research can
now find a coherent home in the perspective of internal tensions.

Third, in developing and systematically applying the idea of internal tensions to strategic alliances, we extended and reinforced the stream of research in management and organizational studies based on contradictions.
The notions of tensions, contradictions, opposites, dilemmas, and paradoxes are significant elements in various management theories. We found
from our review of this stream of research that the idea of organizations
having to face paradoxical choices and manage contradictions has not been
emphasized in the alliance literature. In this chapter, we demonstrated the
relevancy of the tensions view because it helps explain alliance instabilities
in a more comprehensive and integrated manner than the other theoretical approaches.

We should also mention that although the tensions framework emphasizes the determinative effects of alliance conditions as assessed by the balancing of contradictory forces, it is also in consonance with a process view
of alliances. We believe that because the balance of forces shifts over time,
a continuing examination of alliance conditions will inform us about the
alliance evolution process. Given the dearth of evolutionary theories of alliances (Koza & Lewin, 1998), our framework contributes to a new way of
studying alliance process.

Finally, the normative value of the framework is that alliance managers can work to preserve an appropriate balance on an ongoing basis and
therefore, prevent undesired or premature alliance dissolution. As Ring
and Van de Ven (1994, p. 112) also note, "cooperative IORs [interorganiza-
tional relationships] are maintained in this model not because they achieve
stability, but because they maintain balance." In our framework, alliances

suffer from a high instability rate due to internal tensions, so that an appreciation of these tensions should be of help in stabilizing the alliances.

Suggestions for Empirical Testing

We offer in this section our suggestions for the empirical testing of the proposed framework. We believe that both quantitative and qualitative approaches can be used (Das & Boje, 1993). In discussing these two broad approaches, we provide guidelines for collecting pertinent data, identifying respondents, operationalizations of the key variables, and statistical testing of the propositions.

In the quantitative approach, cross-sectional and large datasets covering various types of alliances are needed to test the internal tensions framework. Such data will obviously ensure statistical robustness and generalizability. However, there are significant challenges in collecting data and developing valid measures of the principal constructs. When secondary data are used, the key is to identify comprehensive alliance databases that contain information regarding all the constructs of this framework.[2]

As to instrument development, multi-item survey measures should be developed to capture the proposed constructs. To that end, we note that existing research studies provide the necessary foundation for developing these survey measures.[3] In most propositions (except Propositions 4a and 4b), the dependent variable is either alliance stability (Propositions 1–3) or alliance outcome (Propositions 5a and P5b). Both variables can be captured by a question relating to the outcome of the alliance, namely, whether the alliance is still operating or has been dissolved or terminated through mergers/acquisitions beyond initial plans. To statistically test Propositions 1 to 3, a discriminant analysis can be used to predict the dependent variable "alliance stability." The independent variables will be the discrepancy within each pair, that is, the higher the differences, the more the likelihood of alliance dissolution. Negative relationships between alliance stability and the differences, for example, cooperation minus competition, will support Propositions 1 to 3. Also, Propositions 4a and 4b can be tested by moderated regression analysis using cooperation as the dependent variable, rigidity as the independent variable, and time orientation as the moderating variable. Finally, Propositions 5a and 5b can be tested by a discriminant analysis, but the dependent variable will be "alliance outcome" with two values: dissolution and merger/acquisition. These two propositions will be supported by positive relationships with the following algebraic differences: cooperation minus competition, rigidity minus flexibility, and long-term orientation minus short-term orientation.

In alliance research, the qualitative approach has been used less frequently than quantitative research, with a few notable exceptions (Doz, 1996; Larson, 1992). A smaller number of cases are needed here, but demand more careful study. Experiments and quasi-experiments in "real" organizations are very difficult to design and carry out. Field investigations are clearly preferable, with interviews and in-depth case analyses.[4] Doz's (1996) study is illustrative of open-ended interviews for inductive analysis of alliance cases. We have proposed that competing forces would evolve over time, triggering reconfigured interrelationships, and potential imbalances, among the internal tensions. Thus, interviews and observations should aim at eliciting information on various levels of these forces at different points in alliance operation. We expect that alliance dissolution will follow a process of accelerating imbalance among these internal competing forces in the alliance.

Limitations and Future Research

The internal tension framework proposed here is useful within its theoretical boundaries. We noted that the three internal tensions are either uniquely present or particularly salient in strategic alliances. Because hierarchical organizations do not house such tensions to any significant extent, our framework is clearly applicable to alliances only. Hence, certain interfirm arrangements such as outsourcing (arrangements that are not much different from market transactions) are not covered. Of course, the tension-based approach, in a more general fashion, may well be useful for studying other topics, including hierarchical organizations. Also, the framework focuses on the inordinate instabilities of alliances, that is, terminations that are not planned by both partners. It does not apply to planned terminations, which may be a consequence of achieving the objectives of the alliance.

The framework is also limited in several other ways, indicating the need for further research. First, although it links alliance outcomes with imbalances of several competing forces, it does not clearly depict the evolutionary process by which these forces may develop. However, the three conflicting forces may serve as the foundation for a more process-oriented model, such as the one proposed by Ring and Van de Ven (1994). We have not explicitly examined the consequences from the evolution of competing forces in alliances. The framework essentially suggests that a significant imbalance results in alliance dissolution, but it does not specify the process through which a slight imbalance may be restored into balance or deteriorate into significant imbalance. This topic deserves attention in future research.

Second, because of the complexities of the constructs proposed here, we believe that the interrelationships of the three types of internal tensions would need to be examined further. It is also possible that some additional (though, perhaps, less prominent) competing forces may be at work in strategic alliances.

Third, given that our framework is fairly parsimonious—using only six variables—it leaves out some potentially relevant factors such as resources and bargaining power. For example, it does not discuss external factors such as changing market conditions that cause alliance termination. We should note, though, that market conditions affect alliances and nonalliances alike, so that they cannot be a reason for unusual alliance instability. Nevertheless, it would improve the comprehensiveness of the framework if future research could incorporate other relevant variables using more encompassing theoretical lenses.

Finally, a more elaborate contingency framework may be desirable for explaining alliance instabilities with greater effectiveness. Although we have shown how alliance structures may affect the balance between the competing forces, we did not attempt to discuss the potential contingencies of other important influences that could well moderate the relationship between the imbalances of internal tensions and alliance instabilities, such as different alliance purposes and different stages of industry life cycles. It seems also likely that certain types of alliances with particular goals are more unstable than others. Future research should explore such refinements.

In conclusion, we delineated strategic alliances as systems whose stability is determined by a balancing of multiple internal tensions. We developed a general framework of internal tensions that comprehensively explains the inherent instabilities of strategic alliances and integrates fragmented theoretical views and empirical observations. We discussed alliance change in terms of the shifting dynamic tensions of the various competing forces. In particular, our framework yields insights into what happens when the balance between the different competing forces shifts toward the dominance of one force or the other. We also elaborated on the different ways of alliance terminations and their antecedent conditions, that is, the different kinds of imbalances among various opposing forces. Finally, we offered detailed suggestions for empirical testing of the various propositions developed here, noted the limitations of our framework, and indicated directions for further research. We hope our proposed internal tensions perspective will serve to encourage efforts to understand more fully how instabilities are generated by the conflicting forces that inform the essentially fragile existence of strategic alliances.

NOTES

1. Based on a survey of 750 CEOs of top U.S. firms, Pekar and Allio found that the rate of alliance formation increased 25% annually between 1985 and

1992, with 5,100 formed between 1980 and 1987 and over 20,000 formed between 1988 and 1992 (1994, p. 54). Harbison and Pekar (1998) reported that the revenues generated by the largest 1,000 U.S. companies from alliances increased dramatically from less than 2% in 1980 to 21% in 1997, and was expected to reach 35% by the year 2002 (p. 1). According to Beamish and Delios (1997), the number of alliances in the period 1985–1989 increased substantially from the level of the 1980–1984 period in key industries, For example, 203% in automobiles and 83% in biotechnology (p. 96). They also mention that more than 13,000 technology cooperation agreements can be found in the database of equity and nonequity alliances compiled by Maastricht Economic Research Institution on Innovation and Technology (p. 92).

2. The difficulty lies in the relative scarcity of alliance databases and also, the fact that they often contain sketchy information about the alliances, such as the date of formation, type, equity arrangements, and so on. Available alliance databases exist with *Alliance Analyst* (1994–1998); CATI database of MERIT (see Hagedoorn, 1993; Hagedoorn & Schakenraad, 1994); Bioscan, which covers the pharmaceutical industry collaborations (see Barley, Freeman, & Hybels, 1992; Deeds & Hill, 1996; Lane & Lubatkin, 1998); and UNCTAD reports on world investment trends (see Beamish & Delios, 1997; Burgers, Hill, & Kim, 1993). *Alliance Analyst*, for example, contains information about all the different types of alliances, thus enabling the coverage of all the categories mentioned in Table 12.4. These alliance types include joint ventures, minority equity alliances, joint production, joint marketing, joint R&D, R&D contracts, licensing, and others. The ReCap database (www.recap.com) contains detailed summaries of over 5,000 biotech alliances from 1978 onwards. In addition, researchers have also compiled large-scale alliance databases in various industries by covering the relevant media and industry publications (e.g., Balakrishnan & Koza, 1993; Eisenhardt & Schoonhoven, 1996; Gulati, 1995; Harrigan, 1988; Kent, 1991; Parkhe, 1993b). We should note that the usefulness of many of these databases is fairly time-bound, as more comprehensive sources are likely to be developed in the future.

Starting with a review of these alliance databases in terms of accessibility, researchers will then need to collect additional secondary data and use them as proxies for some of our constructs. For example, Park and Russo (1996) adopted a longitudinal approach and followed 430 joint ventures for five years. The status of the venture (ongoing versus terminated) was recorded at the end of the period. One can also look into alliance contracts for eliciting information on flexibility versus rigidity and short-term versus long-term orientation. For example, regarding flexibility-rigidity, researchers may look for clauses that relate to possible changes in the alliance arrangements. The stated duration of the alliance can also be compared with the actual alliance longevity in order to determine which terminations reflect alliance instability.

The secondary data should be supplemented by primary data, which may be gathered through mail surveys or face-to-face interviews. Whereas the advantages of mail surveys include more in-depth data, the major challenge here is in the identification of potential respondents and the development of suitable instruments. A multirespondents approach is appropriate because it will permit a check of interrespondent reliability and thus, the overall reliability of the data. Potential respondents should be well-informed about alliance activities. The alliance managers and top level corporate managers can be identified from publications such as Standard and Poor's *Register of Corporations, Directors, and Executives.* For example, Parkhe (1993b) selected the executive vice presidents as the initial corporate level for identifying respondents.

3. The construct of cooperation in our framework should be operationalized in terms of the degree to which firms seek mutual interests rather than self-interests in alliances. For example, following Buckley and Casson's (1988) discussion of cooperation in terms of mutual forbearance, an item on cooperation may read, "To what extent do the partner firms exercise mutual forbearance in their dealings with each other?" Another item can be, "Neither partner makes demands that might be damaging to the other partner" (Inkpen & Currall, 1997, p. 328). In contrast to cooperation, competition should be operationalized in terms of the degree to which a firm pursues self-interests rather than mutual interests. Cullen, Johnson, and Sakano (1995) developed a measure on conflict that may help in developing a measure for competition. For instance, one item might read "How often did you and your partner firm disagree on who should have control over the key decisions in the alliance?" Rigidity is the degree of structural formality and connectedness that prevents modifications to alliance arrangements. A question on rigidity might be, "To what extent are the partners precluded from making changes in the alliance relationship?" Flexibility should be operationalized in terms of the degree of adaptability, responsiveness, and agility. Thus, an item on flexibility can be, "In this relationship, our firm and our partner firm expect to be able to make adjustments in the ongoing relationship to cope with changing circumstances" (Aulakh, Kotabe, & Sahay, 1997, p. 189). Short-term orientation should be operationalized in terms of the degree to which partners focus on quick and tangible results. A question, from Venkatraman (1989, p. 959), will ask about "The extent to which the criteria for resource allocation generally reflect short-term considerations." Long-term orientation should be operationalized in terms of the degree to which partners focus on developing the alliance rather than concentrating on achieving short-term goals. Following Ganesan (1994, p. 15), a question for long-term orientation can be about "The extent to which the partners focus on long-term goals in this relationship." All the six measures can use a Likert-type scale. Several items will of course need to be developed for each measure, and the value of each measure will be the average of these items.

The questionnaire should be pretested with a group of alliance managers to ensure acceptable validity and reliability. The scales of the independent variables will measure the levels of the various competing forces when the alliance was formed, for example, the level of initial flexibility in the alliance. Although the balancing of the forces will evolve over time, the assumption is that alliances characterized by initial imbalances are more likely to be unstable. For the study to be comprehensive, though, the surveys will have to be longitudinal. The questionnaire, containing all items except the one on alliance outcome, can be sent to top managers soon after the alliances are formed (*Alliance Analyst* regularly reports on the formation of the latest alliances). In subsequent annual or biannual intervals, further rounds of the questionnaire, with the addition of an item on alliance outcome, should be administered. Thus, it will be possible to measure how the balancing of the competing forces has been evolving and whether an imbalance has led to alliance termination.

4. Researchers may consult Larson (1992) for a detailed account of such an interview process. As with mail surveys, researchers should endeavor to include multiple, informed top managers for this purpose. Identifying appropriate respondents will be relatively easy for the interviews because researchers will usually be on-site for the purpose. Larson (1992), for example, worked on locating managers involved in initial alliance formation or consequent alliance management. The design will be better if it is longitudinal in nature, that is, if it involves multiple visits during various stages of alliance operation. Researchers probably do not have to follow the alliances for a very long period, because Harrigan (1988) found that only 42% of alliances lasted more than 4 years. Hence, a 5-year cutoff point may be reasonable for such studies. In these interviews, both close-ended questions (see Larson, 1992) or open-ended questions (see Uzzi, 1997) may be employed. The process of developing these questions will be similar to that of the survey measure development we discussed earlier.

ACKNOWLEDGMENT

This chapter, save some minor changes, was earlier published as Das, T. K., & Teng, B. (2000). Instabilities of strategic alliances: An internal tensions perspective. *Organization Science, 11,* 77–101.

REFERENCES

Alexander, E. R. (1995). *How organizations act together: Interorganizational coordination in theory and practice.* Luxembourg: Gordon and Breach.

Alliance Analyst. (1994–1998). Newcap Communications, Inc., Philadelphia, PA.

Astley, W. G., & Van de Ven, A. H. (1983). Central perspectives and debates in organization theory. *Administrative Science Quarterly, 28,* 245–273.

Aulakh, P. S., Kotabe, M., & Sahay, A. (1997). Trust and performance in cross-border marketing partnerships. In P. W. Beamish & J. P. Killing (Eds.), *Cooperative strategies* (Vol. 1) *North American perspectives* (pp. 163–196). San Francisco, CA: New Lexington Press.

Axelrod, R. (1984). *The evolution of cooperation.* New York, NY: Basic Books.

Bacharach, S. B., & Lawler, E. J. (1981). *Bargaining: Power, tactics, and outcomes.* San Francisco, CA: Jossey-Bass.

Balakrishnan, S., & Koza, M. P. (1993). Information asymmetry, adverse selection and joint-ventures. *Journal of Economic Behavior and Organization, 20,* 99–117.

Barley, S. R., Freeman, J., & Hybels, R. C. (1992). Strategic alliances in commercial biotechnology. In N. Nohria & R. G. Eccles (Eds.), *Networks and organizations: Structure, form, and action* (pp. 311–347). Boston, MA: Harvard Business School Press.

Barley, S. R., & Kunda, G. (1992). Design and devotion: Surges of rational and normative ideologies of control in managerial discourse. *Administrative Science Quarterly, 37,* 363–399.

Beamish, P. W. (1985). The characteristics of joint ventures in developed and developing countries. *Columbia Journal of World Business, 20*(3), 13–19.

Beamish, P. W. (1987). Joint ventures in LDCs: Partner selection and performance. *Management International Review, 27,* 23–37.

Beamish, P. W., & Delios, A. (1997). Incidence and propensity of alliance formation. In P. W. Beamish & J. P. Killing (Eds.), *Cooperative strategies* (Vol. 3) *Asian Pacific perspectives* (pp. 91–114). San Francisco, CA: New Lexington Press.

Beamish, P. W., & Inkpen, A. C. (1995). Keeping international joint ventures stable and profitable. *Long Range Planning, 28*(3), 26–36.

Benson, J. K. (1977). Organizations: A dialectical view. *Administrative Science Quarterly, 22,* 1–21.

Bleeke, J., & Ernst, D. (1991). The way to win in cross-border alliances. *Harvard Business Review, 69*(6), 127–135.

Blodgett, L. L. (1991). Partner contributions as predictors of equity share in international joint ventures. *Journal of International Business Studies, 22,* 63–78.

Blodgett, L. L. (1992). Factors in the instability of international joint ventures: An event history analysis. *Strategic Management Journal, 13,* 475–481.

Bradach, J. L., & Eccles, R. G. (1989). Price, authority, and trust: From ideal types to plural forms. *Annual Review of Sociology, 15,* 97–118.

Brouthers, K. D., Brouthers, L. E., & Wilkinson, T. J. (1995). Strategic alliances: Choose your partners. *Long Range Planning, 28*(3), 18–25.

Buckley, P. J., & Casson, M. (1988). A theory of cooperation in international business. In F. J. Contractor & P. Lorange (Eds.), *Cooperative strategies in international business* (pp. 31–53). Lexington, MA: Lexington Books.

Bucklin, L. P., & Sengupta, S. (1993, April). Organizing successful co-marketing alliances. *Journal of Marketing, 57,* 32–46.

Burgers, W. P., Hill, C. W., & Kim, W. C. (1993). A theory of global strategic alliances: The case of the global auto industry. *Strategic Management Journal, 14,* 419–432.

Cameron, K. S., & Quinn, R. E. (1988). Organizational paradox and transformation. In R. E. Quinn & K. S. Cameron (Eds.), *Paradox and transformation: Toward a theory of change in organization and management* (pp. 1–18). Cambridge, MA: Ballinger.

Cauley, L. (1996, March 19). US West and Time Warner CEOs offer conflicting testimony in Turner suit. *Wall Street Journal,* p. B4.

Cullen, J. B., Johnson, J. L., & Sakano, T. (1995). Japanese and local partner commitment to IJVs: Psychological consequences of outcomes and investments in the IJV relationship. *Journal of International Business Studies, 26,* 91–115.

Das, T. K. (1984). Portmanteau ideas for organizational theorizing. *Organization Studies, 5,* 261–267.

Das, T. K. (1986). *The subjective side of strategy making: Future orientations and perceptions of executives.* New York, NY: Praeger.

Das, T. K. (1987). Strategic planning and individual temporal orientation. *Strategic Management Journal, 8,* 203–209.

Das, T. K. (1991). Time: The hidden dimension in strategic planning. *Long Range Planning, 24*(3), 49–57.

Das, T. K. (1993). Time in management and organizational studies. *Time & Society, 2*(2), 267–274.

Das, T. K., & Boje, D. M. (1993). Interorganizational networks: A meaning-based perspective. *International Journal of Organizational Analysis, 1,* 161–183.

Das, T. K., & Teng, B. (1996). Risk types and inter-firm alliance structures. *Journal of Management Studies, 33,* 827–843.

Das, T. K., & Teng, B. (1997). Sustaining strategic alliances: Options and guidelines. *Journal of General Management, 22*(4), 49–64.

Das, T. K., & Teng, B. (1998a). Resource and risk management in the strategic alliance making process. *Journal of Management, 24,* 21–42.

Das, T. K., & Teng, B. (1998b). Between trust and control: Developing confidence in partner cooperation in alliances. *Academy of Management Review, 23,* 491–512.

Das, T. K., & Teng, B. (1999). Managing risks in strategic alliances. *Academy of Management Executive, 13*(4), 50–62.

Das, T. K., & Teng, B. (2000). A resource-based theory of strategic alliances. *Journal of Management, 26,* 31–61.

Deeds, D. L., & Hill, C. W. L. (1996). Strategic alliances and the rate of new product development: An empirical study of entrepreneurial biotechnology firms. *Journal of Business Venturing, 11,* 41–55.

Deephouse, D. L. (1999). To be different, or to be the same? It's a question (and theory) of strategic balance. *Strategic Management Journal, 20,* 147–166.

DiMaggio, P. J., & Powell, W. W. (1983). The iron cage revisited: Institutional isomorphism and collective rationality in organizational fields. *American Sociological Review, 48,* 147–160.

Dollinger, M. J., Golden, P. A., & Saxton, T. (1997). The effect of reputation on the decision to joint venture. *Strategic Management Journal, 18,* 127–140.

Doz, Y. L. (1996, Summer). The evolution of cooperation in strategic alliances: Initial conditions or learning processes? *Strategic Management Journal, 17*[Special Issue], 55–83.

Economist. (1995, July 22). Airline alliances: Flying in formation. *Economist,* 59–60.

Eisenhardt, K. M., & Schoonhoven, C. B. (1996). Resource-based view of strategic alliance formation: Strategic and social effects in entrepreneurial firms. *Organization Science, 7,* 136–150.

Ford, J. D., & Ford, L. W. (1994). Logics of identity, contradiction, and attraction in change. *Academy of Management Review, 19,* 756–785.

Franko, L. G. (1971a). Joint venture divorce in the multinational company. *Columbia Journal of World Business, 6*(3), 13–22.

Franko, L. G. (1971b). *Joint venture survival in multinational corporations.* New York, NY: Praeger.

Ganesan, S. (1994). Determinants of long-term orientation in buyer-seller relationships. *Journal of Marketing, 58*(2), 1–19.

Gates, S. (1993). *Strategic alliances: Guidelines for successful management.* New York, NY: Conference Board.

Geringer, J. M., & Woodcock, C. P. (1995). Agency costs and the structure and performance of international joint ventures. *Group Decision and Negotiation, 4,* 453–467.

Ghoshal, S., & Moran, P. (1996). Bad for practice: A critique of the transaction cost theory. *Academy of Management Review, 21,* 13–47.

Glaister, K. W., & Buckley, P. J. (1996). Strategic motives for international alliance formation. *Journal of Management Studies, 33,* 301–332.

Gomes-Casseres, B. (1987). Joint venture instability: Is it a problem? *Columbia Journal of World Business, 22*(2), 97–102.

Gomes-Casseres, B. (1996). *The alliance revolution: The new shape of business rivalry.* Cambridge, MA: Harvard University Press.

Gray, B., & Wood, D. J. (1991). Collaborative alliances: Moving from practice to theory. *Journal of Applied Behavioral Science, 27,* 3–22.

Greiner, L. E. (1972). Evolution and revolution as organizations grow. *Harvard Business Review, 50*(4), 37–46.

Gulati, R. (1995). Does familiarity breed trust? The implication of repeated ties for contractual choice in alliances. *Academy of Management Journal, 38,* 85–112.

Gulati, R., Khanna, T., & Nohria, N. (1994). Unilateral commitments and the importance of process in alliance. *Sloan Management Review, 35*(3), 61–70.

Hagedoorn, J. (1993). Understanding the rationale of strategic technology partnering: Interorganizational modes of cooperation and sectoral differences. *Strategic Management Journal, 14,* 371–385.

Hagedoorn, J., & Schakenraad, J. (1993). Strategic technology partnering and international corporate strategies. In K. S. Hughes (Ed.), *European competitiveness* (pp. 60–86). Cambridge, England: Cambridge University Press.

Hagedoorn, J., & Schakenraad, J. (1994). The effect of strategic technology alliances on company performance. *Strategic Management Journal, 15,* 291–309.

Hallen, L., Johanson, J., & Seyed-Mohamed, N. (1991). Interfirm adaptations in business relationships. *Journal of Marketing, 55*(2), 29–37.

Harbison, J. R., & Pekar, P., Jr. (1998). *Smart alliances: A practical guide to repeatable success.* San Francisco, CA: Jossey-Bass.

Harrigan, K. R. (1988). Strategic alliances and partner asymmetries. In F. J. Contractor & P. Lorange (Eds.), *Cooperative strategies in international business* (pp. 205–226). Lexington, MA: Lexington Books.

Hatfield, L., & Pearce, J. A., II. (1994). Goal achievement and satisfaction of joint venture partners. *Journal of Business Venturing, 9,* 423–440.

Heide, J. B. (1994). Interorganizational governance in marketing channels. *Journal of Marketing, 58*(1), 71–85.

Heide, J. B., & Miner, A. S. (1992). The shadow of the future: Effects of anticipated interaction and frequency of contact on buyer-seller cooperation. *Academy of Management Journal, 35,* 265–291.

Hennart, J.-F., Kim, D.-J., & Zeng, M. (1998). The impact of joint venture status on the longevity of Japanese stakes in U.S. manufacturing affiliates. *Organization Science, 9,* 382–395.

Heydebrand, W. (1977). Organizational contradictions in public bureaucracies: Toward a Marxian theory of organizations. *Sociological Quarterly, 18,* 83–107.

Hill, C. W. L. (1990). Cooperation, opportunism, and the invisible hand: Implications for transaction cost theory. *Academy of Management Review, 15,* 500–513.

Inkpen, A. C., & Beamish, P. W. (1997). Knowledge, bargaining power, and the instability of international joint ventures. *Academy of Management Review, 22,* 177–202.

Inkpen, A. C., & Currall, S. C. (1997). International joint venture trust: An empirical examination. In P. W. Beamish & J. P. Killing (Eds.), *Cooperative strategies* (Vol. 1) *North American perspectives* (pp. 308–334). San Francisco, CA: New Lexington Press.

Jensen, M. C., & Meckling, W. H. (1976). Theory of the firm: Managerial behavior, agency costs and ownership structure. *Journal of Financial Economics, 3,* 305–360.

Jones, C., Hesterly, W. S., Fladmoe-Lindquist, K., & Borgatti, S. P. (1998). Professional service constellations: How strategies and capabilities influence collaborative stability and change. *Organization Science, 9,* 396–410.

Joskow, P. (1985). Contract duration and relationship-specific investments: Empirical evidence from coal markets. *American Economic Review, 77,* 168–185.

Joskow, P. (1991). Asset specificity and the structure of vertical relationships: Empirical evidence. In O. E. Williamson & S. G. Winter (Eds.), *The nature of the firm: Origins, evolution, and development* (pp. 117–137). New York, NY: Oxford University Press.

Kahn, J. (1996, May 22). Clipped wings: McDonnell Douglas's high hopes for China never really soared. *Wall Street Journal,* pp. A1, A12.

Kanter, R. M. (1994). Collaborative advantage: The art of alliances. *Harvard Business Review, 72*(4), 96–108.

Kent, D. H. (1991). Joint ventures vs. non-joint ventures: An empirical investigation. *Strategic Management Journal, 12,* 387–393.

Khanna, T., Gulati, R., & Nohria, N. (1998). The dynamics of learning alliances: Competition, cooperation, and relative scope. *Strategic Management Journal, 19,* 193–210.

Killing, J. P. (1983). *Strategies for joint ventures.* New York, NY: Praeger.

Killing, J. P. (1988). Understanding alliances: The role of task and organizational complexity. In F. J. Contractor & P. Lorange (Eds.), *Cooperative strategies in international business* (pp. 55–68). Lexington, MA: Lexington Books.

Kogut, B. (1988). Joint ventures: Theoretical and empirical perspectives. *Strategic Management Journal, 9,* 319–332.

Kogut, B. (1989). The stability of joint ventures: Reciprocity and competitive rivalry. *Journal of Industrial Economics, 38,* 183–198.

Kogut, B. (1991). Joint ventures and the option to expand and acquire. *Management Science, 37,* 19–33.

Koot, W. T. M. (1988). Underlying dilemmas in the management of international joint ventures. In F. J. Contractor & P. Lorange (Eds.), *Cooperative strategies in international business* (pp. 347–368). Lexington, MA: Lexington Books.

Koza, M. P., & Lewin, A. Y. (1998). The co-evolution of strategic alliances. *Organization Science, 9,* 255–264.

Kuhn, T. S. (1977). The essential tension: Tradition and innovation in scientific research. In T. S. Kuhn (Ed.), *The essential tension: Selected studies in scientific tradition and change* (pp. 225–239). Chicago, IL: University of Chicago Press.

Lado, A. A., Boyd, N. G., & Hanlon, S. C. (1997). Competition, cooperation, and the search for economic rents: A syncretic model. *Academy of Management Review, 22,* 110–141.

Lane, P. J., & Lubatkin, M. (1998). Relative absorptive capacity and interorganizational learning. *Strategic Management Journal, 19,* 461–477.

Larson, A. (1992). Network dyads in entrepreneurial settings: A study of the governance of exchange relationships. *Administrative Science Quarterly, 37,* 76–104.

Leonard-Barton, D. (1992, Summer). Core capabilities and core rigidities: A paradox in managing new product development. *Strategic Management Journal, 13*[Special Issue], 111–125.

Li, J. (1995). Foreign entry and survival: Effects of strategic choices on performance in international markets. *Strategic Management Journal, 16,* 333–351.

Lourenco, S. V., & Glidewell, J. C. (1975). A dialectical analysis of organizational conflict. *Administrative Science Quarterly, 20,* 489–508.

Macneil, I. R. (1974). The many futures of contracts. *Southern California Law Review, 47,* 691–816.

Macneil, I. R. (1980). *The new social contract.* New Haven, CT: Yale University Press.

Maybury-Lewis, D. (1989). The quest for harmony. In D. Maybury-Lewis & U. Almagor (Eds.), *The attraction of opposites: Thought and society in the dualistic mode* (pp. 1–17). Ann Arbor: University of Michigan Press.

McGuire, J. B. (1988). A dialectical analysis of interorganizational networks. *Journal of Management, 14,* 109–124.

Miles, R. E., & Snow, C. C. (1991). Causes of failure in network organizations. *California Management Review, 34*(4), 53–72.

Newman, W. H. (1992). Focused joint ventures' in transforming economies. *Academy of Management Executive, 6*(1), 67–75.

Orton, J. D., & Weick, K. E. (1990). Loosely coupled systems: A reconceptualization. *Academy of Management Review, 15,* 203–223.

Oye, K. A. (Ed.). (1986). *Cooperation under anarchy.* Princeton, NJ: Princeton University Press.

Park, S. H., & Russo, M. V. (1996). When competition eclipses cooperation: An event history analysis of joint venture failure. *Management Science, 42,* 875–890.

Park, S. H., & Ungson, G. R. (1997). The effect of national culture, organizational complementarity, and economic motivation on joint venture dissolution. *Academy of Management Journal, 40,* 270–307.

Parkhe, A. (1993a). Partner nationality and the structure-performance relationship in strategic alliances. *Organization Science, 4,* 301–324.

Parkhe, A. (1993b). Strategic alliance structuring: A game theory and transaction cost examination of interfirm cooperation. *Academy of Management Journal, 36,* 794–829.

Parkhe, A., Rosenthal, E. C., & Chandran, R. (1993). Prisoner's dilemma payoff structure in interfirm strategic alliances: An empirical test. *Omega, 21,* 531–539.

Pekar, P., Jr., & Allio, R. (1994). Making alliances work—Guidelines for success. *Long Range Planning, 27*(4), 54–65.

Pearce, R. J. (1997). Toward understanding joint venture performance and survival: A bargaining and influence approach to transaction cost theory. *Academy of Management Review, 22,* 203–225.

Pennings, J. M., Barkema, H., & Douma, S. (1994). Organization learning and diversification. *Academy of Management Journal, 37,* 608–640.

Pfeffer, J., & Nowak, P. (1976). Joint ventures and interorganizational dependence. *Administrative Science Quarterly, 21,* 394–418.

Pfeffer, J., & Salancik, G. R. (1978). *The external control of organizations: A resource dependence perspective.* New York, NY: Harper and Row.

Poole, M. S., & Van de Ven, A. H. (1989). Using paradox to build management and organization theories. *Academy of Management Review, 14,* 562–578.

Porter, M. E. (1980). *Competitive strategy: Techniques for analyzing industries and competitors.* New York, NY: Free Press.

Porter, M. E. (1985). *Competitive advantage: Creating and sustaining superior performance.* New York, NY: Free Press.

Porter, M. E. (1990). *The competitive advantage of nations.* New York, NY: Free Press.

Provan, K. G., & Skinner, S. J. (1989). Interorganizational dependence and control as predictors of opportunism in dealer-supplier relations. *Academy of Management Journal, 32,* 202–212.

Quinn, R. E. (1988). *Beyond rational management: Mastering the paradoxes and competing demands of high performance.* San Francisco, CA: Jossey-Bass.

Quinn, R. E., & Cameron, K. S. (Eds.). (1988). *Paradox and transformation: Toward a theory of change in organization and management.* Cambridge, MA: Ballinger.

Quinn, R. E., & Rohrbaugh, J. (1983). A spatial model of effectiveness criteria: Towards a competing values approach to organizational analysis. *Management Science, 29,* 363–377.

Ramanathan, K., Seth, A., & Thomas, H. (1997). Explaining joint ventures: Alternative theoretical perspectives. In P. W. Beamish & J. P. Killing (Eds.), *Cooperative strategies,* (Vol. 1) *North American perspectives* (pp. 51–85). San Francisco, CA: New Lexington Press.

Ring, P. S., & Van de Ven, A. H. (1992). Structuring cooperative relationship between organizations. *Strategic Management Journal, 13,* 483–498.

Ring, P. S., & Van de Ven, A. H. (1994). Developmental processes of cooperative interorganizational relationships. *Academy of Management Review, 19,* 90–118.

Rosman, A., Lubatkin, M., & O'Neill, H. (1994). Rigidity in decision behaviors: A within-subject test of information acquisition using strategic and financial informational cues. *Academy of Management Journal, 37,* 1017–1033.

Sankar, C. S., Boulton, W. R., Davidson, N. W., Snyder, C. A., & Ussery, R. W. (1995). Building a world-class alliance: The Universal Card-TSYS case. *Academy of Management Executive, 9*(2), 20–29.

Saxton, T. (1997). The effects of partner and relationship characteristics on alliance outcomes. *Academy of Management Journal, 40,* 443–461.

Serapio, M. G., Jr., & Cascio, W. F. (1996). End-games in international alliances. *Academy of Management Executive, 10*(1), 62–73.

Sharfman, M. P., & Dean, J. W., Jr. (1997). Flexibility in strategic decision making: Informational and ideological perspectives. *Journal of Management Studies, 34,* 191–217.

Smith, K. K., & Berg, D. N. (1987). *Paradoxes of group life: Understanding conflict, paralysis, and movement in group dynamics.* San Francisco, CA: Jossey-Bass.

Stafford, E. R. (1994). Using co-operative strategies to make alliances work. *Long Range Planning, 27*(3), 64–74.

Stuckey, A. (1983). *Vertical integration and joint ventures in the aluminum industry.* Cambridge, MA: Harvard University Press.

Teece, D. J. (1992). Competition, cooperation, and innovation: Organizational arrangements for regimes of rapid technological progress. *Journal of Economic Behavior and Organization, 18,* 1–25.

Uzzi, B. (1997). Social structure and competition in interfirm networks: The paradox of embeddedness. *Administrative Science Quarterly, 42,* 35–67.

Van de Ven, A. H. (1992, Summer). Suggestions for studying strategy process: A research note. *Strategic Management Journal, 13*[Special Issue], 169–188.

Van de Ven, A. H., & Poole, M. S. (1995). Explaining development and change in organizations. *Academy of Management Review, 20,* 510–540.

van Heigenoort, J. (1967). Logical paradoxes. In P. Edwards (Ed.), *The encyclopedia of philosophy* (Vol. 5, pp. 45–51). New York, NY: Macmillan and Free Press.

Venkatraman, N. (1989). Strategic orientation of business enterprises: The construct, dimensionality, and measurement. *Management Science, 35,* 942–962.

Weick, K. E. (1976). Educational organizations as loosely coupled systems. *Administrative Science Quarterly, 21,* 1–19.

Williamson, O. E. (1975). *Markets and hierarchies: Analysis and antitrust implications.* New York, NY: Free Press.

Williamson, O. E. (1983). Credible commitments: Using hostages to support exchange. *American Economic Review, 73,* 519–540.

Williamson, O. E. (1985). *The economic institutions of capitalism.* New York, NY: Free Press.

Yamawaki, H. (1997). Exit of Japanese multinationals in US and European manufacturing industries. In P. J. Buckley & J.-L. Mucchielli (Eds.), *Multinational firms and international relocation* (pp. 220–237). Cheltenham, England: Edward Elgar.

Yan, A., & Gray, B. (1994). Bargaining power, management control, and performance in United States-China joint ventures: A comparative case study. *Academy of Management Journal, 37,* 1478–1517.

Yoshino, M. Y., & Rangan, U. S. (1995). *Strategic alliances: An entrepreneurial approach to globalization.* Boston, MA: Harvard Business School Press.

Zaheer, A., & Venkatraman, N. (1995). Relational governance as an interorganizational strategy: An empirical test of the role of trust in economic exchange. *Strategic Management Journal, 16,* 373–392.

Zeitz, G. (1980). Interorganizational dialectics. *Administrative Science Quarterly, 25,* 72–88.

ABOUT THE CONTRIBUTORS

Andreas Al-Laham is chair in Strategic and International Management at the University of Mannheim (Germany). Before taking this position, he was a Visiting Professor for Strategic Management and Organization Theory at the J. L. Rotman School of Management, University of Toronto (Canada) from 2000 until 2002. From 2002 until 2004 he held a professorship for International and Strategic Management at the SIMT Business School, University of Stuttgart (Germany). Thereafter, Dr. Al-Laham worked as a professor for General Management and International Strategy at the CASS Business School, City University of London (UK) (2004–2006) and at the University of Kaiserslautern (Germany) (2006–2009). Since 2006, he has been a Visiting Professor at the CASS Business School. Prof. Al-Laham has published extensively in leading international journals in International Management, Strategic Management, and Innovation Management, such as *Journal of Business Venturing, Management International Review,* and *British Journal of Management.* E-mail: al-laham@uni-mannheim.de

David Arditi is a professor in the Department of Civil, Architectural and Environmental Engineering at Illinois Institute of Technology, Chicago. He is the founder and current director of the Construction Engineering and Management Program. His teaching and research focus on all aspects of construction management, engineering, and support. He is the author of many papers published in professional journals and conference proceedings. He serves on the editorial board of several journals and is an active member of several professional societies. E-mail: arditi@iit.edu

Management Dynamics in Strategic Alliances, pages 315–323
Copyright © 2012 by Information Age Publishing
315

Ariela Caglio is associate professor of Management Accounting and Control at Università Bocconi and Professor of SDA Bocconi School of Management. She has published several contributions in books and academic journals. Her research interests relate to the evolution of the accounting profession, CFOs compensation, and interorganizational management accounting. She is Book Review Editor of the *European Accounting Review*. E-mail: ariela.caglio@sdabocconi.it

T. K. Das is professor of Strategic Management and Area Coordinator (Strategic Management and Business & Society) at the Zicklin School of Business, Baruch College, City University of New York. He is concurrently a member of the University's Doctoral Faculty. Professor Das received his PhD in Organization and Strategic Studies from the Anderson Graduate School of Management, University of California at Los Angeles (UCLA). He also has degrees in physics, mathematics, and management, and a professional certification in banking. Prior to entering the academic life, Professor Das had extensive experience as a senior business executive. He has research interests in strategic alliances, strategy making, organizational studies, temporal studies, and executive development. Professor Das has published several books and monographs, and his research has appeared in over 45 journals, of which some of the later ones include *Academy of Management Executive, Academy of Management Review, British Journal of Management, Journal of International Management, Journal of Management, Journal of Management Studies, Organization Science, Organization Studies*, and *Strategic Management Journal*. Professor Das currently serves as a senior editor of *Organization Studies*, and is or has been associate editor or editorial board member of a number of other journals. He is the founding Series Editor of *Research in Strategic Alliances* (Information Age Publishing). E-mail: TK.Das@baruch.cuny.edu

Pat H. Dickson is associate professor and director of the Business and Enterprise Management degree program in the Schools of Business at Wake Forest University. He has also served as a professor of strategy and entrepreneurship on the faculties of Georgia Tech and the University of Louisville. Prior to earning his PhD in 1997 from the University of Alabama, he spent 15 years as an entrepreneur, co-founding companies in the automotive parts and service industry and as a corporate executive serving as Director of Franchising for a regional retail and manufacturing company in the same industry. He is currently a fellow and a vice president of the United States Association of Small Business and Entrepreneurship (USASBE). He has served as Proceedings Editor for both USASBE and the International Congress for Small Business and Entrepreneurship (ICSB). He has two areas of unique expertise: new venture creation, including opportunity assessment, resource acquisition, technology commercialization and the strategic management of new ventures; and strategic alliances, including formation and structure and the use of alliances for resource acquisition, technology transfer, and internationalization. His research has appeared in leading journals in the management and entrepreneurship fields, and he has been awarded a Certificate of Distinction for Outstanding Research by the Academy of Management and the National Federation of Independent Business. E-mail: dicksoph@wfu.edu

Angelo Ditillo is associate professor of Management Accounting and Control at Università Bocconi and professor of the SDA Bocconi School of Management. He has published several contributions in academic journals. His current research interests relate to interorganizational management accounting and management control in knowledge-intensive firms and creative settings. E-mail: angelo.ditillo@unibocconi.it

Natsuko Fujikawa is a Postdoctoral Fellow at the Economic Research Center, Graduate School of Economics, Nagoya University, Japan. She received her PhD in economics from the School of Economics, Nagoya University, Japan, in 2008. Her primary research interests are organizational learning, interorganizational learning, organization designs, and organizational change. Fujikawa is currently pursuing research on the dynamics of organizational learning and the barriers to organizational learning. Her recent publications appeared in the *Annual Bulletin of the History of Management* and *Journal of International Business Research*. E-mail: fujikawa@soec.nagoya-u .ac.jp

Varghese P. George is assistant professor of management at the University of Massachusetts at Boston. He received his PhD from MIT. His principal area of research is managing technological innovation. He is interested in strategies for managing external relationships and in issues related to trust, power, and flow of knowledge. He also does research on organizational communication networks and is interested in the influence of communication on innovation and in the influence of architecture and organizational structure on communication networks. He has recently turned his attention to communication for learning in an educational environment. *E-mail:* vpgeorge@gmail.com

Michael Hitt is a Distinguished Professor of Management at Texas A&M University and holds the Joe B. Foster Chair in Business Leadership. He received his PhD from the University of Colorado. Dr. Hitt has coauthored or co-edited 26 books and authored or co-authored many journal articles. A recent article in the *Journal of Management* listed him as one of the ten most cited authors in management over a 25-year period. Additionally, the *Times Higher Education* in 2010 listed him among the top scholars in economics, finance, and management based on the number of articles with a high citation rate on the Web of Science. He has served on the editorial review boards of multiple journals and is a former editor of the *Academy of Management Journal* and the *Strategic Entrepreneurship Journal*. He is a Fellow in the Academy of Management and in the Strategic Management Society, a Research Fellow in the National Entrepreneurship Consortium, and received an honorary doctorate from the Universidad Carlos III de Madrid. He is a former president of the Academy of Management, a former president of the Strategic Management Society, and a member of the Academy of Management Journal's Hall of Fame. He received awards for the best article published in the *Academy of Management Executive* (1999), *Academy of Management Journal* (2000), and the *Journal of Management* (2006). He received the Irwin Outstanding Educator Award and the Distinguished Service Award from the Academy of Management and the Falcone Distinguished Entrepreneurship Scholar Award from Syracuse University. E-mail: mhitt@indiana.edu

Niki Hynes is professor of marketing at ESC Clermont. Prior to this, she worked as a full-time research fellow at Ecole Polytechnique Federale in Lausanne, Switzerland, and as a lecturer in marketing at the University of Strathclyde in Glasgow. She received a BSc (Hons) degree in biochemistry from the University of London and an MBA from the University of Edinburgh. After 8 years of work experience in a variety of international sales and marketing roles, she undertook her PhD in marketing at Lincoln University in New Zealand. She has extensive experience in teaching at undergraduate and postgraduate levels both on campus and in an online environment and has been teaching for laureate for over 3 years. Her present research interests include marketing in high-technology firms, market and technological orientation, strategic alliances, and the use of simulation games in teaching and learning, and she has published in *Industrial Marketing Management, International Journal of Technology Management, Technological Forecasting and Social Change*, and *Journal of Brand Management*. E-mail: niki. hynes@esc-clermont.fr

Tsutomu Kobashi is associate professor in the Faculty of Management, Aichi Institute of Technology, Japan. He received a PhD in economics from the School of Economics, Nagoya University, Japan, where he previously worked. He did his research at Anderson School of Management, University of California, Los Angeles (UCLA), as a visiting scholar from 2009 to 2010. His research interests include interorganizational relationships (IOR), organizational structure, research methodology, and strategic management. In the field of IOR, he has published many papers dealing with interorganizational learning (IOL), interorganizational dynamics, and interorganizational structure. He is currently working on research focusing on the dynamics of maker-supplier networks in the automobile industry and horizontal alliances in the airline industry. In the field of organizational structure, his focus is on front-back organization. Through a comparison with other organizational structures, such as multidivisional structure and matrix organization, he has identified the idiosyncrasies of front-back organization. In the field of methodological research, his interests lie mainly in determining the relationship between methodology and theory development, and the practical application of knowledge. E-mail: kobashi@aitech.ac.jp

Kazuyuki Kozawa is associate professor in the Faculty of Management, Aichi Gakuin University, Japan. He received a PhD in economics from the School of Economics, Nagoya University, Japan. Previously, he was assistant professor in the Faculty of Management, Shizuoka Sangyo University, Japan. He has been a visiting research scholar at the Department of Philosophy, College of Humanities and the Arts, San Jose State University, San Jose, California. His research interests include organizational learning, knowledge, practice, and artifacts. He is focusing on the relationship between knowledge and learning through engaging in practice with artifacts in an organizational context. He is currently researching artifacts and the differences between data, information, and knowledge and what this implies for supporting innovation and organizational effectiveness. Artifacts in an organizational context have many meanings that must be known if one is to understand what organizational members do and what their culture is. He is interested in determining how changes in the relationship between artifacts and these meanings affect organizational learning. E-mail: kozawa@dpc.agu.ac.jp

Rajesh Kumar is associate professor of international business strategy at the University of Nottingham. His expertise lies in the management of alliances, international negotiations, and managing in emerging markets with a specific focus on India. Professor Kumar has a PhD degree from New York University. He has taught at Penn State, Ohio State, and Babson College in the United States and in numerous institutions throughout Europe. Prior to moving to Nottingham in January 2008, he was associate professor at the Aarhus School of Business, University of Aarhus. Professor Kumar's work on alliances has looked at the microbehavioral processes involved in alliance development. Past work has highlighted the importance of interpartner legitimacy, emotions, process and outcome discrepancies, and more recently regulatory focus on alliance evolution. Professor Kumar has published in leading international journals such as *Journal of Management, Journal of Management Studies, Organization Science, Journal of World Business, Industrial Marketing Management, Journal of Applied Behavioral Science, International Marketing Review,* and *International Journal of Conflict Management* and continues to maintain an active research agenda. E-mail: Rajesh.Kumar@nottingham.ac.uk

Spyros Lioukas is professor of business strategy at the Athens University of Economics and Business. He is currently teaching courses on strategy and on ethics/corporate governance in the "International MBA" and the "Athens MBA," and directs the MSc in Public Policy & Management. He also directs the Laboratory of Strategy and Entrepreneurship, where he is currently is directing research projects in the areas of innovation and competitive strategy, entrepreneurship, corporate reputation, and governance. He received a PhD from the London Business School, and formerly he was in the teaching faculty of the London Business School. He has published several papers in leading academic journals including, *Strategic Management Journal, Organization Science, Management Science, British Journal of Management, Information & Management, International Management Review, Long Range Planning, Industrial Economics, European Economic Review, Transportation*, and others. He served as Ambassador of Greece to the OECD (1996–2001) and has been national representative in the EC on technology and innovation. He acted as advisor to OKE (the Economic and Social Committee) and has served as member on several committees for industrial policy, entrepreneurship, transport infrastructure, and investment appraisal for subsidized projects. He has also been advisor to the Public Power Corporation for many years. He is involved in small enterprise startups and serves as independent nonexecutive director in the board of two companies. E-mail: scl@aueb.gr

Jan Mouritsen is a professor at Copenhagen Business School. His research is oriented toward understanding the role of management technologies and management control in various organizational and social contexts. He focuses on empirical research and attempts to develop new ways of understanding the role and effects of controls and financial information in organizations and society. He is interested in translations and interpretations made of (numerical) representations (e.g., as in budgets, financial reports, nonfinancial indicators, and profitability analysis) in the contexts they help to illuminate. His interests include intellectual capital and knowledge management, technology management, operations management, new accounting, and management control. He is currently an editorial board member of a number of academic journals in the various areas of management and business research including accounting (e.g., CAR and AOS), operations management, IT, and knowledge management. He has published in journals including *Accounting, Organizations and Society; Management Accounting Research; Scandinavian Journal of Management; Accounting, Auditing and Accountability Journal; Journal of Intellectual Capital*, and *Critical Perspectives on Accounting.* E-mail: jm.om@cbs.dk

Beliz Ozorhon is assistant professor of construction management in the Department of Civil Engineering at Bogazici University, Turkey. Her research initiatives focus on innovation management, international joint ventures, strategic decision making, performance management, and knowledge management. Her recent projects investigate the innovative processes in built environment and the role of academic engagement in innovation. She has published 10 papers in leading journals and 20 conference papers. E-mail: beliz.ozorhon@boun.edu.tr

Adamantia Pateli is a lecturer at the Department of Informatics of the Ionian University, Corfu, Greece. She holds a BSc degree in informatics (specialization in information systems) from the Athens University of Economics and Business (AUEB), a master's degree in electronic commerce from the University of Manchester, and a PhD degree from the Department of Management Science and Technology of the Athens University of Economics and Business (AUEB). She has presented her research at major international conferences and has published in leading academic journals, such as *Management Decision, International Journal of Technology Management, Journal of Organizational Change Management, Electronic Markets, European Journal of Information Systems, Journal of Theoretical and Applied Electronic Commerce Research, Information & Management, International Journal of Web Engineering and Technology,* and *International Journal of Mobile Communications.* She serves as an associate editor of the *International Journal of E-Services and Mobile Applications.* E-mail: pateli@ionio.gr

Bing-Sheng Teng is associate professor of strategic management and associate dean for MBA at Cheung Kong Graduate School of Business in Beijing, China. He was previously associate professor of strategic management with tenure at George Washington University (GWU), as well as the lead professor of the departmental doctoral program at GWU. Professor Teng's research has been published in a variety of top academic journals including *Academy of Management Review* and *Organization Science.* Professor Teng also serves on the editorial boards of *Journal of Business Research* and *International Entrepreneurship and Management Journal.* He was awarded the Wendell and Louis Crain Research Scholarship at GWU. Professor Teng's current research interests include strategic alliances, mergers and acquisitions, business model innovation, and international strategies (especially of Chinese firms). His expertise on Chinese management led to frequent interviews by the popular media such as the *Wall Street Journal* and *Business Week.* E-mail: bsteng@ckgsb.edu.cn

Sof Thrane is an associate professor at Copenhagen Business School, where his research is focused on the ways in which interfirm relationships and innovation networks develop and change, often taking into account the role of managerial technologies in developing and maintaining relationships and organizational networks. This research interest has led to a range of studies on the paradoxical ways in which managerial technologies shape organizational life and on innovative approaches to the use of management accounting for creating and overcoming boundaries within and between organizations. Professor Thrane has published in journals such as *Research Policy, Accounting Organization and Society,* and *Management Accounting Research.* He received his PhD from Copenhagen Business School, where his thesis work provided fresh insights on the problem of managing interorganizational relationships. He currently heads the PhD School, LIMAC, at Copenhagen Business School and is involved in research on cost disclosure in interfirm networks, and research focusing on how management accounting shapes and develops innovation networks, specifically in terms of increasing sustainability of products. E-mail: sth.om@cbs.dk

K. Mark Weaver is the Ben May Chair of Entrepreneurship at the University of South Alabama and the executive director of the Melton Center for Innovation. He received his PhD in management from Louisiana State University. Since 1972, he has taught at Bradley University, the University of Alabama, University of Twente–Netherlands, University College Dublin, and the Oslo Business School. He has also held endowed chairs in entrepreneurship at Rowan University and Louisiana State University. He has been a principal investigator/coPI on over $10 million in external grants and funding. His research interests have been in strategic alliances, international entrepreneurship, social entrepreneurship, and family business. He has received best paper awards from USASBE, Babson Kaufmann, and the Academy of Management. He is an elected fellow in USASBE, ICSB, and SBIDA. His research publications include *Academy of Management Journal, Journal of Business Venturing, Entrepreneurship Theory and Practice, Journal of International Business Studies, Journal of Small Business Management,* and several others. He currently (2011) serves as president of the United States Association for Small Business and Entrepreneurship (USASBE). E-mail: kmarkweaver@gmail.com

Juliette Wilson is a lecturer in marketing at the University of Strathclyde, Glasgow, and Deputy Director of the Masters in International Marketing Programme. She has received degrees from the University of Aberdeen and the University of Strathclyde. Her present research interests include strategic alliances, supply chains and networks, and small businesses. She worked for a number of years as a research fellow in the department, most notably conducting research in the food industry where she worked extensively with large and small companies, both nationally and internationally, examining issues related to relative competitiveness in the industry. Before pursuing an academic career, Professor Wilson worked as an economic researcher for the Sea Fish Industry Authority in Edinburgh. She has published in *Technological Forecasting and Social Change, Journal of Marketing Channels, In-*

ternational Review of Retail Distribution and Consumer Research, International Journal of Retail and Distribution Management, and the *British Food Journal.* E-mail: juliette.wilson@strath.ac.uk

Florian Zock is a PhD student in management at the Center for Doctoral Studies in Business (part of the Graduate School of Economic and Social Sciences) at the University of Mannheim (Germany). He holds a Diploma in International Cultural and Business Studies from the University of Passau (Germany). He also holds a BA with Honors in International Management from the University of Stirling (Scotland). Focusing on strategic management, his research interests include alliance portfolio management and business model management. E-mail: fzock@mail.uni-mannheim.de

INDEX

Management Dynamics in Strategic Alliances, pages 325–339
Copyright © 2012 by Information Age Publishing

CPSIA information can be obtained at www.ICGtesting.com
Printed in the USA
BVOW021246240612

293415BV00002B/9/P